W9-AFB-826

Front Cover: Edwin E. Aldrin, Jr., on the moon, photographed by Neil A. Armstrong.

Back Cover: Apollo 11 lunar module, back in orbit after leaving moon's surface, nears command module for docking. Both photos, NASA.

FLIGHT TIME	FLIGHT HIGHLIGHTS
1 hr. 48 mins.	First manned flight; 1 orbit
0 hrs. 15 mins.	Suborbital flight; first American in space
0 hrs., 16 mins.	Suborbital flight; capsule sank
25 hrs. 18 mins.	More than 1 day in space; 17.5 orbits
4 hrs. 55 mins.	First American in orbit; 3 orbits
4 hrs. 56 mins.	Splashdown 250 miles from recovery target; 3 orbits
94 hrs. 22 mins.	Two spacecraft in orbit at same time (Vostok 3 and Vostok 4); 64 orbits
70 hrs. 57 mins.	On first orbit Vostok 4 came within 3.1 miles of Vostok 3; 48 orbits
9 hrs. 13 mins.	Splashdown 5 miles from recovery target; 6 orbits
34 hrs. 20 mins.	Extended U.S. flight; 22 orbits
119 hrs. 6 mins.	Group flight with Vostok 6; 81 orbits
70 hrs. 50 mins.	First woman in space; 48 orbits
24 hrs. 17 mins.	First 3-man space crew; 16 orbits
26 hrs. 2 mins.	First space walk; 17 orbits
4 hrs. 53 mins.	First manned spacecraft maneuvers in orbit; 3 orbits
97 hrs. 48 mins.	First American space walk; 66 orbits
190 hrs. 56 mins.	Extended space flight equal in length to a trip to the moon and back; 128 orbits
330 hrs. 35 mins.	Extended space flight; 220 orbits
25 hrs. 51 mins.	Rendezvous with Gemini 7; 17 orbits
10 hrs. 42 mins.	Docked with Agena rocket; 6.5 orbits
72 hrs. 21 mins.	Rendezvous, space walk, and on-target splashdown; 47 orbits
70 hrs. 47 mins.	Rendezvous with two Agena targets; 46 orbits
71 hrs. 17 mins.	Attained altitude of 850 miles; rendezvous and docking with Agena target; 47 orbits
94 hrs. 33 mins.	3 space walks; splashdown and recovery live on television; 63 orbits
26 hrs. 40 mins.	Komarov killed when spacecraft parachute snarled and craft plunged to earth; 18 orbits
260 hrs. 9 mins.	First Apollo flight; first live television from a manned spacecraft; 163 orbits
95 hrs.	Rendezvous but no docking with unmanned Soyuz 2; 64 orbits
147 hrs.	First manned voyage around moon; first live television from lunar orbit; 10 moon orbits
71 hrs. 14 mins.	First rendezvous and docking of manned spacecraft (Soyuz 4 and Soyuz 5); 48 orbits
72 hrs. 46 mins.	First transfer of crew from one craft to another; 49 orbits
241 hrs. 1 min.	Testing of lunar module in earth orbit; 151 orbits
192 hrs. 3 mins.	Lunar module descended to within 9 miles of surface of moon; 31 moon orbits
195 hrs. 18 mins.	Lunar module lands on moon; men walk on moon; moon rocks retrieved
118 hrs. 42 mins.	First metal-welding experiment carried out in a spacecraft; 80 orbits
118 hrs. 41 mins.	Maneuvered to within several hundred yards of Soyuz 8; 80 orbits
118 hrs. 41 mins.	With Soyuz 6 and Soyuz 7, first 7-man, 3-spacecraft group flight; 80 orbits
244 hrs. 36 mins.	Second moon voyage; on-target landing on the Ocean of Storms

1970

THE
NEW BOOK
OF
KNOWLEDGE
ANNUAL

THE YOUNG PEOPLES
BOOK OF THE YEAR

A REVIEW OF THE EVENTS OF 1969

Grolier Grolier
LIMITED   INCORPORATED
MONTREAL   NEW YORK

STAFF

CONTENTS

SPECIAL ARTICLES

CONTRIBUTORS

Barber, Alden G., L.H.D.
Chief Scout Executive, Boy Scouts of America
Boy Scouts   page 393

Ben-Horin, Meir, Ph.D.
Professor of Education and Chairman, Division of Education, Dropsie University
Jews and Judaism   page 305

Berrill, N.J., Ph.D., D.Sc.
Lecturer, Swarthmore College
Biology   page 105

Birch, Guy
News Editor, *Toronto Star*
Canada   page 108

Blatchford, Joseph H.
Director, Peace Corps
Peace Corps   page 278

Bohle, Bruce, A.B.
Usage Editor, American Heritage Dictionaries
Dictionary Supplement   page 399

Bone, Hugh A., Ph.D.
Professor of Political Science, University of Washington
Governors   page 193

Brackman, Arnold C.
Consultant, Asian affairs; Author, *The Communist Collapse in Indonesia*
Asia   page 87
China   page 119
India   page 204
Japan   page 211
Korea   page 214
Vietnam   page 382

Buder, Leonard
Education writer, *The New York Times*
Education   page 163

Buitenhuis, Peter, Ph.D.
Professor of English, McGill University
Literature, Canadian   page 231

Caras, Roger A.
Author, *Panther!; North American Mammals*
The Animal Kingdom   page 136

Carlson, Jerry A., B.S.
Managing Editor, *Farm Journal*
Agriculture   page 72

Castagno, Alphonso A., Ph.D.
Director, African Studies Center, Boston University
Castagno, Margaret F.
Freelance editor
Africa   page 60
Nigeria   page 263

Clotworthy, John H., B.E.E.
President, Oceans General, Inc.
Oceanography   page 266

Cohen, Geraldine M., B.A.
Scientific Assistant, American Museum of Natural History
Anthropology   page 76

Cook, Robert C.
Editor and Senior Consultant, Population Reference Bureau
Population   page 293

Craib, Roderick, A.M.
Contributing Editor, *Business Week*
Aviation   page 102
Transportation   page 354

Cronkite, Walter
CBS News Correspondent
Top of the News   page 32

Doan, Richard K.
Columnist, *TV Guide*
Television   page 347

Duddleson, William J., B.A.
Director of Policy Studies, The Conservation Foundation
The Environment   page 138

Duff, John B., Ph.D.
Professor of History, Seton Hall University
United States   page 370

Field, Carolyn Wicker, B.S.
Coordinator, Work with Children, Free Library of Philadelphia
Literature for Children   page 233

Fox, Hazel Metz, Ph.D., D.Sc.
Regents Professor and Chairman, Department of Food and Nutrition, University of Nebraska
Food   page 184

Frederick, Pauline, A.B., A.M.
NBC News United Nations correspondent
United Nations   page 364

Geliebter, David Carl, B.A.
Deputy Director, Division on Civil Rights, New Jersey Department of Law and Public Safety
Civil Rights   page 122

Gilruth, Robert R., B.S., M.S., D.Sc.
Director, NASA Manned Spacecraft Center, Houston, Texas
Man in Space   page 10

Goodsell, James Nelson, Ph.D.
Latin America Editor, *The Christian Science Monitor*
Latin America   page 215

Gordon, Leonard I., B.S., M.D.
Medical Consultant, *Medical Tribune*
Medicine and Health   page 238

Gustafson, Barry S., M.A., Dip. Ed.
Lecturer in Political Studies, University of Auckland, New Zealand
New Zealand   page 261
Pacific Islands   page 271

Harris, Leonard, B.S.S.
Arts Editor, CBS News
Theater   page 350

Hattersley, Ralph
Contributing Editor, *Popular Photography*
Photography   page 284

Herst, Herman, Jr., B.A.
Author, *Nassau Street; Fun and Profit in Stamp Collecting*
Stamps   page 199

Howard, C. Edwin, B.S.E.E., M.A.
Automotive writer
Automobiles   page 101

Hoyt, Robert G., A.B.
Editor, *National Catholic Reporter*
Roman Catholicism   page 304

Hudson, Audrey M.
Assistant National Public Relations Director, Camp Fire Girls, Inc.
Camp Fire Girls   page 395

industry developed the necessary space hardware for the trip to the moon. They developed the operational know-how. And they trained the astronauts who would perform this mission.

Within one year of President Kennedy's decision, the master plan for the lunar landing was worked out. This plan was made up of many very important parts.

The first part of the plan called for a giant rocket to boost the spacecraft into orbit. This rocket, the Saturn, would have five huge F-1 engines powering the first stage. Each of these engines would have a thrust greater than 1,500,000 pounds. High-energy hydrogen fuel was to be used for the five engines powering the second stage, and for the single engine of the third stage.

On top of this three-stage rocket would be the moonship and the lunar lander. It was planned that three astronauts would make the trip. One would stay in lunar orbit while his crewmates entered the lunar lander and proceeded to land, work on the moon, and then rejoin him and the mother ship in orbit.

Cape Canaveral was chosen as the launch site for the lunar missions. A new space center was built in Houston, Texas. Here the spacecraft systems would be designed and managed. Here the astronauts would be selected and trained. And from here the moon missions themselves would be controlled. This new facility was called the Manned Spacecraft Center.

Russian Cosmonaut Yuri Gagarin, first man to orbit the earth, was lifted aloft by the then-huge Vostok rocket. Unlike U.S. astronauts, Soviet cosmonauts touch down on land.

PROJECT GEMINI

A very important action was taken during the latter part of 1961. This was the decision to begin Project Gemini. The purpose of Gemini was to gain the flight experience and advanced technology needed for the mission to the moon.

Project Gemini had several major goals. First, it would determine if man could fly in space in a weightless condition for more than ten days. This would be the time required to fly to the moon and back. That man could fly in space for this amount of time was proven by the flight of Gemini 7. Aboard this spacecraft, Colonel Frank Borman and Captain James Lovell orbited the earth for 14 days in December 1965.

The second goal of Project Gemini was to develop rendezvous and docking techniques. These would be required when the lunar lander returned from the moon's surface to join the mother ship. The world's first space rendezvous was accomplished in December 1965. Aboard Gemini 6, Captain Walter Schirra and Colonel Thomas Stafford maneuvered their spaceship to a rendezvous with Gemini 7 during its long-duration flight. Docking was first done by Neil Armstrong and Colonel David Scott in Gemini 8. On March 16, 1966, they docked their spacecraft to an unmanned target vehicle.

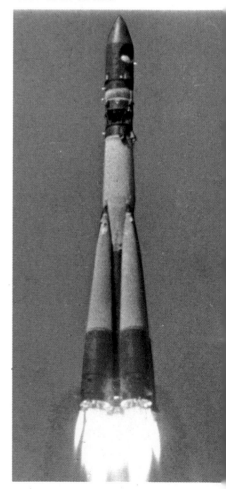

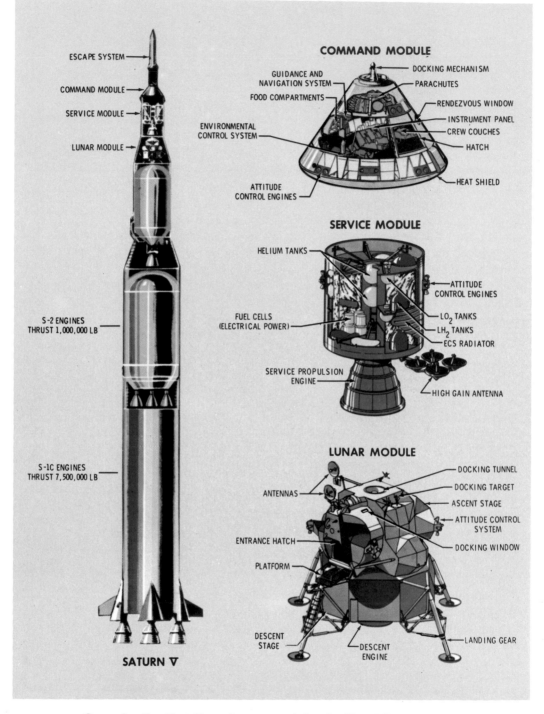

COMMAND MODULE

ESCAPE SYSTEM

COMMAND MODULE

SERVICE MODULE

LUNAR MODULE

DOCKING MECHANISM

GUIDANCE AND
NAVIGATION SYSTEM

PARACHUTES

FOOD COMPARTMENTS

RENDEZVOUS WINDOW

ENVIRONMENTAL
CONTROL SYSTEM

INSTRUMENT PANEL

CREW COUCHES

HATCH

ATTITUDE
CONTROL ENGINES

HEAT SHIELD

SERVICE MODULE

HELIUM TANKS

ATTITUDE
CONTROL ENGINES

FUEL CELLS
(ELECTRICAL POWER)

LO_2 TANKS

LH_2 TANKS

ECS RADIATOR

SERVICE PROPULSION
ENGINE

HIGH GAIN ANTENNA

S-2 ENGINES
THRUST 1,000,000 LB

S-1C ENGINES
THRUST 7,500,000 LB

LUNAR MODULE

DOCKING TUNNEL

DOCKING TARGET

ANTENNAS

ASCENT STAGE

ATTITUDE CONTROL
SYSTEM

ENTRANCE HATCH

DOCKING WINDOW

PLATFORM

DESCENT
STAGE

DESCENT
ENGINE

LANDING GEAR

SATURN Ⅴ

Soon after President Kennedy announced that the United States would send a man to
the moon, work was begun on the giant Saturn launch vehicle, the command module,
the service module, and the lunar module, which would make the actual landing.

The Gemini Project also was to gain experience with activities where the astronaut is outside the spacecraft. The first American astronaut to do this was Colonel Edward White. (A Russian became the first man to walk in space in March 1965.) On June 3, 1965, White ventured out of the Gemini 4 capsule for a 20-minute walk in space. This experience and the later space walks in the Gemini flights were to prove very valuable. They helped develop space-suit technology. They also helped develop procedures for getting out on the lunar surface.

Scientists also wanted astronauts to be able to maneuver the capsule when it re-entered the earth's atmosphere upon return from the moon. In the Gemini program, a technique was developed to accomplish this. The heat shield was used as a gliding surface so that the spacecraft could literally be directed by the astronaut to a desired landing area.

Finally, and of great importance, Gemini Project gave the astronauts invaluable experience. It helped train the men who could form the nucleus of the team that would go to the moon. It was in Gemini that superb techniques were devised for flight management and rendezvous. It was with Gemini that the Mis-

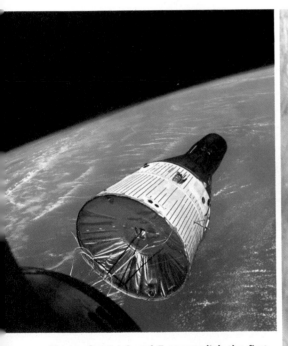

Above, Gemini 6 and 7 accomplish the first rendezvous in space. At right, Gemini 4 Astronaut Edward White becomes the first American to walk in space. His extravehicular activity (EVA) lasted for 20 minutes.

Mission Control Center at the NASA Manned Spacecraft Center, Houston, Texas.

sion Control Center developed to where it was ready for the complex Apollo missions. And it was with Gemini that astronauts and ground controllers learned to work as a team.

CHARTING THE MOON

While NASA was learning to fly men in space in Project Gemini, unmanned satellites were charting the moon.

Just before they crashed onto the moon's surface, the Ranger spacecraft sent back television pictures of the moon. The Surveyor spacecraft actually landed on the moon. They determined the ability of the lunar soil to bear the weight of a spacecraft. They also determined the configuration of the lunar surface in some detail. A lunar orbiter was later used to photograph and map the landing sites that might be used in future manned-landing missions. The lunar orbiters were very successful. They charted the back side and front side of the moon. From their findings, the sites for the Apollo landings were selected.

PREPARING FOR APOLLO

While Project Gemini was going on, work continued on the moonship and the lunar lander. Several unmanned flights were

In preparation for a lunar landing, Ranger 7 was sent to the vicinity of the moon. It returned more than 4,000 photos of the moon's surface.

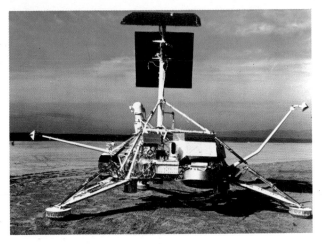

A Surveyor spacecraft. Surveyor 1, which made the first soft landing on the moon, in June 1966, sent over 10,000 photos back to earth.

made with prototypes, or early models, of the moonship. These consisted of a command module and a service module. The moonship command module had the same basic characteristics as the Mercury and Gemini spacecraft. It had a blunt heat shield and a conical afterbody. It was, however, much larger, for it had to have room for three astronauts. It also had an escape tower, as did the Mercury capsule, for launch-escape purposes. The heat shield of the command module used the same principles as Mercury and Gemini. However, the ablation material was much thicker. This was because a spacecraft returning from the moon and re-entering the earth's atmosphere would travel at a greater speed than Mercury or Gemini. As a result, it would generate much more heat.

The service module of the moonship had a powerful space rocket. This was used to steer the ship toward the moon and to slow it down so that it went into orbit around the moon. This rocket has a thrust of over twenty thousand pounds.

The lunar lander, or lunar module as it was called, was designed with two rocket engines. The landing engine powers the descent from lunar orbit to the moon's surface. In the final phases of landing, this engine must be able to be throttled to permit maneuvering to a gentle landing. The second rocket engine of the lunar module is used for ascent only. It powers the takeoff from the moon and the return to lunar orbit.

The navigation and guidance systems of the lunar lander and the mother ship must be very accurate. Both vehicles must perform precision rendezvous maneuvers when the lunar lander

Photograph of the Crater Copernicus, taken by Lunar Orbiter 2.

returns to the mother ship in lunar orbit. Even if communications with the ground are lost, the command module can make its way safely back to earth.

TRAGEDY AT CAPE KENNEDY

In January 1967 a tragedy occurred at Cape Kennedy while plans were under way for the first manned Apollo flight. Astronauts Virgil Grissom, Edward White, and Roger Chaffee were killed by a flash fire in the spacecraft cabin. At the time, the spacecraft and launch vehicle were undergoing a simulated mission on the gantry. In the year that followed the fire, efforts were made to reduce as much as humanly possible the threat of fire in the spacecraft. New materials were found for the cabin interior. These virtually could not burn. Space suits were redesigned. These new suits used beta cloth, a type of fiber-glass material that will not burn. Wiring and plumbing systems were redesigned. And pad operations were modified to use a mixture of oxygen and nitrogen in place of pure oxygen to reduce the fire hazard.

SATURN 5 LAUNCHED

In November 1967 the first huge Saturn 5 rocket was launched. It performed beautifully. It placed the Apollo capsule on a trajectory from which it could be driven back into the earth's atmosphere at the same speed at which it would return from the moon on later flights. The service-module engine was used to help increase the speed of re-entry by driving the command module back to earth. Both spacecraft and the rocket worked perfectly in this mission. NASA thus obtained its first combined, full-scale test of both rocket and spacecraft systems.

NASA was not ready yet, however, to fly on to the moon. On the second flight of the Saturn 5, an instability—called the pogo effect—developed in the Saturn rocket. The pogo effect is a vibration along the axis of the vehicle. This vibration causes undesirable "g" forces throughout the rocket system and in the spacecraft itself. Intensive efforts were made to correct this instability.

APOLLO 8: AROUND THE MOON

In December 1968, NASA was ready for the first manned flight to the moon. However, this flight was not designed to land on the moon. Rather, it was designed to fly to the moon, go into lunar orbit, take pictures of the lunar-landing sites, and then return to earth. This flight was Apollo 8. Aboard this craft, Captain Frank Borman, Captain James Lovell, and Colonel William Anders made man's first trip to the moon. The way was paved for this flight by Apollo 7, which occurred in October of

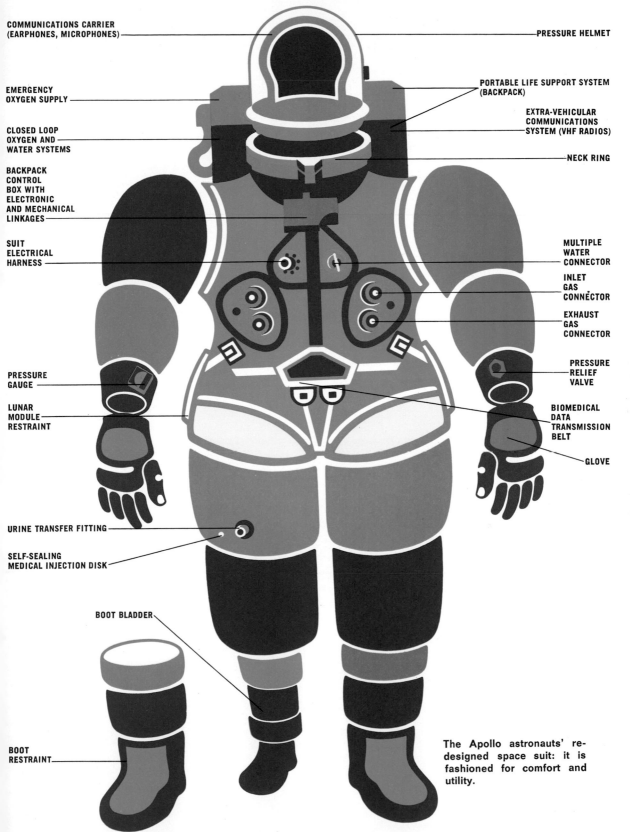

COMMUNICATIONS CARRIER
(EARPHONES, MICROPHONES)

PRESSURE HELMET

EMERGENCY
OXYGEN SUPPLY

PORTABLE LIFE SUPPORT SYSTEM
(BACKPACK)

CLOSED LOOP
OXYGEN AND
WATER SYSTEMS

EXTRA-VEHICULAR
COMMUNICATIONS
SYSTEM (VHF RADIOS)

NECK RING

BACKPACK
CONTROL
BOX WITH
ELECTRONIC
AND MECHANICAL
LINKAGES

SUIT
ELECTRICAL
HARNESS

MULTIPLE
WATER
CONNECTOR

INLET
GAS
CONNECTOR

EXHAUST
GAS
CONNECTOR

PRESSURE
GAUGE

PRESSURE
RELIEF
VALVE

LUNAR
MODULE
RESTRAINT

BIOMEDICAL
DATA
TRANSMISSION
BELT

GLOVE

URINE TRANSFER FITTING

SELF-SEALING
MEDICAL INJECTION DISK

BOOT BLADDER

BOOT
RESTRAINT

The Apollo astronauts' redesigned space suit: it is
fashioned for comfort and
utility.

Apollo 7 photograph of a hurricane (October 18, 1968) taken from an altitude of 97 miles.

This photograph of a nearly full moon was taken from the Apollo 8 spacecraft, December 1968.

The moon's Crater Langrenus, photographed by Apollo 8 from an altitude of 150 miles.

This view of the rising earth greeted Apollo 8 astronauts as they came from behind the moon.

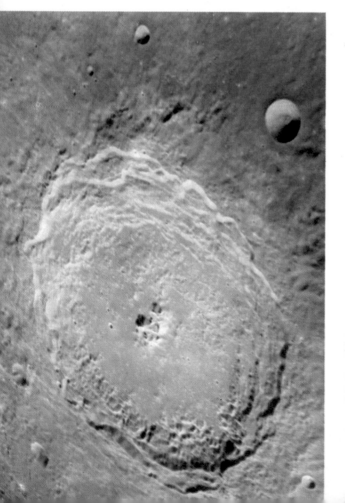

the same year. Aboard Apollo 7, Astronauts Walter Schirra, R. Walter Cunningham, and Donn Eisele orbited the earth in the Apollo command and service modules for 11 days. Apollo 7 had been so successful that it allowed NASA to fly the lunar mission of Apollo 8 without further testing in earth orbit.

APOLLO 9

Apollo 8 was followed in March 1969 by Apollo 9. This flight tested, in earth orbit, the lunar module and the command and service modules. This was the first manned flight of the lunar module. Rendezvous and docking between the command and service modules and the lunar module were also tested. Astronauts James McDivitt and Russell Schweickart piloted the lunar module. Colonel David Scott controlled the mother ship. The transfer through the tunnel system of the spacecraft was first accomplished in this test. As in previous flights, the space engines of the service module performed flawlessly, so too did

Apollo 9 Astronaut David R. Scott is half out of the command module. The photo was taken by Astronaut Russell Schweickart, from the docked lunar module.

the landing and ascent engines of the lunar module. During the last few days of flight in Apollo 9, the astronauts took many fascinating and useful photographs of the earth for earth-resources studies.

APOLLO 10: DRESS REHEARSAL

NASA was now ready for the final dress rehearsal for the lunar-landing mission. Apollo 10 was launched in May 1969. It was to do all phases of the lunar-landing mission except the actual landing itself. It was to develop the timelines for the crew. And it was to work out thermal-control procedures during the translunar and transearth trajectories. The landing module was to be separated from the mother ship in lunar orbit, and descend into a low orbit around the moon for photographing the landing sites. Colonel Thomas Stafford and Commander Eugene Cernan flew to within nine miles of the lunar surface. They then returned successfully to rendezvous with Commander John Young in the mother ship.

In July 1969, final preparations had been made for landing on the moon. Astronauts Neil Armstrong, Colonel Mike Col-

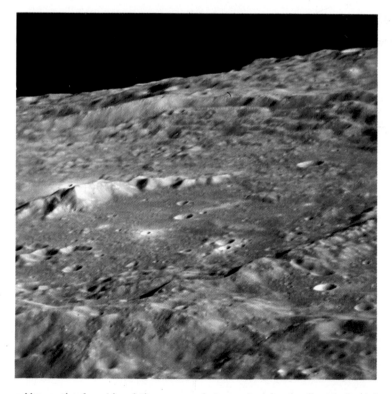

Above, the far side of the moon, photographed by Apollo 10. At right, during Apollo 9 flight the lunar module is tested in earth orbit.

lins, and Colonel Buzz Aldrin had spent hundreds of hours training with ground simulators for this key mission. Neil Armstrong had made many flights with a lunar-landing trainer. Scientific equipment had been carefully developed and checked out. It was then stowed aboard the lunar lander for deployment on the lunar surface. The deep-space communications network was ready. So too were the ground-control teams at the Mission Control Center and the recovery forces at sea. It had been decided to quarantine the lunar samples and the astronauts when they returned to earth. The National Academy of Sciences believed these precautions were necessary to protect the earth against the remote possibility that undesirable organisms might be brought back from the moon.

APOLLO 11: MAN ON THE MOON

Apollo 11 was launched on the morning of July 16, 1969. The landing on the moon was made on July 20, 1969, at the Sea of Tranquility. Armstrong's historic words after touchdown were, "Houston, Tranquility Base here. The *Eagle* has landed." Almost 50 pounds of lunar rocks and fines were collected. These were stowed in special vacuum-type boxes for transportation back to earth. A special laser reflector was placed on the lunar surface. It is being used for determining the precise motions of the moon and its distance from the earth to a degree never before possible. A special lunar seismometer also was placed on the moon's surface. It has given measurements of the seismic activity of the moon.

The astronauts found that it was quite pleasant to walk on the moon in spite of their heavy space suits and life-support equipment. The 1/6 gravity of the moon allowed them to walk and even

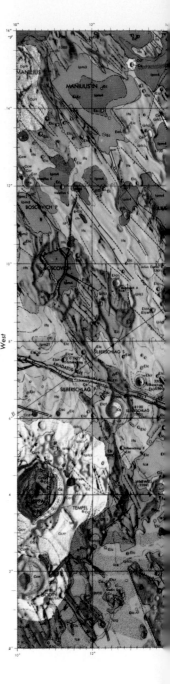

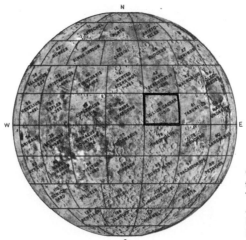

Color map of the moon shows the Sea of Tranquility (Mare Tranquillitatis), where the Apollo 11 touched down. Landing site was 0° 41′ 15″ north latitude, 23° 26′ east longitude.

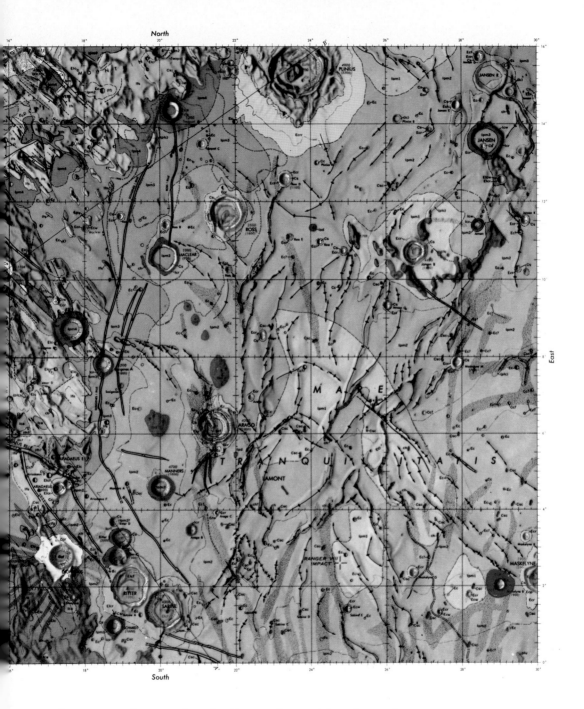

to lope at speeds up to 5 or 6 miles per hour without becoming very tired. They placed an American flag on the surface and drove core-sampling equipment 5 inches into the lunar surface. These core samples were brought back to earth for scientific analysis.

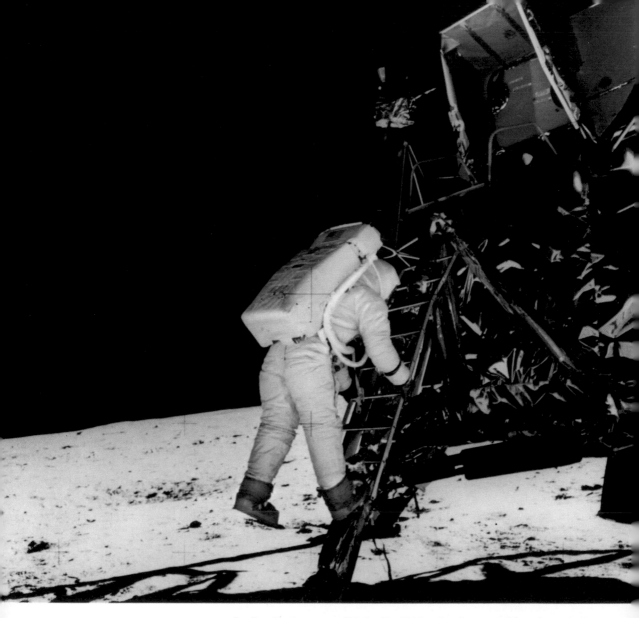

Apollo 11 Astronaut Edwin E. Aldrin, Jr., lunar-module pilot, climbs down the steps of the lunar-module ladder as he prepares to walk on the moon. Photograph was taken by Astronaut Neil A. Armstrong.

After several hours on the lunar surface, the astronauts returned to the lunar lander. They were able to rest before the check-out and countdown for lift-off back to orbit around the moon. Here again, all systems, including the ascent engine, performed perfectly. The rendezvous and docking with the mother ship were done in a routine fashion. The transfer of lunar-sample boxes was made without difficulty. The return from lunar orbit to the transearth trajectory was done according

Astronaut Aldrin, on the lunar surface, deploys one of the Apollo 11 scientific experiments: a seismometer that will measure vibrations on the moon. Behind him is the lunar lander and American flag.

to plan as was the landing in the Pacific. The astronauts and the samples were placed in a sealed van aboard the aircraft carrier and transported back to the Lunar Receiving Laboratory at Houston. Here they were quarantined for 21 days from the time they set foot on the lunar surface. Elaborate tests have shown no evidence of any organisms on the lunar surface.

The lunar rocks and fines have proved to be of great interest to scientists all over the world. Analysis has already shown the

An astronaut's footprint on the powdery lunar surface.

A lunar rock, showing glass-lined surface pits.

moon to be of very ancient origin, over 3,000,000,000 years old. The composition of the rocks is unlike anything found on earth. They give high promise of unlocking many secrets of the universe and of our own origin here on earth. The flight of Apollo to the moon surely marks a great milestone in human endeavor. The machines that made the trip possible are the most powerful and yet the most accurate ever designed and built by mankind. The teamwork demonstrated by government and industry teams was extraordinary. Apollo 11 fulfilled the national goal of landing men on the moon and returning them safely to earth in this decade.

APOLLO 12

On November 14, 1969, Apollo 12, the second landing expedition to the moon, was launched from Cape Kennedy. Astronauts Charles Conrad, Jr., Richard F. Gordon, Jr., and Alan L. Bean made up the crew of this flight.

On November 19, Commander Conrad successfully landed the lunar craft *Intrepid* on the Ocean of Storms, about 950 miles farther west than the landing site of Apollo 11. After the landing, Conrad and the lunar-module pilot, Commander Bean, set up a small nuclear-power generating station for the long-life scientific experiments that they carried with them. They then performed the first lunar geologic traverse and collected over 60 pounds of lunar rocks. On their second lunar walk they collected more rocks as well as parts from a Surveyor spacecraft, which had been on the moon for a long time. These were brought back for study of the effects of the lunar environment on mechanical and electronic systems. While Conrad and Bean explored the lunar surface, Commander Gordon maintained the command module in lunar orbit.

Apollo 12 splashed down in the Pacific on schedule on November 24, 1969. The scientific experiments left by the astronauts have already given much new and valuable data. It appears that the moon will have many new and unexpected characteristics which will puzzle and fascinate scientists for some time to come.

THE FUTURE

There will be more Apollo missions over the next few years. Scientists the world over agree that there is much to be learned about the universe from further exploration of the moon. There is great incentive at the present time to perform more lunar landings at other places on the lunar surface. Scientists are anxious to place seismometer networks on the moon to help determine the internal makeup of that body and the secrets of

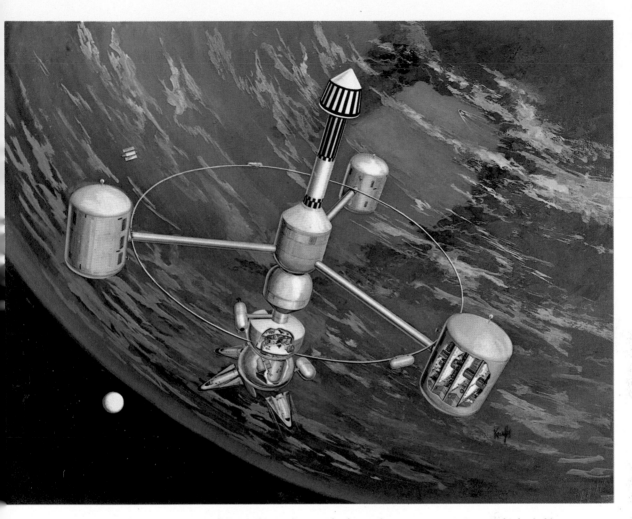

An artist's rendering of what a future space station might look like. Space shuttles would ferry men between the orbiting station and earth.

its origin. Just how many Apollo landings will be made will, however, depend on the scientific return in relation to the effort required. Only the future can give the answer to this.

What does the future hold? Surely the next decade in space will be even more exciting and productive than the past. Plans are under way for a huge space base in earth orbit. There also are plans for a reusable shuttle vehicle. This spacecraft will be able to move men and materials back and forth from the space base to earth, routinely, so that scientists and engineers as well as astronauts can fly in space. Unmanned missions to Mars, Venus, and to the outer planets will certainly take place in the future. And someday, man himself will visit Mars and the outer planets.

TOP OF THE NEWS

By WALTER CRONKITE

1969 will be remembered as the year in which man first set foot on an alien celestial body. The two Apollo lunar landings, watched on television by millions of earthbound people, were a testament to the technical creativity and the will to succeed of the American people. To many this achievement gave hope that the same will to succeed, the same creativity—and the necessary funds—would be applied to the more earthly problems that plagued the United States and, indeed, the entire world.

In 1969, these problems were legion. The lands of Latin America, Africa, and Asia continued to suffer from the effects of overpopulation and underdevelopment. In Latin America and Africa, military coups took their toll of civilian governments. In Africa, too, Nigeria, the nation that had offered greatest promise of success, remained torn by civil war. In Asia, the Vietnam war continued to take too many lives—and to cause domestic turmoil in the United States. In Asia there were the beginnings of what could be a world tragedy: armed confrontation between the two communist superpowers—China and the Soviet Union. The Middle East also contained the seeds of total war, as the Arabs and Israelis maintained rigid positions that precluded any possibility of peace.

There were, however, some bright spots on the world scene during the year. In Germany, Willy Brandt, the new chancellor, took important steps to bring about some accommodation between East and West. In the United States, President Nixon, during his first year in office, made important moves toward reducing world tensions. The Senate passed and he signed the nuclear-nonproliferation treaty. Talks were begun with the Soviet Union on limiting strategic arms. And an effort was made to begin the slow process of disengagement from the Vietnam war. Perhaps one sign of Mr. Nixon's success was the fact that thousands of college students were beginning to shift their efforts from demonstrations against the war to demonstrations against pollution of our natural environment. A concerted national effort, hopefully, will lead to the elimination of pollution as well as a host of other domestic ills.

JANUARY

			1	2	3	4
5	6	7	8	9	10	11
12	13	14	15	16	17	18
19	20	21	22	23	24	25
26	27	28	29	30	31	

4. Ifni in North Africa, a territory of Spain since 1934, was ceded to Morocco.

7. France banned the sale and shipment of military arms to Israel.

10. Sweden extended full diplomatic recognition to North Vietnam.

13. A Scandinavian Airlines DC-8 crashed into Santa Monica Bay in California; 15 were killed.

14. Explosions aboard the nuclear-powered aircraft carrier USS *Enterprise* on a training cruise in the Pacific killed 27 crew members.

16. Soviet spacecraft Soyuz 4 and Soyuz 5 completed the first docking of manned spacecraft in space and the first transfer of crew members between orbiting spacecraft.

18. A United Airlines Boeing 727 exploded in the air and fell into Santa Monica Bay, California; all 38 aboard were killed.

20. In Coronado, California, a U.S. Navy court of inquiry into the capture of the USS *Pueblo* on January 23, 1968, by North Korea, opened.

don Johnson, Hubert Humphrey, and the presidential party looked on as the oath of office was administered to the President by Chief Justice of the Supreme Court Earl Warren. In his inaugural speech, Mr. Nixon called for international peace.

						1
2	3	4	5	6	7	8
9	10	11	12	13	14	15
16	17	18	19	20	21	22
23	24	25	26	27	28	

5. Millions of workers in Italy demanding higher pensions staged a 24-hour strike.

8. An oil well offshore at Santa Barbara, California, was capped after 11 days of leaking oil into the Pacific Ocean. Governor Ronald Reagan declared the shores blackened by the oil as "disaster areas."

13. National Guardsmen used tear gas against student rioters to restore order at the University of Wisconsin in Madison. . . . Police and students clashed at Duke University in Durham, North Carolina. . . . An administration building at City College in New York City was seized by students.

14. Two tuna fishing boats from the United States were attacked by a Peruvian Navy gunboat; the boats were within the 200-mile territorial-water limit claimed by Peru.

18. In the U.S. House of Representatives, the name of the House Un-American Activities Committee (HUAC) was changed to House Internal Security Committee (HISC).

25. The Government of Tanzania canceled its U.S. Peace Corps program.

MIDDLE EAST CONFLICT. Bitter fighting between Israel and its Arab neighbors continued to be a daily occurrence. During February, Arab commandos, such as those training in Jordan, above, were responsible for an attack against an Israeli airplane at the Zurich, Switzerland, airport, and for the bombing of a supermarket in Jerusalem, which killed two Israeli youths. In response to guerrilla activity, Israeli planes attacked guerrilla concentrations in Jordan and Syria. Israeli armed forces (right) also retaliated against sniping attacks across the Suez Canal by Egyptian soldiers. On February 12, in the United Nations Security Council, Israel charged that Egypt was organizing and directing Arab guerrilla forces and that between June 6, 1967, and December 31, 1968, Israel had been the target of 1,288 acts of sabotage and border incidents. During this period, 281 Israelis were killed, more than 1,000 Arab guerrillas were killed, and 1,500 were arrested or captured. In an effort to bring about peace, the big-four powers (United States, U.S.S.R., Great Britain, and France) began preliminary discussions on February 5. At the end of February, Gunnar Jarring, special UN envoy, resumed his peace efforts. But the level of fighting and the intensity of passions seemed to doom peace efforts before they started.

MARCH

						1
2	3	4	5	6	7	8
9	10	11	12	13	14	15
16	17	18	19	20	21	22
23	24	25	26	27	28	29
30	31					

1. Clay L. Shaw was acquitted in New Orleans, Louisiana, on a charge of conspiring to assassinate President John F. Kennedy.

9. Fighting between Israel and Egypt across the Suez Canal resulted in heavy damage to Egyptian oil storage tanks in the city of Suez. General Abdel Moneim Riad, Egypt's armed forces chief of staff, was killed.

10. In Memphis, Tennessee, James Earl Ray pleaded guilty to the murder of Dr. Martin Luther King, Jr. He was sentenced to 99 years in prison.

11. The "black lung" law was enacted in West Virginia.

13. Apollo 9 splashed down in the Atlantic, ending a 10-day flight in earth orbit to test the lunar module.

16. In Venezuela a jet crashed after take-off from Grano de Oro airport, Maracaibo; all 84 persons aboard and 71 on the ground were killed.

19. British paratroopers landed in the Caribbean island of Anguilla after the island tried to set itself up as an independent republic.

Chinese and Soviet border guards approach each other during a lull in the fighting along the frozen Ussuri River, where, in March, the long-standing feud between Communist China and the Soviet Union flared into open warfare. Two major clashes, on March 2 and March 15, resulted in dozens of deaths on both sides. The fighting began over conflicting claims to a small island in the Ussuri River. The Russians call the island Damansky; the Chinese call it Chenpao. Situated on the Manchurian border, 250 miles north of Vladivostok, it is strategically unimportant. Conflicting claims to the island date back to 1860, when the Russians and Chinese signed a treaty establishing the Far Eastern boundaries between the two states. China has repudiated this treaty.

		1	2	3	4	5
6	7	8	9	10	11	12
13	14	15	16	17	18	19
20	21	22	23	24	25	26
27	28	29	30			

1. The UN Security Council censured Israel for its air attack on a Jordanian town on March 26 in which 18 civilians were killed.

2. In Ghana, Joseph A. Ankrah, head of state, resigned after admitting that he had gotten money for political purposes from a private company.

8. Haskell Karp, 47, the first person to receive an artificial heart, died in St. Luke's Episcopal Hospital, Houston, Texas. A man-made plastic and Dacron heart had been implanted in him on April 4 by a team of surgeons headed by Dr. Denton A. Cooley. The artificial heart was used for 65 hours. It was replaced by a human heart on April 7.

14. North Korea shot down a U.S. Navy EC-121 unarmed reconnaissance plane over the Sea of Japan.

17. In a Los Angeles, California, court, Sirhan Sirhan was found guilty of the murder of Senator Robert F. Kennedy . . . . Alexander Dubcek resigned as first secretary of Czechoslovakia's Communist Party. He was succeeded by Gustav Husak.

27. President René Barrientos Ortuño of Bolivia was killed in a helicopter crash.

Georges Pompidou

DE GAULLE RESIGNS. On April 28, President Charles de Gaulle of France resigned. His resignation came after his proposals for government reform lost in a national referendum on April 27. De Gaulle's reforms would have strengthened regional governments and weakened the powers of the French Senate. On April 28, Alain Poher, president of the Senate, became acting president of France. On April 29, former Premier Georges Pompidou announced his candidacy for president.

Charles de Gaulle

MAY

6. U.S. Secretary of the Navy John H. Chafee overruled a Navy court of inquiry into the capture of the *Pueblo* by North Korea in 1968. He announced that Commander Lloyd M. Bucher and the crew members would not be disciplined.

9. More than 200 saints were dropped from the official liturgical calendar of the Roman Catholic Church. The saints included St. Nicholas, St. Valentine, and St. Christopher—favorites of Catholics and non-Catholics throughout the world.

14. Supreme Court Justice Abe Fortas resigned under public pressure after it was disclosed that he had accepted and later returned money from a private foundation.

20. In Vietnam, the U.S. 101st Airborne Division and South Vietnamese forces took Apbia Mountain, called "Hamburger Hill." The battle for the mountain had begun on May 10.

21. President Nixon named U.S. Court of Appeals Judge Warren Earl Burger to be chief justice of the Supreme Court.

25. In Sudan, a military coup overthrew the Government of Premier Ahmed Mahgoub.

APOLLO 10. On May 18, in a dress rehearsal for the Apollo 11 lunar landing, Apollo 10 blasted off with astronauts Thomas Stafford, Eugene Cernan, and John Young aboard. On May 21 the craft went into lunar orbit. On the following day, Cernan and Stafford separated the lunar module from the command module and maneuvered it to within 9 miles of the moon. After 2 orbits, they returned to the command module for the trip back to earth.

NEW SUPREME COURT CHIEF JUSTICE. On May 21, President Richard Nixon nominated Warren Earl Burger, 61, a judge of the U.S. Court of Appeals for the District of Columbia, to be chief justice of the United States. Justice Burger succeeds Earl Warren, who retires in June, at the end of the Supreme Court's current term.

1	2	3	4	5	6	7
8	9	10	11	12	13	14
15	16	17	18	19	20	21
22	23	24	25	26	27	28
29	30					

2. The U.S. destroyer *Frank E. Evans* and the Australian aircraft carrier *Melbourne* collided in the South China Sea; 74 crewmen from the *Evans* were lost.

4. New York Governor Rockefeller's fact-finding mission to Chile for President Nixon was called off because of the threat of demonstrations and strikes against the visit. Rockefeller's visit to Venezuela was canceled on June 1; his visit to Peru had been canceled on May 23.

9. The prime interest rate on bank loans in the United States was raised from 7½ to 8½ per cent. It was the third and biggest increase in 1969.

15. Georges Pompidou was elected president of France in a runoff election with Alain Poher. Pompidou won 58.2 per cent of the vote.

16. The Supreme Court ruled that the U.S. House of Representatives had acted unconstitutionally when it barred New York Representative Adam Clayton Powell from the Ninetieth Congress.

25. In Vietnam, the U.S. Navy turned over 64 river patrol boats to the South Vietnamese Navy.

SOME U.S. TROOPS TO LEAVE VIETNAM. Following talks with South Vietnamese President Nguyen Van Thieu at Midway Island, President Richard Nixon announced on June 8 that 25,000 American soldiers, largely Army and Marine combat troops, would be withdrawn from South Vietnam by the end of August. President Nixon called the move a "significant step forward" toward peace. U.S. Secretary of Defense Melvin Laird, who had attended the Midway conference, stated the following day that more American soldiers could be withdrawn from South Vietnam if the South Vietnamese Army continues to take on more and more of the burden of fighting. At the time of President Nixon's statement on the withdrawal of combat soldiers, there were some 540,000 United States troops serving in Vietnam.

JULY

3. The UN Security Council censured Israel for annexing the Arab section of Jerusalem.

5. Tom Mboya, Kenya's minister of economic affairs, was assassinated in Nairobi by an unidentified gunman. . . . Mariano Rumor's center-Left coalition Government resigned, plunging Italy into a political crisis.

7. In Canada, the House of Commons approved a bill making French, along with English, an official language of Canada.

18. Mary Jo Kopechne was killed when a car driven by Senator Edward M. Kennedy plunged off a bridge into a pond on Chappaquiddick Island in Massachusetts. . . . El Salvador and Honduras accepted a peace plan by the Organization of American States to end their five-day undeclared war.

22. Prince Juan Carlos was named the future king of Spain by Generalissimo Francisco Franco.

31. U.S. space probe Mariner 6 flew past Mars within 2,132 miles of the Martian surface. Mariner 6 sent its first photographs of Mars back to earth on July 29.

MAN ON THE MOON. On July 20, astronaut Neil Armstrong piloted the Apollo 11 lunar module to the surface of the moon. Soon Armstrong and his fellow astronaut, Edwin Aldrin (seen above), were walking on the lunar surface as millions of people watched on TV. For over two hours they took photos, collected rock and soil samples, set up experiments, and enjoyed being the first men ever to set foot on a celestial body other than earth. On July 21, their work done, the two astronauts blasted off in the lunar module. They rejoined command-module pilot Michael Collins in lunar orbit, and then headed back to earth, where they splashed down July 24.

A NEW PRINCE OF WALES. At Caernarvon Castle, Wales, on July 1, Charles Philip Arthur George, eldest son of Queen Elizabeth II, was invested as the 21st Prince of Wales.

AUGUST

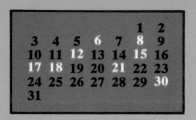

					1	2
3	4	5	6	7	8	9
10	11	12	13	14	15	16
17	18	19	20	21	22	23
24	25	26	27	28	29	30
31						

6. An amendment that would have halted the Safeguard missile defense system (ABM) lost in the U.S. Senate.

8. France devalued the franc 11.1 per cent.

12. North Vietnamese and Vietcong forces attacked more than 150 allied cities, towns, and bases in South Vietnam. It was the heaviest fighting of the war in several months.

15. The U.S. Department of Agriculture banned the use of DDT and two other pesticides, dieldrin and heptachlor, in Government-sponsored projects.

17. Hurricane Camille hit the Gulf Coast of the United States with 150 mph winds.

18. President Nixon nominated U.S. Court of Appeals Judge Clement F. Haynsworth to the Supreme Court.

21. Troops and police were used to put down anti-Soviet demonstrations in Prague, Czechoslovakia. It was the first anniversary of the Soviet invasion.

30. In the first free elections in Ghana since 1956, the Progress Party headed by Kofi A. Busia won a majority in Parliament.

STRIFE IN NORTHERN IRELAND. Severe rioting between Roman Catholics and Protestants broke out in Belfast, Northern Ireland, on August 2. In the violence, scores were injured, stores were looted, and homes were burned down (below). New clashes erupted on August 12 in Londonderry and spread to Belfast, Armagh, and other cities. On August 19 the British Army took control of all security for Northern Ireland. British troops were used to patrol barricaded streets (above).

PRESIDENT NIXON ON 9-DAY TOUR IN ASIA AND EUROPE.
On August 2, President Nixon arrived in Rumania for a 27-hour visit. He became the first American president to visit a communist country since 1945 when President Franklin D. Roosevelt met with Stalin in Yalta in the Soviet Union. The Rumanians warmly greeted President Nixon (seen riding in a motorcade in Bucharest with President Nicolae Ceausescu of Rumania) with cheers of "Sa traite Domnule Presedinte!" (Long life, Mister President!). Three times President Nixon left his car to shake hands with some of the 500,000 people lining the motorcade route. Rumania was one stop in the President's 24,500-mile, 9-day tour, which also included the Philippines, Indonesia, Thailand, South Vietnam, India, Pakistan, and Great Britain. The President conferred with the heads of government of each country on his tour.

SEPTEMBER

	1	2	3	4	5	6
7	8	9	10	11	12	13
14	15	16	17	18	19	20
21	22	23	24	25	26	27
28	29	30				

7. In Brazil, U.S. Ambassador C. Burke Elbrick was released after being kidnaped on September 4 by terrorists. In exchange, the Brazilian Government freed 15 political prisoners.

8. President Nixon and President Gustavo Diaz Ordaz of Mexico dedicated the Amistad Dam on the Rio Grande, on the Texas-Mexico border.

9. An Israeli amphibious tank force crossed the Gulf of Suez for a ten-hour assault on Egyptian military targets.

10. Alaska's North Slope oil lands were leased for a record $900,220,590.

26. A military junta overthrew President Luis Adolfo Siles Salinas of Bolivia; General Alfredo Ovando Candia assumed the presidency.

28. In West Germany, Chancellor Kurt Kiesinger's Christian Democratic Union failed to win a majority in national elections.

29. The U.S. Army dropped charges against six Green Beret soldiers. They had been arrested in August for the alleged murder of a Vietnamese double agent.

Premier Chou En-lai   Premier Aleksei N. Kosygin

KOSYGIN AND CHOU EN-LAI MEET IN PEKING. On September 11, Soviet Premier Aleksei N. Kosygin and Chinese Premier Chou En-lai met and held frank talks at the Peking airport. This was the first meeting between leaders of the two disputing powers since 1965. Kosygin and Chou had both just come from paying respects in Hanoi, North Vietnam, following the death of North Vietnamese leader Ho Chi Minh. (Chou left Hanoi September 5, and Kosygin arrived September 6.) It was thought that a plea in Ho's will and a call from the North Vietnamese had brought about the meeting. After the Peking meeting, both countries called for talks on their border dispute. Kosygin in Peking had asked for border talks, a cease-fire, and mutual withdrawal of troops.

S.S. MANHATTAN CONQUERS NORTHWEST PASSAGE. On September 14 a huge ice-breaking tanker emerged from the ice-filled Prince of Wales Strait in the North American Arctic and entered the Beaufort Sea. By doing this the *Manhattan* completed the first commercial trip through the largely icebound Northwest Passage. The ship made the journey to prove that large ships can travel through the passage. If they can do this regularly, the oil discovered on the Alaska North Slope and other minerals of the Arctic can be carried by this route to ports on the east coast of the United States.

OCTOBER

			1	2	3	4
5	6	7	8	9	10	11
12	13	14	15	16	17	18
19	20	21	22	23	24	25
26	27	28	29	30	31	

5. Severe flooding in western Algeria left more than 100,000 homeless.

7. Policemen and firemen went on strike for higher wages in Montreal, Canada. Quebec's provincial Parliament ordered the men back to work.

10. President Nixon announced that Lt. Gen. Lewis B. Hershey would no longer be director of the Selective Service System (the draft) as of February 16, 1970.

13. The Soviet Union launched a manned spacecraft, Soyuz 8, to orbit at the same time as two other manned spacecraft, Soyuz 6, launched on October 11, and Soyuz 7, launched on October 12.

15. President Abirashid Ali Shermarke of Somalia was assassinated by a policeman.

21. Willy Brandt, leader of the Social Democratic Party, was sworn in as the fourth chancellor of West Germany.

27. An earthquake in Banja Luka, Yugoslavia, left more than 60,000 homeless.

29. The U.S. Supreme Court ordered desegregation "at once" of all schools.

THE AMAZIN' METS WIN THE WORLD SERIES. On October 16 the New York Mets beat the Baltimore Orioles 5–3 to win the World Series, 4 games to 1. The Orioles, the powerhouse team of the American League, won only the first game. The Mets, piloted by manager Gil Hodges, were sparked by the incredible fielding of center fielder Tommy Agee and by strong pitching from Jerry Koosman, Tom Seaver, and Gary Gentry. Met first baseman Donn Clendenon was the Most Valuable Player of the World Series.

MORATORIUM DAY. Across the United States, on October 15, hundreds of thousands of people marched in candle-lit parades, attended rallies, wore black armbands, and carried peace signs to show their opposition peacefully to the war in Vietnam. The event was Moratorium Day. It was planned at first as a youth protest against the war. The idea spread to other groups. The Moratorium received the support of clergymen and many members of Congress. President Nixon, however, said that the antiwar protests would not have any effect on the policies of the United States. The President was supported by many people who felt that the antiwar protests aided North Vietnam and were harmful to the United States effort in Vietnam. And on Moratorium Day many demonstrated support of the President by displaying American flags.

NOVEMBER

						1
2	3	4	5	6	7	8
9	10	11	12	13	14	15
16	17	18	19	20	21	22
23	24	25	26	27	28	29
30						

3. The Lebanese Army and Arab guerrillas reached an agreement to end fighting between them that had begun in mid-October. The agreement provided for the guerrillas to keep their bases in Lebanon.

5. Bobby G. Seale, chairman of the Black Panther Party, and on trial in Chicago with seven other persons for conspiracy to incite a riot during the 1968 Democratic national convention, was convicted of contempt of court and sentenced to four years in prison.

20. U.S. Secretary of Agriculture Clifford M. Hardin ordered that the use of the pesticide DDT in residential areas be ended within thirty days; the use of DDT in other areas was to be ended by 1971. . . . Henry Cabot Lodge resigned as chief U.S. negotiator at the Paris peace talks.

21. The U.S. Senate voted 55–45 against the nomination of Clement F. Haynsworth, Jr., to the Supreme Court.

25. President Nixon renounced the use of germ warfare by the United States and ordered all germ-warfare weapons destroyed.

WAR PROTEST IN WASHINGTON, D.C. More than 300,-000 demonstrators massed in the capital on November 15 to protest United States military involvement in the Vietnam war. It was the largest single antiwar demonstration in American history.

APOLLO 12. On November 19, Apollo 12 astronauts Charles Conrad and Alan Bean became the third and fourth men ever to set foot on the moon. After 31½ hours there, the two blasted off and rejoined command-module pilot Richard Gordon in lunar orbit. The return trip to earth was on schedule and without incident. Left to right: Conrad, Gordon, Bean.

DECEMBER

1. A national draft lottery, the first since World War II, was held in Washington, D.C., to assign draft numbers to young men between the ages of 19 and 26 who have not been in military service.

5. Two Israeli civilians held by Syria since the plane they were on was hijacked on August 29 were released in exchange for 13 Syrians held in Israel.

12. The National Commission on the Causes and Prevention of Violence ended its 18-month inquiry with a final report that called for $20,000,000,000 a year to be spent on domestic problems to fight the social causes of unrest.

15. President Nixon announced that 50,000 additional U.S. troops would be withdrawn from Vietnam by April 15, 1970. The troop withdrawals announced in 1969 thus totaled 110,000 men.

22. In Northern Ireland, civil-rights leader Bernadette Devlin was sentenced to six months in prison for her activities during religious rioting in Londonderry in August 1969. . . . The United States and the Soviet Union agreed at the Helsinki, Finland, arms talks to open full arms talks in Vienna, Austria, on April 16, 1970.

VIETNAM: THE CONDUCT OF WAR. To generations of Americans, the image of U.S. troops has always been the positive one of weary GI's taking time out from war to pass out candy and food to hungry children (right, top). On occasion, the burning of villages that harbor enemy troops (above) has been accepted as a necessary evil of war. In December, however, Americans saw pictures that revealed a different story: American troops had allegedly taken part in a 1968 massacre at the Vietnamese village of Songmy. As many as 567 men, women, and children were reportedly killed. The story tore at the conscience of America. First Lieutenant William Calley, Jr., leader of the platoon that entered the village, faced charges in the murder of 109 of the civilians. Captain Ernest Medina, commander of the infantry company involved, denied that he had ordered or seen any massacre. Paul Meadlo, a former soldier, said during a television interview that at Songmy he had shot 35 to 40 civilians on orders from superior officers.

William L. Calley, Jr.

Ernest L. Medina

Paul D. Meadlo

THE
YEAR
IN
REVIEW

1969

BY 1969, there were 37 independent nations in Africa south of the Sahara. This count does not include Rhodesia, Biafra, Namibia (South-West Africa), and a number of territories still under colonial rule. Nor does it include the northern African countries of Algeria, Tunisia, Libya, Morocco, and the United Arab Republic. These northern states, though located on the continent of Africa, are included in the classification "Middle East." They are members of the Organization of African Unity (OAU), however, and they play an important role in the cultural and political affairs of Africa.

All Africa's independent nations except South Africa belong to the OAU, which holds meetings each year and tries to solve some of the continent's problems. During 1969 it was concerned with finding a settlement for the Nigeria-Biafra civil war. It was also concerned with the refugee problem in Africa. (Some 900,000 Africans live as refugees outside their home countries.) The OAU is also concerned with independence movements in the nonindependent territories, such as Angola, Mozambique, and Namibia. It has asked the UN to pressure the white leaders of Rhodesia and South Africa to give the black people in these countries more freedom and more say in how the countries are run.

The Nigerian civil war attracted the world's greatest attention in 1969 (see the article NIGERIA, which begins on page 263). But important events occurred in other countries too. Ghana approved a new constitution, held free elections, and returned to civilian rule. Uganda welcomed Pope Paul VI on the first trip by a pope to Africa. Kenya lost a progressive leader when Tom Mboya was assassinated. Rhodesia, ruled by a white minority, approved a constitution that was condemned as racist by most African countries. And military coups toppled existing governments in Sudan and Somalia.

Although drama and conflict most often make the headlines, other events are sometimes more significant. Regional organizations, such as the African-Malagasy Common Organization, and the one calling itself East and Central African States promoted co-operation among their members in agriculture, industry, communications, and trade. Most African countries, with aid from the UN and the more developed nations, are also trying to improve their education, medical services, and transportation, and to raise the standard of living. Most wish also to reduce the problems caused by differences of language and tradition among their peoples.

United States aid to Africa was $186,000,000 in 1969 ($4,000,000 less than in 1968). Peace Corps groups continued to serve in many African countries as teachers and community-development workers.

▶ BOTSWANA

Elections were held in October. President (Sir) Seretse Khama and members of the Democratic Party won a majority of the 34-seat Assembly.

Diamond discoveries give Botswana hope for economic improvement.

▶ BURUNDI·

President Michel Micombero's Government made efforts to ease border tensions with Rwanda and Congo (Kinshasa). The three countries also tried to find ways to solve economic problems on a regional basis.

▶ CAMEROUN

A new "unification road" now links East (French-speaking) and West (English-speaking) Cameroun. Under President Ahmadou Ahidjo, the country is trying to develop food-processing industries and diversify agriculture. With French aid, new training schools for nurses and a University Center for Health Services were set up.

▶ CENTRAL AFRICAN REPUBLIC

The leader of an attempted coup was executed in April. In May, President (General) Jean Bedel Bokassa tightened censorship regulations of foreign newspapers and of the local press and radio.

▶ CHAD

President François Tombalbaye was the sole candidate in the June presidential elections. He received 93 per cent of the votes. Unrest among the Arab population in the interior continued, and thousands of people were killed. The President called in over 1,500 French troops to help preserve order.

▶ CONGO DEMOCRATIC REPUBLIC (KINSHASA)

In January and April, a number of persons, including former rebel leader "General" Ngalo, were executed for subversive activities. In March, the death was announced of Joseph Kasavubu, the first president of the country (until President Joseph Mobutu's coup in 1965). A former Premier, Moise Tshombe, died of a heart attack in June in Algiers, where he was in prison.

A convention of the ruling People's Revolutionary Movement was held in May. It was attended by leaders of 19 other African nations and over three thousand Congolese officials. The convention stressed the nationwide strength of the party.

During student riots at Lovanium University, a number of students, soldiers, and police were killed or wounded. Colleges were temporarily closed, and all student organizations were banned except the Youth Section of the ruling party, the People's Revolutionary Movement.

Relations with the Central African Republic (CAR) continued to be strained since the CAR quit the Union of Central African States in 1968.

A National Security Council, headed by President Mobutu, was created in July 1969 to help ensure internal and external security.

▶ CONGO REPUBLIC (BRAZZAVILLE)

President (Major) Marien Ngouabi took office in January. A purge of the Army and police followed discovery of two antigovernment groups in February. In May, the President visited Algeria and the United Arab Republic, where he indicated his support of the Arabs in the Middle East, of the North Vietnamese, and of the African liberation movements.

▶ DAHOMEY

President Emile Derlin Zinsou visited the United States in March and discussed with President Nixon the problem of relief for victims of the Nigerian war. In 1969 Dahomey was one of the main bases for planes carrying relief to Biafra.

In May and July, two plots to overthrow the Government were discovered, and the plotters were arrested. In December, however, a third plot was successful. Following an assassination attempt on President Zinsou, the Army took control of the country. Lieutenant Colonel Maurice Kouandete, chief of the armed forces, announced that President Zinsou had been ousted.

▶ EQUATORIAL GUINEA

President Francisco Macias Nguema banned flights by the Red Cross from Fernando Po to Biafra and condemned the Biafran separatists. He asked the UN for refugee aid for Nigerians, mainly Ibos, who live on Fernando Po, and who were threatening to revolt.

In March a state of emergency was declared when Spain sent in ships to evacuate Spanish citizens after anti-Spanish disturbances. Almost all Spaniards left the country. In March, too, an attempted coup, led by the Foreign Minister, was put down.

▶ ETHIOPIA

The Haile Selassie University and all secondary schools were closed in March because of antigovernment student agitation. Over a thousand students were arrested, but most were promptly released.

In June, parliamentary elections were held. There were two thousand candidates for the 250 seats. Political parties are banned in Ethiopia, so the candidates ran as independent persons committed to the Emperor.

Members of the Eritrean Liberation Front, composed of Muslims living in the northeastern province, Eritrea, sabotaged Ethiopian Airlines planes in Pakistan and West Germany. They also hijacked a plane en route from Addis Ababa to Southern Yemen and forced it to land in Sudan. The Ethiopian Government believes the movement is armed and trained by the Government of Syria.

Antitax protests by Somali nomads in the Ogaden region of southern Ethiopia led to a number of deaths.

In July, Emperor Haile Selassie met with President Nixon in Washington, D. C. They discussed the Middle East, Nigeria, and U.S.-Ethiopian relations.

▶ **GABON**

President Albert Bongo was elected in February by a 100 per cent vote. In June a ministerial session of the Equatorial Africa Heads of State (Chad, Central African Republic, Congo [Brazzaville], and Gabon) was held in Gabon to work out means for economic and political co-operation.

Gabon is one of the four African states that have recognized Biafra, and reports continue that Gabon is a middleman in the shipment of French arms to Biafra. In September, President Bongo announced that the Nigerian head of state, Lieutenant Colonel Gowon, had asked him to try to arrange a meeting between him and the Biafran leader, General Ojukwu.

▶ **THE GAMBIA**

In July, the ruling People's Progressive Party urged Prime Minister (Sir) Dauda Jawara to hold a referendum to introduce a republican constitution. The opposition United Party opposes the change and claims that it would concentrate too much power in the hands of the proposed president.

Smuggling between Gambia and Senegal led to strained relations between the two countries.

▶ **GHANA**

The constituent assembly approved a new constitution, political parties were formed, and elections were held in August, returning the country to civilian control. Dr. K. A. Busia, leader of the Progress Party, was elected premier and took office in September. The Progress Party won 101 out of 140 seats in the National Assembly; the National Alliance of Liberals, led by K. A. Gbedemah, won 29. A Presidential Committee, composed of three members of the National Liberation Council (NLC) —the military-police Government that ousted President Kwame Nkrumah in 1966—will serve as advisers to the new Government. Brigadier Akwasi Amankwa Afrifa, former chairman of the NLC, heads the Presidential Committee. A National House of Chiefs will handle matters involving traditional chiefs.

Ghana's economic problems were aggravated in 1969 by a fall in cacao production, caused by abnormally heavy rains in 1968.

▶ **GUINEA**

Relations with Ivory Coast continued to be strained. In June an assassination attempt on Sékou Touré led to the on-the-spot lynching of the assailant, who was a Guinean. President Sékou Touré accused the Ivory Coast of training Guinea mercenaries to bring about an overthrow of the Guinea Government. The Ivory Coast denied the charge.

▶ **IVORY COAST**

In May, President Felix Houphouet-Boigny closed Abidjan University following a student strike.

In a reorganization of the country, it was announced in June that Ivory Coast's four large regions will be divided into 24 regions so that they can be administered more efficiently.

The Ivory Coast broke diplomatic relations with the Soviet Union. The Soviet Union had criticized Ivory Coast for its recognition of Biafra. (See also Guinea.)

Tom Mboya, Kenya's minister for economic planning and development, was assassinated July 5.

Kenyan President Jomo Kenyatta tried to quell tribal strife which followed Mboya's death.

▶ KENYA

The Government closed University College in Nairobi for two weeks in January and February after students protested the Government's refusal to allow the leader of the opposition Kenya People's Union, Oginga Odinga, to address them.

In October, Oginga Odinga and the seven Kenya People's Union members of Parliament were arrested. They were charged with organizing anti-Government demonstrations in which 11 persons were killed and 78 wounded. The Government also banned the Kenya People's Union.

On July 5, Tom Mboya, the 38-year-old minister for economic planning and development, was shot dead in Nairobi. Mboya, a member of the Luo tribe, was considered a possible successor to the aging President, Jomo Kenyatta, a member of the Kikuyu tribe. Clashes broke out between Luos and Kikuyus. A Kikuyu was charged with the murder, and was tried and found guilty in September. He was hanged secretly.

Nahashon Isaac Njenga Njoroge, a Kikuyu, was hanged for Mboya's murder.

Following Mboya's funeral, schoolgirls deliver flowers to his home in Nairobi.

▶ LESOTHO

The kingdom of Lesotho is economically dependent on South Africa, and Prime Minister (Chief) Leabua Jonathan continued to maintain good relations with that Government. Seventy-one political refugees from South Africa were told in August 1968 to return to South Africa and face criminal charges. An appeal against the order was dismissed by the Lesotho Supreme Court in 1969. The case was then taken to the Privy Council in London.

▶ LIBERIA

William V. S. Tubman celebrated his 25th year as president of Liberia in January. Tubman has been active in efforts to seek an end of the Nigerian civil war.

In March, President Tubman visited Mauritania and signed an agreement of co-operation with that country.

In September, Miss Angie E. Brooks, assistant secretary of state of Liberia, was elected president of the 24th General Assembly of the UN. Miss Brooks has represented Liberia at the UN since 1953.

▶ MALAGASY REPUBLIC

In April, President Philibert Tsiranana visited Malawi and Kenya. He and President Hastings K. Banda of Malawi stated that they did not approve of either armed conflict or boycotting as suitable ways of dealing with racial problems in Rhodesia, Mozambique, and South Africa. President Tsiranana also met with Prime Minister Ramgoolam of Mauritius, and together they denounced the Rhodesian constitutional referendum.

▶ MALAWI

In April, eight men were hanged for their part in a 1967 attempt to assassinate President Hastings K. Banda.

Malawi continues its policy of retaining good relations with neighboring Rhodesia and South Africa, on which Malawi is economically dependent. Malawi is planning rail links to Rhodesia and to Mozambique so that it will have better access to southern Africa and to the sea. South Africa has a technical-assistance program in Malawi.

▶ MALI

Former Head of Government Modibo Keita, overthrown in November 1968, is under arrest and will be tried by the present military Government. In March the new chief of state, Captain Yoro Diakite, met with former President de Gaulle in France. A meeting between Mauritanian and Mali officials was held to discuss a settlement of their common boundary line.

▶ MAURITANIA

President Moktar Ould Daddah and President Tubman of Liberia signed a convention of co-operation in March. Also, Mauritanian and Mali officials met to discuss a settlement of their frontier.

▶ MAURITIUS

At a June meeting, Prime Minister Seewoosagur Ramgoolam and President Tsiranana of Malagasy denounced the Rhodesian constitutional referendum.

The opposition Social Democratic Party rejected the governing Labor Party's conditions for a coalition Government. It especially criticized the Government's proposal to postpone elections to the legislature for five years. Elections are now scheduled to be held in 1972.

▶ NIGER

At the invitation of President Hamani Diori, delegations from 28 French-speaking countries in Europe, Asia, Africa, and the Americas met in February to discuss the creation of an agency for cultural and technical co-operation.

▶ RHODESIA

Rhodesia continued to be led by the white-dominated regime of Prime Minister Ian Smith, who had declared Rhodesia independent of Great Britain in 1965. In the international community, Rhodesia is still regarded as a nonindependent territory. Since 1965, Rhodesia has been heavily

Rhodesian Prime Minister Ian Smith faced new problems as Britain broke diplomatic relations.

criticized for not allowing more black Rhodesians to take part in government. There are about 4,000,000 blacks, compared with 220,000 whites. The OAU has asked the UN Security Council to take steps to prevent the Government from carrying out policies that might lead to racial conflicts.

In June, Rhodesia held a referendum on constitutional proposals and on whether Rhodesia should become a republic. The total vote cast was less than 77,000. A majority of those voting favored both questions. Almost 90 per cent of the eligible voters are white; about 0.07 per cent are black; the remainder are "colored" (mixed) or Asian. The Zimbabwe African People's Union and the Zimbabwe African National Union oppose the present Government and seek to liberate the country from the rule of the white minority. They are led by black Rhodesian refugees now living in neighboring countries. Neither group was very active in 1969.

South Africa is Rhodesia's chief ally in Africa. Botswana, Malawi, and Swaziland, which are heavily dependent on Rhodesia and South Africa economically, maintain good relations with Smith's Government. Britain ended diplomatic ties with Rhodesia in June.

▶ RWANDA

In June, under President Gregoire Kayibanda, Rwanda met with officials from Congo (Kinshasa) and Burundi in an effort to improve relations, find solutions to problems of economic development, and study the formation of a regional economic organization.

▶ SENEGAL

From March to May, student unrest at the University of Dakar and in secondary schools was touched off when 25 students were expelled from the university. In May, the Government, under President Leopold Senghor, closed the university residences

A new library at the University of Dakar (Senegal), which, in the spring of 1969, was the scene of student unrest, caused by the expulsion of 25 students.

and arrested the leaders of the protest. Post Office workers, petroleum workers, and employees of the National Office of Cooperation and Assistance for Development launched strikes. In June a state of emergency was declared after a strike by bank employees and the threat of further strikes by other workers.

SIERRA LEONE

In March, the Government revoked the state of emergency declared in November 1968 when violence swept the Southern and Eastern provinces. Earlier, 200 political prisoners had been released.

In June, Prime Minister Siaka Stevens called a constitutional committee to rewrite the constitution and establish a republican form of government. Opposition leaders, who had held office in the coalition Government, then ended the coalition in June. They oppose the rewriting of the constitution because they think it already contains provisions allowing for a republic.

SOMALI REPUBLIC

Elections were held in March, and the ruling Somali Youth League (SYL) was returned to power. Most of the 28 parties who won seats in the elections later joined the SYL after the formation of the new Government. In incidents preceding and during the elections, 25 persons lost their lives. Prime Minister Mohammed Haji Ibrahim Egal, who favors a policy of friendship with Kenya and Ethiopia, was re-elected.

In July, clashes between Somali nomads and Ethiopian troops in the Ogaden region of Ethiopia resulted in about 50 deaths. Violence erupted when the Somalis resisted Ethiopian demands for the *gibir,* a head tax on animals.

In October, President Abdirashid Ali Shermarke was assassinated. Following his death the Army overthrew the Government on the pretext that corruption and weakness in the Government had led to the President's death. All government ministers, including Prime Minister Egal, were arrested. The new Supreme Revolutionary Council proclaimed a policy of nonalignment.

SOUTH AFRICA

Elections for the Representative Council for South Africa's 1,800,000 "colored" people (persons of mixed race) were held in September. The 60-member Council (40 elected and 20 appointed by the Government) will take the place of a council wholly appointed by the Government. About 600,000 colored people are registered to vote. The Labor Party, the one party that openly opposes the Government's apartheid policies, won a majority of the votes, but not enough to assure it a majority in the Council. The body will have few powers. Any action taken by it must be approved by the national Parliament.

In September, Prime Minister Balthazar J. Vorster called for parliamentary elections to be held in early 1970 instead of in 1971, as originally scheduled. He hoped to hold the elections before ultraconservative elements were able to build up effective support against him. There are 3,500,000 white people out of a total population of 20,070,000. Voters come mainly from this group. Practically all blacks are excluded.

South Africa and Portugal are co-operating on a giant hydroelectric project in Mozambique.

SUDAN

The Government of Prime Minister Ahmed Mahgoub was overthrown by the military in May. The coup was led by Colonel Gafaar Mohammad al-Nimeiry, who is chairman of the Revolutionary Council and premier. A civilian, Abu Bakr Awadallah is Sudan's minister of foreign affairs. The new Government is composed of Muslims from the northern part of the country. The Constituent Assembly and all political parties were dissolved after the coup, and the former members of government were arrested. The new Premier promised to seek a solution to the continuing rebellion

HEADS OF GOVERNMENT

Botswana	SIR SERETSE KHAMA, president	Malawi	H. KAMUZU BANDA, president
Burundi	MICHEL MICOMBERO, president	Mali	YORO DIAKITE, chief of state
Cameroun	AHMADOU AHIDJO, president	Mauritania	MOKTAR OULD DADDAH, president
Cent. Afr. Rep.	JEAN BEDEL BOKASSA, president	Mauritius	SIR SEEWOOSAGUR RAMGOOLAM, prime minister
Chad	FRANCOIS TOMBALBAYE, president	Niger	HAMANI DIORI, president
Congo (Brazzaville)	MARIEN NGOUABI, president	Nigeria	YAKUBU GOWON, chief of state
		Rhodesia	IAN SMITH, prime minister
Congo (Kinshasa)	JOSEPH D. MOBUTU, president	Rwanda	GREGOIRE KAYIBANDA, president
		Senegal	LEOPOLD SENGHOR, president
Dahomey	PAUL EMILE DE SOUZA, head, military junta	Sierra Leone	SIAKA STEVENS, prime minister
Equatorial Guinea	FRANCISCO MACIAS NGUEMA, president	Somali Rep.	MOHAMMAD SIYAD BARREH, president, Supreme Revolutionary Council
Ethiopia	HAILE SELASSIE I, emperor	S. Africa	B. J. VORSTER, prime minister
Gabon	ALBERT B. BONGO, president	Sudan	GAAFAR MOHAMMAD AL-NIMEIRY, premier
Gambia	D. K. JAWARA, prime minister		
Ghana	KOFI A. BUSIA, premier	Swaziland	SOBHUZA II, king
Guinea	SEKOU TOURE, president		MAKHOSINI DLAMINI, prime minister
Ivory Coast	FELIX HOUPHOUET-BOIGNY, president	Tanzania	JULIUS NYERERE, president
		Togo	ETIENNE EYADEMA, president
Kenya	JOMO KENYATTA, president	Uganda	MILTON OBOTE, president
Lesotho	MOSHOESHOE II, king	Upper Volta	SANGOULE LAMIZANA, president
Liberia	WILLIAM V. S. TUBMAN, president		
Malagasy Rep.	PHILIBERT TSIRANANA, president	Zambia	KENNETH K. KAUNDA, president

	POPULATION	CURRENCY *	OAU	EAEC
Botswana	612,000	1 rand = $1.40	X	
Burundi	3,570,000	87.5 francs = $1.00	X	
Cameroun	5,825,000	277.7 francs = $1.00	X	
Central African Rep.	1,525,500	277.7 francs = $1.00	X	
Chad	3,552,500	277.7 francs = $1.00	X	
Congo (Brazzaville)	915,000	277.7 francs = $1.00	X	
Congo (Kinshasa)	17,493,000	1 zaire = $2.00	X	
Dahomey	2,778,000	277.7 francs = $1.00	X	
Equatorial Guinea	300,000	70 pesetas = $1.00	X	
Ethiopia	24,888,000	2.5 Ethiopian dollars = $1.00	X	X
Gabon	504,500	277.7 francs = $1.00	X	
Gambia	408,000	1 pound = $2.40	X	
Ghana	8,815,000	1 new cedi = $1.00	X	
Guinea	3,978,000	277.7 francs = $1.00	X	
Ivory Coast	4,296,000	277.7 francs = $1.00	X	
Kenya	10,918,000	7.1 shillings = $1.00	X	X
Lesotho	916,000	1 rand = $1.40	X	
Liberia	1,222,000	1 Liberian dollar = $1.00	X	
Malagasy Rep.	6,860,000	277.7 francs = $1.00	X	
Malawi	4,407,500	1 pound = $2.40	X	
Mali	4,998,000	555.4 francs = $1.00	X	
Mauritania	1,122,000	277.7 francs = $1.00	X	
Mauritius	816,000	5.6 rupees = $1.00	X	
Niger	3,800,000	277.7 francs = $1.00	X	
Nigeria	55,042,000	1 pound = $2.80	X	
Rhodesia	4,944,000	1 pound = $2.80		
Rwanda	3,594,500	100 francs = $1.00	X	
Senegal	3,997,500	277.7 francs = $1.00	X	
Sierra Leone	2,555,000	1 leone = $1.20	X	
Somali Republic	2,887,000	7.1 shillings = $1.00	X	X
South Africa	20,070,000	1 rand = $1.40		
Sudan	15,656,000	1 pound = $2.87	X	
Swaziland	411,500	1 rand = $1.40	X	
Tanzania	13,274,000	7.1 shillings = $1.00	X	X
Togo	1,847,000	277.7 francs = $1.00	X	
Uganda	8,500,000	7.1 shillings = $1.00	X	X
Upper Volta	5,406,000	277.7 francs = $1.00	X	
Zambia	4,330,000	1 kwacha = $1.40	X	X

* US $; 1969 exchange rates

OAU—Organization of African Unity
EAEC—East African Economic Community

of the non-Muslim African population in the three southern provinces.

In June the Government announced that the south would be given more self-rule, but said that the Army could not be withdrawn as long as southern civilians were armed and engaged in military rebellion. A leader of southern Sudanese refugees in Uganda said in July that his people wanted independence from the central Government.

The new Government stated that it would not restore diplomatic relations with the United States (broken in 1967) until the United States abandons its "pro-Israel" stand.

▶ SWAZILAND

To a large extent the kingdom of Swaziland, led by Prime Minister (Prince) Makhosini Dlamini, is economically dependent upon South Africa and on its associations with Mozambique, Malawi, and Rhodesia. In June, the Prime Minister paid state visits to Uganda, Kenya, and Tanzania.

▶ TANZANIA

Prime Minister Julius K. Nyerere announced the nation's second five-year development plan, which stresses agricultural development and efforts to build a socialist state. The voting age for parliamentary elections was lowered to 18. A textile mill, developed with French aid and aimed at making Tanzania self-sufficient in clothing production, was opened in 1969.

▶ TOGO

A constitutional committee appointed in 1967 finished its work on a new constitution. President (Brigadier General) Etienne Eyadema announced in January that civilian political activities would once more be permitted. There were protests against this decision, and it was reversed. President Eyadema remained in power.

▶ UGANDA

A conference on refugees was held in February. Over 170,000 refugees from Rwanda, southern Sudan, and Congo (Kinshasa) now live in Uganda. President Milton Obote announced in June a government decision to protect people living near the border from raids by Sudanese troops. The Sudan has paid reparations for past attacks, but the raids have continued.

In July, Pope Paul VI arrived to bless the altar of a shrine to 22 Ugandans who were martyred in the late nineteenth century. Out of a population of 8,500,000, Uganda has 3,000,000 Catholics. Africa as a whole has 30,000,000 Catholics.

While in Uganda, the Pope met with representatives of Nigeria and Biafra in a vain effort to bring about a solution of the Nigerian civil war.

▶ UPPER VOLTA

The Government is led by President (Lieutenant Colonel) Sangoule Lamizana. In May, former President Maurice Yameogo, who was ousted by the military in 1966, was convicted of embezzlement during his 6 years in office and sentenced to 5 years at hard labor. He was fined $220,000 and was divested of all political and civic rights. The sentence was later reduced to 2 years.

▶ ZAMBIA

In March, Zambia, under President Kenneth D. Kaunda, recognized the independence of Biafra.

The outcome of a referendum held in June granted the Government more freedom to revise the constitution. Some of the proposed constitutional revisions were aimed at relaxing safeguards of property rights (mainly of foreign companies). In October the owners of two foreign copper-mining companies reached an agreement with Zambia, which will purchase controlling interests in the companies.

MARGARET F. CASTAGNO and
ALPHONSO A. CASTAGNO
Director, African Studies Center
Boston University

See also MIDDLE EAST; NIGERIA; UNITED NATIONS.

AGRICULTURE

Faster planting means greater profit to farmers. This special machine can plant twenty 30-inch rows and apply insecticide and fertilizer at the same time.

FARMERS faced an uncertain year in 1969. Morale among cash-crop growers sank along with prices for their products. Huge supplies of wheat, corn, soybeans, and cotton piled up worldwide. Livestock producers took advantage of low feed costs to add to some of the best profits they have seen. A consumers' meat-eating surge pushed beef, pork, and lamb prices up. And prices for milk, eggs, fruit, and vegetables did well.

Aside from prices, farmers were mostly concerned about the kind of farm program the Nixon administration would propose to replace the one expiring at year-end. The uncertainty over the farm program, along with low grain prices, drove many farmers into a conservative mood. Farmers did not buy new equipment. They patched their machinery for another year. Equipment dealers grimly watched their sales charts plunge 5 to 10 per cent on tractors, combines, and other crop equipment.

▶ FARM PROGRAM CHALLENGED

The new Secretary of Agriculture, Clifford M. Hardin, conducted several "listen-ins" at universities around the nation to hear farm policy proposals directly from farmers. All summer he considered alternatives to the current program. But he elected to pass the final choice of a program along to Congress, rather than endorse one of his own. As political pressures mounted in the fall and winter, these directions emerged for farm policy:

Congress voted against limiting the amount of direct government payment any one producer could receive.

Emphasis would shift toward the "negative income tax" idea. That is, small farmers would receive help based more on their net income, less on crop production.

Massive land retirement, proposed by many groups early in the year, probably would not get legislative support.

▶ **FARM INCOME**

Farmers had a healthy total income. The 1969 total net income from farming was estimated at $16,000,000,000. This was above the $14,800,000,000 level of 1968. Farmers' wages and returns from off-farm activities added nearly $15,000,000,000 more to their net.

▶ **GRAIN PRODUCTION**

In 1969 the corn output in the United States was 4,300,000,000 bushels, 1 per cent below 1968. Soybean production was at 1,100,000,000 bushels, 2 per cent below 1968. The production of all wheat was 1,500,000,000 bushels, 7 per cent below 1968. Sorghum grain, however, was 3 per cent above 1968 and at a new record with 785,000,000 bushels.

There was heavy wheat and feed-grain production worldwide, and stocks of left-over grain accumulated. Farmers in the United States foresaw that they would be planting fewer acres under government programs in 1970.

▶ **EXPORT BATTLE**

Farmers in the United States shipped less than the hoped-for $6,000,000,000 in farm goods during 1969. But farmers resolved to regain wider markets. The United States has been the world's largest exporter of farm products, with 20 per cent of all agricultural world trade.

There were several reasons for the decline in farm exports in 1969. One was that competing nations undercut prices in a major wheat price war that shattered the International Wheat Agreement.

The 103-day dock strike in the United States in early 1969 cost farmers untold millions in future grain-export sales. It scared the best customer of the United States, Japan, into a long-term policy of buying more grain elsewhere.

The European Common Market countries have increased dairy production with high subsidies and import duties. In 1964 the United States export sales of dry milk and butter were over $50,000,000. But in 1969, sales were down to almost zero.

▶ **PURE FOOD, AIR, AND WATER**

Hopes rose that animals may help eat up much of the United States' growing trash pile. Before you get visions of billy goats champing paper cups, here is how biochemists see it: Helpful bacteria would digest cellulose and related compounds that make up about two thirds of a city's solid waste. The cellulose ration would be laced with minerals from sewage sludge. Then the crop of microbes would be processed into a wholesome high-protein feed for animals. It is a bit far out, but wastes can no longer be simply diluted into air and water. They must be converted into materials that are useful or at least harmless.

Concern over pesticides grew into a widely popular cause during 1969. However, a U.S. Department of Agriculture study over four years shows that there has been no buildup of pesticide residues in soil. Several states curbed the use of the insecticide DDT, which remains potent long after application. DDT use has been dwindling for many years as farmers switch to better insect killers which decompose rapidly.

▶ **FARMERS PROMOTE THEIR PRODUCTS**

Farmers were looking for new ways to sell their products. They wanted to sell more to the consumers they already have, and they wanted to find new consumers around the world.

Pork producers took 5 cents from each hog sold and gave it to finance research on new ways of promoting pork. An Iowa

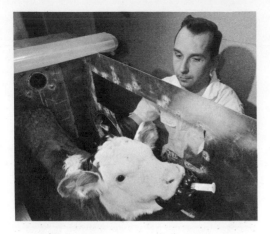

A veterinarian experiments with a calf in efforts to develop vaccine against scours, a viral disease.

A "mechanical sow." Pigs too weak to be nursed by a real sow have been saved by this machine.

pork producer came up with a new way of serving pork. Called "Hawkeye Delight Fillet," it is pork loins wedged together, wrapped with bacon, and baked, fried, or broiled.

Soybean producers pressed for state laws allowing checkoffs of ½ cent per bushel to help widen foreign markets. Cotton growers stepped up research and promotion to save cotton's share of the textile market against competing synthetic fibers.

Beef feeders, sensing that market information can help them sell beef, extended their private *Cattle-Fax* service to cover nearly half of all fed beef sold. At the Denver, Colorado, headquarters of *Cattle-Fax,* information on inventories and prices is received from all over the nation. A computer analyzes what is happening and what is likely to happen to prices. Experts add to the report with their own judgment, then teletype the daily summary to subscribing cattle feeders.

▶ LIVESTOCK RESEARCH

An animal-health breakthrough at the University of Nebraska may lead to a vaccine for calf scours. This serious disease hampers beef and dairy production. Veterinarians found that a specific virus causes the disease. It was previously thought that bacteria caused calf scours. The vaccine is being tested.

In Illinois a new treatment for a deadly hog disease called TGE passed its first field trials. The technique may apply to human medicine. Immunity comes from inoculation with a live virus. The live virus is too strong to handle as an ordinary "shot." So the vaccine is frozen in a capsule, then popped down the hog's throat.

An international transplant of unborn pigs aroused speculation on what might be possible for other species. University of Illinois scientists removed 4 fertilized eggs from a pregnant gilt and flew the eggs to a waiting gilt in Canada. Within 10 hours the eggs were implanted. The Canadian gilt gestated the 4 eggs, which developed into 4 healthy pigs born normally. If such transplants could be made routinely, the best animals could be used to upgrade herds rapidly while cheaper animals took over the time-consuming gestation chores.

▶ GIANT LIVESTOCK OUTFITS

Several "gee-whiz"-size livestock outfits entered the ring in 1969:

A $10,000,000 egg factory to turn out 4,500,000 eggs a week was to be built near Ft. Dodge, Iowa.

A beef-processing plant that will handle 10,000 head a week—the world's largest—was planned for Plainview, Texas, by Missouri Beef Packers Inc.

There was a merger between the world's largest beef feedlot, Monfort of Colorado Inc., and Denver meat purveyor Mapelli Bros. Inc. This integrates production all the way from feedlot to chefs' grills.

Two dairymen's co-ops merged into a giant bargaining group of 30,000 dairymen linked in 21 states from Minnesota to Texas. Soon there may be as few as 5 supercorporations formed to give dairymen the strength they need to bargain with processors.

A "factory" turning out 25,000 hogs a year from 1,200 sows went into production in British Columbia, Canada. The investment was about $1,000 per sow.

▶ CROP TECHNOLOGY

A new Plant Protection Center at Oregon State University is building a massive computer-based "memory" on the world's weeds and the chemicals that control them. The weed will be described to the computer. The computer then searches its memory for the scientist's recommendation, and in seconds the computer prints out the proper control for the weed.

Experimental machines were used for crops once thought impossible to mechanize. Soft, sweet, tree-ripened peaches were shaken mechanically into a foam-plastic honeycomb to save hand harvest. Rubber-fingered machines picked ripe strawberries. Electronic eyes on a huge new tomato harvester sorted red tomatoes from green ones. On giant potato-digging machines, sensing devices picked out potato-shaped rocks from real potatoes.

▶ SPACE PLATFORMS WILL PREDICT YIELDS

The Apollo space program will perhaps lead to more information about earthly crops than about moon rocks. A spin-off from the space project calls for orbiting spacecraft by 1971 to supply continuous crop data worldwide. Using infrared and other multiband scanners, scientists will probably be able to estimate crop yields and detect pollution sources.

Farmers adopted other electronic gadgetry closer to earth. Dairy cows began wearing personalized transponders. With the transponder on, a cow gives off a signal that is picked up by a receiver in an electronic feeder. The signal from the cow tells the feeder how much the cow has eaten lately. The feeder then calculates how much to give the cow. The more milk the cow gives, the more feed it gets.

Other producers installed closed-circuit television in hog and cow maternity wards. When the owner hears a prospective mother's labor noises over the intercom, he can see by television if the animal needs help.

▶ NEW FARM PATTERNS EMERGE

New farm patterns were predicted from 1963–68 growth rates. By 1972 there will be 27 per cent more farmers producing $40,000 or more of farm products a year. There will be 19 per cent more producing over $20,000 a year. The same number of farmers will produce less than $20,000 but more than $10,000. The greatest change will be in the number of farmers in the lowest category. Fewer, some 1,640,000 farmers in 1972, will produce less than $10,000 a year.

On balance, government demographers figure that the historic decline in total farm population has leveled off at 10,000,000.

▶ BATTLE OVER UNIONS ON FARMS

In the drive to unionize farm workers there was little action on any of the eight collective-bargaining bills pending in the Congress. The showcase event was the grape boycott and strike led by Cesar Chavez to organize the vineyard workers in California.

Growers, most of whom rose to ownership from laborer status themselves, want a new labor law that creates a Federal Farm Labor Relations Board. They want strikes prohibited at harvesttime. Union organizers want farmers compelled to bargain under rules set by the National Labor Relations Board and the Wagner Act. And they insist that harvesttime strikes be legal.

JERRY A. CARLSON
Managing Editor, *Farm Journal*

See also FOOD; POVERTY.

ALBANIA. See EUROPE, EAST.

ALGERIA. See MIDDLE EAST.

ANIMALS AND WILDLIFE. See CONSERVATION.

ANTHROPOLOGY

A TRIBE of Indians who still use stone tools and who speak a language unlike any other known language was discovered during the year in the jungles of Colombia. The Indians, according to Dr. Robert L. Carneiro of The American Museum of Natural History, may belong to the Yuri, a tribe believed to have become extinct fifty years ago.

Reports of the discovery of another group of "stone age" Indians in South America appeared in 1969. The elusive, almost legendary Akuriyo were found thirty years after a Dutch expedition had made contact with them for one day. The nomadic tribe, known earlier as the Wama, are a Carib-speaking people of Surinam. They still use stone axes and live by hunting and fishing.

Anthropologists must now undertake the urgent task of making studies of them. But the scientists are deeply concerned. How will the Akuriyo's sudden encounter with the attractions and pressures of modern civilization affect their way of life? How long will they be able to survive as a cultural group? Indeed, questions Dr. Carneiro, how long will the Akuriyo survive at all?

Scientists and governments alike share a general concern: the probability of mortal damage to unsophisticated minorities by continued contact with our technological world. To those concerned, urgency to find out about such minorities and a feeling of responsibility for them are joined.

Anthropologists all over the world are directing considerable effort to the themes of urgency, social responsibility, and relevance, or what matters in today's world.

▶ SCIENTIFIC MEETINGS

The question of urgency was a leading topic of several major scientific meetings in 1969. A report was issued by the Working Group on Urgent Anthropology of the 8th International Congress of Anthropological and Ethnological Sciences, in Tokyo. The group urged workers to capture data, not only about disappearing tribes, but about changing social and cultural forms, as well.

The committee made several concrete suggestions. Some disappearing tribes are isolated, hunting-gathering peoples, such as the Akuriyo, Bushmen, Eskimo, Ona, Vedda, and Andamanese. Immediate studies of these groups must be started and continued in the little time left before they are totally wiped out.

Certain peasant societies scattered all over the world are in a special, critical relationship with expanding urban centers. Anthropologists must examine the nature and effects of culture change.

The committee also pointed out that close co-operation between pure research and applied research at this time can be especially fruitful. Out of this effort can come new approaches to guiding and training young workers in the newer nations, whose need is greatest.

Thor Heyerdahl's "Ra" sets sail from Morocco.

EXPERIMENTS

A common problem met by anthropologists, sociologists, and astronomers alike is that of conducting controlled experiments. Neither man nor the stars can be manipulated to isolate and test programed reactions. Therefore, scientific experiments must be performed in an artificially produced environment.

However, there are certain conditions in nature that provide a kind of natural laboratory. Under these conditions, anthropologists can do experiments of lesser magnitude relating directly to man's basic functioning. Caves—both land and sea caves—provide such an environment. In them, it is possible to examine problems of ecology (the study of living things in their surroundings), and evolution, in addition to mineralogy and hydrology (the science of water).

The Cave Research Foundation, the Institute of Speleology at the University of Kentucky, and the Cave Research Associates are sponsoring an examination of such problems. The organizations hope to uncover rules govering the evolution of animals.

STUDIES AND REPORTS

An investigation of the changing identity of an American Indian culture was reported by John H. Bushnell of the New York State Commission for Human Rights. His examination shows how the Hoopa of northwestern California have been developing a culture that is largely American in content. At the same time, the culture is able to maintain a vivid sense of its ethnic identity.

On the other hand, negative aspects of culture change can lead to "culture fatigue." These negative aspects were the topic of a report on the "Hawaiian Cultural Revolution" by William Davenport of the University of Pennsylvania.

Dr. Margaret Mead gave an address at ceremonies marking her retirement as curator of ethnology of the American Museum of Natural History. She compared the nature of the changes she found among the Manus of New Guinea on a recent tour with her pioneer work on the island more than 25 years ago. She found the Manus had made a successful transition to a different, but still healthy, form of culture.

The expanding field of evolution and genetics is producing perhaps the most significant work being done in physical anthropology today.

Not too widely separated from this area of research, studies of "race" differences have had immediate impact. A highly debated report from Dr. A. R. Jensen in the *Harvard Educational Review* sets forward the claim that United States Negroes are inherently less intelligent than their white countrymen. Behavioral scientists criticize this position. They point out: (1) the need to revise Western concepts of intelligence, (2) the need to evaluate value systems in determining which abilities are given priority in each society, (3) possible paralyzing conflicts between "school" learning and primary home ideologies, and (4) the long-range adverse effects of ill health and poor nutrition on brain size and function.

BRIEFS

A. P. Okladnikov has reported on petroglyphs, or rock drawings, found along Siberian rivers, and spanning a period of 20,000 years. The rock drawings, painted or stamped in red mineral or red ocher, indicate some kind of communication among wide-ranging northern Eurasian nomads.

The Norwegian explorer, Thor Heyerdahl, set out from Morocco in May to cross the Atlantic in a papyrus reed boat, the *Ra*. He was trying to show how Egyptian culture might have been carried accidentally to Central America 3,000 years ago. Heyerdahl abandoned the voyage when his boat became waterlogged in July. He and his men were picked up in mid-Atlantic by another ship.

GERALDINE COHEN
American Museum of Natural History
See also ARCHEOLOGY.

Restored forecourt of the synagogue at Sardis, which dates from the second century.

ARCHEOLOGY

THE amount of work being done by archeologists continued to increase in 1969. In most countries of the world, people are feeling a growing national pride. This has awakened an interest in origins, and thus in archeological work. Another cause of increased archeological activity is the effort to save historic and prehistoric monuments. In many cases these are threatened with destruction by modern dams and building projects.

Efforts to save the monuments are not always successful, however. In the United States, the building of Lower Monumental Dam in Washington resulted in the flooding of most of an important archeological site. It was here that bones from the skull of Marmes man, who lived 13,000 years ago, were found in 1965.

Archeological research during 1969 continued the shift away from the search for one-of-a-kind museum pieces and works of art. Instead, researchers carried out orderly investigations. These are intended to provide information from which people can judge what the everyday lives of men of the past were like.

Instead of exploring at random, archeologists organize their work to look for answers to certain key questions about man's past. The major discoveries of 1969 may be considered in terms of six main foci, or problems, which research seeks to explain.

▶ **EARLIEST MAN-LIKE CREATURES**

Archeologists have been looking for the earliest man-like creatures who walked erect, used tools, and had large brains. In 1969, F. Clark Howell commented on his recent discovery in Ethiopia of 2 human jaws and 40 human teeth. He said that they are between 3,500,000 and 4,000,000 years old, or almost twice the age of the oldest human remains ever found before.

Several fossilized fragments or other, very old man-like creatures have been found in the same general region of east-central Africa. Therefore, many scientists think of the area as the birthplace of mankind.

SPREAD AND DEVELOPMENT OF MAN

One very exciting discovery was made in 1969. The remains of a man and a child, believed to have lived 30,000 years before Christ, were found in a cave in Spain by Gonzales Echegaray, a Spaniard, and Leslie Freeman, of the University of Chicago. The discovery added to our knowledge of ancient man because special conditions in the cave preserved more than just the bones of the skeletons. Dr. Freeman, in describing what they found, said that "as the body decayed, fine sediment of clay filled the cavities. The clay took the appearance of the original man."

The spread of man over the world has been the subject of much archeological research. The most recent discoveries come from Australia, Mexico, and Alaska and Washington in the United States. New evidence hints that men who looked very much like us were living on all the major land areas of the world about 20,000 years ago.

FOOD PRODUCTION

During the first 3,000,000 years of man's existence he obtained food by hunting, fishing, and gathering wild fruits, nuts, vegetables, and roots. About 10,000 years ago some communities in the Near East began to produce food by taming and raising certain animals, and by planting and growing certain plants. The first attempts to grow food were made in different places at different times. The shift from hunting and food gathering to food producing is thought by many to be the single most important change in man's long history.

Archeological research during 1969 concentrated on searching for early examples of this new way of life. Several expeditions in the Old World exposed large and complex villages 9,000 to 10,000 years old. A Turkish-American expedition directed by Halet Cambel and Robert Braidwood has been working on an important early village site in Turkey named Cayonu. Its prehistoric inhabitants raised wheat and barley, herded sheep, goats, and cattle, and built large buildings with stone foundations.

Other interesting villages from this period were excavated by two Canadian expeditions in Iran. More evidence of early food-producing communities has been discovered recently in Thailand, Yugoslavia, Afghanistan, and the Sudan.

Evidence of like developments has been found in Mexico and the Southwestern United States. These remains date from 6,000 to 8,000 years ago. During 1969, Richard MacNeish began a large-scale project to find evidence of early food production in Peru. He had already done such work successfully in Mexico.

DEVELOPMENT OF CITIES

Another focus of 1969 research was on evidence of the development of the first cities, and on the changes in social structure that went along with this development. The earliest evidence of cities is found in

Figure of a sphinx (a mythological half-lion, half-woman) found in Lydian houses at Sardis. The piece is part of a painted storage jar more than four feet tall. It dates from 600–550 B.C.

Iraq (Ancient Mesopotamia) and Mexico. These areas continue to be the centers of thorough research.

In 1969, Robert Adams went on with his study of the pattern of prehistoric and historic settlements and their relation to irrigation systems in central Iraq. Donald Hansen uncovered important parts of the ancient city of Lagash in southern Iraq. These may help to connect historical records with archeological work.

In the New World during 1969, Kent Flannery continued his investigation of the prehistoric settlement patterns in the Oaxaca Valley of Mexico. René Millon began the final stages of research on his mapping of the huge ancient city of Teotihaucan in the Valley of Mexico. The project is designed to outline the city limits and the nature of its various districts during Teotihaucan's many periods of occupation. This type of work has begun to unearth facts that help explain political, social, and economic factors surrounding the growth of the first cities.

▶ CLASSICAL AND BIBLICAL ARCHEOLOGY

Archeological discoveries in Greece, Rome, and the Holy Land have always been followed by the public with great interest. Work during 1969 produced a variety of exciting material. In Jerusalem, an Israeli expedition directed by B. Mazar uncovered more of the original Hebrew Temple complex of King Solomon and the Second Temple of Herod.

Also in Israel, further advances were made in understanding the methods of making glass used in antiquity. Several years of work by an American expedition directed by Saul and Gladys Wienberg reached a climax. The expedition discovered a complete glass-working furnace from the tenth century.

Archeologist Yigael Yadin discovered the water system used in the Old Testament city of Hazor in northern Israel. The site of the city was found in 1875, but its waterworks had remained a puzzle. In the Negev desert, Dr. Beno Rothenberg and a group of volunteers unearthed a royal Egyptian temple dating to the time of Moses.

Other discoveries of special interest were made in Turkey in the classical city of Sardis by a team of archeologists led by George Haufmann of Harvard University. In 1968 a building found there was identified as a gold refinery complete with crucibles and furnaces. It is believed that Sardis is the place where the earliest coins in the world were minted for King Croesus, ruler of the Lydian Empire in the seventh century B.C. Discoveries in 1969 at Sardis included a new quarter of the ancient city and evidence of several more gold refineries, and some sculptures. Also in 1969 in Turkey, the temple of the Aphrodite of Cnidus was found by an expedition led by Iris C. Love of Long Island University. The Greek temple is of the Doric order and circular. It is believed that it dates from the fourth century B.C.

▶ HISTORICAL ARCHEOLOGY IN THE NEW WORLD

The newest area of interest in archeology is the colonial period of American history, and later periods. Interest is so great that The Society for Historical Archeology was formed recently to promote research. An example of work in this field is the help archeologists have given in the investigation and reconstruction of Jamestown in Virginia and Plymouth Plantation in Massachusetts.

Some of the most interesting discoveries of 1969 came from Port Royal, Jamaica. Archeologists uncovered part of a seventeenth- and eighteenth-century settlement, as well as a large and varied collection of glass objects. Perhaps the single most interesting piece was a seventeenth-century clay pipe made in the shape of a small man. From this kind of discovery, archeologists are able to add new and valuable details to historical records.

CHARLES L. REDMAN
University of Chicago
See also ANTHROPOLOGY.

ARCHITECTURE

Architect Richard Foster's circular glass house has 9 wedge-shaped rooms: 3 bedrooms, den, living room, dining room, kitchen, dressing room, and laundry.

SOME extraordinary buildings and building complexes were completed in 1969. And some important architectural ideas were conceived during the year. Government and citizens came to see that the problems of today's societies and cities are the result in part of physical decay. There was the hope that better environment, especially better housing, might help these problems.

▶ SOME VERY SPECIAL HOUSES

In architecture, houses are a very special problem. Every architect likes to design them, because they combine in small scale all the problems of designing spaces for people. Also they offer, if the client is willing, a chance for the kind of experimentation that is not possible because of cost in a large building. Marcel Breuer said it just right when he called houses "laboratories of design."

One such house is architect Richard Foster's house in Connecticut for his own family. The 72-foot-diameter house rotates, at speeds up to 5 feet per minute, on a 14-foot-wide ball-bearing ring. But the house is not a stunt. Foster's design is his response to a breathtaking site. It has farmland hills and a lake to the west, a meadow and a pond to the east, and a pine forest to the north. Foster rotates his house on its pedestal for changing landscape, sun, and moon.

In sharp contrast is architect Richard Meier's house on Long Island, New York, for a client. It is made of white-painted wood and great sheets of glass. It is almost a piece of cubist sculpture on its meadow site.

As elegant as both of these special houses is architect John Bloodgood's more conservative house for a client. The owners wanted a "cross between an early European chateau and a Midwestern farmhouse." Bloodgood's design accomplishes this unlikely combination in a house that seems just right for its Iowa site.

At a time when the city and its housing problems are uppermost in everyone's mind, these houses are examples of a kind of housing to which few people can aspire. But they are important because houses of this kind advance the cause of all architecture through innovative design.

▶ IMPORTANT AND INNOVATIVE BUILDINGS

Perhaps the year's most-talked-about architecture was Boston's new City Hall. It was designed by a firm of three young architects: Gerhard Kallmann, Noel McKinnell, and Edward Knowles. They won the commission through a nationwide competition in 1962. The building is bold and exciting. It has few conventional shapes and spaces.

Cincinnati's Playhouse in the Park was surely the year's most enjoyable building. The building is officially called the Robert S. Marx Theater. Designed by architect Hugh Hardy, the 672-seat theater was built entirely with community funds. The exterior has a free shape built with simple cinder block and a stainless-steel roof.

The interior is wild and wonderful. For example, the air ducts and diffusers, normally carefully hidden in a building, are here made of stainless steel and used as decoration. The lighting in the lobby is a cluster of everyday fluorescent tubes, hung just as if they were a chandelier. In the lobby, sound-absorbing carpet—a bold green—is on the ceiling. In the theater itself, the concrete blocks are left exposed. And the great trusses spanning from wall to wall to support the roof and support the stage lights are not just left exposed. They are painted a bright red.

The plaza outside is lighted at night by airport-runway lights in the standard beautiful (if you think about it) blue. Perhaps this building is pop art. That is, it uses

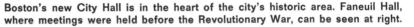

Boston's new City Hall is in the heart of the city's historic area. Faneuil Hall, where meetings were held before the Revolutionary War, can be seen at right.

Cincinnati's Playhouse in the Park—simply but beautifully constructed of cinder block.

familiar things in fresh ways. But like pop art, this building is fun. And it is real architecture.

Perhaps the most important public building of the year was the new Hawaii State Capitol. It was designed by two firms: Belt, Lemmon & Lo, and John Carl Warnecke & Associates. Its unique design seems fitting for Hawaii. The great central court, under a roof reminiscent of the island's volcanic mountains, is open to the mild climate. Both the Senate and House chambers are within circular cones. And the building is set in a broad pool—much as the beautiful Hawaiian Islands are set in the middle of the Pacific Ocean.

The boldest architectural proposal of 1969 was Battery Park City in New York City. A city agency and a public, nonprofit corporation plan to build this huge city-within-a-city on New York's lower west side. It is planned by a number of architectural firms. They include Harrison & Abramovitz, Philip Johnson & John Burgee, and Conklin & Rossant. The project has impressive statistics. The total site will be 118 acres, 91 acres of which will be landfill created in the river. There will be 5,000,000 square feet of new office space and 19,000 new apartment units for 55,000 residents. The project will cost more than $1,000,000,000.

The new Hawaii State Capitol in Honolulu, completed in 1969, has a uniquely designed roof reminiscent of the islands' volcanoes.

One of the year's most exciting engineering accomplishments was the Blossom Music Center. It is the summer home of the Cleveland Symphony. The shape of the building grew almost entirely out of functional needs for acoustics. The structure in turn grew out of the shape. The shell has a shape somewhat like a sliced-off cone. The roof slants down from a height of 94 feet above the stage floor to 25 feet at the center to 15 feet at the sides. The steel arch framing the roof supports spans 400 feet.

And the roof itself is carried on a cobweb of light-steel-pipe trusses. Thus the music center is a column-free space for 4,500 listeners. Architect for this innovative structure was Schafer, Flynn and vanDijk. The structural engineer was R. M. Gensert Associates.

The year's most beautiful building? It is always risky to make such a judgment. But many will award that rating to Paul Rudolph's chapel for Tuskegee Institute in Alabama. The design seems simple, but it is most complex. The chapel has a warped roof plane and skylights that create inside incredibly beautiful natural lighting.

▶ EUROPEAN ARCHITECTURE

The New National Gallery in Berlin, designed by Mies van der Rohe, opened in 1969. It has Mies' usual simplicity and fanatic attention to detail. This beautiful pavilion was one of the last works of the master architect, who died in August 1969.

The University of East Anglia in Norwich, Norfolk, England, by British architect Denys Lasdun, was completed in 1969. The sprawling series of buildings is interconnected by a complex of walkways and bridges.

In France, architects Marcel Breuer and Robert Gatje created a new town. The town, called Flaine, is a ski resort. There are several hotels, apartment buildings, many shops, a school, a church, a theater, and government offices. All the buildings were made with the same precast-concrete panels.

The fourth building is the Rosenthal glass factory in Amberg, Germany. It is a 66-foot-high, tent-shaped building supported by a series of huge precast-concrete ribs. The concrete ribs carry broad precast-concrete louvers which can be adjusted to control light and carry off the heat and fumes of the glassmaking process inside. The building was designed by famed architect Walter Gropius (who died in July) with Alex Cvijanovic, one of the principals of the firm Gropius founded, The Architects Collaborative.

Paul Rudolph's design provides natural lighting for the new chapel at Tuskegee Institute.

NEW APPROACH TO URBAN HOUSING

Two forces joined to mount a strong new attack on the problems of in-city housing. One force was the growing militancy of the urban poor. The other was a developing commitment by taxpayers and government to raise the living standards of the poor.

One way to help pay the cost of new housing is for government to subsidize it. Often when government is paying part of the costs it also becomes involved in the planning and design. A most successful program of government-aid housing was begun in 1969 in New York City. There Mayor John Lindsay set up a new housing agency with a specific goal to raise the level of design. The agency's design team developed new plans for the use of land in the city. Those parts of run-down urban neighborhoods that were worth saving would be preserved. This would include parks, landmark buildings, and churches. New housing would be planned around the preserved structures.

New York City has begun to build housing following these plans. One project is Tracey Towers. It is being built on air rights over a subway yard in the Bronx. Tracey Towers is the design of the distinguished architect Paul Rudolph, with architect Jerald Karlan. The complex includes a 40-story and a 42-story tower, plus 36 town houses.

A nationwide attack on problems of urban housing was mounted in midyear by Secretary George Romney of the Department of Housing and Urban Development. Secretary Romney invited the nation's corporations to submit proposals for mass-produced housing. That is, large components would be made in the factory and assembled into homes on the building site.

At the same time, state and local governments were asked to make up lists of land on which new housing could be built. Local governments were asked to abandon in part their local zoning and building code restrictions against factory-produced housing. Evaluation of these proposals was begun in the fall of 1969. The ten or twenty most promising proposals will be test-built on sites throughout the United States. Families will be urged to visit them. It was Secretary Romney's hope that this plan, called "Operation Breakthrough," would cut the cost of housing and make many more homes available.

OTHER ARCHITECTURAL NOTES

The nation's architects through the American Institute of Architects involved themselves officially and deeply with the struggle for better housing in the cities. Architectural students, led by Taylor Culver, president of the 17,000-member Association of Student Chapters, A.I.A., came to the 1969 convention of the American Institute of Architects in a militant mood. They went away with a commitment from the architects to raise $15,000,000 toward helping urban problems.

In other actions, the convention resolved that "members shall not accept commissions which appear to strengthen or support racial discrimination."

The year saw the death of two of the country's most influential architects: Walter Gropius and Ludwig Mies van der Rohe. Both men had been longtime friends. They had worked together in Germany before the rise of Hitler forced them to move to the United States. They shared—with Frank Lloyd Wright and Le Corbusier—a rare status. They were the last of the masters who conceived and shaped what we now call modern architecture.

Both men were in active practice up to the time of their death. Gropius worked in Boston, with The Architects Collaborative. Mies headed an office in Chicago. Both men had received a host of awards for their work, including the gold medal of the American Institute of Architects.

WALTER F. WAGNER, JR.
Editor, *Architectural Record*
See also HOUSING.

ARGENTINA. See LATIN AMERICA.
ARMED FORCES. See UNITED STATES.
ART. See PAINTING.

ASIA

MANY important events took place in Asia during 1969. In Vietnam, the United States carried out its first troop withdrawals. The war seemed to lessen in intensity in the field. Meanwhile, the two opposing sides sparred in the political arena, seeking a settlement. To the north, Communist China's 76-year-old Chairman Mao Tse-tung named Defense Minister Lin Piao as his political heir. The Chinese-Soviet border dispute erupted during the year in a series of sharp clashes.

In India, the powerful Congress Party, which has ruled the country since independence in 1947, split into two hostile factions. The ceremonies marking the 100th anniversary of Gandhi's birth were marred by Hindu-Muslim violence in

A member of the U.S. Marines' Ninth Battalion prepares to leave South Vietnam.

Gandhi's home state of Gujarat. Japan showed signs for the first time since the end of World War II of becoming a major Asian political power once again. Korea was racked by a political crisis when the National Assembly amended the constitution to permit President Chung Hee Park to run for a third term.

On balance, Asian highlights for 1969 showed the area to be very unstable politically. But maybe the most important development, which was less dramatic and therefore received less attention, was the "Green Revolution." This is the phrase used in Asia to describe the results obtained from planting new hybrid wheat and rice seeds developed in Mexico and the Philippines. The seeds produced bumper harvests in many parts of Asia, and gave the Far East hope of growing enough food to feed itself.

Here follow descriptions of events in Asia during 1969 in every country but those discussed in separate articles. Separate coverage is accorded to China, India, Japan, Korea, and Vietnam.

▶ AFGHANISTAN

This Central Asian nation entered its fourth year under a democratic constitution in 1969. Although it was too early to make a judgment, the experiment appeared to be working. Afghanistan's second free parliamentary elections were held during 1969. And the king, Mohammad Zahir Shah, was thought to be ready to withdraw his opposition to the forming of political parties.

▶ BHUTAN

This small kingdom, nestling in the Himalayas, also experimented in democracy. King Jigme Dorji Wangchuk amended the constitution to provide that if two thirds of Parliament passed a "no confidence" vote against the king, he must step down in favor of the next royal successor in the Wangchuk dynasty. The king must also

Cambodian mercenaries are airlifted to a battle in South Vietnam.

receive a vote of confidence by the Parliament every three years to remain in power.

▶ BRUNEI

The oil-rich Sultanate of Brunei in northern Borneo expressed concern about its future defense arrangements, since Britain plans to withdraw from the region by 1971. The Sultan of the British-protected state flew to London to open talks for a new defense compact between the two states.

▶ BURMA

Once the world's largest rice exporter, Burma approached famine conditions in 1969. This situation was the result of the unwise nationalization policies of General Ne Win. (Ne Win came to power in 1962 by deposing the popularly elected U Nu.)

In 1966, after four years' imprisonment, U Nu was released and permitted to leave Rangoon. In August 1969, U Nu, on a visit to London announced plans to overthrow Ne Win and restore democracy in Burma—by force, if necessary. Although U Nu retains popular support in Burma, there are few signs that the military regime is near collapse.

▶ CAMBODIA

Sharing a common frontier with South Vietnam, Cambodia felt uneasy as the U.S. tried to remove itself from the Vietnam conflict. Cambodia's sense of insecurity deepened when the Communists put new pressure on Prince Norodom Sihanouk's government. Communist strength inside the Buddhist kingdom is made up of regular North Vietnamese Army units and Vietcong irregulars. These use Cambodia as a base for their raids against South Vietnam.

During the year, the Prince was troubled to find that he could not enter certain parts of his own kingdom because they had been "occupied" by the Communists. As a result of this discovery, Cambodia moved closer to the United States and the two countries

restored diplomatic relations. Cambodia had broken off relations with the United States in 1965 in a bid to appease the Communists and steer a neutral course at the time that the war in Vietnam was being stepped up.

▶ CEYLON

Ceylon's hopes for unity between the Sinhalese majority and the Tamil-speaking minority were shattered during the year. The Tamil Federal Party withdrew from the government of Prime Minister Dudley Senanayake. The party was forced to take this action because at its annual convention Tamil militants had carried the day. The militants demanded a self-governing Tamil-speaking state within a Ceylonese federation. The Tamil demand, however, may play into the hands of Sinhalese extremists who want to excite racial passions as they did in 1958. In that year, the Tamils suffered heavy losses when the worst racial strife in Ceylon's history swept the island.

▶ HONG KONG

The last British crown colony in Asia, Hong Kong continued to play the role of haven for refugees fleeing mainland China. In 1949, at the time of the Communist take-over in Peking, Hong Kong had a population of 1,800,000, made up largely of refugees from the Chinese civil war. In 1969, the island's population soared above 4,000,000 as refugees continued to stream into the crown colony's 29 square miles at a rate of 400 monthly. British efforts to turn them back have in recent years prevented an even larger influx.

▶ INDONESIA

This island nation ended its 20-year drive to add West Irian (western New Guinea) to its territory. Following a controversial plebiscite in September, to which the United Nations sent observers, the territory was formally incorporated into the Republic of Indonesia.

West Irian was excluded from the Dutch transfer of sovereignty to Indonesia in

Troops of the Royal Laotian Government train with American-made weapons.

1949, pending negotiations partly because the region's Papuan population differed from the majority of Indonesians in race, language, and culture. In 1962 President Sukarno, in collaboration with the Communists, attacked West Irian. Under pressure from their allies, including the United States, the Dutch acceded to Indonesia's pressure and signed an accord at the UN. This agreement provided for a plebiscite in West Irian by 1969. The plebiscite, or "act of free choice," as it was called, was held on schedule. Through a complicated system of consultation, 1,025 delegates were selected in West Irian to represent the 800,000 Papuans of the territory, many of whom dwell in a Stone Age culture.

Although the interim Indonesian rule of West Irian has been dotted by small-scale Papuan revolts since 1962, in mid-1969 the delegates "unanimously" voted that West Irian should be part of the Indonesian Republic. The unanimity of the balloting made the outcome suspect and the plebiscite was widely criticized. Ironically, Sukarno was no longer in power when the struggle for West Irian ended.

▶ LAOS

This Southeast Asian country, site of "the forgotten war," moved back into the headlines in 1969. In a series of skirmishes in and around the Plain of Jars, the neutralist Royal Laotian Government, backed by the Royal Thai Army and the U.S. Air Force, engaged the Communist Pathet Lao. The latter was aided by 50,000 regular North Vietnamese Army troops. At stake was the future control of this strategically located Buddhist kingdom. (Laos has common frontiers with Communist China, North Vietnam, South Vietnam, Thailand, Cambodia, and Burma.)

In the U.S. Congress, there was growing concern that the Laotian fighting might draw the United States into "another Vietnam." In September the Senate passed an amendment to the Pentagon's budget forbidding the use of U.S. funds for American combat support of "local forces" in Laos or Thailand.

▶ MACAO

This oldest of European outposts in the Far East pressed ahead with its economic development. In 1969 a new multimillion-dollar textile plant, the largest in this Portuguese territory, began full-scale operation.

▶ MALAYSIA

This nation, which includes the Malay Peninsula and parts of northern Borneo, was shaken in 1969 by clashes between Malays and Chinese on the Malay Peninsula. Prime Minister Abdul Rahman's government collapsed and was succeeded by an emergency National Operations Council (NOC). The violence broke out in May following a general election in which the Malay-dominated Alliance Party was returned to power but lost much ground to the Chinese-controlled Democratic Action Party. Because the Chinese community controls business in Malaysia, the Malays feared that the Chinese electoral gains foreshadowed a Chinese political take-over as well. The Malays panicked, and 143 Chinese and 25 Malays were slain in riots. With the coming of National Operations Council rule, the Malays held that "democracy is dead" in Malaysia. The Chinese responded by declaring that parliamentary government must be revived as soon as law and order are fully restored. They said there would be no lessening of racial tensions so long as the country was ruled by emergency decree.

▶ MALDIVE ISLANDS

Maldivians mourned the death in May 1969 of Sultan al-Amir Mohammad Farid Didi, who led the Indian Ocean island nation to independence in 1965. On November 11, 1968, when the Maldive Islands became a republic, the Sultan abdicated and went into retirement.

▶ MONGOLIA

As a Soviet ally in Central Asia, Mongolia found itself affected by the Chinese-Soviet border confrontation in 1969. Chinese-Soviet clashes erupted to the east and west of Mongolia. During the summer, the Mongolian Defense Minister visited Moscow to plan joint strategy in the event of a war with China. Thousands of Russian troops are stationed in Mongolia.

▶ NEPAL

Nepal's Prime Minister Thapa, who headed the government for four years, resigned "to strengthen democracy and to give a chance to others." His resignation coincided with a steady deterioration in Nepal's relations with India. The Himalayan kingdom canceled an arms agreement with New Delhi. Nepal also called for the withdrawal of the small Indian military mission in Katmandu and some Indian civilian radio operators stationed near the Nepal-China border.

▶ PAKISTAN

Strikes, student demonstrations, and uncontrolled rioting plagued both West and East Pakistan in early 1969. In East Pakistan, a major demand was for self-rule in the face of the dominance of West Pakistanis in the central government. Protests nationwide were directed against the ruling elite for repression of political parties and for failure to end extreme economic inequality.

Unable to quell the unrest, President Mohammad Ayub Khan resigned in March. He turned the presidency over to General Agha Mohammad Yahya Khan, commander-in-chief of the Army. The new Government proclaimed a state of martial law and announced that constitutional government would be restored with the return of law and order.

▶ PHILIPPINES

President Ferdinand Marcos, the leader of the Nacionalista Party, became the first president in the history of the Republic to win a second term. He defeated the Liberal Party standard-bearer, Sergio Osmeña, Jr.

Marcos' triumph paved the way for him to push through a vigorous land-reform program. The biggest political problem facing the Philippines is a feudal system of agriculture. Tenant farming or sharecropping is commonplace and landlordism is rampant. Marcos, like previous presidents, found that one term in office did not give him enough time to carry out land reform.

The program is strongly opposed by the dominant conservative class. In 1969, the Free Farmers Federation, a reform movement led by Roman Catholic laymen sup-

HEADS OF GOVERNMENT

Afghanistan MOHAMMAD ZAHIR SHAH, king
NOOR AHMAD ETEMADI, prime minister

Bhutan JIGME DORJI WANGCHUK, king

Burma NE WIN, chief of state

Cambodia PRINCE NORODOM SIHANOUK, chief of state

Ceylon DUDLEY SENANAYAKE, prime minister

China, Communist CHOU EN-LAI, premier
MAO TSE-TUNG, Communist Party chairman

India V. V. GIRI, president
INDIRA GANDHI, prime minister

Indonesia SUHARTO, president

Japan HIROHITO, emperor
EISAKU SATO, prime minister

N. Korea KIM IL-SUNG, premier

S. Korea CHUNG HEE PARK, president
CHUNG IL KWON, premier

Laos SAVANG VATTHANA, king
SOUVANNA PHOUMA, premier

Malaysia TUNKU ABDUL RAHMAN, prime minister

Maldive Is. IBRAHIM NASIR, president

Mongolia ZHAMSARANGIN SAMBU, chief of state

Nepal MAHENDRA BIR BIKRAM SHAH DEVA, king
KIRTINIDHI BISTA, prime minister

Pakistan AGHA MOHAMMAD YAHYA KHAN, president

Philippines FERDINAND E. MARCOS, president

Singapore YUSOF IBN ISHAK, president
LEE KUAN YEW, prime minister

Taiwan CHIANG KAI-SHEK, president

Thailand BHUMIBOL ADULYADEJ, king
THANOM KITTIKACHORN, prime minister

N. Vietnam TON DUC THANG, president
PHAM VAN DONG, premier
LE DUAN, Communist Party chairman

S. Vietnam NGUYEN VAN THIEU, president
NGUYEN CAO KY, vice-president

	POPULATION	ARMED FORCES	CURRENCY*
Afghanistan	16,879,000	75,000	45 Afghani = $1.00
Bhutan	822,000	20,000	. . . .
Burma	27,594,000	142,500	4.8 kyat = $1.00
Cambodia	6,847,000	38,500	54 riels = $1.00
Ceylon	12,595,000	. . . .	5.9 rupees = $1.00
China, Communist	750,664,000	2,821,000	2.5 yuan = $1.00
India	539,584,000	925,000	7.5 rupees = $1.00
Indonesia	118,170,000	365,000	350 new rupiahs = $1.00
Japan	103,223,000	250,000	360 yen = $1.00
North Korea	13,619,000	384,500	2.6 won = $1.00
South Korea	32,074,000	620,000	280 won = $1.00
Laos	2,975,000	65,000+	500 kip = $1.00
Malaysia	11,032,000	44,750	3.1 Malaysian dollars = $1.00
Maldive Islands	102,000	. . . .	6 rupees = $1.00
Mongolia	1,236,000	17,500	4 tugrik = $1.00
Nepal	11,110,000	20,000	10.1 rupees = $1.00
Pakistan	135,943,000	324,000	4.8 rupees = $1.00
Philippines	38,399,000	32,500	3.9 pesos = $1.00
Singapore	2,152,000	14,250	3.1 Singapore dollars = $1.00
Taiwan	13,910,000	555,000	40 Taiwan dollars = $1.00
Thailand	35,775,000	126,400	21 baht = $1.00
North Vietnam	22,063,000	457,000	3.7 dong = $1.00
South Vietnam	18,300,000	472,500++ 573,500+++	118 piastres = $1.00

* US $; 1969 exchange rates
+ Royal Lao Forces
++ Regular forces
+++ Paramilitary forces

Ferdinand Marcos: Philippine president.

ported by young priests, organized demonstrations against Rufino Cardinal Santos, the Archbishop of Manila. They accused the church of failing to take the lead in demanding land and other social reforms. The church crisis gives Marcos the chance to mobilize popular support behind the reform.

▶ **SIKKIM**

Sikkim remained the most closely aligned to India of the three Himalayan kingdoms (Bhutan, Nepal, and Sikkim). In 1969 Sikkim continued to play a pivotal role in the defense of the Indian subcontinent against Chinese pressure from the north.

▶ **SINGAPORE**

Singapore marked the 150th anniversary of its founding as a British colony. The celebration's emphasis was on the defense of the independent state, which is peopled mostly by "overseas Chinese." Singapore is developing a "citizen army" on the Israeli pattern with the aid of senior Israeli military advisers. The increased stress on Singapore's military self-reliance stems

from Britain's decision to close the big Singapore naval base by 1971.

▶ **TAIWAN**

This island fortress of the Chinese Nationalist Government of President Chiang Kai-shek gave attention in 1969 to choosing a potential successor to the 81-year-old Generalissimo. The issue was raised at the tenth Nationalist (Kuomintang) Party congress. Chiang's elder son, 59-year-old Chiang Ching-kuo, emerged as the probable heir. In mid-year Chiang appointed his son deputy premier.

▶ **THAILAND**

Thailand held its first general election in 11 years. The five-year-old military government of Field Marshal Thanom Kittikachorn retained power. The United States and Thailand also announced plans to withdraw 6,000 of the 49,000 American troops stationed in the kingdom. The force is largely made up of U.S. Air Force personnel who carry out air operations against Communists in Laos and South Vietnam. The cutback was requested by the Thais, who were irked by charges in the U.S. Congress that U.S. involvement in Thailand's defense could lead the United States into "another Vietnam."

▶ **TIBET**

Tibet observed the tenth anniversary of the Tibetan uprising against the Chinese Communists. The Dalai Lama, in exile in India, pledged to return one day to an independent Tibet. "Our hope remains with young Tibetans," he said. "They have a strong sense of resistance." During the year, new outbreaks in fighting were reported between Tibetans and their Chinese Communist overlords. In late March, China was said to be increasing its security guards along the Tibet-Sinkiang border.

ARNOLD C. BRACKMAN

See also CHINA; INDIA; JAPAN; KOREA; VIETNAM.

ASTRONAUTS. See PEOPLE IN THE NEWS; SPACE EXPLORATION.

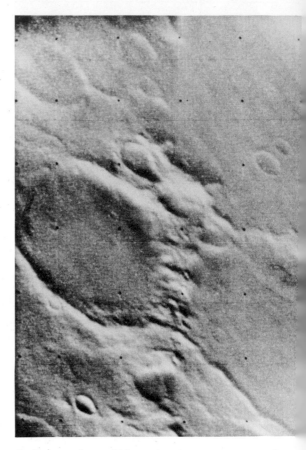

Photograph of Mars taken by Mariner 7 from a distance of 281,000 miles. The South Polar cap covered by frozen carbon dioxide is visible.

A close-up photo of Mars taken by Mariner 7 reveals craters somewhat similar to those on the moon. The area seen is 75 by 200 miles.

ASTRONOMY

DURING 1969, astronomical research continued to advance. No branch failed to make worthwhile progress.

▶ NEW FINDINGS ABOUT THE MOON

On July 20, 1969, Neil A. Armstrong and United States Air Force Colonel Edwin E. "Buzz" Aldrin, Jr., of the Apollo 11 mission landed on the moon. They were the first human beings to leave the earth and visit another body in space. Their mission was an important leap forward in astronomy, as well as in space technology. The astronauts, or more exactly, the lunanauts were able to place delicate scientific equipment on the moon and bring lunar rock back to earth.

The scientific apparatus on the moon includes a seismometer. This device can measure shocks, or seisms, that might occur on the moon. Similar devices are used to measure earthquake seisms on our own planet. The seismometer on the moon has to send its measurements back by radio. So far, these have shown that there are seisms on the moon. Although it is too early to say much, it seems that some seisms are the result of heavy landslides. Some of these are caused by the fierce heat of the sun and the extreme cold of the lunar night. Other landslides may be caused by eruptions inside the moon.

The lunanauts also set up a screen to collect atomic particles from the sun. This was taken back to earth for tests. The men placed a special mirror on the moon, as well. This mirror reflects light beams sent from earth by a laser, which gives a strong, narrow beam. Using this, astronomers can determine very precisely the moon's distance from earth. The first measurements made have already produced some new figures correct to within a few inches, and far more accurate than any before.

The samples of lunar rock that the lunanauts brought back are being studied by scientists in many countries. So far, the scientists have found that some of the rocks are as much as 3,500,000,000 years old. Scientists have also found that the chemical composition of the rocks is unlike that of any rocks known on earth. The moon rocks are also unlike any meterorites that have fallen to earth. The composition of the moon rocks seems to rule out the theory that the moon is a fragment of the earth that was torn off billions of years ago.

Rock samples from the Ocean of Storms brought back by the Apollo 12 astronauts may be at least a billion years younger than the rocks brought back by Apollo 11. These rocks also contained a great deal less titanium but more iron and nickel.

▶ MARS

Farther out from the earth is the planet Mars. Mariners 6 and 7 flew within 2,000 miles of it in July and August. The pictures radioed back to earth show a host of large and small craters like those on the moon. However, the pictures also showed that some parts of Mars have a terrain unlike the moon and the earth.

The pictures showed the air on Mars to be made up mostly of carbon dioxide. There is very little water vapor. There is frozen carbon dioxide, or "dry ice," covering the South Pole ice cap. This means that the climate of much of Mars is very cold.

The two Mariners have confirmed that there are no canals on the planet. Astronomers cannot yet be certain what causes certain dark areas on Mars. Some astronomers thought these might be covered with lichens or mosses. But the Mariner pictures make this explanation seem unlikely. The areas could be dark because their rocks are discolored. The probes show that Mars' atmosphere is very thin.

▶ VENUS

Venus was studied by the landing of two Russian probes, Venus 5 and Venus 6, in May. These gave somewhat the same results as the American Mariner 5 and the Russian Venus 4, launched in 1967. The probes showed that Venus is very hot, with a temperature more than 4 times that of boiling water. The pressure from its atmosphere is immense: about 80 to 120 times the air pressure on earth. Astronomers now feel that it is not likely that there is life of any kind on Venus.

▶ THE SUN

Farther than Mars and Venus lies the sun, our nearest star. During the year, astronomers continued their study of it. They have been studying it with space probes in particular, so that they can measure how much ultraviolet radiation the sun gives off. It is ultraviolet radiation that makes people sunburned, even though the atmosphere keeps most of it from reaching the ground. Out in space, instruments can observe all the ultraviolet. New facts can be discovered about the sun's radiation that light, heat, and radio waves cannot give. The information comes from an Orbiting Solar Observatory (OSO) 5 launched in January. It shows the astronomer what is happening in the upper parts of the sun's gases. The observations have shown that sunspots extend their effects strongly right through the gases that form the sun's atmosphere.

OBSERVING THE STARS

Other space probes have been launched to observe ultraviolet radiation and X rays from the stars. In 1969 the Orbiting Astronomical Observatory (OAO) 2 was at work, observing almost 600 stars. OAO 2 carries 11 telescopes. So far, it has shown astronomers that the stars of the Pleiades all emit between 3 and 6 times more ultraviolet than was expected. Some other stars have been found that radiate up to 40 times more. These new facts mean that astronomers will have to revise their ideas about the precise way stars radiate energy.

X-ray observations have shown that there is a new place in the sky between the constellations of Centaurus and Lupus from which intense X rays are being received. The strength of the X rays varies.

During 1969, astronomers continued to study weak radio radiation that seems to spread all over space. They had a theory that the radiation was caused by heat, coming from a time when the universe was very young. Astronomers expected that observations made from rockets from above the earth's atmosphere would confirm their theory. The observations made so far do not give the expected result. Astronomers will now have to seek other explanations.

PULSARS

In 1967, radio astronomers discovered a pulsar, a source that sent out rapid pulses of radio waves. Since then many other pulsars have been found, some also emitting X rays and light waves. During 1969, astronomers spent much time looking into them further. Astronomers discovered that some pulsars show a slowing down of their pulses.

But the most exciting discovery during the year occurred in January at the Steward Observatory, Tucson, Arizona. Scientists there saw for the first time a pulsar associated with an observable star. The pulsar is in the Crab nebula (the remains of an exploded star), and its light, as well as its radio waves, undergoes pulses.

At the moment, astronomers think that pulsars may be neutron stars lying in our own galaxy. Scientists think that when a large star burns out its heat, the atoms pack tightly together to become dense balls of collapsed atoms, or neutrons. With the collapse of the atoms, energy is converted to rotational energy. This causes the tightly packed atoms, or neutrons, to spin very fast. It is this spin that is thought to cause the pulse. Neutron stars are about 10 miles in diameter. No neutron star—if that is what a pulsar is—has ever been observed before.

QUASARS

During 1969 the study of quasi-stellar radio sources, or quasars, continued. Astronomers are trying to decide whether they are really the most distant objects observed. Quasars look like stars on a photograph, although on deeper study, they are obviously not. They are strong radio sources and strong emitters of heat rays and X rays.

Many astronomers believe that quasars are galaxies in an early stage of formation. One theory put forward during the year suggests that there is at the center of our galaxy the remains of a quasar. Another theory much developed during the year is that quasars are huge, collapsing superstars.

In addition, some British astronomers at Cambridge University are looking into another theory. According to this theory, quasars are bodies that are far bigger than superstars and are undergoing the most complete collapse. This theory is linked with a new theory of gravitation, one that is also concerned with the behavior of the atom. More facts are needed to decide which of the theories is the most likely.

COLIN A. RONAN
Editor, *The Journal of the British Astronomical Association*

Prime Minister John G. Gorton's Liberal-Country coalition narrowly defeated the Labor Party.

Poet, history teacher, and diplomat, Sir Paul Hasluck is Australia's new governor-general.

AUSTRALIA

AUSTRALIANS entered 1969 on a wave of economic prosperity. Few problems distracted them from the task of developing the vast mineral riches of their country. There was, however, some dissent on the war in Vietnam. The Government of Australia continued to support the United States in the war. But the war seemed to have less support among the people. This was seen in the national elections held in October.

The Labor Party campaigned on a pledge to bring all Australian troops home by June 30, 1970. (There were about 8,000 Australian troops in Vietnam in 1969.) As a result, the Labor Party cut into the majority of Prime Minister John G. Gorton's Liberal-Country Party coalition. In the elections, the Liberal-Country coalition won 66 of 125 seats in the House of Representatives. It had held 80 of 124 seats in the old House.

▶ POLITICS

After a long and distinguished political career, the Governor-General of Australia, Lord Casey, retired in April. He was succeeded by Sir Paul Hasluck. An intellectual and poet, Sir Paul was minister of external affairs.

The Federal Government, a coalition of the Liberal and Country parties, is led by Prime Minister John G. Gorton. He and the two parties continued to benefit from the country's economic progress though the Labor Party made some gains. The Labor Party had been splintered by the breaking away of the Democratic Labor

Party. Dissatisfaction with existing political parties was shown in July when Senator Reginald J. D. Turnbull of Tasmania announced the formation of the new Australia Party, an anti-Establishment, non-Leftist reform group.

▶ THE PRIME MINISTER'S TRAVELS

In January, Prime Minister Gorton attended a Commonwealth meeting in London. He also made two trips to the United States. One was to attend the funeral of Dwight Eisenhower in Washington, D.C., on March 31. While there Gorton met briefly with President Nixon. He then went on to Canada to meet with Prime Minister Trudeau. Gorton returned to the United States in early May for a three-day official visit. Gorton and Nixon discussed Australia's security under ANZUS.

▶ DEFENSE

Australia in 1969 maintained a foreign policy based on the defense of Southeast Asia against the spread of communism. To this end, Australia continued to rely on the ANZUS Pact, a treaty alliance with New Zealand and the United States for mutual defense. It is because of its membership in SEATO (Southeast Asia Treaty Organization), however, that Australia has aided the United States in Vietnam with a force of eight thousand troops. It was on SEATO naval maneuvers in the South China Sea in June 1969 that the Australian aircraft carrier *Melbourne* sliced the American de-

U.S. Navy helicopters join search and rescue operations over the stern of the "Frank E. Evans" (left), cut in two in a collision with the "Melbourne."

stroyer *Frank E. Evans* in half with the resulting loss of 74 American lives.

During the year a secret defense research station was set up in co-operation with the United States at Pine Gap, south of Alice Springs in the Northern Territory. Yet, in spite of much public criticism, the Australian Government refused to sign the nuclear-nonproliferation treaty, which the United States supports.

Britain intends to withdraw its armed forces from east of Suez. Because of this, Australia must plan a foreign policy independent of Britain. In the face of pleas and warnings from Malaysia and Singapore, Mr. Gorton decided to keep Australian armed forces in both countries. In view too of American intentions to withdraw troops from Vietnam and to pull out of Southeast Asia, Australia is worried that a power vacuum may occur. There have been signs that Mr. Gorton may be prepared to come to terms with the Soviet Union, which has a growing interest in the area.

▶ COMMUNICATIONS

Although Australia may feel uncertain about future U.S. policy in Southeast Asia, it still co-operates with the United States in vital space and defense-communications activities. The Carnarvon satellite-tracking station, one of six operated by the Australian Government for the U.S. National Aeronautics and Space Administration (NASA), played a major role in tracking Apollo 11 and 12 on their moon-landing missions. And expansion of the $80,000,000 Harold E. Holt communications base on Australia's Northwest Cape, a vital U.S. Navy installation used mainly to send radio messages to submarines, was announced in the spring of 1969.

▶ THE ECONOMY

With the rapid development of the great mineral discoveries of the past decade, Australia is about to make a tremendous economic leap forward. Since most of the newly found mineral wealth is in Western Australia, the old American slogan "Go west, young man" has taken on a special Australian meaning.

The iron-ore boom of the northwest, in the Hamersley Range, Mount Newman, and the Robe River district, will lead to the export of several hundred million tons of iron ore, principally to Japan. From the vast deposits of bauxite in Western Australia, Queensland, and the Gove Peninsula of the Northern Territory came over A$224,000,000 worth of products in 1969. Lead and zinc production, mainly from Broken Hill in New South Wales, continued at levels of about 360,000 tons and 230,000 tons a year respectively. Copper, mainly from Mt. Isa in Queensland, amounted to about 100,000 tons for the year. Chief among the most recent mineral finds is nickel, again in Western Australia.

Australia's overall economic growth has also been helped by oil discoveries. Crude-oil production from Barrow Island in Western Australia and the Moonie and Alton fields in southern Queensland supplied about 9 per cent of Australia's needs in 1969. Offshore drilling in Bass Strait, between southeastern Australia and Tasmania, has revealed major new sources of supply. These promise to meet all of Australia's oil needs within a few years. Already natural gas from the Bass Strait area is being used in Melbourne.

In 1969 nothing like the same spectacular development was enjoyed in Australia's agricultural and livestock industries as was experienced in the mining sector. Agricultural production was at record high levels. But there were difficulties in finding export markets—especially for meat and wheat. Therefore the Federal Government limited the acreage to be sown in wheat and increased its drive to find overseas markets for surplus foodstuffs. It also lifted a long-standing ban on the export of Merino rams, known for the quality of their wool.

On the other hand, industry expanded in all its major sectors in 1969. Its exports contributed about $560,000,000. This is nearly one fifth of Australia's total export

HEAD OF GOVERNMENT	POPULATION	ARMED FORCES	DEFENSE BUDGET *	IMPORTS *	EXPORTS *
John G. Gorton	12,406,000	87,150	$1,225	$3,600	$3,350

* US $ ('000,000)

STATE	POPULATION	CAPITAL	PREMIER	PARTY
NEW SOUTH WALES	4,436,000	Sydney	R. W. Askin	Liberal
QUEENSLAND	1,750,000	Brisbane	J. Bjelke-Petersen	Country
SOUTH AUSTRALIA	1,200,000	Adelaide	Raymond Hall	Liberal
TASMANIA	390,000	Hobart	W. A. Bethune	Liberal
VICTORIA	3,500,000	Melbourne	Henry Bolte	Liberal
WESTERN AUSTRALIA	930,000	Perth	David Brand	Liberal

TERRITORIES	POPULATION	CAPITAL	ADMINISTRATOR
CAPITAL TERRITORY	130,000	Canberra	R. Marsh
NORTHERN TERRITORY	70,000	Darwin	R. L. Dean

earnings. During 1969, Australia manufactured its two millionth Holden car.

To maintain the economy at its present almost perfect balance between exports and imports, the Federal Government introduced tighter monetary controls in 1969. It ordered banks to keep more money on deposit with the Australian Reserve Bank. This kept $67,200,000 out of circulation. The Government also raised the rate of bank interest on overdrafts.

In spite of continued high immigration (over 150,000 new Australians came from Europe in 1969), unemployment was at a record low level. Moreover, fewer man-hours were lost in 1969 through strikes than at any time since World War II.

▶ SOCIAL WELFARE AND EDUCATION

The good condition of Australia's economy was reflected in what in a Federal election year was called "a voters budget." Under this, old-age pensions were increased. More people became eligible for public-assistance benefits. And free health insurance for low-income families was provided. Greater social-welfare benefits and educational facilities were also given to the aborigines.

Increased public concern for education led to increased Federal aid. Education remains chiefly the responsibility of the states. But the Federal Government increased grants for college-level education by 40 per cent and began to set up "Colleges of Advanced Education." All political parties agreed on the need to give aid also to denominational non-state schools, which are mainly Catholic.

▶ STUDENT UNREST

Australian universities escaped serious student unrest in 1969. But almost all had some disturbances. In response to their demands, students were given greater participation in university administration by the Australian National University in Canberra and by some state universities.

E. J. TAPP
The University of New England (Australia)

AUSTRIA. See EUROPE, WEST.

AUTOMOBILES

Maverick, Ford's new subcompact, sells for under $2,000.

THE United States automobile industry had another boom year in 1969, even though sales of American-made passenger cars dropped slightly to 8,500,000. Imported cars sold over a million for the first time. This brought total passenger-car sales for 1969 close to the record 9,600,000 sales of 1968. The new record in import sales was achieved despite a drop in Volkswagen sales.

Truck sales also increased during the year, to some 1,900,000. This was an increase of about 100,000 over 1968.

▶ **COMPACTS AND SPORTS CARS**

The newest thing on the scene, at least so far as American manufacturers were concerned, was the subcompact—something close to the size of the Volkswagen Beetle. First on the market, in April, was Ford's Maverick. Costing less than $2,000, it is designed to compete with imported compact cars. The Maverick is a little larger and a little more powerful than the imports. But like them, it emphasizes simplicity and easy repair and maintenance.

When the 1970 models appeared in September, American Motors unveiled its Hornet. American Motors also plans to offer the still-smaller Gremlin in the spring of 1970. Also coming: the Ford Phoenix (not necessarily its final name); the Chevrolet XP887, sometime in the summer of 1970; and Chrysler's "25 car," scheduled to appear sometime in 1971.

Two new General Motors specialty cars aimed to compete with the Ford Thunderbird were among the 1970 models. These were Chevrolet's Monte Carlo and Oldsmobile's Cutlass Supreme.

▶ **AUTOS AND AIR POLLUTION**

Air pollution was often in the spotlight of government attention in 1969. In August, Dr. Lee A. DuBridge, President Nixon's science adviser, announced a new Federal program to persuade the auto industry to compete in producing a low-pollution vehicle by the 1990's. Funds for research amounting to $2,200,000 were provided in 1969 and were to be doubled or tripled in the new few years. But in point of fact, car makers had already made substantial progress in cutting exhaust fumes.

The High Cost of Repairs

A growing concern of car owners in 1969 was the rising cost of insurance and repairs. A major selling point for Ford's Maverick was that it was simple to maintain and repair. Indeed, Ford said that the average car owner could handle some of the work himself by following instructions in the owner's manual. Many items commonly damaged in minor accidents, such as the radiator grill, can be quickly replaced.

During 1969, automotive diagnostic centers were given support by car makers. Such centers use simple computers and other electronic equipment to detect potential problems. This has helped reduce repair costs. By the end of 1969, more than four hundred centers were in operation.

C. E. HOWARD

AVIATION

Aviation problems in 1969 included airport congestion and hijacking. Left: Travelers face delays at Kennedy Airport. Right: Raffaele Minichiello, who hijacked a plane from California to Rome.

THE biggest problem facing civil aviation in 1969 was that air traffic had outgrown the ground facilities for handling it. In the United States, there were more planes in the air than the air traffic controllers' network could take care of safely. There were too few airports, too few runways, and too few highways leading to the airports to handle the existing planes and the hordes of passengers traveling on them. People living near airports found them increasingly bad neighbors in terms of noise, air pollution, and traffic congestion on the approaching highways.

▶ **CONGESTION AND REMEDIES**

The skies above the major airports have no more room. The waiting time needed to get clearance to use a runway for landing or takeoff grows longer. Passengers find that parking lots at airports are jammed, with cars waiting in line to enter. The terminal facilities are often too far from both the parking lots and the planes. And when the traveler does reach the terminal, he finds it inefficient and overcrowded.

The big question in 1969 was whether anyone would take action to deal with the aviation industry's problems. As often happens, the whole matter was referred to Congress. The Nixon administration, for its part, proposed a bill calling for spending $250,000,000 a year for 10 years to modernize airways facilities and equipment.

The proposal calls for installing new automated control centers for the airways system; for more instrument landing systems at airports; for better communications and long-range radar coverage; and for new air traffic control towers equipped to make the job of controlling air traffic easier. There would also be money in the program for more research and development work. If adopted, the program would provide $2,500,000,000 in the next 10 years. Less than $1,000,000,000 had been appropriated for the same purposes over the past 10 years. In addition, another $2,500,000,-000 would be made available for airport construction and development in the form of 50/50 matching grants to local governments (city and state).

Two new commercial jetliners made their maiden flights in 1969: the Soviet Union's supersonic transport, the TU-144 (top); and the American-built Boeing 747 jumbo jet.

An important feature of the administration bill is that it promises funds for a 10-year period, during which there would be no need for further votes each year by different Congresses. The money would come primarily from user taxes, including an 8 per cent tax on domestic passenger tickets, a 5 per cent tax on freight waybills, a 9 cent per gallon levy on noncommercial aviation fuel, and a tax of $3.00 per person for international departures in the United States and for flights to Hawaii and Alaska.

Most aviation observers give the bill a better than even chance for success. It does not entirely please any segment of the aviation industry. But it is the only full-scale plan of attack that anyone has put forward. Even the elements that feel themselves to be the most damaged by the bill admit that it is better than nothing.

The fact is that after 10 years of feast or famine in which large safety appropriations were passed only in the years following major air disasters, time by 1969 had run out. Without some kind of immediate action in the near future the whole structure of air travel could grind to a halt.

▶ FINANCIAL PROBLEMS

For the airlines, 1969 brought financial problems too. Expenses had risen much faster during the year than had revenues, and airline earnings took a nose dive.

Domestic airlines asked for fare increases, which the Civil Aeronautics Board agreed were needed. A big surprise, however, came at the end of summer when the Italian government airline, Alitalia, rejected a bulk rate (for group travelers) proposed by the International Air Transport Association. Without approval by all 104 members, the IATA proposal had to be renegotiated. A conference of IATA members met in October and November to try to reach agreement on fares before the opening of the 1970 peak season beginning April 1. In the meantime, "open rates," under which each company could set its own fares for its own routes, prevailed. In practice, this proved not to be the air war that many carriers had feared.

Basically, the new rates that took effect on November 1 followed the rate proposed by Alitalia in its initial rejection of the IATA fares. Temporarily at least, the lines set fares across the North Atlantic that were great bargains ($299 for a round trip New York-Rome tourist fare is an example). In fact, though, the difference in terms of revenue to the airlines between the open rate fares and the IATA group-tour fares (which included a minimum of $100 in ground accommodations and services) was very small. For the long run, the 1969 fare struggle suggested an eventual lowering of the international fare structure.

The dispute over fares arose in part because of competition with cheaper, nonscheduled transatlantic airlines. Late in 1969 the International Air Transport Association listed new transatlantic fare rates. The fare rates are designed to meet the competition of the nonscheduled airlines. The fares will be for March 1, 1970, to March 31, 1971, only. Under the plan, 14-to-21-day excursion fares will be extended to 28 days. A 29-to-45-day excursion series will be offered. And new fares for groups of 80 or more persons will be available.

▶ SUPERSONIC PASSENGER JETS

In 1969, the supersonic jet airliner—referred to as the supersonic transport, or SST—made real progress. First the U.S.S.R. TU-144 made its maiden flights; then the Anglo-French Concorde was successfully flown. In the United States, meanwhile, the Boeing 2707, which had won the competition to be the American SST, went through a series of last-minute rescues from oblivion.

Late in September, President Nixon made a policy decision to keep the United States in the supersonic transport race. Still, the program he advanced was far less than the full support backers of the SST had hoped for. What the administration proposed stretched out the earliest date by which an American SST could fly with passengers to 1978. This would be several years behind the date on which the Russian and Anglo-French SST's will be in service.

Under the administration plan, a separation of the "prototype" (model) and "production" stages will add two years to the original schedules, in which these stages would have overlapped. Congress was asked to appropriate $96,000,000 in fiscal 1970. With $99,000,000 already appropriated but as yet unspent, this would permit Boeing to start building a full-scale metal mock-up of the plane and to schedule the first prototype flight in 1972.

When it is completed, the American SST will be considerably advanced technically over its foreign rivals. They are designed to carry about 130 passengers transatlantic distances at speeds up to 1,400 mph. The U.S. design is expected to carry 280 passengers at speeds up to 1,800 mph.

▶ HIJACKING

A new and bizarre hazard of air travel mushroomed in 1969. About 60 passenger planes were hijacked the world over in 1969. The figure is particularly staggering if compared to the total of 59 hijackings from 1950 through 1968. Most of the planes seized in 1969 had been commandeered to Cuba from other Western Hemisphere countries, but no part of the world was immune. In one spectacular hijack, an AWOL U.S. marine forced the pilot of a TWA plane to fly from California all the way to Rome, Italy, with stops being made at Denver; New York City; Bangor, Maine; and Ireland.

By the end of 1969 no practical way to keep potential hijackers out of airplanes had been found. No major air tragedies had as yet resulted—but, in the words of one concerned airline pilot, the unstemmed rash of hijackings continued to be "a disaster waiting to happen."

RODERICK CRAIB
Contributing Editor
Business Week

BELGIUM. See EUROPE, WEST.

BIAFRA. See NIGERIA.

BIOLOGY

IN 1969 great steps were taken in the search for life in space and time. The search for life in space was spectacular but, as expected, the first men on the moon found no traces of living organisms there. And spacecraft sent to the vicinity of Mars and Venus recorded that conditions on these planets could not support life of any kind. On earth, however, the search for traces of the beginnings of life was more rewarding.

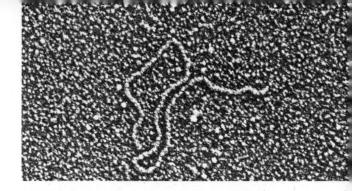
Electron-microscope photo of a single gene.

▶ UNDERSTANDING HEREDITY

While some scientists probe the vast solar system and the distant past for traces of life, others probe the basic unit of heredity, the gene, for ways to improve life. In this area of scientific investigation, very important steps were taken in 1969. Led by Dr. Jonathan Beckwith, a team of scientists at the Harvard Medical School isolated for the first time a single gene from an organism—a common bacterium called *Escherichia coli.*

This achievement has made it possible that in the future scientists will be able to control the process by which genes determine human traits. Someday scientists may be able to make artificial genes and substitute them for unwanted or harmful genes, such as those that cause hereditary diseases.

Another achievement in the area of heredity was the making of the so-called multimouse. A very young embryo of only eight cells, of dark-hair parentage, was incubated with another eight-cell embryo, of white-hair parentage. The two embryos were made to fuse together. The combined cluster of small cells was then placed in the womb of a third mouse. Nineteen days later a female mouse—which actually had four parents—was born. A week after birth, hair began to appear. The mouse had bands of white and dark hair all over its body, a real mixture of what originally was going to be two separate white and dark mice. By means of this sort of experiment, scientists hope that a further understanding of heredity will become possible.

Just as important in this area of biological sciences were the new procedures whereby individual tissue cells of mouse and man or chick and man can be made to combine to form cells with the genes of both inside a single cell membrane.

▶ STUDYING ANIMALS

Animal behavior studies in 1969 were unusually interesting. Communications with chimpanzees employing a "deaf-and-dumb" type of sign language showed much greater promise than did efforts to communicate with them by ordinary speech sounds. On the other hand, analysis by computers of the complicated sound languages of porpoises made steady progress.

Another creature under study was the Weddell seal of the Antarctic. Like man, the Weddell seal is a mammal which breathes air. Yet it can swim for several miles under water beneath the ice without coming up for air. Its underwater swims often last for an hour or more. Moreover, it can dive to a depth of from 1,000 to 2,000 feet and swim back to the surface in about 15 minutes. These performances were measured and studied in a temporary laboratory (a heated hut) set up on a shelf of ice in the Antarctic, with 2,000 feet of water below.

N. J. BERRILL
Swarthmore College

See also CHEMISTRY; CONSERVATION.

BOLIVIA. See LATIN AMERICA.

BOOKS. See LITERATURE; PUBLISHING.

BOTSWANA. See AFRICA.

BRANDT, WILLY

ON October 21, 1969, Willy Brandt, leader of the Social Democratic Party since 1961, was sworn in as West Germany's fourth chancellor. He became the first socialist leader of a German Government since 1930.

Willy Brandt was born on December 18, 1913, in Lübeck, Germany. His political views were shaped at an early age by his mother and grandfather, both of whom were strong Socialists.

When Hitler came to power in 1933, Brandt fled Germany. Except for two years in Spain, he lived in Scandinavia, working as a journalist. In 1945, after World War II, Brandt returned to Germany. Three years later he married Rut Hansen; they have three sons. Brandt was elected mayor of West Berlin in 1957, and since that time has become a dynamic national figure with a wide appeal. In 1966, when the ruling Christian Democrats headed by Chancellor Kiesinger found it necessary to form a coalition Government with the Social Democrats, Brandt was named vice-chancellor and foreign minister. He remained at these posts until the elections of 1969 enabled him to become chancellor.

See also EUROPE, WEST.

BRAZIL. See LATIN AMERICA.
BULGARIA. See EUROPE, EAST.

BURGER, WARREN EARL

DURING the 1968 presidential campaign Richard Nixon promised to appoint as chief justice of the Supreme Court a man who would strictly and objectively interpret the Constitution. He also promised a man whose strong views on "law and order" would become the majority opinion of the court. On May 21, 1969, with the nomination of Warren Burger, President Nixon seemingly fulfilled his pledge.

Burger was regarded as a man with moderate views on civil-rights issues. But he was also regarded as a man who was a tough "law and order" judge in criminal cases. He was openly critical of the liberal Warren court. In speeches and dissenting opinions he was against the Supreme Court's trend of broadening the rights of suspected criminals.

The Senate swiftly confirmed Burger. He was sworn in on June 23. Burger became the fifteenth chief justice of the Supreme Court. He succeeded Earl Warren, who had served 16 years on the bench.

Burger was born on September 17, 1907, in St. Paul, Minnesota. He attended the University of Minnesota, and graduated *magna cum laude* from the St. Paul College of Law. He then combined teaching with a private legal practice. From 1935 to 1953 he was a partner in the firm of Faricy, Burger, Moore and Costello. During that time he argued many cases before the Supreme Court. In 1933 he married Elvera Stromberg. They have two children.

At the 1952 Republican national convention, Burger first supported Harold Stassen, Minnesota's favorite-son delegate. Burger later was instrumental in switching the Minnesota delegation to Dwight Eisenhower. A year later, President Eisenhower nominated him to be assistant attorney general in charge of the Justice Department's Civil Division. Burger remained at that post until 1956.

Prior to his becoming chief justice, Burger had been a judge of the U.S. Court of Appeals for the District of Columbia for 13 years. During that time, his decisions were thought to be the most conservative of the highly liberal court.

See also LAW.

BURMA. See ASIA.
BURUNDI. See AFRICA.

CABINET, U.S.

Secretary of State: WILLIAM P. ROGERS
Secretary of the Treasury: DAVID M. KENNEDY
Secretary of Defense: MELVIN R. LAIRD
Attorney General: JOHN N. MITCHELL
Postmaster General: WINTON M. BLOUNT
Secretary of the Interior: WALTER J. HICKEL
Secretary of Agriculture: CLIFFORD M. HARDIN
Secretary of Commerce: MAURICE H. STANS
Secretary of Labor: GEORGE P. SHULTZ
Secretary of Health, Education, and Welfare:
  ROBERT H. FINCH
Secretary of Housing and Urban Development:
  GEORGE W. ROMNEY
Secretary of Transportation: JOHN A. VOLPE

The Cabinet of the Nixon administration faced critical problems in domestic and foreign affairs in 1969. Secretary of Defense Melvin R. Laird (top, left) gave the "highest priority" to the Vietnamization of the war, or the taking on of more responsibility for the war by South Vietnam. Laird indicated at the end of the year that U.S. troops in Vietnam would now be fighting in response to enemy actions. And he predicted that the Vietnam war costs would be lower in 1970. Secretary of Housing and Urban Development George W. Romney (bottom, left) predicted a housing shortage. He said that with the current rate of construction "we will fall more than 10,000,000 units short of our housing needs." Secretary of Health, Education, and Welfare Robert H. Finch (above) supported the Supreme Court's "at once" school-desegregation ruling. In 1969, Finch's department licensed a vaccine for rubella and banned the future use of cyclamates in beverages. In other areas, Secretary of the Interior Walter J. Hickel grappled with an offshore oil leak near Santa Barbara, California. Secretary of Labor George P. Shultz spoke of a "hands-off" policy for labor negotiations. And Secretary of the Treasury David M. Kennedy supported a tight fiscal policy to fight inflation.

CAMBODIA. See ASIA.
CAMEROUN. See AFRICA.

CANADA

TO many Canadians, it seemed that most of the problems of 1969 centered on the city of Montreal.

To be sure, there were nationwide problems too. Chief among these were inflation, pollution, and a continued high level of unemployment. A desperate housing shortage, and a serious glut of wheat on the prairies, with little prospect of increased sales on the world market, were among the other problems facing Canadians during the year.

But in 10 months the citizens of Canada's largest metropolis had been continually harassed by bombings by separatists (people wanting French-speaking Quebec to secede from Canada)—including the explosion of 10 sticks of dynamite at the home of Mayor Jean Drapeau. Two serious incidents of student unrest and a 16-hour strike of police and firemen added to the atmosphere of disruption.

The strike brought a night of lawlessness and destruction to the city of 2,000,000, causing one death and $2,350,000 in damage. Prime Minister Pierre Trudeau saw in the October 7 night of anarchy elements of "a society that is running amok, or surely that is a little out of control."

October 7, 1969, Montreal's worst day, began when the city's 3,700 policemen learned that their demand for pay equal to the pay of Toronto police had been denied them by an arbitration-board report. It gave them a 16 per cent raise to $8,480, well below a Toronto constable's $9,112.

Officers left their beats, abandoned patrol cars, and gathered in a north-end arena to denounce the arbitration award. They were joined by 2,400 firemen equally displeased with a similar wage award.

As the day wore on, the policemen rejected pleas by city officials to return to work. Quebec Premier Jean-Jacques Ber-

trand ordered 800 Quebec Provincial Police into the city and asked Ottawa to send Federal troops. By the time most of the Provincial Police and Army troops arrived, the damage had been done. A mob sacked a garage and burned a bus. Sniper fire broke out, and a Provincial Policeman was fatally wounded. Then the mob moved on downtown Montreal, smashing store windows and carrying off loot. In all, 175 stores, hotels, and offices were damaged and looted.

In Quebec city, the provincial capital, the National Assembly approved emergency legislation ordering the strikers back to work on pain of heavy fines for each policeman. The police returned to duty, and looting ceased. Before the night was over, 104 arrests had been made.

As Montreal cleaned up, Lucien Saulnier, chairman of Montreal's Executive Committee, charged that members of the Company of Young Canadians (CYC) were responsible for many of the city's

Canadian soldiers guard Montreal City Hall on October 8, one day after widespread rioting followed a strike by policemen.

problems. He listed 12 charges against the Federally sponsored CYC, including illegal possession of weapons and possession of manuals on how to make Molotov cocktails. His demand for an inquiry brought a reply from Ottawa that the CYC was already under investigation.

Six weeks later Montreal's City Council passed a bylaw giving police the right to prohibit in advance parades or open-air gatherings that "endanger tranquility, peace, or public order."

▶QUEBEC

Only a month earlier, in the Montreal suburb of St. Léonard, about 1,500 separatists and teen-age vandals led by unilinguist agitator Raymond Lemieux swarmed through the streets. They attacked groups of Italian-born residents and smashed the storefronts and windows of Italian-owned businesses. The issue that caused the violence was the teaching of English in French-language schools.

Nearly half of St. Léonard's residents are Italian immigrants who have demanded the right to have their children taught in English. The predominantly French-speaking school board decided in 1968 that English would be phased out of the school system. The decision was based on the fear that unless Quebec insists on schooling in French for all, the survival of the language and ultimately of French Canada cannot be assured.

In defiance of the school board's ruling, Italian-born residents set up their own basement school for 205 first graders to study English. Just ten days before the school was to open, Quebec's Education Minister, Jean-Guy Cardinal, said the government would not tolerate basement schools. He suggested that the Italians build a private school of their own.

Cardinal's decision created an uneasy feeling in some parts of Canada that the Quebec government led by Premier Bertrand no longer supports "the right of Canadian parents to have their children educated in the official language of their choice," the principle advocated by the Royal Commission on Bilingualism and Biculturalism.

While public indignation grew, Premier Bertrand hastily introduced a bill that was passed by the National Assembly. The new law makes Quebec French in principle, but bilingual in practice. It ensures the right of parents to choose the language of instruction of their children. At the same time it insists that students in English-language schools acquire a "working knowledge" of French in elementary schools, high schools, and junior colleges.

In June, at a leadership convention of Quebec's ruling Union Nationale Party, Bertrand fought off a challenge by Cardinal by 1,327 votes to 938. But the closeness of the vote indicated a lack of unity in the party.

Quebec Liberals also prepared to challenge Premier Bertrand in an election expected early in 1970. Their longtime leader Jean Lesage announced his retirement in August. Shortly afterward, a Gallup poll on voting trends showed that 27 per cent would support Premier Bertrand's Union Nationale Party (not a separatist party, but one critical of Canada's Liberal Prime Minister Trudeau); 27 per cent would vote for the Liberals; and a surprising 23 per cent favored separatist René Lévesque's Parti Québecois.

▶ THE PRIME MINISTER

Prime Minister Pierre Elliott Trudeau had the approval of most Canadians for his leadership during his first twenty months in office (his term began April 20, 1968). However, during most of this period, his efforts were concerned with shepherding through Parliament legislation remaining from Lester B. Pearson's Government.

The address Trudeau prepared for the opening of Parliament on October 23, 1969, was thought to be the first comprehensive statement of his own plans for Canada. He proposed many economic and social-welfare programs aiming toward what he called the "Just Society." His plans included lowering the voting age to 18; new approaches to collective bargaining; tax reform; and changes in some of the laws governing unemployment insurance and foreign investments in industry.

Earlier in October, Trudeau had reacted with anger and dismay at the behavior of France's Secretary of State for Foreign Affairs, Jean de Lipkowski. De Lipkowski, during eight days spent in Canada talking with Quebec provincial officials, had ignored the leaders of the Canadian Federal Government and their invitation to visit Ottawa. De Lipkowski took it upon himself not only to urge Quebeckers to "fight" for freedom but also to interpret the Canadian Constitution as allowing direct relations in the field of culture between a Ca-

continued on page 112

Canadian Prime Minister Pierre Elliott Trudeau continued efforts to bring about a "Just Society."

BILINGUALISM IN CANADA

By PIERRE ELLIOTT TRUDEAU
Prime Minister of Canada

CANADA is a very large and exciting country. But it is not an easy country to know. Even under modern conditions, it is a long and expensive trip from St. John's to Vancouver, or from Windsor to Inuvik. There are great differences of geography, history, and economics within our country. These differences have produced a rich diversity of temperament, viewpoint, and culture.

The most important example of this diversity is the existence of two major language groups, French and English. Both of these are strong enough in numbers and in material and intellectual resources to resist the forces of assimilation.

For many Canadians, Canada has seemed to be an English-speaking country with a number of minority groups speaking other languages. There are places where such groups as Italian Canadians, Ukrainian Canadians, or Chinese Canadians outnumber French-speaking Canadians.

But if we look at Canada as a whole, we find that there are two major language groups in the country: English-speaking and French-speaking. This has been the case throughout our history as a nation. No other group forms a majority in any province. No other group has its own public educational systems or radio and television networks. No other group makes up more than a small percentage of our population. According to the most recent census figures, the three largest groups whose mother tongue is neither English nor French are German (3.1 per cent of the population), Ukrainian (2 per cent), and Italian (1.9 per cent).

To build and maintain a strong and united country, both French- and English-speaking Canadians should be able to feel

Street signs in Montreal are in French and English, the two major Canadian languages.

at home in all parts of Canada. And it is essential that their rights as members of our major language groups should be respected by the Federal Government. These are the objectives of the Official Languages Act and of our policy of bilingualism.

I believe that our two major languages are a great advantage for Canada. A country that has learned to speak two great world languages will be able to make full use of the skills and energies of all its citizens. Such a country will be more interesting, more stimulating, and, in many ways, richer than it has ever been. Such a country will be much better equipped to play a useful role in the world of today and tomorrow.

nadian province and a foreign power (in this case, France). Prime Minister Trudeau saw these statements as a surprising continuation by the Pompidou regime of former French President Charles de Gaulle's support to Quebec's separatists.

▶FOREIGN RELATIONS

For years Canada has been reviewing its role in the North Atlantic Treaty Organization (NATO). In September, Prime Minister Trudeau announced plans to trim the country's NATO forces in Europe by half to 5,000 and abandon the unit's nuclear-strike role entirely by 1972. The announcement brought protests from spokesmen of several countries who fear other NATO members may follow Canada's lead.

The troop cutback was part of a reduction of the country's armed forces from 98,000 to 82,000 and decision to scrap the country's only aircraft carrier, the *Bonaventure*.

Canada became the 69th country to establish diplomatic relations with the Vati-

A grain elevator in the heart of Saskatchewan's wheatlands. Surplus wheat caused economic problems in Canada.

The antifilibuster rule sets a time limit on debates. Any government bill introduced in the House of Commons can now be voted on ten sitting days after it has been introduced.

One such debate that showed the need for some form of control concerned the Government's omnibus bill, a series of amendments and changes in the Criminal Code. For weeks a small group of Quebec-based Créditistes led by Réal Caouette talked endlessly against passage of the bill, objecting to two clauses. One clause would allow therapeutic abortions. The other would permit homosexual acts between consenting adults. The bill, finally passed, also controls the sale and ownership of firearms, sets up more-liberal lottery laws, and requires breathalyzer tests for persons suspected of driving under the influence of alcohol.

▶ THE ECONOMY

In 1969, Canada seemed to be on an economic treadmill. The gross national product (the total production of goods and services) exceeded $75,000,000,000, yet price and wage increases almost nullified any gains.

Government cutbacks on spending, and the reduction of civil-service jobs by 25,000 did little to halt price inflation. The cost of living increased by 5 points. Interest rates on prime bank loans reached 8.5 per cent. And mortgage interest rates ranged from 9 to 11 per cent.

Strikes not only slowed down the economy, but the resulting wage settlements brought new fears of inflation. After 20,000 steelworkers returned to work with a wage increase of 29 per cent, over a 3-year contract, the steel companies raised their prices by 6 per cent. When 19,000 employees of the International Nickel and the Falconbridge Nickel companies ended a 4-month walkout with a similar wage settlement, the price of nickel was raised 25 per cent.

can. And there were signs that there would be an exchange of envoys between Canada and Communist China in the near future. Secret talks with representatives from Peking had been held in the Canadian Embassy in Stockholm for six months.

▶ PARLIAMENT

Like all democratic forms of government, Canada's parliamentary system has many flaws. One, which allowed opposition members to delay the passage of bills by endless debate, has disappeared.

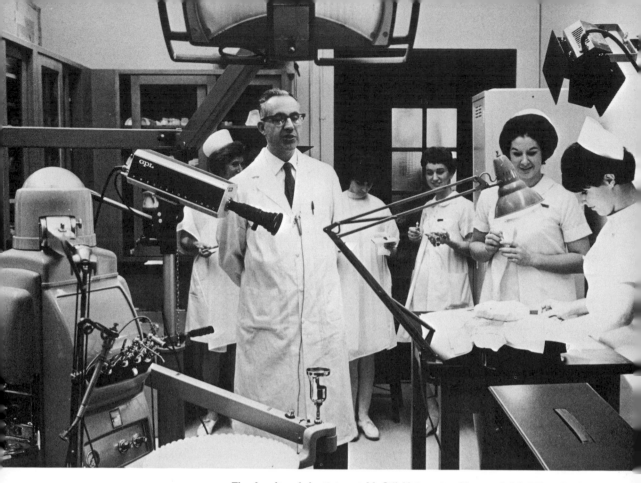

The faculty of dentistry at McGill University, Montreal. McGill and other Canadian universities faced growing student unrest during the year.

Government officials became angry at the increases. They threatened to "use less than voluntary measures" to curb wage and price increases. Prime Minister Trudeau said that the Government was considering price controls.

The Prairies: Farm Problems

In the great wheat-growing provinces of Manitoba, Saskatchewan, and Alberta, 190,000 grain farmers suffered one of the most disastrous years since the drought-ridden 1930's. It was caused not by crop failure but by an overabundance of grain production and a lack of foreign markets. At year's end, farmers had a surplus of nearly 1,000,000,000 bushels of unsold wheat, enough to supply domestic and foreign demand for three years.

Farm income in many cases was cut by 50 per cent, and many farmers offered to trade wheat for appliances and trucks. The University of Saskatchewan even allowed some students to pay for their tuition with grain. The offer brought 1,000 applications, but the university was able to accept only 300.

The worldwide surplus of wheat (production has increased from 8,700,000,000 to 11,200,000,000 bushels in the past decade) has brought a price-cutting war in all export countries. Under the International Grains Agreement of 1968, Canada reduced the price of No. 1 wheat from $1.97 to $1.90, but it was still far above the U.S. export price of $1.55 a bushel. Canada's chief customers, Communist China and the Soviet Union, are still buying wheat, but in diminishing quantities. Russia has agreed to take delivery of 135,000,000 bushels of grain, but this is part of a deal made several years ago.

HOUSING

In January, Paul Hellyer, Federal minister of transport, made 47 recommendations to Parliament that his task force on housing felt might help solve the country's housing crisis. The 7-member task force had toured 27 cities across Canada seeking ways to end a chronic shortage of 200,000 homes at prices low-income families could afford. Among the recommendations: Extending government-guaranteed mortgages from 35 to 40 years; raising their value from the present ceiling of $18,000 to over $30,000; and gradually ending down payments for low-wage earners.

After three months passed with no government action, Hellyer resigned from the Cabinet. He declared that he was "increasingly disturbed with the directions and policies being followed by the government."

UNIVERSITIES

Nowhere was student unrest more apparent than at two Montreal universities. In February, rampaging militants destroyed the $2,000,000 computer center at Sir George Williams University after black students claimed a biology professor had given them low marks because of their color. Still awaiting trial on charges of conspiracy to commit arson are 97 persons, a number of them black students from Caribbean islands.

At McGill University in March, 6,000 students and separatists demanded that the university be changed into a French-speaking institution. They stormed the university gates but were turned back by police.

The 300,000 students at colleges and universities elsewhere in Canada were content to seek educational restructuring by more-peaceful means. In a majority of the country's 50 universities, students have won a voice on administrative and academic committees without resorting to violence or disruptive demonstrations.

HEALTH AND WELFARE

Ontario and Alberta both joined Medicare in 1969. These two provinces were the last big holdouts from the Federally sponsored scheme. Only three provinces have not yet joined the program: New Brunswick and Prince Edward Island, because they feel they cannot afford it; and Quebec, because it hopes to begin its own program in 1970.

THE PROVINCES

Two provincial elections were held during the year, and both produced surprises. The Social Credit Party government of British Columbia, led by Premier W. A. C. Bennett, was returned to office with an increased majority despite a determined bid by the socialistic New Democratic Party (NDP). Bennett emerged with 39 seats in the 55-member legislature, 6 more than in the last election. The NDP won only 11 seats, and the Liberals 5.

It was a different story in Manitoba. The New Democrats, with 33-year-old Edward R. Schreyer as their new leader, defeated the Conservative government of Walter Weir by winning 28 of the 57 seats in the legislature to Weir's 22. It is Manitoba's first NDP government and the first socialist government ever elected in any province except Saskatchewan.

THE FAR NORTH

In September 1969 the voyage of the huge U.S. oil tanker SS *Manhattan* through the Northwest Passage (the seaway through the North American Arctic islands) proved that this route can be used to transport oil from Alaska's North Slope to the Atlantic Ocean and the eastern ports of the United States. This development prompted Prime Minister Trudeau, in the opening speech to Parliament, to assert Canada's "exclusive right to explore and exploit" the North American Arctic islands and the adjacent continental shelf.

GOVERNMENT OF CANADA

Governor-General: ROLAND MICHENER

THE CANADIAN MINISTRY

Prime Minister: PIERRE ELLIOTT TRUDEAU
Leader of the Government in the Senate: J. J. MARTIN
Secretary of State for External Affairs: MITCHELL SHARP
Solicitor General: GEORGE MC ILRAITH
Public Works: ARTHUR LAING
Manpower and Immigration: ALLAN MAC EACHEN
Treasury Board President: CHARLES M. DRURY
Finance and Receiver General: EDGAR J. BENSON
National Defense: LEO-ALPHONSE CADIEUX
Industry, Trade, and Commerce: JEAN-LUC PEPIN
Regional Economic Expansion: JEAN MARCHAND
Energy, Mines, and Resources: JOHN J. GREENE
National Revenue: JEAN-PIERRE COTE
Justice and Attorney General: JOHN N. TURNER
Indian Affairs and Northern Development: JEAN CHRETIEN

Labor: BRYCE STUART MAC KASEY
Privy Council President: DONALD S. MAC DONALD
National Health and Welfare: JOHN C. MUNRO
Secretary of State: GERARD PELLETIER
Fisheries and Forestry: JACK DAVIS
Agriculture: HORACE A. OLSON
Veterans Affairs: JEAN-EUDES DUBE
Consumer and Corporate Affairs: RONALD BASFORD
Transport: DONALD C. JAMIESON
Communications: ERIC W. KIERANS
Minister without Portfolio: ROBERT K. ANDRAS
Supply and Services: JAMES A. RICHARDSON
Minister without Portfolio: OTTO E. LANG
Minister without Portfolio: HERB GRAY
Minister without Portfolio: ROBERT D. STANBURY

POPULATION	ARMED FORCES	DEFENSE BUDGET *	IMPORTS *	EXPORTS *	ANNUAL PER CAPITA INCOME *
21,550,000	98,300	$1,678,000,000	$11,748,500,000	$12,895,600,000	$2,530

* US $

PROVINCE	POPULATION	CAPITAL	PREMIER	PARTY
ALBERTA	1,581,000	Edmonton	Ernest C. Manning	Social Credit
BRITISH COLUMBIA	2,101,000	Victoria	W. A. C. Bennett	Social Credit
MANITOBA	987,400	Winnipeg	Edward R. Schreyer	New Democratic
NEW BRUNSWICK	633,400	Fredericton	Louis J. Robichaud	Liberal
NEWFOUNDLAND	520,000	St. John's	Joseph R. Smallwood	Liberal
NOVA SCOTIA	771,400	Halifax	George I. Smith	Conservative
ONTARIO	7,697,000	Toronto	John P. Robarts	Conservative
PRINCE EDWARD ISLAND	110,700	Charlotte-town	Alexander B. Campbell	Liberal
QUEBEC	6,133,700	Quebec	Jean-Jacques Bertrand	Union Nationale
SASKATCHEWAN	969,600	Regina	W. Ross Thatcher	Liberal

TERRITORIES	POPULATION	CAPITAL	COMMISSIONER
NW TERRITORIES	30,000	Yellowknife	Stuart M. Hodgson
YUKON	15,000	Whitehorse	James Smith

Jean Chrétien, minister of Indian affairs and northern development.

Canada's claim to the Arctic land areas was not new. But Trudeau also pledged Canada's intention to protect the Arctic seas and coastal regions from pollution caused by future industrial development —and even promised legislation spelling out what the "protective" measures should be. Thus Trudeau, in a tactful way, asserted Canada's "responsibility" for the Northwest Passage, which the United States claims to be international waters.

Canadian External Affairs Minister Mitchell Sharp had said that it is pointless for Canada to claim blanket sovereignty over the Arctic archipelago without thought for the attitudes of other countries. It must be noted, however, that Prime Minister Trudeau's remarks stopped short of a claim of outright ownership by Canada of the seaway.

▶ INDIAN AFFAIRS

Canada's 237,490 Indians had their first look at proposals intended to end a century of segregation and give them full equality. Jean Chrétien, minister of Indian affairs and northern development, said the new policy hopefully would end the government's "white fathers" image and bring Indians into the Canadian mainstream.

Chrétien then set out to sell the new plan to the Indians. In place of Federal guardianship, which has treated Indians as a race apart, he proposed that the Indian Affairs department be dissolved. The provincial governments would provide all social services, schools, housing, and medical care for the Indian population. The 2,274 reservations, totaling 6,000,000 acres, would be turned over to the Indians without government interference.

The Indians have long complained that treaty and aboriginal rights have been abrogated or never paid for. Chrétien promised the appointment of a commissioner to sift through the claims, which would then be laid before a court or tribunal. Conceivably the claims might run as high as $3,000,000,000.

The Indians' first reaction to the proposals was critical. Some Indian leaders feared integration would be "cultural genocide." Others saw in it hope for the economic lot of the Indians. The Indians' per capita annual income is only $360, compared with a national per capita average of $1,540. Their unemployment rate is 50 per cent, 10 times higher than the national average.

Chrétien promised full discussions before the new act is presented to Parliament. It probably will not receive approval until late 1970. But already one provincial government has shown that Indians have some rights. A $1,000,000,000 Manitoba hydroelectric project which would have flooded out two prosperous Indian fishing and trapping villages on Southern Indian Lake, 500 miles north of Winnipeg, is being cancelled and an alternative plan is being sought.

GUY BIRCH
News Editor, *Toronto Star*

CENTRAL AFRICAN REPUBLIC. See AFRICA.
CENTRAL AMERICA. See LATIN AMERICA.
CEYLON. See ASIA.
CHAD. See AFRICA.

CHARLES, PRINCE OF WALES

CHARLES, 20, knelt and placed his hands in the hands of his mother, Queen Elizabeth II. "I, Charles, Prince of Wales, do become your liege man of life and limb and of earthly worship, and faith and truth I will bear unto you to live and die against all manner of folks." With these words, Charles Philip Arthur George Windsor was invested 21st Prince of Wales and Earl of Chester.

This colorful, hour-long pageantry, which took place at Caernarvon Castle, Wales, on July 1, 1969, was watched on television by millions of people.

Prince Charles, the future king of England, was born on November 14, 1948, at Buckingham Palace. When he was three years old his grandfather, King George VI, died, and his mother, Elizabeth, became queen. At that time, Charles became heir apparent to the throne. Charles' father is Prince Philip, Duke of Edinburgh.

In 1967 Charles was graduated from Gordonstoun, the school in Scotland where his father had been educated. He now attends Trinity College, Cambridge University, where he first studied archeology and anthropology before switching to history. He plays the cello in the college orchestra and acts in drama-society plays. He loves to sail, pilot his own plane, and play polo and cricket.

He has two brothers, Andrew, 9, and Edward, 5, and a sister, Anne, 19.

CHEMISTRY

IN 1969 the field of chemistry was expanded by a number of new developments. Some of these were major scientific advances which will ultimately change the life of man.

Scientists have long known that if enzymes (complicated biochemical catalysts) could be made synthetically, a whole new era in chemistry would be ushered in. In January 1969 this era began, with the announcement of the synthesis of the enzyme ribonuclease, used in the body to get rid of unwanted nucleic acids.

The existence of a fascinating substance called polywater was confirmed by American and British scientists in 1969. (It had been announced several years earlier by Soviet scientists, but had not before been confirmed in the West.) Polywater has the same chemical composition as ordinary water (H_2O), but it is far more stable and does not appear to freeze. Instead, at $-40°$ C., it changes to a glasslike state rather than the crystal state of ice. And its boiling point is much higher than ordinary water's. Polywater is made by condensing ordinary water in quartz capillary tubes the thickness of a human hair. The new form of water is 40 per cent denser than ordinary water.

In 1969, American scientists made element No. 104, the heaviest element in the periodic table. There is no official name for it yet, but the element is called kurchatovium (Ku) by the Soviets, who announced its synthesis earlier, but by a different and unreported method.

The deciphering of the structures of the bigger molecules is always big news. In 1969 the major breakthrough was the deciphering of insulin, the protein hormone necessary in the body to prevent diabetes. Others deciphered in 1969 were gamma globulin, the blood protein that helps the body ward off disease, and catalase, the "janitor" enzyme that rids the body of waste hydrogen peroxide.

A. RAE PATTON
Colorado State University

CHILE. See LATIN AMERICA.

Chinese in Peking protest against Soviet part in clash at Chenpao Island.

CHINA, COMMUNIST

IN 1969 the People's Republic of China commemorated the twentieth anniversary of the communist take-over of the Chinese mainland. The celebration was held at a time of continuing though lessening domestic political unrest and economic problems caused by the Cultural Revolution. It was held, too, at a time when China and the Soviet Union—the two communist superpowers—were engaged in a bitter, often bloody struggle.

▶ **FOREIGN AFFAIRS**

China's relations with the Soviet Union, already strained, took a dramatic turn for the worse in 1969.

At ninth congress of the Chinese Communist Party, a new party constitution was approved.

Starting on March 2, Chinese and Soviet troops fought pitched battles along the Siberian-Manchurian border and in Central Asia, where the Soviet Republic of Kazakhstan and China's Sinkiang Province join. Each side accused the other of starting the fighting. In one incident, it was reported that as many as 3,000 Soviet troops and 2,000 Chinese troops had taken part. Casualties were reported to be high. In China, organized anti-Soviet demonstrations started in front of the Soviet Embassy in Peking and quickly spread throughout the country. At the Ninth Communist Party Congress, which was held a short time after the two major clashes in March, Lin Piao, heir-apparent to Chairman Mao Tse-tung, called the Soviet Union a fascist state.

It was estimated that China and the Soviet Union massed a combined total of 1,500,000 men along their frontiers. There were also rumors that the Soviet Union had thought about attacking China's nuclear arsenal in Sinkiang Province. (During 1969, China exploded another atom bomb in the atmosphere and conducted its first underground nuclear test.) The Chinese told their people to prepare for the possibilty of nuclear war with the Soviets.

Tensions lessened in September. In a move to avert the outbreak of major hostilities, Soviet Premier Aleksei Kosygin and Chinese Premier Chou En-lai held a surprise meeting at Peking. This was the first high-level meeting between the two countries since 1965. Further talks were held beginning in October. Nevertheless, the two countries remained far apart on the border question and on ideological issues.

United States-Chinese Relations

The United States in 1969 tried cautiously to improve relations with China. For one thing, President Nixon maintained a strictly neutral position in the Soviet-Chinese dispute. He relaxed trade restrictions so that American tourists visiting such places as Hong Kong can buy up to $100 worth of goods made in Communist China. And he eased travel restrictions, allowing congressmen, scientists, doctors, scholars, teachers, journalists, and members of the Red Cross to visit China.

Early in the year, however, Liao Ho-shu, the Chinese chargé d'affairs in The

Hague, Netherlands, defected and was granted political asylum in the United States. Peking denounced the United States, accusing it of wanting to send Liao to Taiwan (Nationalist China) in order to create "anti-China incidents."

▶ **DOMESTIC AFFAIRS**

During the Cultural Revolution, which was launched in 1965, the Communist Party and the Government were purged. Education was suspended. And economic development suffered greatly. During the Cultural Revolution, too, the Army became the strongest force in China, assuming almost complete control of the country. Against this background, Mao Tse-tung summoned the long-delayed ninth congress of the Communist Party. It was the first congress held since 1958.

Lin Piao, named in April to succeed Mao Tse-tung.

The Ninth Communist Party Congress

More than 1,500 delegates from all over China traveled to Peking to attend the ninth congress of the Chinese Communist Party, held from April 1 to April 24. The two major items of business were the approval of a new Communist Party Constitution and the election of a new Communist Party Central Committee.

Most of the delegates to the congress were supporters of Mao Tse-tung. These men and women were from the military-dominated revolutionary committees Mao had set up in China's 29 provinces, autonomous regions, and special municipalities.

The new constitution, which was approved on April 14, formally named Defense Minister Lin Piao, 62, as Mao's successor. Many observers believe that Lin has already taken over many duties from the aging (76) Mao. Lin, a field marshal, had directed the Chinese Communist Army during the Korean war.

The congress elected a Central Committee of 170 delegates, and 109 alternate members. Of these, more than 100 are from the armed forces, making the military the most powerful group in the Central Committee. The new Central Committee

then elected its Political Bureau (Politburo). Mao Tse-tung was, of course, reelected chairman and Lin Piao vice-chairman. Military people also dominated this 21-member body.

Aftermath of the Cultural Revolution

During the summer, public mass trials were held, and some "counter-revolutionaries" were sentenced to death. Nevertheless, there were signs that the Cultural Revolution was easing in 1969. Many Chinese ambassadors returned to their posts abroad. And some of the regime's foreign prisoners were released, including Anthony Grey. A British correspondent, Mr. Grey had been held under house arrest for more than two years.

Economic problems created by the Cultural Revolution were evident in 1969. Peking was forced to import more grain from the West, notably Canada, France, and Australia. China's purchase of 2,200,000 tons of wheat from Australia was a record single grain transaction for both countries.

ARNOLD C. BRACKMAN

See also ASIA; UNION OF SOVIET SOCIALIST REPUBLICS.

CIVIL RIGHTS

THOSE people concerned with civil rights in the United States faced a difficult time in 1969. The radical and moderate factions in the black community remained split over many issues. There were also more signs of ill will between lower- and middle-class whites on the one hand and minority groups on the other. And, for the first time in recent history, the U.S. Justice Department and the National Association for the Advancement of Colored People (NAACP) were opponents instead of allies in a major court case on desegregation (the ending of separation of the races).

There were, however, some other government actions favorable to civil rights during 1969.

▶ SCHOOL DESEGREGATION

On August 28, 1969, at the Government's request, the U.S. Fifth Circuit Court of Appeals granted 30 Mississippi school districts permission to delay desegregation. The government move was at once denounced by civil-rights groups. On the following day, August 29, the NAACP asked the U.S. Supreme Court to overturn the lower-court decision. The United

A Negro student at the University of Wisconsin calls for black-studies programs. Similar demands were made on campuses across the United States.

THE BLACK PANTHERS

Black Panther Party Chairman Bobby Seale, one of the most vocal leaders of the militant Negro group, in jail. Seale had been sentenced to four years in prison for contempt of court during the "Chicago Eight" case, in which eight defendants were being tried for conspiracy to incite a riot during the 1968 Democratic national convention in Chicago. During 1969, too, several Black Panthers were killed in gun battles with police in various cities. The Panthers charged that the United States Justice Department and city police forces are engaged in a conspiracy to wipe them out. To find the truth of the matter, no less than eight investigations were begun. One citizens group looking into the slayings includes former Attorney General Ramsey Clark and former Supreme Court Justice Arthur Goldberg. The Black Panthers, a revolutionary group, recruits members from jails, colleges, and the streets. Attorney General John Mitchell has called them a threat to national security.

States Civil Rights Commission joined in the protest against the "go-slow" policy of the Government.

On October 29 the Supreme Court ruled unanimously that the school districts must desegregate "at once." This ruling will apply to all Southern school districts. It replaces the 1955 Supreme Court decision that schools should desegregate with "all deliberate speed."

The Government did not always team up with "go-slow" views on civil rights during 1969. On January 16 the Department of Health, Education, and Welfare (HEW) charged Louisiana with running a segregated state college system. Louisiana was given 60 days to draw up plans for ridding the system of segregation. And on August 1 the Justice Department filed a suit against the state of Georgia to end segregation in its schools. This was the first time in U.S. history that an entire state had

been so charged by the Federal Government.

De Facto Segregation

School segregation can be ended in the South by legal means. Ending it in the North is more complicated, because there it is not a matter of law. In the North, school segregation happens because of residence patterns: schools in all-Negro neighborhoods are attended mainly by Negro children and staffed mostly by Negro teachers.

As a way of ending this type of segregation, some cities have begun bussing Negro children to mainly-white schools. This is being done in Rochester, N.Y., Boston, Hartford, and elsewhere. In February, however, plans to bus Negro children to schools in the well-to-do Long Island city of Great Neck caused a great deal of protest. In a referendum the people of Great

Neck defeated the plan. The Great Neck school board, however, went ahead with an experimental bussing plan.

It is partly because of the difficulty of ending de facto segregation in the North that many civil-rights supporters and Negro parents have turned to other means of securing a good education for their youngsters. Some have sought community control of schools, giving parents more to say about the actions of the local board of education. Others have asked for outright, frank separation. Along with separation they want the introduction of ethnic studies and a more meaningful approach used in textbooks and teaching.

▶ SEPARATISM AND BLACK STUDIES

Separatism was demanded by many blacks on college and university campuses in the United States in 1969. Much of the year's campus unrest was based on demands by blacks for black-studies programs and for separate dormitories and other facilities. Mexican-American students in California and Puerto Rican students in New York also presented demands for ethnic-study programs.

At Cornell University, in April, black students seized the Student Union building and held it with guns smuggled in to them later. The black students claimed they acted in fear of hostile white students gathering outside. The black students were given lenient treatment by Cornell. As a result, some of the faculty members quit in protest. After this incident New York State passed a law against having guns on college campuses.

The development of demands for separatism raised the question of just what civil rights are supposed to be in the United States. Do these rights include the right for one group to separate itself from others? The chief aim of most civil-rights workers in the United States has been to make possible the sharing of the good things in our society by all people regardless of race. It was in 1969 that an increasing number of voices asked for the right not to get

together with their fellowmen of other races, but to be apart. This view is not held by the majority of American Negroes now, but the spokesmen for it are young, articulate, and vigorous.

▶ EQUAL EMPLOYMENT

A drive for full and equal employment opportunities was important in 1969. The U.S. Labor Department began a pilot program in Philadelphia to ensure more jobs for minority-group members in the building craft unions. The program is known as the Philadelphia Plan. If successful, it will be used in other major cities. The plan would require a percentage of minority-group workers to be employed on Federally financed housing. The plan was criticized in some quarters for being a "quota system." As such, it would violate the Civil Rights Act of 1964. But Attorney General John N. Mitchell gave an opinion in September rejecting this view.

In Pittsburgh, where the Philadelphia Plan had not yet gone into effect, protests by blacks and white supporters against discrimination in the building crafts unions closed down many construction sites from August 25 to August 29. Counterdemonstrations by white workers made the dispute last even longer. City officials were able to make arrangements in September for more job opportunities for minority-group members on future jobs.

On March 20, 1969, a strike of hospital workers, most of them Negro, began in Charleston, South Carolina. The strike, at two hospitals, was backed by the Southern Christian Leadership Conference (SCLC). Mass demonstrations were held, and more than four hundred people were arrested. Among those jailed was Dr. Ralph Abernathy, leader of the SCLC. The strike was settled at just one hospital more than three months after it had started.

▶ CIVIL DISORDERS

Violence and civil disorder are not an aim of the civil-rights movement. Quite the contrary. However, even peaceful protest can create an air of tension, and violence sometimes breaks out accidentally. In cases where groups cause civil disorders on purpose, they are hurting civil rights. When peaceful people of any race are prevented from walking on the streets freely because a riot is taking place, the rioters have taken away the civil rights of other people.

There was less violence in U.S. cities in 1969 than there was in 1968. Still, there were more than 170 "civil disturbances." Among the cities where disturbances occurred in 1969 were Cairo, Illinois; Miami, Florida; Detroit, Michigan; Winston-Salem, North Carolina; Port Gibson, Mississippi; Newark, New Jersey; Passaic, New Jersey; and Hartford, Connecticut.

From April 4 to April 6 there was a series of disorders and demonstrations sparked by the first anniversary of the death of Dr. Martin Luther King, Jr.

▶ ELECTIONS

As a result of the 1965 Voting Rights Act, which banned the literacy test in Southern states, it is now possible for more Negroes to register to vote. In 1969 a number of Negroes were elected to important offices in different parts of the United States, including the South.

Charles Evers, brother of slain civil-rights leader Medgar Evers, was elected mayor of Fayette, Mississippi. He was sworn in on July 7. Chapel Hill, North Carolina, elected its first black mayor, Howard Lee, in May. And in November, Carl B. Stokes, the first black mayor of a major city, was re-elected in Cleveland, Ohio.

In July, six black candidates gained control of the Greene County, Alabama, school board and county commission after intervention by the U.S. Supreme Court to get them on the ballot.

▶ COURT MATTERS AND DECISIONS

The U.S. Supreme Court took up a number of civil-rights issues besides school desegregation in 1969. The Court ruled in favor of peaceful student antiwar demonstrators who had staged a protest in Des Moines, Iowa. And in welfare, the Court ruled that one-year-residency rules for welfare applicants were unconstitutional. The Court said that such rules interfered with freedom to travel—that is, to move one's residence from one city or state to another.

In November the Senate defeated President Nixon's appointment to the Supreme Court of Judge Clement F. Haynsworth. This was a victory for civil-rights leaders. The Haynsworth appointment had been made to "help restore balance" to the Court that for some 15 years had handed down rulings favorable to civil-rights legislation.

▶ AMERICAN INDIANS

In 1969, American Indians began to speak out militantly in their own interest. In August a three-day all-Indian study group met in Denver, Colorado. The first such meeting ever held, it was attended by Indian professional men and technicians from many tribes, and whites were not permitted. The overall intent of the meeting was to define Indian problems and propose solutions desired by the Indians rather than by white men.

The note of self-reliance voiced in the Denver meeting was heightened to one of militancy by Indians attending the annual convention of the National Congress of American Indians in October, in Albuquerque, New Mexico. The younger Indians were outspoken in their pessimism over getting better treatment from the Federal Government unless Indians themselves take part in the planning of Indian affairs.

DAVID GELIEBTER
Deputy Director
Division of Civil Rights
New Jersey Department of Law
and Public Safety

CONGRESS, U.S.

THE first session of the Ninety-first Congress convened on January 3, 1969. Three main facts or developments shaped the character of the Ninety-first Congress as the session unfolded.

First, the pace of law-making activity during most of 1969 was the slowest in modern U.S. history. Second, giant strides were taken toward the widest reform of the U.S. tax laws ever made. And third, the session saw a dramatic change in attitude toward military commitments.

This session marked the first year of the administration of President Richard M. Nixon. Because the executive branch spent the early months of 1969 developing the outlines of a program of laws it could live with for at least 4 years, Congress had to mark time waiting for the legislative package.

▶ **COMPOSITION AND LEADERSHIP**

The Ninety-first Congress convened with the following party lineup: In the Senate were 57 Democrats and 43 Republicans. In the House of Representatives were 243 Democrats and 192 Republicans.

Before the Congressional session began, party caucuses (closed meetings) had met in the Senate and House to elect leaders for the Ninety-first Congress. In a surprising upset, Senator Edward M. Kennedy (D. Mass.) defeated the incumbent (office-holding) Assistant Majority Leader, Russell B. Long (D. La.). Kennedy had captured the second-ranking post in the Democratic Senate leadership. Democratic Majority Leader Mike Mansfield (Mont.) was re-elected.

Among Senate Republicans, Hugh Scott of Pennsylvania beat Roman L. Hruska of Nebraska for the post of Assistant Minority Leader under Senate Republican leader Everett McKinley Dirksen. Later in the year, on September 24, Scott was to move up to Minority Leader on the death of Senator Dirksen. Often called "Mr. Republican," Dirksen had been one of the best-known and most colorful figures in American politics for many years.

In the House, aging Speaker John W. McCormack (D. Mass.) and Majority Leader Carl Albert (D. Okla.) were re-elected. Gerald Ford of Michigan was re-elected as Republican Minority Leader of the House.

▶ **BUSINESS OF THE CONGRESS**

Among the Senate's first important actions was its confirmation in January of President Nixon's appointments of his Cabinet. The Senate confirmed 11 of 12 nominations by voice vote. Confirmation of Walter Hickel as secretary of the interior came three days later by roll-call vote after debate over whether or not he was concerned enough about conserving the nation's wilderness resources.

During the first three months of the session there was little legislative activity, although many hearings were held before Congress' various committees. By the Easter recess, Congress had approved a pay raise for the president and for Senate members. It had increased the limit on the national debt. It had extended the president's authority to re-organize certain government programs. Perhaps most important, the Senate ratified the treaty halting the spread of nuclear weapons (Treaty on the Nonproliferation of Nuclear Weapons).

In April Congress received a message from President Nixon containing the broad outlines of his domestic program and recommendations "to redirect the course of the nation." The next day Congress received the President's plan to revise the 1970 Federal budget proposals he had inherited from Lyndon B. Johnson.

Mike Mansfield (Dem.), Senate Majority Leader.

Hugh Scott (Rep.), Senate Minority Leader.

President Nixon's budget recommendations were aimed at cutting approximately $4,000,000,000 from Mr. Johnson's budget. The plan was to reduce Federal spending to $192,900,000,000 and leave a budget surplus of $5,800,000,000, the fourth largest in history.

Mr. Nixon's budget proposed to cut domestic outlays by $2,900,000 and defense spending by $1,100,000. One of the main goals of the Nixon budget was to fight inflation (soaring prices and wages) by reducing the amount of Federal money flowing into the economy. Inflation had become a very serious problem by 1969, and was to worry Congress all during the year.

The Nixon legislative program received in April proposed: (1) increased social security benefits; (2) improved equal employment opportunities; (3) a broad program of manpower training and job placement; (4) action against organized crime; (5) development of airways, airports, and mass transit; (6) re-organization of the Post Office Department; (7) home rule and Congressional representation for the District of Columbia; (8) tax-credit incentives to induce the private sector to help solve social problems; (9) revenue sharing by the Federal Government with the states and cities; and (10) tax reform. The President also promised proposals later to cover the problems of inflation, welfare, and crime. Although the first ten recommendations were stated in broad outline in April, Congress was to wait months before receiv-

John McCormack (Dem.), Speaker of the House

Carl Albert (Dem.), House Majority Leader.

ing the proposals in specific enough form to be acted upon.

▶ THE SLOW PACE OF ACTION

By the time Congress went on a 3-week vacation in August, it had passed only one piece of major legislation. This was an extension of the surcharge on Federal income taxes, sought by the President to help fight inflation. All 15 of the regular appropriations bills, needed to provide money to run the government, were still unpassed. The first money bill to get through Congress was not approved until late September, three months into the new fiscal year. To permit the government agencies and departments to operate, Congress had to pass a series of stop-gap resolutions.

In early August, Mr. Nixon submitted his recommendations for major reforms in the country's welfare system, manpower training, and poverty programs. He also put forward the specifics of his plan for revenue sharing with state and local governments.

▶ ACTION BEGINS

In a major move, President Nixon on October 13 sent a message to Congress to speed up the business of law-making to meet the needs of "a nation in distress." In his message he urged Congress to begin a decade of reform "such as this nation has not witnessed in half a century." He asked for twelve reforms in particular, and foremost of these were: (1) revision of the draft law so that 19-year-olds will be drafted first, by lottery; (2) revamping of the welfare system to provide a minimum income to the "working poor"; (3) changes in the election system to provide for direct popular election of the president and vice-president; (4) federal tax reform; (5) conversion of the post office to a government corporation to make it more efficient; (6) cost-of-living adjustments in social security benefits; (7) re-organization of job training programs; and (8) revenue sharing with the states. A mine-safety law and proposals to help eliminate hunger in the United States were also among the requests included in this message.

In late October Mr. Nixon asked swift action on the thirteen money bills still stalled in Congress. He warned that unless the bills were passed promptly it might be impossible for him to send Congress his budget for the next fiscal year in time to meet the requirements of law.

Despite the slow pace of legislation, lengthy studies and debates on two major subjects were taking place during the year. These subjects were tax reform and military expansion.

▶ TAX REFORM

When Congress convened in January, demands for tax reform were sweeping Washington. The out-going Johnson administration had revealed that some of the wealthy were paying no Federal income taxes because of tax loopholes. The revelation stirred a great public outcry.

In April President Nixon sent Congress a tax-reform message along with a proposal to extend the surtax, reducing the rate from 10 per cent to 5 per cent for the first half of 1970. The House finally passed the surtax extension but not before Congressional liberals had obtained a promise of tax reform to go with it. A broad tax reform-surtax package was finally passed by Congress in December. President Nixon signed the tax bill on December 30.

The new tax law reduces individual income taxes by about $9,100,000,000 a year by 1973. However, because of tax reforms and heavier taxes on corporations, tax collections will be increased by $6,600,000,000. Also included in the tax law were a 15 per cent increase in social security benefits, an increase in the personal exemption from $600 to $650, and a reduction of the oil and gas depletion allowance from 27½ per cent to 22 per cent.

Gerald Ford (Rep.), House Minority Leader.

▶ MILITARY SPENDING

The first real signs of friction between the President and Congress came in March. In that month Mr. Nixon decided to ask Congress to approve the building of a modified version of the controversial antiballistic missile (ABM) system.

The President said that the Safeguard ABM system would protect U.S. missile sites against Soviet or Chinese missile attack, ensuring the ability to fire back. But his critics charged that he was giving in to the military, hurting U.S.-Soviet relations, and spending too much money for a system that might not work.

Finally, after a long and bitter debate, the Senate on August 6 narrowly backed the Safeguard system. In suspenseful voting a bloc made up mainly of Republicans and Southern Democrats won the day in favor of the Safeguard.

The whole defense budget came under fire as uneasiness grew over the war in

Vietnam and Nixon's policies for dealing with it. Although Vietnam war costs were being reduced from $30,000,000,000 a year to $25,000,000,000, charges of mismanagement and waste by the military grew more frequent. Despite the questions raised, however, Congress voted all the monies requested by the Pentagon before the end of the year.

War-related disputes among the lawmakers included one over the testing of a new type of missile system, the MIRV. The MIRV (Multiple Independently-targeted Reentry Vehicle), a sort of "missile bus," if built, would carry several warheads. Each could be dropped on a different target.

The draft laws were also criticized, as was the Navy for allowing conditions to exist that made possible the seizure of the *Pueblo* by North Korea. The arms buildup the world over was viewed with alarm.

Dissatisfaction with the United States' overseas commitments and the military spending they entail led Congress to criticize U.S. defense arrangements with other countries, particularly in Asia. In June the Senate adopted a "national commitments" resolution that stated its opposition to committing the United States to the defense of other countries without the consent of Congress.

▶ FINAL MONTHS OF 1969

If the most of the Ninety-first Congress' first session was noted for its sluggish pace, it could not be faulted on committee work. In both House and Senate, committees delved into such subjects as college disorders, defense contracts, electoral-college reform, medical care, drug-abuse control, hunger, inflation, organized crime, civil rights, the ethics of judges, foreign trade, and tax reform.

Haynsworth Rejected

In June the Senate had given quick confirmation to President Nixon's choice of Judge Warren E. Burger as chief justice of the United States. But his appointment of Judge Clement F. Haynsworth of the Fourth Circuit Court of Appeals to fill the seat left vacant by Justice Abe Fortas engaged the attention of the Senate for three months of heated debate. Objections were raised to Judge Haynsworth's appointment on the grounds that he had shown insensitivity to conflict of interest questions (he had in several cases rendered judicial decisions on companies in which he owned stock). And some legislators frankly objected to the Southern conservative cast of his thinking, apparent in some of the decisions he had handed down. When the appointment came to a vote, on November 21, Haynsworth was defeated by 55 to 45. Of special interest was the fact that Senate Republican leader Hugh Scott had cast a "no" vote, following the dictates of conscience over party loyalty.

Legislation Passed

Among the laws passed in 1969 were the following:

Amendment of the Selective Service Act to permit introduction of a lottery system.

A toy safety act, to protect children from toys made dangerous by electricity, heat, or mechanical hazards.

A tough mine safety act providing for closing of mines, restriction of coal dust, and compensating ailing miners.

A measure allowing the Federal Government to set water-quality standards and control oil spillage.

Acts to set up the William Howard Taft National Historic Site in Cincinnati, Ohio, and the Lyndon B. Johnson National Historic Site in Johnson City, Texas; and an act to provide for the development of the Eisenhower National Historic Site in Gettysburg, Pennsylvania.

A national plan for volunteer service programs for older Americans.

Congress also enlarged housing and urban development programs, and increased spending for education and Federal food stamps for the poor.

TAIT TRUSSELL
Senior Editor, *Congressional Quarterly*

THE CONGRESS OF THE UNITED STATES

UNITED STATES SENATE

ALABAMA
John J. Sparkman (D)
James B. Allen (D)

ALASKA
T. F. Stevens (R)
Mike Gravel (D)

ARIZONA
Paul Fannin (R)
Barry Goldwater (R)

ARKANSAS
J. William Fulbright (D)
John L. McClellan (D)

CALIFORNIA
George Murphy (R)
Alan Cranston (D)

COLORADO
Peter H. Dominick (R)
Gordon Allott (R)

CONNECTICUT
Thomas J. Dodd (D)
Abraham Ribicoff (D)

DELAWARE
John J. Williams (R)
J. Caleb Boggs (R)

FLORIDA
Spessard L. Holland (D)
Edward Gurney (R)

GEORGIA
Herman E. Talmadge (D)
Richard B. Russell (D)

HAWAII
Hiram L. Fong (R)
Daniel K. Inouye (D)

IDAHO
Frank Church (D)
Len B. Jordan (R)

ILLINOIS
Ralph T. Smith (R)
Charles H. Percy (R)

INDIANA
Vance Hartke (D)
Birch E. Bayh (D)

IOWA
Jack Miller (R)
Harold Hughes (D)

KANSAS
James B. Pearson (R)
Robert Dole (R)

KENTUCKY
John S. Cooper (R)
Marlow W. Cook (R)

LOUISIANA
Allen J. Ellender (D)
Russell B. Long (D)

MAINE
Margaret Chase Smith (R)
Edmund Muskie (D)

MARYLAND
Joseph Tydings (D)
C. M. Mathias, Jr. (R)

MASSACHUSETTS
Edward M. Kennedy (D)
Edward Brooke (R)

MICHIGAN
Philip Hart (D)
Robert Griffin (R)

MINNESOTA
Eugene J. McCarthy (D)
Walter Mondale (D)

MISSISSIPPI
John Stennis (D)
James O. Eastland (D)

MISSOURI
Stuart Symington (D)
T. F. Eagleton (D)

MONTANA
Mike Mansfield (D)
Lee Metcalf (D)

NEBRASKA
Carl Curtis (R)
Roman Hruska (R)

NEVADA
Howard W. Cannon (D)
Alan Bible (D)

NEW HAMPSHIRE
T. J. McIntyre (D)
Norris Cotton (R)

NEW JERSEY
Clifford Case (R)
H. A. Williams, Jr. (D)

NEW MEXICO
Clinton P. Anderson (D)
Joseph M. Montoya (D)

NEW YORK
Jacob K. Javits (R)
Charles E. Goodell (R)

NORTH CAROLINA
B. Everett Jordan (D)
Samuel J. Ervin, Jr. (D)

NORTH DAKOTA
Quentin Burdick (D)
Milton Young (R)

OHIO
Stephen Young (D)
William Saxbe (R)

OKLAHOMA
Fred R. Harris (D)
Henry Bellmon (R)

OREGON
Mark Hatfield (R)
R. W. Packwood (R)

PENNSYLVANIA
Hugh Scott (R)
R. S. Schweiker (R)

RHODE ISLAND
John O. Pastore (D)
Claiborne Pell (D)

SOUTH CAROLINA
Strom Thurmond (R)
Ernest Hollings (D)

SOUTH DAKOTA
Karl Mundt (R)
George S. McGovern (D)

TENNESSEE
Albert Gore (D)
Howard Baker, Jr. (R)

TEXAS
Ralph Yarborough (D)
John G. Tower (R)

UTAH
Frank E. Moss (D)
Wallace F. Bennett (R)

VERMONT
Winston L. Prouty (R)
George D. Aiken (R)

VIRGINIA
William Spong, Jr. (D)
Harry F. Byrd, Jr. (D)

WASHINGTON
Henry M. Jackson (D)
Warren G. Magnuson (D)

WEST VIRGINIA
Robert C. Byrd (D)
Jennings Randolph (D)

WISCONSIN
William Proxmire (D)
Gaylord A. Nelson (D)

WYOMING
Gale W. McGee (D)
Clifford Hansen (R)

UNITED STATES HOUSE OF REPRESENTATIVES

ALABAMA
J. Edwards (R)
W. L. Dickinson (R)
George Andrews (D)
William Nichols (D)
W. W. Flowers (D)
John Buchanan (R)
Tom Bevill (D)
Robert Jones (D)

ALASKA
H. W. Pollock (R)

ARIZONA
John Rhodes (R)
Morris Udall (D)
Sam Steiger (R)

ARKANSAS
Bill Alexander (D)
Wilbur Mills (D)
J. Hammer-
schmidt (R)
David Pryor (D)

CALIFORNIA
Don Clausen (R)
H. T. Johnson (D)
John Moss (D)
R. L. Leggett (D)
Phillip Burton (D)
W. S. Mailliard (R)
J. Cohelan (D)
G. P. Miller (D)
Don Edwards (D)
C. S. Gubser (R)
P. McCloskey (R)
Burt Talcott (R)
C. M. Teague (R)
J. R. Waldie (D)
John McFall (D)
B. F. Sisk (D)
G. M. Anderson (D)
R. B. Mathias (R)
C. Holifield (D)
H. A. Smith (R)
A. F. Hawkins (D)
J. C. Corman (D)
Del Clawson (R)
G. P. Lipscomb (R)
C. E. Wiggins (R)
Thomas Rees (D)
Barry Gold-
water, Jr. (R)
Alphonzo Bell (R)
G. E. Brown, Jr. (D)
E. R. Roybal (D)
C. H. Wilson (D)
Craig Hosmer (R)
Jerry Pettis (R)
R. T. Hanna (D)
James Utt (R)
Bob Wilson (R)
L. Van Deerlin (D)
John Tunney (D)

COLORADO
Byron G. Rogers (D)
D. G. Brotzman (R)
Frank Evans (D)
W. N. Aspinall (D)

CONNECTICUT
E. Q. Daddario (D)
W. L. St. Onge (D)
R. N. Giaimo (D)
L. P. Weicker, Jr. (R)
J. S. Monagan (D)
T. J. Meskill (R)

DELAWARE
W. V. Roth, Jr. (R)

FLORIDA
R. L. F. Sikes (D)
Don Fuqua (D)
C. E. Bennett (D)
W. Chappell, Jr. (D)
Louis Frey, Jr. (R)
Sam Gibbons (D)
James Haley (D)
W. C. Cramer (R)
P. G. Rogers (D)
J. H. Burke (R)
Claude Pepper (D)
D. B. Fascell (D)

GEORGIA
G. E. Hagan (D)
Maston O'Neal (D)
Jack Brinkley (D)
Ben Blackburn (R)
F. Thompson (R)
J. J. Flynt, Jr. (D)
J. W. Davis (D)
W. Stuckey, Jr. (D)
Phil Landrum (D)
R. Stephens, Jr. (D)

HAWAII
S. Matsunaga (D)
Patsy Mink (D)

IDAHO
J. A. McClure (R)
Orval Hansen (R)

ILLINOIS
W. L. Dawson (D)
Abner Mikva (D)
W. T. Murphy (D)
E. J. Derwinski (R)
J. C. Kluczynski (D)
Dan Ronan (D)
F. Annunzio (D)
D. Rostenkowski (D)
Sidney Yates (D)
H. R. Collier (R)
R. C. Pucinski (D)
R. McClory (R)
Philip M. Crane (R)
J. N. Erlenborn (R)

Charlotte Reid (R)
J. B. Anderson (R)
L. C. Arends (R)
Robert Michel (R)
T. F. Railsback (R)
Paul Findley (R)
Kenneth Gray (D)
W. L. Springer (R)
George Shipley (D)
Melvin Price (D)

INDIANA
Ray Madden (D)
E. F. Landgrebe (R)
John Brademas (D)
Ross Adair (R)
R. L. Roudebush (R)
William Bray (R)
John Myers (R)
Roger Zion (R)
Lee Hamilton (D)
David Dennis (R)
A. Jacobs, Jr. (D)

IOWA
Fred Schwengel (R)
John Culver (D)
H. R. Gross (R)
John Kyl (R)
Neal Smith (D)
Wiley Mayne (R)
W. J. Scherle (R)

KANSAS
K. G. Sebelius (R)
Chester Mize (R)
Larry Winn, Jr. (R)
G. E. Shriver (R)
Joe Skubitz (R)

KENTUCKY
F. Stubblefield (D)
W. H. Natcher (D)
W. O. Cowger (R)
M. G. Snyder (R)
Tim L. Carter (R)
John C. Watts (D)
Carl Perkins (D)

LOUISIANA
F. E. Hébert (D)
Hale Boggs (D)
P. T. Caffery (D)
J. Waggonner (D)
Otto Passman (D)
J. R. Rarick (D)
E. W. Edwards (D)
Speedy Long (D)

MAINE
Peter N. Kyros (D)
W. D. Hathaway (D)

MARYLAND
R. C. B. Morton (R)
C. D. Long (D)

E. A. Garmatz (D)
George Fallon (D)
L. J. Hogan (R)
J. G. Beall, Jr. (R)
S. N. Friedel (D)
Gilbert Gude (R)

MASSACHUSETTS
Silvio Conte (R)
E. P. Boland (D)
Philip Philbin (D)
Harold Donohue (D)
F. B. Morse (R)
M. J. Harrington (D)
T. H. Macdonald (D)
T. P. O'Neill, Jr. (D)
J. McCormack (D)
M. M. Heckler (R)
James Burke (D)
Hastings Keith (R)

MICHIGAN
John Conyers, Jr. (D)
Marvin Esch (R)
Garry Brown (R)
E. Hutchinson (R)
Gerald Ford (R)
C. Chamberlain (R)
D. W. Riegle, Jr. (R)
James Harvey (R)
G. Vander Jagt (R)
E. A. Cederberg (R)
Philip Ruppe (R)
J. G. O'Hara (D)
C. C. Diggs, Jr. (D)
Lucien Nedzi (D)
William Ford (D)
John Dingell (D)
M. W. Griffiths (D)
W. Broomfield (R)
J. H. McDonald (R)

MINNESOTA
Albert Quie (R)
Ancher Nelsen (R)
C. MacGregor (R)
J. E. Karth (D)
D. M. Fraser (D)
John Zwach (R)
Odin Langen (R)
John A. Blatnik (D)

MISSISSIPPI
T. G. Abernethy (D)
J. L. Whitten (D)
Charles Griffin (D)
G. Montgomery (D)
W. M. Colmer (D)

MISSOURI
William Clay (D)
J. W. Symington (D)
L. K. Sullivan (D)
W. J. Randall (D)
R. Bolling (D)
W. R. Hull, Jr. (D)

Durward Hall (R)
R. H. Ichord (D)
W. L. Hungate (D)
Bill Burlison (D)

MONTANA
Arnold Olsen (D)
John Melcher (D)

NEBRASKA
Robert Denney (R)
G. Cunningham (R)
Dave Martin (R)

NEVADA
W. S. Baring (D)

NEW HAMPSHIRE
Louis Wyman (R)
J. C. Cleveland (R)

NEW JERSEY
John E. Hunt (R)
C. Sandman, Jr. (R)
J. J. Howard (D)
F. Thompson, Jr. (D)
P. Frelinghuysen (R)
W. B. Widnall (R)
Robert A. Roe (D)
H. Helstoski (D)
Peter Rodino, Jr. (D)
Joseph Minish (D)
Florence Dwyer (R)
C. E. Gallagher (D)
D. V. Daniels (D)
Edward Patten (D)
(one seat vacant)

NEW MEXICO
Manuel Lujan, Jr. (R)
Ed Foreman (R)

NEW YORK
Otis G. Pike (D)
J. R. Grover, Jr. (R)
Lester Wolff (D)
John Wydler (R)
A. Lowenstein (D)
S. Halpern (R)
J. P. Addabbo (D)
B. S. Rosenthal (D)
J. J. Delaney (D)
Emanuel Celler (D)
Frank Brasco (D)
S. Chisholm (D)
B. L. Podell (D)
John Rooney (D)
Hugh Carey (D)
John M. Murphy (D)
Edward I. Koch (D)
Adam C. Powell,
   Jr. (D)
L. Farbstein (D)
William F. Ryan (D)
J. H. Scheuer (D)
J. H. Gilbert (D)
J. B. Bingham (D)
Mario Biaggi (D)

R. L. Ottinger (D)
Ogden R. Reid (R)
M. B. McKneally (R)
H. Fish, Jr. (R)
Daniel Button (R)
Carleton King (R)
R. C. McEwen (R)
A. Pirnie (R)
H. W. Robison (R)
James Hanley (D)
S. S. Stratton (D)
Frank Horton (R)
B. B. Conable, Jr. (R)
J. F. Hastings (R)
R. D. McCarthy (D)
H. P. Smith III (R)
T. J. Dulski (D)

NORTH CAROLINA
W. B. Jones (D)
L. H. Fountain (D)
D. N. Henderson (D)
N. Galifianakis (D)
Wilmer Mizell (R)
R. Preyer (D)
Alton Lennon (D)
Earl B. Ruth (R)
C. R. Jonas (R)
J. T. Broyhill (R)
Roy A. Taylor (D)

NORTH DAKOTA
Mark Andrews (R)
Tom Kleppe (R)

OHIO
Robert Taft, Jr. (R)
D. D. Clancy (R)
C. W. Whalen, Jr. (R)
W. M. McCulloch (R)
Delbert Latta (R)
W. H. Harsha (R)
C. J. Brown (R)
J. E. Betts (R)
T. L. Ashley (D)
C. E. Miller (R)
J. W. Stanton (R)
S. L. Devine (R)
C. A. Mosher (R)
W. H. Ayres (R)
C. P. Wylie (R)
Frank T. Bow (R)
J. M. Ashbrook (R)
Wayne Hays (D)
M. J. Kirwan (D)
M. A. Feighan (D)
Louis Stokes (D)
Charles Vanik (D)
W. E. Minshall (R)
D. E. Lukens (R)

OKLAHOMA
Page Belcher (R)
Ed Edmondson (D)
Carl Albert (D)
Tom Steed (D)
John Jarman (D)
J. N. Camp (R)

OREGON
Wendell Wyatt (R)
Al Ullman (D)
Edith Green (D)
J. R. Dellenback (R)

PENNSYLVANIA
W. A. Barrett (D)
R. N. C. Nix (D)
James Byrne (D)
J. Eilberg (D)
W. J. Green (D)
Gus Yatron (D)
L. G. Williams (R)
E. G. Biester, Jr. (R)
G. R. Watkins (R)
J. M. McDade (R)
Daniel Flood (D)
J. I. Whalley (R)
R. L. Coughlin (R)
W. S. Moorhead (D)
Fred Rooney (D)
E. D. Eshleman (R)
H. T. Schneebeli (R)
R. J. Corbett (R)
G. A. Goodling (R)
Joseph Gaydos (D)
John H. Dent (D)
John P. Saylor (R)
A. W. Johnson (R)
J. P. Vigorito (D)
Frank M. Clark (D)
Thomas Morgan (D)
J. G. Fulton (R)

RHODE ISLAND
F. J. St. Germain (D)
R. O. Tiernan (D)

SOUTH CAROLINA
L. M. Rivers (D)
Albert Watson (R)
W. J. B. Dorn (D)
James R. Mann (D)
T. S. Gettys (D)
J. L. McMillan (D)

SOUTH DAKOTA
Ben Reifel (R)
E. Y. Berry (R)

TENNESSEE
J. H. Quillen (R)
John J. Duncan (R)
W. E. Brock III (R)
Joe L. Evins (D)
Richard H. Fulton (D)
W. R. Anderson (D)
Ray Blanton (D)
Ed Jones (D)
D. Kuykendall (R)

TEXAS
Wright Patman (D)
John Dowdy (D)
J. M. Collins (R)
Ray Roberts (D)
Earle Cabell (D)

Olin Teague (D)
George Bush (R)
Bob Eckhardt (D)
Jack Brooks (D)
J. J. Pickle (D)
W. R. Poage (D)
Jim Wright, Jr. (D)
G. Purcell (D)
John Young (D)
E. de la Garza (D)
Richard White (D)
Omar Burleson (D)
Robert Price (R)
George Mahon (D)
H. B. Gonzalez (D)
O. C. Fisher (D)
Bob Casey (D)
A. Kazen, Jr. (D)

UTAH
L. J. Burton (R)
S. P. Lloyd (R)

VERMONT
R. T. Stafford (R)

VIRGINIA
T. N. Downing (D)
G. W. Whitehurst (R)
D. Satterfield III (D)
W. M. Abbitt (D)
W. C. Daniel (D)
Richard Poff (R)
John O. Marsh (D)
W. L. Scott (R)
W. C. Wampler (R)
Joel Broyhill (R)

WASHINGTON
Thomas Pelly (R)
Lloyd Meeds (D)
J. B. Hansen (D)
Catherine May (R)
Thomas Foley (D)
Floyd Hicks (D)
Brock Adams (D)

WEST VIRGINIA
R. H. Mollohan (D)
H. O. Staggers (D)
J. M. Slack (D)
Ken Hechler (D)
James Kee (D)

WISCONSIN
H. C. Schadeberg (R)
R. Kastenmeier (D)
V. W. Thomson (R)
C. J. Zablocki (D)
Henry Reuss (D)
W. A. Steiger (R)
David R. Obey (D)
John Byrnes (R)
Glenn Davis (R)
A. E. O'Konski (R)

WYOMING
John Wold (R)

CONSERVATION

The formation of the Canadian Wild Horse Society and the establishment of a "wild-horse range" in Montana gave only scant hope in 1969 that the magnificent wild mustang could be saved from eventual extinction.

THE ANIMAL KINGDOM

THE year 1969 was not a peaceful one for the animal kingdom or for those concerned with protecting wildlife. From almost every continent there were reports of endangered species.

▶ CANADA'S MUSTANGS

Another animal that faced extinction in 1969 was the mustang of Canada's western provinces. There are very few bands of mustangs remaining. Yet the Canadian Government has not moved forcefully to save them. These horses were often shot for bounty. This has now been outlawed. But many mustangs are still shot, shipped south to the United States, and used for dog food.

The Canadian Wild Horse Society was formed to lead the fight to save these horses. Many important people support this fight. Still, the outlook for the mustangs was not good at the end of 1969.

At year's end, the major battles to save animal wildlife remained inconclusive. It was clear, however, that the biggest problem facing man was not which aspect of the animal kingdom to study, but what fraction would be saved to study at all.

Pesticides and the trade in exotic furs were under the scrutiny of government agencies and private citizens. Moves were made to put an end to the brutal trade in exotic pets. And efforts were started to establish control over roadside menageries, where conditions are very bad.

▶ BEAR CONTROVERSY

In August 1967 two young campers were killed by bears in Glacier National Park, Montana. The deaths and the bears caused a controversy that continued throughout 1969. Many magazine articles called for the removal of the bears. The unpredictable grizzlies were branded as especially dangerous. Other people pointed out, however, that in 97 years only five

Sanctuaries are needed along the seacoasts to save the condor from extinction.

people have been killed by bears in the National Park System.

In 1968, more than 150,800,000 people visited national parks in the United States. Thus the figure of five deaths in almost a century seems less ominous. In fact, it was pointed out, statistically speaking, bear watching is a safer activity than swimming, boating, driving, or taking a shower.

There are bears in only 16 national parks. For the time being, they seemed safe. Though some were killed by park rangers, others were just moved to infrequently visited park areas.

Most people agree that a better educational program is needed. Visitors to national parks must be made aware that *all* bears can be dangerous at *all* times. Because of this fact, many people believe that the symbol of the forest-fire warden, Smoky the Bear, should be changed. They feel that Smoky gives people the idea that the wild bear is in fact a tame animal.

▶ **SEAL-PUP SLAUGHTER**

The annual slaughter of seal pups on the Canadian Arctic ice floes made headline news in 1969. Sealskin coats for the fashion trade are made from the skins of baby seals. Each year thousands of these newborn animals are beaten to death. Motion-picture films and photographs of the slaughter were shown on television and in magazines. This created a storm of protest. The Canadian Embassy began using form letters to answer all the protests that poured in. The Canadian Government responded by banning the hunting of baby seals starting in 1970.

▶ **THE RETURN OF THE BIRDS**

Good news in 1969 included the announcement by the U.S. Department of the Interior that three birds thought to be extinct had reappeared. Two of these birds are from Hawaii. The Molokai creeper (*Loxops maculata flammea*) is found only in the damp forests on the upper slopes of the Hawaiian island of Molokai. The Maui nukupuu (*Hemignathus lucidus affinis*) was also sighted in 1969 in Hawaii. None had been seen since 1896.

The third species rediscovered in 1969 was the Puerto Rico plain pigeon (*Columba inornata wetmorei*). Actually, the report of its existence had been made in 1963 (the last two reports before this were in 1958 and 1912). But the announcement was held off until more proof was obtained. This happened in 1969, and the distinctive pigeon from the mountains of Puerto Rico, and from the Greater Antilles, rejoined the living.

It was confirmed too that the magnificent ivory-billed woodpecker was nesting in Texas. The locations were kept a closely guarded secret.

In 1969 it was finally conceded that the peregrine falcon is an endangered species. The blame was placed on insecticides. Studies have shown that as the amount of DDT in a bird's body increases, the shells of the bird's eggs become thinner and thinner. Finally it becomes impossible for the bird to brood her clutch. When she sits' on them, they break. Indeed, some eggs were produced with no shell at all.

▶ **MYSTERY OF THE LEMMINGS**

One of the great mysteries of the animal kingdom has been the apparent mass suicide of lemmings on the Arctic tundra. At three- and four-year intervals the number of these animals increases dramatically. Then masses of them leave their home range, march into the sea, and drown. In 1969, researchers at Point Barrow, Alaska, discovered that lemmings have a type of "antifreeze" in their bodies. This antifreeze lets them live in very cold weather when all other rodents go into hibernation.

Some scientists believe that as the weather warms up, the antifreeze may affect the lemmings' central nervous system. This causes behavior that ends in a kind of suicide. How this is related to population density and food supply is not yet understood. But the end of this age-old mystery may be in sight.

ROGER A. CARAS

THE ENVIRONMENT

THE photographs taken by the Apollo astronauts enabled man to see his planet in orbit like a spaceship. Those who saw this beautiful sight could better understand that, as Adlai Stevenson once said, "We travel together, passengers on a little spaceship; dependent on its vulnerable reserves of air and soil preserved from annihilation only by the care, the work and the love we give our fragile craft." In 1969, despite some setbacks, the care, work, and love continued in an effort to preserve not only earth's air and soil but its total natural environment.

▶ **PESTICIDES**

DDT is a very powerful chemical pesticide which builds up in the body. It can take a decade or more for DDT to lose its poisonous effect, and many believe that it might cause cancer. In 1969, after years of warnings by some scientists, the United

States Government banned the use of DDT. The Government acted after Coho salmon caught in Lake Michigan were found to contain dangerous amounts of DDT. Previously, polar bears in the Arctic, penguins in the Antarctic, and Bermuda petrels in the Atlantic, which never see land where DDT is used, had been found to have DDT in their fatty tissues. (This is because DDT circulates through rivers, oceans, and even as vapor through the air.) Even breast milk of some human mothers was found to contain more than two times the "safe" level of DDT.

The Government order banned DDT use in spraying trees in residential areas. It also banned its use against house and garden pests and mosquitos and other insects in aquatic areas. By the end of 1970 the Government intends to ban all other uses of DDT except where "needed to prevent human disease" and "other essential uses for which no alternative is available." In 1970 the Government will begin to take action to ban other pesticides whose poisonous properties are long-lasting.

▶ OIL POLLUTION

In January, an oil well drilled from a platform six miles off Santa Barbara, California, "blew out," forcing oil into the sea. The oil polluted nearly two hundred miles of southern California's coastline. Even after the well was controlled, millions of gallons of oil continued to seep through cracks in rocks under Santa Barbara Channel. Oil slicks spread over hundreds of square miles of sea, killing untold numbers of seabirds. In addition, tons of oil sank, causing as yet unknown damage to microscopic sea organisms.

Claims of damage to boats, beaches, fish, and wildlife totaled more than $1,000,000,000. The Santa Barbara city and county governments and the state of California sued the oil companies involved and the Federal Government, which has jurisdiction over off-shore oil drilling. Some Santa Barbara residents formed an organization called Get Oil Out (GOO), and called for the removal of all oil wells from Santa Barbara Channel.

For some time, Interior Secretary Walter Hickel allowed no additional oil wells off Santa Barbara. He issued stronger regulations of off-shore drilling. And he called for better identification of all marine resource values before new offshore areas could be leased for oil production. Then, in June, Secretary Hickel again permitted unlimited drilling off Santa Barbara on the grounds that it would relieve underground

The New York City skyline is all but hidden beneath a blanket of air pollution.

oil pressure and help stop the continuing leaks. Full-scale drilling was resumed, and another platform was erected so that more wells could be drilled.

In part because of the Santa Barbara accident, tighter oil-pollution controls were the subject of bills passed by both houses of Congress. The bills would make operators of oil tankers and of on-shore and off-shore facilities liable for clean-up costs.

▶ OTHER WATER-POLLUTION CONTROL ACTIONS

For the first time, the Federal Government refused to accept water-quality standards proposed by a state for rivers flowing through the state into neighboring states. The Federal Water Pollution Control Administration directed Iowa to require industries and communities which dump wastes into interstate rivers to install stricter pollution controls by the end of 1973.

In another action, Congress took the unusual step of appropriating more money than President Nixon sought to help communities build waste-water treatment plants. The President asked Congress for $214,000,000 for the fiscal year ending June 30, 1970. However, as a result of increasing Congressional concern, encouraged by the Citizens Crusade for Clean Water, the Congress in December appropriated $800,000,000.

▶ AIR POLLUTION CONTROL

Twenty metropolitan areas were designated by the Federal Government for the first time as air-quality control regions. The states involved submitted air-quality standards for the first 11 regions to the National Air Pollution Control Administration (NAPCA). By mid-1970, 37 more air-quality regions will be established. At that time, some 70 per cent of the U.S. urban population will be subject to the Air Quality Act of 1967, the nation's basic air pollution control law.

NAPCA issued tighter emission controls on automobiles. And the first nationwide

pollution standards for diesel buses and heavy trucks were issued, effective January 1970. Despite these steps, however, the air over most American cities, like most of the rivers flowing through them, continued to get dirtier every day. Motor vehicles continued to be the major source of air pollution.

▶ THE EVERGLADES

In Florida an environmental controversy neared a showdown. It involved the first stage of a proposed jetport which would eventually be six times the size of John F. Kennedy International Airport near New York City. The immediate issue was whether the Dade County (Miami) Port Authority would receive the Federal approvals necessary to operate the first stage, a single-runway training airport.

The site is only six miles from the northern edge of Everglades National Park. It is in a swamp that supplies much of the water on which the park's unique plant and animal life depends. The National Park Service and some congressmen warned that "the whole chain of life in the Everglades, from algae to alligators, will be threatened by the inevitable pollution which will accompany the jetport and the facilities which support it."

▶ ENDANGERED SPECIES

Congress enacted a law designed to protect species of wildlife threatened by extinction by man, often because their skins are sold for articles of clothing. The law prohibits importation into the United States of such endangered species as the cheetah and snow leopard and their furs or other products.

▶ OUTDOOR RECREATION

After a five-year study, the Interior Department's Bureau of Outdoor Recreation announced some features of its Nationwide Outdoor Recreation Plan. It calls for less emphasis on large national parks and recreation areas in rural areas and more emphasis on smaller areas near cities. The plan proposes greatly increased Federal investment.

Meantime, however, the Government cut back funds for the existing recreation programs. As a result, a backlog of bills to authorize new recreation areas began to accumulate in Congress. However, Congress completed action to authorize Florissant Fossil Beds National Monument in Colorado, to complete Padre Island National Seashore in Texas, and to establish two new wilderness areas in California.

▶ COASTAL ZONE MANAGEMENT

The Commission on Marine Science, Engineering and Resources called for better management of the coasts and Great Lakes. It urged the thirty coastal states to develop coastal zone planning and management agencies. It also recommended a new Federal grant program to help.

In October the administration proposed a plan to increase spending on coastal problems and marine research. If passed, some $30,000,000 would be spent in fiscal 1971.

Meanwhile, California established such a coastal zone agency: the San Francisco Bay Conservation and Development Commission (BCDC). The California legislature, concerned about haphazard filling of the bay, gave BCDC power over the bay and over a 100-foot-wide strip of land around the bay's 276-mile shoreline.

▶ CONSERVATION BILL OF RIGHTS

The people of New York State voted in 1969 to add to the state constitution a "Conservation Bill of Rights." This put into the state's fundamental law a declaration that a basic policy of the state is "to conserve and protect its natural resources and scenic beauty." The legislature was directed to make "adequate provision for the abatement of air and water pollution and of excessive and unnecessary noise, the protection of agricultural lands, wetlands and shorelines, and the development and regulation of water resources." Rhode Island placed a similar measure on its

1970 ballot. Citizens in other states were drafting similar constitutional amendments.

▶ ENVIRONMENTAL OVERVIEW AGENCIES

The conservation commission movement started in Massachusetts in the 1950's. By 1969 it had spread to six other states in the Northeast. More than 570 such units of local government were advising city and town councils on actions necessary to make their community total environment a better one for people. In 1969 the Federal Government also acted to set up an environmental overview agency. The Congress passed a bill to create a three-member Council on Environmental Quality. The council members are to be appointed by the President and will help him prepare early environmental quality reports to the nation.

▶ NATIONAL ENVIRONMENTAL POLICY

The Board of Environmental Quality Advisers was set up by the National Environmental Policy Act of 1969. This act declares that each person "should enjoy a healthful environment" and that each person "has a responsibility to contribute to the preservation and enhancement of the environment. This important new legislation directs all Federal agencies to "recognize the worldwide and long-range character of environmental problems and lend appropriate support to . . . international co-operation in anticipating and preventing a decline in the quality of mankind's world environment."

In 1969, too, the United Nations Economic and Social Council (UNESCO) issued a report by UN Secretary-General U Thant on *Problems of the Human Environment*. The UN plans to hold a conference on these problems in 1972 "to provide a worldwide focus for worldwide action."

WILLIAM J. DUDDLESON
Director of Policy Studies
The Conservation Foundation

COSTA RICA. See LATIN AMERICA.

CRIME

IN 1969 the National Commission on the Causes and Prevention of Violence issued some disturbing reports. It warned, for one thing, that there may be an increasing number of assassinations in the United States. The commission recommended that the president and other public figures make fewer public appearances.

The commission also warned that the heavily populated cities of the United States are being turned into armed camps as crime increases at an alarming rate. Between 1960 and 1968, the commission reported, the homicide rate increased 36 per cent. Robberies increased 119 per cent. Perhaps most frightening, the greatest percentage of violent crimes was committed by young people between the ages of 15 and 24.

The statistics used by the commission were based on the Federal Bureau of Investigation's *Uniform Crime Reports*. The latest of these reports were issued in August 1969 and contained alarming figures about crime rates during 1968.

There were 4,500,000 serious crimes in the United States in 1968. This figure represents a rise of 17 per cent over the previous year. Crime increased 17 per cent in suburban areas, 18 per cent in large cities, and 11 per cent in rural areas.

California led the nation in all crimes committed, with a rate of 3,763 crimes for every 100,000 people. New York was second with 3,544 crimes for every 100,-000 people.

Murders increased from 12,090 in 1967 to 13,650 in 1968. There were more murders in the South (47 per cent) than in any other area of the country. Firearms were used in 65 out of every 100 murders in the country.

Guns were also used in 65,000 assaults and 99,000 robberies during 1968.

Drug-law-violations arrests were up 64 per cent over 1967. The figure increased so greatly because there were many more arrests for the sale and use of marijuana.

The 1969 *Uniform Crime Reports* also showed that crime rose 11 times as fast as the population of the United States between 1960 and 1968. During the same eight-year period, police solution of serious crimes dropped 32 per cent. The number of serious crimes in 1968 was 122 per cent higher than the figure for 1960.

These statistics show an alarming increase in all kinds of crime. But it should be pointed out that most crimes are committed by people who commit crimes repeatedly. Because of this fact, the Joint Commission on Correctional Manpower and Training warned in 1969 that the crime rate would not be checked until reforms were made in prisons.

The President's Commission on Law Enforcement and the Administration of Justice pointed out another factor. Technically, many actions are violations of laws that are either unrealistic or impossible to enforce. Violations of antimarijuana laws are but one example.

Another factor in the increasing crime rate is the alienation of many groups from society as a whole. Among these groups are the urban poor and a substantial number of young people. Still another factor is the failure of law-enforcement agencies to act when certain violations of the law occur. For example, there are cases in which organized crime is allowed to go on openly. Public faith in law, especially in ghetto areas, is shaken when this occurs.

In the long run, crime prevention depends upon popular support. On a practical level, remodeling of state laws, improvements in the penal system, and the elimination of many social ills will go a long way toward decreasing the United States' high crime rate.

ROBERT K. WOETZEL
Boston College

CUBA. See LATIN AMERICA.
CYPRUS. See MIDDLE EAST.

The Czechoslovak military stands ready to put down anti-Soviet demonstrations in August 1969.

CZECHOSLOVAKIA

FOR most Czechs and Slovaks 1969 was a very bad year. Soviet political control over Czechoslovakia was re-established. The political and human gains of 1968 were almost all lost. Alexander Dubcek and other liberals who tried to give Czechoslovakia "socialism with a human face" were removed from power. They were replaced by conservatives who would follow the Soviet line. In addition, economic signs all boded ill for the nation's future standard of living.

▶ **AFTERMATH OF THE SOVIET INVASION**

As 1969 began, there was an uneasy stalemate in Czechoslovakia. Soviet troops still occupied the country. The Czechoslovak Communist Party had been forced to change its line toward Moscow's position. But in reality many of the gains of the period before the Soviet invasion of August 21, 1968, were preserved. Alexander Dubcek was still first secretary of the Communist Party. And important liberals such as Josef Smrkovsky still played important roles. The press was less free than in the previous year, but it was still the most informative of any in East Europe.

In the early weeks of 1969 a bitter battle went on between liberals and conservatives. The liberals, headed by Dubcek, tried to protect as much as possible the 1968 democratic gains. The conservatives and "realists" felt that Moscow's wishes had to be met far more vigorously and quickly than Dubcek wanted. Moscow, of course, exerted great political and economic pressure. Thus the outcome was never in doubt.

Dubcek Ousted

As winter turned into spring, a Prague celebration of a Czechoslovak sports victory over a Russian team resulted in some anti-Soviet violence. Moscow used this as an excuse to force Dubcek's ouster as first secretary of the Czechoslovak Communist Party. He was replaced by Slovak Communist Party leader Gustav Husak. Mr. Husak had been in jail under the old Novotny regime in the 1950's. Only in the 1968 Dubcek period had he been able to gain major political importance. After taking office, Husak claimed that he wanted to save as much as possible of the 1968 liberal reforms. But he also professed to believe that "realistically" Czechoslovakia had no choice but to bow to Moscow's will.

Liberals Purged

The months that followed Husak's rise to power were nightmares for Czechoslovak democrats and liberals. A purge removed liberals from almost all key posts. They were replaced with men anxious to praise the Soviet Union and denounce the democratic changes of 1968. The purge was very thorough in the communications media. Liberal reporters, editors, commentators, and others were removed from their jobs. They were replaced by "reliable" men.

On the international scene, Husak tried to show that Czechoslovakia was a 100 per cent supporter of the Soviet Union. He pleaded with other communist parties not to make an issue of the August 1968 invasion of his country by Soviet troops.

But Moscow was still not satisfied. And the purges and other backward steps of the Husak regime raised tension in Czechoslovakia. This tension exploded on August 21, 1969, the first anniversary of the invasion. Hundreds of thousands of Czechs and Slovaks observed this day of sorrow by such peaceful gestures as wearing black clothes or boycotting public transportation. But there were also some anti-Soviet riots in Prague, Brno, and other cities. The demonstrations were put down with force.

Even more important, the Husak regime used the demonstrations as an excuse to enact harsh new laws. These laws enabled the Government to punish anyone who spoke out against the Soviet Union or against Czechoslovakia's forced reintegration into the Soviet sphere of influence. The laws also allowed the Government to fire workers from their jobs and expel students from school if they were involved in demonstrations.

Conservatives in Control

Husak worked hard to satisfy Moscow's demands. But he had competition from other political leaders, who wanted an even more severe pro-Soviet policy. Some of these political leaders hoped to succeed Husak as Communist Party first secretary. One such conservative was Lubomir Strougal. A former head of the secret police, Strougal became head of the Communist Party in the Czech lands after the Soviet invasion. He thus became the most important politician in the country after Husak. Alois Indra, Drahomir Kolder, and Vasil Bilak were conservatives who had battled Dubcek and had been defeated by him in 1968. Now they dreamed of new political power. In September the drive of these conservatives reached a new height. They openly denounced Dubcek and other liberals and demanded their punishment. The outcome of this was that on September 27 the Czechoslovak Cabinet resigned. On the following day it was announced that Dubcek had been ousted from the Czechoslovak Communist Party Presidium. He was also removed as chairman of the Federal Assembly. Dubcek retained his seat on the Communist Party Central Committee. But it was packed with conservatives, and Dubcek was the sole liberal voice. At the same time, Josef Smrkovsky, Dubcek's close associate and a liberal, was ousted from the Central Committee. The conservatives were in complete control of the Czechoslovak Communist Party and Government.

▶ ECONOMY

As the political regression gained speed, so too did the deterioration of the Czechoslovak economy. There was inflationary pressure on prices. And there was declining productivity. Many workers felt that to work hard would be to help the Russians. In some places there were acts of sabotage. And, throughout the nation, fear of what might lie ahead caused many people to spend all they could. These people felt that real goods were better than Czechoslovak currency that might become worthless.

HARRY SCHWARTZ
The New York Times

See also EUROPE, EAST; HUSAK, GUSTAV.

DAHOMEY. See AFRICA.

DANCE

Edward Villella, leading dancer of the New York City Ballet, has been called "the best in the land. ...America's most electrifying, most versatile... classical dancer."

THERE continued to be an awareness that dance is not only an art, but that exposure to it is part of human education. This is true not only for someone at a performance or a member of a dance class. It is also true of face-to-face contact with dance artists. Thus, the new policy of the National Endowment for the Arts Coordinated Residence Touring Program was to bring dance artists to meet people. The program brought 10 leading modern-dance companies into communities throughout the United States. The dance groups taught, performed, lectured, and mingled with students.

In 1969 the program was active in over 20 states. Hopefully, more than 30 states will have such programs in 1970. Active in these programs are the Alvin Ailey American Dance Theatre, First Chamber Dance Quartet, and the dance companies of Lucas Hoving, Merce Cunningham, Pearl Lang, Jose Limon, Alwin Nikolais, Don Redlich, Murray Louis, and Paul Taylor.

▶ DANCE IN THE GHETTO

Another active force that has been growing is dance in the ghetto. Karamu in Cleveland, the Gloria Unti Performing Arts Workshop in San Francisco, Hull House in Chicago, and New York's Henry Street Settlement Playhouse School were just a few of the schools and dance workshops bringing dance to inner-city areas.

New groups were also at work. The most ambitious of these is the Harlem Performing Arts School in New York City, which is directed by Arthur Mitchell. He is one of the New York City Ballet's leading dancers. He is also the first black classical dancer to be a regular member of a major ballet company.

The Harlem school offers two to five ballet classes a week. The school has first-rate teachers, and charges 50 cents a week. So far there are over 300 pupils. A new and larger studio is being sought so that more pupils can join. Mitchell is also the director-choreographer of the classical-ballet company, the Harlem Dance Theatre.

▶ DANCES AT A GATHERING

The New York City Ballet had the privilege of presenting one of the year's most important works. This work, Jerome Robbins' *Dances at a Gathering,* is an hour-long masterpiece of simplicity and musicality. The work does not have frenetic mixed-media devices often seen in many new dances. The elements of *Dances at a Gathering* are a pianist playing Chopin pieces and ten dancers in tunics dancing through the music as if they had emerged from its very heart.

Dances at a Gathering was the hit of the New York City ballet season. It was also the high point of the week-long June appearance of the New York City Ballet during the Monte Carlo Festival. The festival marked the fortieth anniversary of the death of Sergei Diaghilev, the great Russian dance impresario. Diaghilev's Ballets Russes during the 1910's and 1920's stimulated a tremendous growth of dance in the West—a growth that continued as the 1960's came to a close.

▶ AMERICAN DANCE IN EUROPE

American dance companies continued to be popular in Europe. The City Center Joffrey Ballet astounded Vienna with *Astarte.* And the Alwin Nikolais Dance Theatre was a success in major cities of Europe.

The Eliot Feld American Ballet Company had its official debut at Italy's Spoleto Festival in the summer of 1969. The com-

The Harlem Dance Theatre rehearses.

The Stuttgart Ballet performs "Eugene Onegin," choreographed by John Cranko.

pany's debut in the United States was at the Brooklyn Academy of Music in late October.

American dancer-choreographer Glen Tetley, who has become even more successful in Europe than in the United States, was named codirector of the Netherlands Dance Theatre in The Hague. In Switzerland, Alfonso Cata, once a dancer with the New York City Ballet, became director of the Geneva Grand Theatre Ballet. John Taras, former ballet master of the New York City Ballet, became artistic director of the Paris Opera Ballet.

▶ **EUROPEAN DANCE IN THE UNITED STATES**

In 1969 the trend worked the other way too. Dancers and dance companies from Europe were popular in the United States. Into the repertoire of the City Center Joffrey Ballet came *Konservatoriet* by Denmark's Auguste Bournonville, Sir Frederick Ashton's *Facade* from England, and Léonide Massine's *Three-Cornered Hat* from the Diaghilev Ballets Russes. The Harkness Ballet took into its repertoire a work on a Spanish theme by Benjamin Harkarvy. He is an American teacher-choreographer who has been codirector of the Netherlands Dance Theatre in The Hague.

England's Royal Ballet had a very successful visit in 1969. It offered a new production of Petipa's *Sleeping Beauty* and the debut of Sir Frederick Ashton's beautiful *Enigma Variations*. The Royal Ballet had one unfortunate production, *Pelléas and Mélisande* by Roland Petit. Even the company's brilliant stars, Rudolf Nureyev and Dame Margot Fonteyn, could not save it.

The Stuttgart Ballet presented two seasons in the United States in 1969. One was its debut at the Metropolitan Opera House in June. The other was a 6-week tour in October and November. The Stuttgart Ballet is an 8-year-old German company directed by Englishman John Cranko. Impresario Sol Hurok brought the company to New York for its debut.

The Stuttgart Ballet presented John Cranko's versions of *The Taming of the Shrew,* Prokofiev's *Romeo and Juliet,* and Pushkin's *Eugene Onegin* among others. The company was at its best in these storytelling ballets. It offered fine dancing and very handsome decor. But it was the warmth and theatricality of the presentations that delighted audiences and turned the company into a popular hit.

LYDIA JOEL
Editor in Chief, *Dance Magazine*

DWIGHT DAVID EISENHOWER
(1890–1969)

Dwight David Eisenhower, general of the army and 34th president of the United States, died on March 28, 1969, at Walter Reed Army Hospital in Washington, D.C. The 78-year-old soldier-statesman had been in the hospital since May 1968, after suffering his fourth heart attack.

On his death, tributes began pouring in from all parts of the world, and President Nixon announced that March 31 would be a day of national mourning. Nixon, who had been Eisenhower's vice-president for eight years, said that the late President "held a unique place in America's history, and in its heart, and in the hearts of people the world over."

Eisenhower's body was taken to Washington National Cathedral on March 29, where the closed coffin was put on public view. The next day, in a three-hour military procession, the body was taken to the Capitol where it lay in state until March 31. Over fifty thousand people walked past the coffin and silently paid tribute. On April 2, President Eisenhower was buried in Abilene, Kansas.

Dwight D. Eisenhower, affectionately known as Ike, was born on October 14, 1890, in Denison, Texas, the third son of David and Ida Stover Eisenhower. Two years later his family moved to Abilene, where Eisenhower spent his youthful years.

In 1916, a year after graduating from the United States Military Academy at West Point, Eisenhower married Mary (Mamie) Geneva Doud. They had two sons, Dwight Doud (who died in infancy) and John, who is today ambassador to Belgium.

In 1935 Eisenhower was assigned to the Philippines to help General Douglas MacArthur organize a Philippine national Army. With the outbreak of World War II, promotions came rapidly, and in 1942 he was put in command of the European Theater of Operations. In this position he directed the Allied invasion of North Africa. A year later, in December 1943, President Franklin D. Roosevelt appointed Eisenhower commander of Supreme Headquarters Allied Expeditionary Forces in Europe (SHAEF). On D day, June 6, 1944, he led the invasion of nazi-occupied Europe. Eisenhower became a five-star general in the same year.

In 1945, at the end of World War II, Eisenhower returned to the United States, where he received a hero's welcome. He then served as Army chief of staff until 1948, when he accepted the presidency of Columbia University. Two years later, however, the General was back in uniform as the supreme commander of NATO forces.

In 1952 Eisenhower left the military for the political arena, winning the Republican presidential nomination on the first ballot. In the November elections he defeated Democrat Adlai Stevenson by more than six million votes. He was re-elected in 1956, again defeating Stevenson.

During his eight years as president, Eisenhower negotiated the Korean-war settlement in 1953; attended the "Big Four" summit conference in Geneva with Britain, France, and the Soviet Union; and ordered Federal troops into Little Rock, Arkansas, to enforce the Supreme Court's decision on school desegregation.

In retirement, Ike assumed the role of elder statesman. He advised his three successors, John F. Kennedy, Lyndon Johnson, and Richard Nixon.

Every American president is remembered not only for specific deeds and actions, but for his personal traits. With Ike it was his frankness, his sincerity, and his broad, charming smile which communicated warmth. He will also be remembered as one of the few presidents who left office after eight years with the same popularity he had enjoyed on his first day as leader of the United States.

FERN L. MAMBERG

ALEXANDER OF TUNIS (HAROLD RUPERT LEOFRIC GEORGE ALEXANDER), 77, British viscount, died June 16. He was a World War II military leader who directed the Allied campaigns in the Middle East, Italy, and North Africa. From 1946 to 1952 he was governor-general of Canada.

ANSERMET, ERNEST (ALEXANDRE), 85, Swiss orchestra conductor, died February 20 in Geneva, Switzerland. Ansermet founded l'Orchestre de la Suisse Romande in 1918 and was its conductor until 1967.

ARENALES, EMILIO, 46, president of the United Nations General Assembly (23d session) and foreign minister of Guatemala, died April 17. He was Guatemala's permanent representative to the UN from 1955 to 1958.

BARRIENTOS ORTUÑO, RENE, 49, president of Bolivia, was killed in a helicopter crash on April 27. He had been elected president in 1966 after heading a military junta and serving as co-president with General Alfredo Ovando Candia.

BLAIBERG, PHILIP, 60, the world's longest-surviving heart transplant patient at the time of his death, died August 17 in Capetown, South Africa. Blaiberg lived for 19 months and 15 days after the heart transplant performed by Dr. Christiaan Barnard.

BRISCOE, ROBERT, 74, Irish nationalist, politician, and textile manufacturer, died May 30. In 1956, Briscoe became the first Jewish Lord Mayor of Dublin, Ireland. He had helped to found the Fianna Fail (Soldiers of Destiny) Party in 1926. He was a member of the Dail Eireann (Chamber of Deputies) from 1927 to 1965.

BROWN, JOHN MASON, 68, drama critic and writer, died March 16. Brown was once a member of the Pulitzer Prize drama jury. He wrote *The Modern Theatre in Revolt* and *The Worlds of Robert E. Sherwood: Mirror to His Times.*

CASTLE, IRENE (FOOTE), 75, ballroom dancer, died January 25. With her husband Vernon, she made famous the "Castle Walk" and "maxixe" dances that were popular before World War I.

COLLYER, CLAYTON (BUD), 61, radio and television master of ceremonies, died September 8. Collyer's television shows included *Beat the Clock, Break the Bank,* and *To Tell the Truth.*

CONNOLLY, MAUREEN, 34, tennis champion, died June 21. Known as "Little Mo," in 1953 she became the first woman ever to win the grand slam of tennis—the national titles of the United States, Britain, France, and Australia.

COSTELLO, WILLIAM A., 65, United States ambassador to Trinidad and Tobago from 1967 to 1969, died June 20. Costello was a former radio and television correspondent who wrote *The Facts About Nixon: An Unauthorized Biography* in 1960.

CURRIE, DANIEL LAUCHLIN, 75, Canadian statesman and chief justice of the Supreme Court of Nova Scotia, died February 4.

DEMPSEY, SIR MILES, 72, British general, died June 6, the 25th anniversary of the D-Day invasion in which he led the British Second Army. After the war in Europe ended, Sir Miles commanded the 14th Army in the British reoccupation of Singapore and Malaya.

DIRKSEN, EVERETT McKINLEY, 73, United States Senator from Illinois and Republican leader of the Senate, died September 7. Dirksen began his national career when he was elected to the House of Representatives in 1932. He won election to the Senate in 1950. Dirksen supported and helped to pass the 1964 Civil Rights Bill and the 1965 Voting Rights Act.

DULLES, ALLEN W., 75, director of the Central Intelligence Agency from 1953 to 1961, died January 29. He was the brother of John Foster Dulles, secretary of state in the Eisenhower Administration.

DUPUY, PIERRE, 72, Canadian diplomat, died May 21 in France. Dupuy served as Canada's ambassador to the Netherlands, France, and Italy. He was commissioner general of Expo 67.

EDISON, CHARLES, 78, politician and industrialist, died July 31. He was the son of inventor Thomas Alva Edison. Charles Edison

Philip Blaiberg   Everett Dirksen   Levi Eshkol

was governor of New Jersey (1941–44) and U.S. secretary of the Navy (1939–40).

ESHKOL, LEVI, 73, prime minister of Israel since 1963, died February 26. Eshkol was born in Oratovo, Russia, and emigrated to Palestine in 1913, where he worked toward founding the nation of Israel.

FRANCIS, THOMAS, Jr., 69, virologist, died October 1. He headed the epidemiology department at the University of Michigan. In 1934, Dr. Francis isolated the A strain of influenza, and in 1940, the B strain. In 1945 he developed a vaccine to fight both influenza strains. He directed the nationwide field trials of the Salk polio vaccine in 1954 that showed the vaccine to be safe and effective.

GARLAND, JUDY, 47, actress and singer, died June 22 in London, England. She starred in *A Star Is Born, Easter Parade,* and *Meet Me in St. Louis.* She won an Academy Award in 1939 for *The Wizard of Oz,* the film in which she sang *Over the Rainbow.* The song became identified with her.

GIMBEL, ADAM, 75, merchant, died September 9. Gimbel, a member of the family that

founded Gimbel Brothers and Saks department stores, was president of Saks Fifth Avenue from 1926 until February 1969.

GORCEY, LEO, 52, motion-picture actor, died June 2. Gorcey starred in the Dead End Kids and Bowery Boys film series of the 1930's and 1940's.

GROPIUS, WALTER ADOLF, 86, architect, died July 5 in Boston. Gropius was born in Germany. He founded the Bauhaus School of Design in Weimar, Germany, in 1919. In 1937, he went to the United States to head the department of architecture at Harvard's Graduate School of Design. At the time of his death he was an active member of The Architects' Collaborative in Boston, which he founded.

HAGEN, WALTER, 76, golf champion, died October 5. From 1914 to 1929, Hagen won 17 major golf titles including 2 U.S. Open championships, 5 PGA titles, and 4 British Opens.

HARTLEY, FRED A., JR., 67, former member of the U.S. House of Representatives from New Jersey, died May 11. Hartley co-authored (with Senator Robert A. Taft) the Taft-Hartley Labor Act of 1947.

HAWKINS, COLEMAN, 64, jazz musician, died May 19. Hawkins played the tenor saxophone, and his recording of *Body and Soul* is a jazz classic.

HAYES, GEORGE FRANCIS (GABBY), 83, motion-picture and television actor, died February 9. Hayes appeared in more than two hundred Westerns as the sidekick of cowboy stars William Boyd, Gene Autry, and Roy Rogers.

HENIE, SONJA, 57, world and Olympic ice-skating champion and motion-picture actress, died October 12. She was born in Norway and won her first figure-skating championship when she was eight years old. She went on to win Olympic medals in 1928, 1932, and 1936 and to make ice-skating films including *One in a Million.*

HO CHI MINH, 79, president of North Vietnam, died September 3. Ho Chi Minh was born Nguyen Tat Thanh on May 19, 1890, in Nghean province (now part of North Vietnam). He left Vietnam in 1911. As a young man, he worked at a number of jobs, including ship's messboy and pastry cook, in Paris, London, and New York. In France in 1919 he tried unsuccessfully to attend the Versailles Peace Conference to present a plan for Asian

Sonja Henie

nationalism. In 1920 he joined the French Communist Party. He studied Marxism and revolutionary tactics in Moscow and was a revolutionary in China in the 1930's. There he planned a revolution for Vietnam. In 1940 he took the name Ho Chi Minh which means Ho, Shedder of Light. He returned to Vietnam in 1941, after a 30-year absence, and formed the Vietminh. The Vietminh fought a guerrilla war against the Japanese during World War II. In 1945 the Vietminh took Hanoi, and on September 2, Ho Chi Minh declared Vietnam's independence from France. France set up a separate government in the south and guerrilla war broke out. The French were defeated at Dienbienphu in 1954.

HUNTER, JEFFREY, 43, motion-picture actor, died May 27. Hunter appeared in more than 30 films including *King of Kings.*

HUSAIN, ZAKIR, 72, president of India since 1967, died May 3. A Muslim, he was India's first non-Hindu head of state.

Gabby Hayes

INGRAM, REX, 73, stage, motion-picture, and television actor, died September 19. Ingram appeared as De Lawd in the film *The Green Pastures.* He also was in *The Emperor Jones* and *Cabin in the Sky.*

JASPERS, KARL, 86, German psychiatrist and philosopher, died February 26 in Switzerland. Jaspers, with, Sören Kierkegaard, Martin Heidegger, and Jean-Paul Sartre, was one of the great existentialist philosophers. He taught that man must pass judgment on himself. Jaspers wrote *The Question of German Guilt* and *The Future of Mankind.*

KARLOFF, BORIS, 81, motion-picture actor, died February 2 in England. Karloff starred in horror films including *Frankenstein, The Body Snatcher,* and *Isle of the Dead.* Altogether he appeared in more than 130 films.

KASAVUBU, JOSEPH, 52 or 59, first president of the Congo (Kinshasa), died March 24. Kasavubu was a Bakongo tribal leader who led the fight for independence from Belgium. He was president from 1960 to 1965 when he was ousted in a bloodless coup by Joseph Mobutu.

KENNEDY, JOSEPH PATRICK, 81, financier and father of President John F. Kennedy and Senators Robert F. Kennedy and Edward M. Kennedy, died November .18 in Hyannis Port, Massachusetts. Joseph Kennedy was the United States ambassador to Great Britain from 1937 to 1940.

KING, ALFRED DANIEL WILLIAMS, 38, clergyman and civil-rights leader, died July 21 in an accidental drowning. He was the younger brother of the Rev. Dr. Martin Luther King, Jr., and a board member of the Southern Christian Leadership Conference.

KOPECHNE, MARY JO, 28, secretary, was killed on July 18 when a car driven by Senator Edward M. Kennedy plunged off a bridge on Chappaquiddick Island, near Edgartown, Massachusetts.

LEHMAN, ROBERT, 77, investment banker, philanthropist, and art collector, died August 9. He was chairman of the board of trustees of the Metropolitan Museum of Art in New York City. His private art collection was valued at $100,000,000.

Boris Karloff as Frankenstein's monster

LEWIS, JOHN L., 89, labor leader, died June 11. Lewis was president of the United Mine Workers Union from 1920 to 1960. He helped found the Congress of Industrial Organizations (CIO) in 1935. Lewis was a fiery unionist who fought for mine safety, mine-inspection legislation, and mechanization of coal production, in addition to better wages.

LEY, WILLY, 62, German-born rocket expert and author, died June 24. Ley wrote *Watchers of the Skies* and *Rockets, Missiles and Men in Space.*

LOCKHEED, ALLAN HAINES, 80, died May 26. With his brother, Lockheed founded the Lockheed Aircraft Corporation.

LOESSER, FRANK, 59, composer, died July 28. Loesser's Broadway musical hits included *Where's Charley?, Guys and Dolls,* and *How to Succeed in Business Without Really Trying.*

LOPEZ MATEOS, ADOLFO, 59, president of Mexico from 1958 to 1964, died September 22 in Mexico City.

MANLEY, NORMAN WASHINGTON, 76, prime minister of Jamaica from 1959 to 1962, died September 2.

MARCIANO, ROCKY (ROCCO MARCHEGIANO), 45, undefeated world heavyweight boxing champion (1952–56), was killed in a plane crash on August 31.

MAXWELL, GAVIN, 55, British naturalist and author, died September 6 in Scotland. Gavin wrote *Ring of Bright Water* and *Harpoon Venture.*

MBOYA, TOM, 38, Kenya's minister of economic affairs, was shot and killed by a gunman in Nairobi on July 5. Mboya was secretary-general of the ruling Kenya African National Union political party.

McCUTCHEON, MALCOLM WALLACE, 62, Canadian statesman, died January 23 in Toronto. McCutcheon was a senator from 1962 to 1968 and minister of trade and commerce in 1963.

McGILL, RALPH, 70, journalist, died February 3. McGill was editor from 1942 to 1960 and publisher since 1960 of *The Atlanta Constitution.* He crusaded for civil rights and won the 1958 Pulitzer Prize for his editorials on civil rights. In 1964 he won a Presidential Medal of Freedom.

MIES VAN DER ROHE, LUDWIG, 83, architect, died August 18. Born in Germany, Mies van der Rohe emigrated to the United States in 1937. His most famous structures include the Illinois Institute of Technology's Crown Hall, the Chicago Federal Center, and the Seagram Building in New York City.

Rocky Marciano

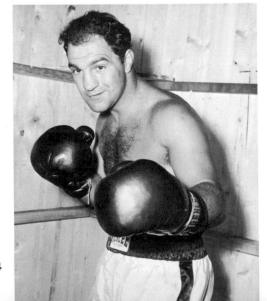

Bishop James Pike

MOORE, DOUGLAS STUART, 75, composer, died July 25. Moore won the 1951 Pulitzer Prize for his music for the folk opera *Giants in the Earth.* His other works include *The Ballad of Baby Doe, The Headless Horseman,* and *The Devil and Daniel Webster.*

OSUNA, RAFAEL, 31, Mexican tennis star, was killed in a plane crash in Mexico on June 4. In May, Osuna had led the Mexican Davis Cup team in an upset victory over Australia in the American Zone semifinals.

PAPEN, FRANZ VON, 89, chancellor of Germany in 1932, died May 2 in West Germany. Von Papen helped Adolf Hitler to become chancellor of Germany in 1933. Von Papen served as vice-chancellor in the nazi regime, 1933–34.

PEARSON, DREW, 71, newspaper political columnist and author, died September 1. Pearson closely watched the activities of people in government. He would disclose information of wrongdoing in his columns. For example, information in Pearson's column led to the censure of Connecticut Senator Thomas J. Dodd in 1967. With Jack Anderson, Pearson wrote *The Case against Congress.*

PEGLER, (JAMES) WESTBROOK, 74, newspaper columnist, died June 24. Pegler won the 1941 Pulitzer Prize for journalism for exposing labor-union corruption.

PIKE, JAMES ALBERT, 56, theologian and former Episcopal bishop of California (1958–

66), was found dead in the Judean hills in Israel on September 7, after being lost and stranded. Pike was in Israel with his wife.

PIRE, DOMINIQUE, 58, Roman Catholic priest, died January 30 in Belgium. Rev. Pire won the 1958 Nobel Peace Prize for his work in helping refugees in Eastern Europe after World War II.

POWELL, CECIL FRANK, 65, British physicist, died August 9. Powell won the 1950 Nobel Prize in Physics for finding a way to photograph nuclear processes and for discovering pi-mesons.

RAND, IVAN C., 84, former justice of the Supreme Court of Canada (1943–59), died January 2. He was the author of the controversial Rand Report on labor relations, published in 1968.

RITTER, THELMA, 63, stage, motion-picture, and television actress, died February 5. She was a character actress who won an Emmy in 1955 (for *The Catered Affair*) and a Tony in 1957 (for *New Girl in Town*). Her films include *All About Eve*, *Rear Window*, and *The Misfits*.

ROLFE, ROBERT A. (RED), 60, baseball player, died July 8. Rolfe was a third baseman for the New York Yankees (1934–42), manager of the Detroit Tigers (1949–52), and athletic director of Dartmouth College (1954–67).

SAUD, IBN ABDUL AZIZ AL-FAISAL AL-SAUD, 67, king of Saudi Arabia from 1953 to 1964, died February 23, in Athens, Greece. He had been in exile since 1964 when he was deposed by his brother Crown Prince Faisal during an economic and political crisis. Income from oil in Saudi Arabia made him one of the richest men in the world.

SHAHN, BEN(JAMIN), 70, artist, died March 14. Shahn was born in Lithuania and emigrated to the United States in 1906. He was a commercial artist, poster maker, and book illustrator who used his art to further political and social causes.

STERN, OTTO, 81, German-born physicist, died August 17 in California. Stern won the 1943 Nobel Prize in Physics for his research at the Carnegie Institute of Technology, Pittsburgh, on the magnetic velocity of protons.

Candid Photographer (Self-Portrait) by Ben Shahn

SWARTHOUT, GLADYS, 64, opera singer, died July 7 in Italy. A mezzo-soprano, she starred with the Metropolitan Opera (1929–45) and was known for her portrayal of Carmen.

TAYLOR, ROBERT, 57, motion-picture and television actor, died June 8. Taylor appeared in more than 70 films including *Ivanhoe*, *Magnificent Obsession*, and *Quo Vadis*.

TSHOMBE, MOISE, 49, former premier of the Congo (Kinshasa), died June 29 in Algeria. Tshombe had been in Algeria, in jail, since June 30, 1967, when his plane was hijacked and he was kidnapped. He led the 1960–63 attempted secession of Katanga Province in the Congo before becoming premier.

WARBURG, JAMES PAUL, 72, financier, government economic adviser, and author, died June 3. Warburg wrote *Germany: Key to Peace* and *The West in Crisis*.

WEINBERG, SIDNEY J., 77, financier, died July 23. He was a partner in Goldman, Sachs & Co., a Wall Street investment-banking firm. Weinberg also served as an unofficial adviser to Presidents Franklin D. Roosevelt, Truman, Eisenhower, Kennedy, and Johnson.

WHITE, JOSH, 61, folk, blues, and spiritual singer, died September 5. White made popular *John Henry*, *One Meatball*, *Hard-Time Blues*, and *Chain Gang*.

DENMARK. See EUROPE, WEST.

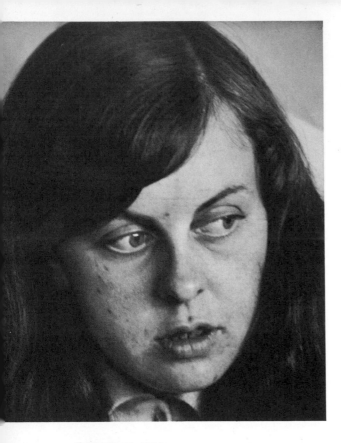

DEVLIN, BERNADETTE

RIOTS and demonstrations were rampant in Northern Ireland (Ulster) as Roman Catholics demanded political and economic equality long denied them by the ruling Protestants. A civil war seemed to be brewing when the British House of Commons called an emergency meeting. During this meeting, on April 22, 1969, a petite, 21-year-old girl from Ulster was sworn in as the youngest member of Parliament. And there Bernadette Devlin rose and held the House of Commons spellbound as she delivered her maiden speech. It was a passionate and eloquent appeal for the poor and oppressed people of Northern Ireland.

Although she had gained a reputation as a champion of Roman Catholic grievances, her appeal was nonsectarian. It was in behalf of the "ordinary people, the oppressed people from whom I come." Miss Devlin charged that Northern Ireland's ruling Unionist Party encouraged religious hatred so that poor Protestants would not rebel against their own poverty.

On April 22, Miss Devlin broke two House of Commons traditions. It was the first time that a member made a speech on the swearing-in day. And it was the first time a new member spoke about a controversial subject. But her twenty-minute speech was highly praised by most members and hailed as one of the best in Parliamentary history.

In August, Miss Devlin visited the United States. She was on a mission to raise $1,000,000 for the many Roman Catholic families that were left homeless by rioting and violence in Northern Ireland in July and August.

One of five children, Josephine Bernadette Devlin was born on April 23, 1947, in Cookstown, County Tyrone, a small market town. Her father was a very poor carpenter who died when she was nine years old.

Until a few months before she won her seat in the House of Commons, Miss Devlin had been a psychology major at Queen's University in Belfast. After the Ulster riots in October 1968, she worked with a student group called Peoples' Democracy. She organized sit-ins, demonstrations, and protest marches. She also waged a strong but losing battle for a seat in the regional Parliament in Belfast.

In a by-election on April 18, in the district of Mid-Ulster, Miss Devlin won her seat in the British House of Commons. She ran as an independent socialist candidate. She defeated the Unionist candidate, a widow whose husband's death had resulted in the by-election. Miss Devlin is the 27th woman now in the House of Commons. And she is one of 12 members from Northern Ireland. Ten of these seats are held by Unionists, who are identified with Britain's Conservative Party.

See also GREAT BRITAIN.

DOMINICAN REPUBLIC. See LATIN AMERICA.
EAST GERMANY. See EUROPE, EAST.

Housewives felt the pinch of inflation in 1969, as their dollars bought less food.

ECONOMY

THE year 1969 was one of economic paradox for the United States. The economy boomed along at a furious, if not record, pace. The gross national product (total value of goods and services produced) topped $900,000,000,000 and was within sight of the magic "trillion dollar" mark. But soaring prices and too-large wage increases in many industries blighted the health of the economy and made the fight against inflation the foremost economic concern for government, business, and labor.

As the year ended there were signs that efforts to halt the inflationary spiral were beginning to work, although rather lightly. Next to ending the Vietnam war, the most important goal for the administration of

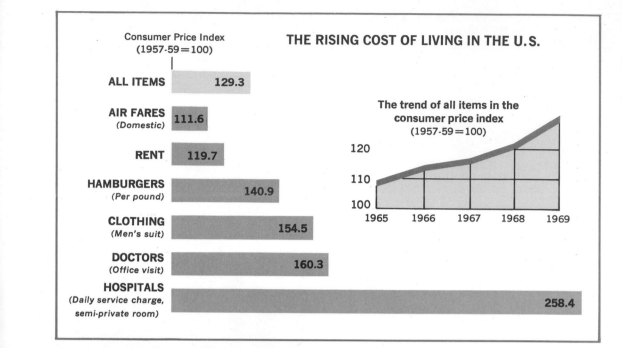

THE RISING COST OF LIVING IN THE U.S.

Consumer Price Index
(1957-59=100)

ALL ITEMS	129.3
AIR FARES (Domestic)	111.6
RENT	119.7
HAMBURGERS (Per pound)	140.9
CLOTHING (Men's suit)	154.5
DOCTORS (Office visit)	160.3
HOSPITALS (Daily service charge, semi-private room)	258.4

The trend of all items in the
consumer price index
(1957-59=100)

120
110
100

1965   1966   1967   1968   1969

The rising cost of living brought many protests. At left, housewives from Long Island, New York, show their displeasure with high meat costs.

President Nixon was to halt inflation. Increased taxes, high interest rates, a shortage of money available for borrowing, and a deliberate cutback in spending by the Federal Government on many programs all were a part of the fight against inflation.

Consumers (the people who buy goods and services) played a part, too. They showed an increased willingness to postpone purchases of automobiles, refrigerators, television sets, and other "hard goods." Many economists saw this as a healthy reaction to the "inflation psychology" of the last several years, when consumers believed that since prices were bound to continue to rise, they should buy quickly before the next price hike.

▶ **INFLATION**

Inflation was largely blamed on the nearly $40,000,000,000 annual cost of the Vietnam war. In the United States, prices rose at a faster rate in the first 7 months of 1969 than they had in any period since 1951. Wages also continued their upward spiral, with most unions setting a goal of at least a 10 per cent hike.

The consumer price index, the most widely watched barometer of price inflation, rose at an annual rate of 6.4 per cent in the first half of 1969. This was a 4.6 per cent increase over a comparable period in 1968. Most economists expected the price increases to average out at about 5 per cent over the entire year as some signs of a slowing of the spiral showed in the final quarter of 1969. Among a vast array of price increases, food and medical costs rose the most.

Another indication of inflation was rising interest rates; in other words, the amount you have to pay to borrow money. In 1969, interest rates reached record levels. At one point, banks were charging 8.5 per cent to prime customers (those with the best credit rating). Students taking out loans to go to college had to pay up to 10 per cent.

The high interest rate and the demand for money by all sorts of borrowers caused many industries to sag. This was especially true in the housing-construction market.

To combat inflation, the Federal Government slashed its spending by $7,000,-000,000. The Federal Reserve Board continued its "tight money" policy, restricting the growth of the nation's supply of money in circulation. A 10 per cent surtax on income was extended until the end of 1969. The President proposed elimination of a 7 per cent tax-incentive credit on business investment for expansion purposes.

Despite inflation and the stern measures taken to curb it, there was every expectation that the economy would continue to boom. At the end of the fiscal year, June 30, 1969, the Government reported a surplus in the budget of $2,400,000,000. This was in sharp contrast with the $25,200,000,000 deficit it had reported a year before, in June 1968.

Personal income was running at an adjusted rate of $756,600,000,000, the Department of Commerce reported after looking over figures for the first 9 months of the year. The average weekly earnings of rank-and-file workers reached $117.80 in September, according to the Department of Labor's tabulation of the latest figures. Their average workweek was 37.8 hours.

For the year, the nation's gross national product was expected to reach $932,000,-000,000, and the consensus of the govern-

In less than twenty years, spending by the Federal Government has nearly tripled. National defense consumes close to half the budget. (Figure for fiscal year 1971 is estimated.)

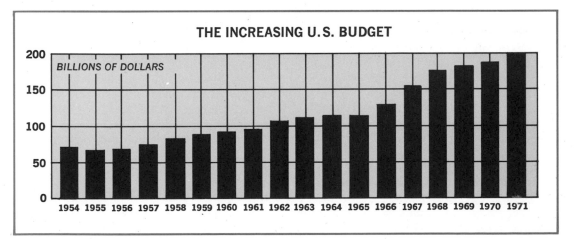

THE INCREASING U.S. BUDGET

BILLIONS OF DOLLARS

200
150
100
50
0

1954 1955 1956 1957 1958 1959 1960 1961 1962 1963 1964 1965 1966 1967 1968 1969 1970 1971

ment's economic indicators was that the trillion-dollar mark would be reached by the last quarter of 1970 or early in 1971.

The purchasing power of the dollar continued to decline. As an example, the Bureau of Labor Statistics reported its latest full-year compilation showed $5.00 in 1968 would purchase 2 pounds, 13 ounces of round steak and 2 pounds of cheese. By contrast, in 1913, $5.00 purchased 3 pounds of steak and 2 pounds of cheese, plus 10 pounds of flour, 3 pounds of rice, 2 loaves of bread, 5 pounds of chuck roast, 2 pounds of bacon, 4 quarts of milk, 1 pound of butter, 15 pounds of potatoes, 5 pounds of sugar, 1 dozen eggs, and 1 pound of coffee with 2 cents left over for candy.

▶ TAXES

A totally unexpected "taxpayer's revolt" exploded early in the year. As a result Congress proposed the most sweeping revision of the nation's tax code in history.

Undersecretary of the Treasury Charls E. Walker gave this opinion of the cause of the revolt: "For years the individual taxpayer has been willing to bear what he believes to be a very heavy tax burden. But once he learned that some people better off than himself—indeed, individuals with incomes in the millions—were paying little or no federal income taxes, then he raised the roof."

It was revealed that 154 persons with incomes of $200,000 or more a year paid little or no income taxes in 1966. This caused a widespread demand by taxpayers and congressmen that loopholes in the tax code be closed. These so-called loopholes included incentives or special credits, such as tax-exempt interest on municipal and state bonds; unlimited exemptions for charitable contributions; business-expansion credits; and the special 27½ per cent allowance to the oil industry for exploration and discovery.

The new tax code means generally lower rates for middle-income taxpayers and gives a special tax allowance to those in the very low income bracket. Single people are no longer asked to pay vastly higher taxes than married people with the same income. The tax rates on business are sharply increased. The income of private foundations, such as Ford, Rockefeller, and Carnegie, is for the first time subject to a tax.

The Nixon administration urged modification of some of the tax bill's provisions. It claimed that under the present bill the overall revenues received by the Government would be cut too sharply at a critical time.

State and Local Taxation

The matter of taxes was not solely a concern at the federal level. State and local taxes continued to show sharp increases, adding to the discontent of the average taxpayer. This taxpayer in 34 states faces higher state-tax bills as the result of action by state legislatures in 1969. Several other states indicated raises are coming.

President Nixon noted the financial plight of the states and proposed the first step toward their long-sought plan to share in revenues collected by the Federal Government from the states. The President asked Congress to approve a plan that would return to the states on a prorata basis a total of $500,000,000 to be spent as they saw fit. He said he hoped that by 1975, $5,000,000,000 annually could be returned to the states.

Eventually this revenue-sharing plan is designed to replace some or all of the 379 Federal programs that grant states money to be used for specific projects. The funds, when actually authorized by Congress, would be given each state in accordance with a formula based on their percentage of national population and the amount of Federal income taxes paid by residents.

▶ THE STOCK MARKET

Wall Street had its ups and downs in 1969. The tremendous volume of trading

New trading area at the New York Stock Exchange. During the year, stock prices fell considerably. One indicator, the Dow Jones industrials average, fell almost 200 points.

on the New York and American stock exchanges swamped brokerage houses with so much paper work that for a time the exchanges curtailed hours of trading. Days when 14,000,000 to 16,000,000 shares of stock were traded were not uncommon. The dollar value of stock held by individuals in companies was $600,000,000,000. Prices of some stocks fluctuated widely over the year, and generally the market value of stocks was below that of 1968.

The trend toward mergers by companies continued, especially by the so-called "conglomerates." These are companies that acquire firms in unrelated fields. Statistical data for the last complete year available, 1968, showed that such conglomerate mergers represented 84 per cent of all acquisitions and 89 per cent of dollar-asset values. The number of mergers for 1968 reached a total of over 4,000 according to Federal Trade Commission figures.

Income-tax-return figures of the Internal Revenue Service showed a total of 1,468,725 corporations in the United States in 1968. The number of proprietorships that year was 9,086,714, and there were 922,680 partnerships.

▶ **LABOR**

The two most significant events affecting relations between labor unions and management were (1) the announcement by President Nixon that the Government would take a "hands off" attitude in contract negotiations and (2) the creation of a new labor-union alliance.

In previous years, in prolonged union-management contract disputes involving vital industries, it had become regular policy for the Government to step in and try to force an acceptable agreement to end or prevent strikes. The President and his Secretary of Labor, George P. Shultz, disavowed such "arm twisting." They expressed confidence that unions and companies could reach new agreements in the free collective-bargaining process without government interference.

There were fewer strikes in 1969 than in 1968. But many contracts involving hundreds of thousands of workers are due to expire in 1970, including those involving the manufacture of automobiles and virtually the entire trucking industry.

As the fiscal 1970 year began (on June 30, 1969), 21,000,000 man-days had been lost to strikes in the first half of calendar 1969, involving 1,377,000 workers in 3,520 work stoppages.

The creation of a new Alliance for Labor Action resulted in the joining of forces by the United Automobile Workers, headed by Walter Reuther, and the Teamsters Union, headed by Acting President Frank E. Fitzsimmons. (Teamster President James Hoffa is serving a Federal prison sentence.) This new labor federation poses a serious threat to the AFL-CIO, the organization to which most individual unions belong. The expected outlook is for bitter rivalry between the two organizations to sign up members. Shortly after the new group was born, the International Chemical Workers Union pulled out of the AFL-CIO to join it.

A step that could have far-reaching consequences on the membership of individual unions was taken by the Government to ensure more representation in unions by Negroes and other minority groups. Under a plan announced by Labor Secretary Shultz for Philadelphia and other large cities, contractors bidding on Federally financed projects would have to assure that a specific number of craftsmen employed would be from these minority groups.

Construction unions generally opposed this step, claiming it was establishing a "quota system" by race in the hiring of skilled craftsmen. The construction craft unions have long been the target of criticism by Negro leaders who contend the unions have refused to accept more than token numbers of minority workers.

▶ **MANPOWER**

More than 78,000,000 people held jobs in the United States in 1969. The number of unemployed hovered around the 3,500,-000 mark. The rate of unemployment rose sharply as the fall work season began, jumping from 3.5 per cent to 4 per cent. This later figure was the highest percentage of unemployment since 1967.

Teen-agers showed a high percentage of unemployment. The number of jobless Negroes continued at about twice the rate of jobless white workers.

Overall, the nation's full-time civilian labor force over 16 years of age increased by about 2,000,000. The number of women over 20 years of age employed totaled more than 20,000,000.

WILBUR MARTIN
Managing Editor
Nation's Business

In April, when black students at Cornell University armed themselves, allegedly for self-protection, and were not disciplined, several faculty members resigned.

EDUCATION

MANY of the problems that beset American education in 1968 were still present in 1969. There were student disruptions in many colleges and high schools. Some educational programs were criticized by those who questioned their relevance and effectiveness. Teacher strikes hit many communities. Money was tight. And educators who looked to the Federal Government for help received little encouragement.

Yet, despite all the problems, there seemed to be a new note of cautious optimism. Student demonstrators found new targets: the war in Vietnam, and poverty and injustice at home. Very often, students were allied with their professors and administrators in protests that united the generations. This, together with new and wiser responses by the colleges and universities to student demands, helped avert many campus disturbances. In the cities, constructive activism seemed to be replacing confrontation as a tactic for hastening public-school reform.

To be sure, the optimism was often built on a fragile foundation. But it offered hope that in 1970 American education would enter a new era as well as a new decade.

▶ TROUBLE ON THE CAMPUS

Student demonstrations and disorders hit several colleges and universities that had managed to avoid serious troubles in previous years.

At City College of New York, the oldest unit of the City University, black students seized the south campus. They demanded that the college admit more black and Puerto Rican students whether or not they could meet the high entrance requirements. Their action led to some violence and a polarization between white and black students.

The demonstration finally ended without its major demands being met. But later the trustees of the City University announced that they would begin in 1970 a new "open admissions" policy originally intended to begin in 1975. Under this policy, the university will admit every high-school graduate in the city who wants to attend either a public community college or a senior college. This would give the university a 1970 freshman class of about 35,000 students, 14,000 more than in 1969. The trustees also promised to provide special programs and services to students who need academic help to overcome disadvantaged backgrounds.

At Harvard University, members of the Students for a Democratic Society (SDS) occupied the main administration building. The students were opposed to the Reserve Officer Training Corps on campus, and demanded a greater role in university affairs. These were also issues on many other campuses. Nathan M. Pusey, Harvard's president, called in the police and a bloody raid ensued. This shocked many on campus who did not take part in the SDS demon-

stration, and led to a student strike. These troubles shook the university administration. But out of them came a greater faculty assertiveness and a larger voice for students. And the ROTC program was stripped of academic status.

At Cornell University, black students occupied the student-union building. Then, allegedly for protection, they armed themselves with rifles and shotguns. Shortly thereafter James A. Perkins, Cornell's president, resigned in the face of criticism that he had not stood up forcefully to the student demonstrators.

These and other acts of student rebellion attracted much attention. Nevertheless, a study by the Educational Testing Service found that only about 2 per cent of the nation's college students were campus activists.

The use of court injunctions at the first signs of trouble headed off major confrontations on many campuses. More important, it appeared that many college presidents were trying to meet legitimate student demands before serious conflicts developed.

▶ HIGH SCHOOL UNREST

Student protests and disruptions spread from the college campus to many high schools and junior high schools during 1968-69. A survey made by the National Association of Secondary School Principals declared: "Three out of five principals report some form of active protest in their schools. Many who note no protest as yet add that they expect it in the near future."

High-school protests, sometimes accompanied by violence, flared in the large cities and in suburban and rural areas. New York, Chicago, and San Francisco were among those hardest hit. In some instances, the disruptions were triggered by racial conflicts. But in most cases they stemmed from nonracial causes, such as student demands for a greater voice in school affairs.

Taking note of the rising tide of student protest, Dr. James E. Allen, Jr., the new

Chicago school teachers strike for higher salaries, improved classroom conditions, and a guarantee against teacher layoffs. It was the first teacher strike in Chicago history.

United States commissioner of education, urged school principals to tackle the issues that underlie student unrest. He urged that steps be taken to prevent school disturbances. His recommended steps ranged from long-term changes in basic educational practices to short-range actions for resolving such common causes of student tensions as dress codes and ethnic studies.

▶ CURRICULUM

Black studies programs were introduced on many American campuses and at some urban high schools. This came about largely in response to pressure from black students. At Yale University, an undergraduate major was established in Afro-American Studies. Harvard University created a department in the area, with 15 courses including an analysis of the black revolution. The American Council on Edu-

cation estimated that hundreds of campuses have begun some form of black studies programs.

In other curriculum areas, a study by the Educational Testing Service found that dramatic changes had taken place in the past decade in the content and teaching methods of high-school courses in mathematics, science, and modern foreign languages. The study also brought out that curriculum reform movements appeared to have had less influence on English and history courses. One of every five college-bound high-school seniors had never read a play by Shakespeare, the study showed.

U.S. Commissioner Allen called for "a total national commitment" to end reading failures in the public schools by 1980. The Commissioner urged support for a crash program that would assure that "no one shall be leaving our schools without the

THE MAGNITUDE OF THE AMERICAN EDUCATIONAL ESTABLISHMENT (1969–70)

More than sixty-one million Americans are engaged full-time as students, teachers, or administrators in the nation's educational enterprise. Another 132,000 make education a time-consuming avocation as trustees of local school systems, state boards of education, or institutions of higher learning. The breakdown is given here:

TEACHERS

Elementary School Teachers	
Public	1,099,000
Nonpublic	152,000
Secondary School Teachers	
Public	904,000
Nonpublic	88,000
College and University Teachers	
Public	344,000
Nonpublic	188,000
Total	**2,775,000**

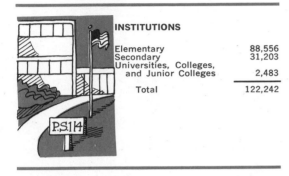

INSTITUTIONS

Elementary	88,556
Secondary	31,203
Universities, Colleges, and Junior Colleges	2,483
Total	**122,242**

ADMINISTRATORS AND SUPERVISORS

Superintendents of Schools	13,106
Principals and Supervisors	119,365
College and University Presidents	2,483
Other College Administrative and Service Staff	82,000
Total	**216,954**

SCHOOL DISTRICTS 20,440

BOARD MEMBERS

Local School Board Members	106,806
State Board Members	500
College and University Trustees	25,000
Total	**132,306**

STUDENTS

Pupils in Elementary Schools (Kindergarten through eighth grade)	
Public Schools	32,600,000
Nonpublic (Private and Parochial)	4,300,000
Total	**36,900,000**

Secondary School Students	
Public High Schools	13,200,000
Nonpublic	1,400,000
Total	**14,600,000**

College and University full- and part-time students enrolled for credit toward degrees	
Public Institutions	5,100,000
Nonpublic	2,000,000
Total	**7,100,000**

Total Students Enrolled   58,600,000

COST (IN BILLIONS)

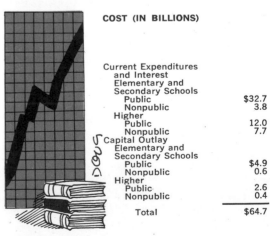

Current Expenditures and Interest	
Elementary and Secondary Schools	
Public	$32.7
Nonpublic	3.8
Higher	
Public	12.0
Nonpublic	7.7
Capital Outlay	
Elementary and Secondary Schools	
Public	$4.9
Nonpublic	0.6
Higher	
Public	2.6
Nonpublic	0.4
Total	**$64.7**

skill and desire necessary to read to the full limits of his capability."

DESEGREGATION

In May 1954, the United States Supreme Court handed down its historic ruling prohibiting segregation in the public schools. A year later the court said that desegregation must be achieved "with all deliberate speed."

Yet in 1969, school segregation was still a fact of life in many Southern communities. In October, however, the court ruled: " 'All deliberate speed' for desegregation is no longer constitutionally permissible . . . The obligation of every school district is to terminate dual school systems [one for white pupils, the other for Negro children] at once."

On the heels of the "at once" edict of the court, the Department of Health, Education, and Welfare announced plans to seek faster school desegregation in the South under the Civil Rights Act of 1964.

FEDERAL AID

Federal aid to education felt the impact of President Nixon's attempt to curb inflation partly through reduced government spending. In his budget for the 1969-70 fiscal year, the President proposed spending $3,000,000,000 for education. This was $400,000,000 below the amount spent the previous year. The House of Representatives, in an unusual move, added $1,000,000,000 to the budget bill it sent to the Senate.

In another development, a staff report to the Task Force on Urban Education urged a vast increase for 1970 in Federal funds for city school systems. The Task Force had been set up by Robert H. Finch, the Secretary of Health, Education, and Welfare.

TEACHERS

Teacher strikes for higher pay and better working conditions continued to plague many school systems in 1969. There were strikes in Chicago (the first in that city's history), Los Angeles, Denver, and in scores of other communities.

The National Education Association (NEA), which used to frown on teacher strikes as being "unprofessional," urged Congress to legalize teacher strikes and to require local school boards to negotiate.

In New York City, the American Federation of Teachers' local affiliate, the United Federation of Teachers, negotiated a record three-year contract with the Board of Education. The contract will give the city's 60,000 teachers an annual pay scale of $9,400 (for beginners) to $16,950 in 1971. This is the highest teacher salary scale of any large city in the nation.

SCHOOL DECENTRALIZATION

The New York City school system, with more than 1,000,000 pupils, is the nation's largest. In 1969, it moved closer to a decentralized operation. The State Legislature passed a bill providing for a shift of substantial operating powers from central headquarters to community school districts that will be set up within the city. The districts will be governed by locally elected school boards. These boards will have jurisdiction over elementary, intermediate, and junior high schools in their areas. Senior high schools will remain under central authority.

The decentralization bill did not go so far as proponents of total community control of local schools had wanted. It also appeared to do away with the city's three small experimental decentralized districts. One of those projects—the predominantly black and Puerto Rican Ocean Hill-Brownsville district in Brooklyn—had figured in the dispute that triggered the 1968 citywide teachers' strikes.

But the decentralization of New York City's school system was expected to give new impetus to similar efforts in other large cities to bring about greater community participation—and, hopefully, improvements—in education.

LEONARD BUDER
The New York Times

EUROPE, EAST

DURING 1969, events within the Soviet Union, Czechoslovakia, and Rumania dominated the news from East Europe.

More than one hundred Russian soldiers were reported killed in several clashes with Communist Chinese troops. These clashes took place in the Far East, along the Ussuri River, and along the border between China's Sinkiang Province and Soviet Central Asia. For some time it seemed that a full-scale war might erupt. But in October the Chinese and Russians opened talks in an effort to defuse the situation.

Delegates from 75 countries met in Moscow June 5–17 to attend the international congress of communist and workers' parties. With the exception of Albania and Yugoslavia, all of the nations of Eastern Europe were represented. For details of these and other events in the Soviet Union during 1969, see the article UNION OF SOVIET SOCIALIST REPUBLICS, which begins on page 360.

Czechoslovakia, with Soviet troops still on its soil, witnessed a retreat from the liberalism of Alexander Dubcek. Indeed, Mr. Dubcek, who had tried to give Czechoslovakia "socialism with a human face," was ousted from his major government and Communist Party positions. Under Soviet pressure, conservatives once again took control of Czechoslovakia. Gustav Husak was named first secretary of the Czechoslovak Communist Party. (A biography of Mr. Husak appears on page 203.) Such freedoms that the Czechoslovak people had obtained under Dubcek all but disappeared. Complete details on these events may be found in the article CZECHOSLOVAKIA, which begins on page 143.

President Nixon's trip to Bucharest, Rumania, made world headlines in early August. His visit underlined United States concern for Rumania's independence. Under Nicolae Ceausescu, Rumania has maintained an independent foreign policy. Indeed, on many occasions it has done just the opposite of what was requested by the Soviet Union. Because of this, many observers felt that Soviet troops might invade Rumania as they had done Czechoslovakia in 1968. In the article RUMANIA, which begins on page 308, Mr. Ceausescu's policies and problems during 1969 are discussed in depth.

Events in other countries of East Europe during 1969 were also deeply affected by relations with the Soviet Union.

Soviet Premier Aleksei Kosygin (third from left), Communist Party Secretary General Leonid Brezhnev, and President Nikolai Podgorny are flanked by other members of the Soviet delega- tion at the international conference of communist and workers' parties, held in Moscow June 5-17. At the conference, the Soviet Union tried to win support in its dispute with China.

ALBANIA

Albania lived in 1969 in fear that it might be invaded by troops of the Soviet Union and its allies. At times during the year, pro-Soviet sources started rumors that Communist China would install mis- siles and nuclear warheads in Albania. When these rumors spread, fears of a Soviet invasion increased.

Albania is allied with Communist China. But it is politically and geographically iso- lated in East Europe. It did not even at- tend the world communist congress in Moscow in 1969. Because of its isolation, during the year the Albanian Government tried to improve relations with Rumania.

Albanian fears of a Russian invasion began when border fighting broke out be- tween Communist China and the Soviet Union. These fears were increased by re- ports that the Soviet Union planned a strike against Chinese nuclear installations. Also, the growth of the Soviet fleet in the Medi- terranean increased concern that the So- viets might land an invasion force in Albania. Nevertheless, Albanian Com- munist Party leader Enver Hoxha and his associates continued to support China. They also continued to denounce the Soviet Union as they had done in earlier years. In return, Albania received Chinese economic and technical aid.

BULGARIA

In 1969 the chief trend in Bulgaria was the movement toward closer political and economic integration with the Soviet Union. As it had been earlier, Bulgaria in 1969 was a loyal ally of the Soviet Union.

Progress continued toward economic integration with the Soviet Union. This was reflected in such moves as the sending of Bulgarian workers to the Soviet Union. Many Bulgarian lumberjacks, for example, worked in Russian forests to fell timber, some of which was then exported to Bul- garia. Bulgaria also began to produce parts for Soviet automobiles, computers, and other machines. By agreeing to make such parts, Bulgaria in effect decided not to make its own autos, computers, or other complex equipment which the Soviet Union prefers to make in its own factories.

EAST GERMANY

The key development of 1969 in East Germany was continued economic develop- ment. This economic progress, however, was not accompanied by any movement toward liberalization. There was no easing of repressive policies under Communist Party leader Walter Ulbricht. The Berlin Wall continued to stand. It remained the symbol of the extreme measures used by the East German regime to keep its people from leaving the country. Escape attempts continued in 1969. Some ended in success. Some ended in the death of those who tried to flee.

In 1969, East Germany continued to seek Western and world recognition as a fully independent state. Some additional countries did grant recognition. But this progress was marginal. East Germany wanted the Soviet Union to exert pressure on West Germany to recognize the legitimacy of the Ulbricht regime. Early in 1969 the Soviet Union seemed willing to exert such pressure on West Germany. At the time, a crisis seemed to build up about the West German decision to hold the parliamentary election of a new president in West Berlin. This crisis ended quickly when Soviet-Chinese fighting broke out in the Far East.

During much of the rest of the year, the Soviet Union seemed anxious to woo West German friendship. Ulbricht could hardly have welcomed this development. But he had little room to maneuver, even if he wanted to. The reason for this is that East Germany is dependent upon the Soviet Union for most of its raw materials. And East Germany must export most of its manufactured goods to the Soviet Union. Also, East Germany is very dependent on the Soviet Union for military and political support.

▶ **HUNGARY**

When Hungary helped the Soviet Union invade Czechoslovakia in August 1968, many Hungarians were shocked. These people still remembered the brutal way in which the Hungarian revolt of 1956 had been put down by Soviet troops. Fears were also raised in Hungary because of the Soviet charges made against Czechoslova-kia in 1968. These charges included the one that Czechoslovakia's economic reform was somehow a step toward capitalism. The Hungarians thus were fearful because they had one of the most radical economic reforms in the Soviet bloc. They feared that the Soviet attitude toward Czechoslovakia's economic policy would lead to a crackdown against the Hungarian system. This did not happen, however. Perhaps this was because Hungary continued its very close political co-operation with the Soviet Union.

Hungary's political co-operation with the Soviet Union was evident at the international communist congress in Moscow in mid-1969. It was also evident in the all-out support the Hungarian regime gave the Soviet Union in the Soviet-Chinese conflict.

Within Hungary the political atmosphere continued to be one of the most relaxed in the Soviet bloc. Janos Kadar remained the dominant figure in the Hungarian ruling group.

▶ **POLAND**

Several striking developments highlighted Polish political life in 1969. On the international scene, Poland followed the Soviet line. The Poles, for example, softened their attitude toward West Germany. They eased their conditions for a normalization of relations with the West German Government.

At the same time, Communist Party leader Wladyslaw Gomulka tried to patch up relations with Czechoslovakia. The Czechoslovak people had deeply resented the participation of Polish troops in the August 1968 invasion.

Domestically, the Gomulka regime tried to wind up the consequences of the internal convulsions of 1968. In 1968 there had been anti-Semitic outbursts in Poland. As a result, the Polish Government introduced voluntary Jewish emigration to Israel. In early summer 1969, however, this emigration was restricted. But presumably by that time most of Poland's few remaining Jews who wished to leave had done so.

YUGOSLAVIA

The Ninth Congress of the Yugoslav League of Communists was held in March 1969. This was the key political event of the year. This Congress generally reaffirmed the independent internal and foreign political positions of the Yugoslav Communists. It also made some key organizational changes. The most important of these changes was the creation of a new Executive Bureau under President Tito. This Bureau is composed of the most important political figures in the country. They include such men as Edvard Kardelj, Vladimir Bakaric, Veljko Vlahovic, and Krste Crvenkovski. The Executive Bureau was obviously created to provide a way to transfer power after President Tito leaves the scene because of illness or death. Tito, who has been prime minister or president of Yugoslavia since the end of World War II, was 77 years old in 1969.

The leaders in the new Executive Bureau come from the republics and provinces that make up Yugoslavia. The reason for this clearly is to try to keep the country unified despite the growing independence and nationalism of the six republics. These republics are Serbia, Croatia, Slovenia, Bosnia and Herzegovina, Macedonia, and Montenegro. They had first united into a single state in 1918.

The most industrialized and wealthiest provinces are Croatia and Slovenia. There has been some conflict between these two provinces and the poorer and less-developed provinces. The latter want capital transferred from Croatia and Slovenia to them so that they can industrialize at a faster pace.

Another important event in 1969 was the visit of Soviet Foreign Minister Andrei Gromyko to Belgrade in the late summer. The purpose of this visit was to improve

Yugoslav President Tito welcomes Apollo 11 astronauts. Left to right: Mrs. Aldrin, Edwin Aldrin, Tito, Mrs. Collins, Michael Collins, Tito's wife, Neil Armstrong and his wife.

Soviet Foreign Minister Andrei Gromyko arrives in Yugoslavia. The purpose of his visit was to improve relations between the two communist countries.

relations between Yugoslavia and the Soviet Union. These relations had been badly strained by the Soviet invasion of Czechoslovakia. The Yugoslavs had reacted very strongly to this event, and had supported the Czechoslovaks.

Apparently to improve the atmosphere for the Gromyko visit, President Tito spoke out a few days before the Soviet official arrived. In this speech, he demanded that the Yugoslav Communists tighten their rule over the country. He also demanded that the Communists crack down on excessive demonstrations of local independence and of political nonconformity.

The Gromyko visit ended with a communiqué which stressed areas of agreement between the two countries. In that statement, Mr. Gromyko appeared to reaffirm earlier Soviet recognition of Yugoslavia's right to independent development. However, President Tito later met with Nikolai Ceausescu of Rumania. Tito indicated that the Gromyko visit had by no means made Yugoslavia a conforming member of the Soviet bloc. Earlier, the Yugoslav refusal to attend the world communist congress in

Moscow had emphasized the continuing breach between Moscow and Belgrade.

Economically, Yugoslavia continued to be the Eastern European country with the closest ties to the West. Vacationers from West Europe crowded Yugoslavia's resorts on the Adriatic Sea during the summer months. And hundreds of thousands of Yugoslav workers were permitted to leave the country to work in Western European factories. These men sent home part of their wages to help support their families.

In Yugoslavia itself, the peculiar Yugoslav combination of socialist ownership and free-market operation continued to forge ahead despite some problems.

A visitor to Belgrade, Zagreb, or other major Yugoslav cities could see that in many ways the country was the most prosperous of all the communist-ruled nations in Eastern Europe. It was also the most Western.

HARRY SCHWARTZ
The New York Times

See also CZECHOSLOVAKIA; HUSAK, GUSTAV; RUMANIA; UNION OF SOVIET SOCIALIST REPUBLICS.

HEADS OF GOVERNMENT

EAST EUROPE

Albania	ENVER HOXHA, 1st secretary
Bulgaria	TODOR ZHIVKOV, 1st secretary
Czechoslovakia	LUDVIK SVOBODA, president
	GUSTAV HUSAK, 1st secretary
East Germany	WALTER ULBRICHT, 1st secretary
	WILLI STOPH, premier
Hungary	JANOS KADAR, 1st secretary
Poland	WLADYSLAW GOMULKA, 1st secretary
Rumania	NICOLAE CEAUSESCU, 1st secretary
U.S.S.R.	LEONID BREZHNEV, 1st secretary
	ALEKSEI KOSYGIN, premier
Yugoslavia	JOSIP BROZ TITO, president

WEST EUROPE

Austria	JOSEF KLAUS, chancellor
Belgium	BAUDOUIN I, king
	GASTON EYSKENS, prime minister
Britain	ELIZABETH II, queen
	HAROLD WILSON, prime minister
Denmark	FREDERIK IX, king
	HILMAR BAUNSGAARD, premier
Finland	URHO KEKKONEN, president
France	GEORGES POMPIDOU, president
West Germany	GUSTAV HEINEMAN, president
	WILLY BRANDT, chancellor
Greece	CONSTANTINE II, king (in exile)
	GEORGE PAPADOPOULOS, premier
Iceland	KRISTJAN ELDJARN, president
	BJARNI BENEDIKTSSON, prime minister
Ireland	EAMON DE VALERA, president
	JOHN M. LYNCH, prime minister
Italy	GIUSEPPE SARAGAT, president
	MARIANO RUMOR, premier
Luxembourg	JEAN, grand duke
	PIERRE WERNER, prime minister
Malta	GIORGIO B. OLIVIER, prime minister
Netherlands	JULIANA, queen
	PIET DE JONG, prime minister
Norway	OLAV V, king
	PER BORTEN, prime minister
Portugal	MARCELO CAETANO, premier
Spain	FRANCISCO FRANCO, chief of state
Sweden	GUSTAF VI, king
	OLOF PALME, prime minister
Switzerland	HANS PETER TSCHUDI, president

	POPULATION	ARMED FORCES	CURRENCY*	COMECON	EFTA	EEC
EAST EUROPE						
Albania	2,157,000	38,000	4 leks = $1.00			
Bulgaria	8,451,000	154,000	1.2 leva = $1.00	X		
Czechoslovakia	14,472,000	230,000	8.5 korunas = $1.00	X		
East Germany	16,016,000	137,000	3.4 Ostmarks = $1.00	X		
Hungary	10,331,000	97,000	17.4 forints = $1.00	X		
Poland	32,760,000	275,000	15.9 zloty = $1.00	X		
Rumania	20,036,000	193,000	9.4 lei = $1.00	X		
U.S.S.R.	243,410,000	3,300,000	1 ruble = $2.40	X		
Yugoslavia	20,624,000	218,000	12.5 dinars = $1.00			
WEST EUROPE						
Austria	7,437,000	50,000	25.9 schillings = $1.00		X	
Belgium	9,710,000	102,400	50.2 francs = $1.00			X
Britain	56,034,000	405,000	1 pound = $2.40		X	
Denmark	4,944,000	45,500	7.5 kroner = $1.00		X	
Finland	4,728,000	36,400	4.2 markkas = $1.00			
France	50,500,000	503,000	5.5 francs = $1.00			X
West Germany	58,332,000	465,000	3.7 marks = $1.00			X
Greece	9,007,000	159,000	30 drachmas = $1.00			
Iceland	204,000	none	88 kronur = $1.00			
Ireland	2,914,000	13,000	1 pound = $2.40			
Italy	53,471,000	420,000	625 lire = $1.00			X
Luxembourg	301,000	560	50.2 francs = $1.00			X
Malta	302,000	none	1 pound = $2.40			
Netherlands	13,042,000	124,000	3.6 guilders = $1.00			X
Norway	3,830,000	38,000	7.1 kroner = $1.00		X	
Portugal	9,706,000	182,000	28.7 escudos = $1.00		X	
Spain	32,962,000	289,500	70 pesetas = $1.00			
Sweden	8,064,000	76,000	5.2 kronor = $1.00		X	
Switzerland	6,255,000	26,500	4.3 francs = $1.00		X	

* US $; 1969 exchange rates
Comecon—Council for Mutual Economic Aid
EFTA—European Free Trade Association
EEC—European Economic Community (Common Market)

As 1969 ended, East and West Germany called for better mutual relations, raising hopes that one day the Berlin Wall may come down.

EUROPE, WEST

IN 1969, President Richard M. Nixon of the United States visited Europe for eight days, from February 23 to March 2. Mr. Nixon met government leaders in Brussels, London, Paris, Rome, and Bonn, and he also visited West Berlin. Despite some heckling and demonstrations, Nixon won general approval of his mission by press and public in the five countries he visited. His meeting with French President Charles de Gaulle was credited with improving relations between the two countries. One purpose of the President's journey was to establish a personal relationship with key Western government leaders. He also wanted to get their opinions before pursuing arms-limitation talks with the Soviets.

The resignation of President De Gaulle (see the article FRANCE on page 186) brought the possibility of an easing of rigid French views that had prevented British membership in the European Economic Community (EEC). But in Britain, opinion cooled toward the step because, among other changes, it would increase the prices of foods that at present enjoy farm subsidies and tariff benefits when imported from Commonwealth countries.

(British relations with Common Market countries, as well as other items, are discussed in full in the article GREAT BRITAIN, which begins on page 194.)

At an EEC meeting in December, France did not block a statement that the Common Market was ready to begin new talks on British membership. The EEC also hinted that in the future the Common Market may include Norway, Denmark, and Ireland as well as Britain.

Italy faced still another governmental crisis in 1969. Premier Mariano Rumor resigned in July only to form a new Government the following month. (Full details of these events will be found in the article ITALY on page 210.)

Other countries of Western Europe were not without their own changes and crises during the year.

▶ AUSTRIA

On May 29, Theodor Piffl-Percevic resigned as minister of education and was replaced by Dr. Alois Mock, chief of Cabinet to Chancellor Josef Klaus. The cabinet crisis was the result of a petition signed by 340,000 persons (6.78 per cent of the electorate) calling for the revocation of a new law prescribing a ninth year of study in Austrian grammar schools.

▶ BELGIUM

Joseph-Jean Merlot, 55, deputy premier and minister for economic affairs in the cabinet of Premier Gaston Eyskens, died on January 21 from injuries received in an automobile accident. Andre Cools, minister of the budget and a socialist, as Merlot had been, was named deputy premier on January 27, retaining his budget post. Edmond Leburton joined the Cabinet as minister for economic affairs, the second post left vacant by Merlot's death.

▶ DENMARK

A proposal to lower the voting age from 21 years to 18 was rejected in a referendum June 24, despite its passage earlier in the month by Parliament. A total of 63.8 per cent of eligible Danes voted in the referendum, and only 445,066 (13.6 per cent) voted for the reduction. The voting age in Denmark had been lowered from 23 years to 21 in May 1961.

▶ FINLAND

On June 4, the Government announced it had decided to order Finland's first nuclear power plant from the Soviet Union.

Late in the year representatives of the United States and the Soviet Union met in Helsinki, the Finnish capital, for preliminary discussions on strategic arms limitation talks.

▶ GERMANY, WEST

In February, still another crisis over West Berlin brought new restrictions on the city's road and rail ties with the West. The confrontation was caused by a Bonn Government decision to hold elections of a new Federal German president in West Berlin. Despite the communist harrassment, West German members of Parliament held the elections. After three ballots, they chose Justice Minister Gustav Heinemann, a Social Democrat. Diplomats credited Soviet concern over frontier clashes with Communist China for the failure of the crisis to reach the danger level.

Willy Brandt Becomes Chancellor

In September, parliamentary elections were preceded by bitter campaign battles between Christian Democrats and Social Democrats who had governed in a "grand coalition" since 1966. With both major parties sharing responsibility for government policies, campaign debate focused on the personalities of their leaders—Chancellor Kurt Kiesinger of the Christian Democrats, and Social Democratic Willy Brandt, vice-chancellor and foreign minister. Because polls reported that the Christian Democrats and the Socialists were almost equally matched, attention centered on two lesser parties. They were the Free Democrats, who had supported Heine-

Willy Brandt, West Germany's new chancellor.

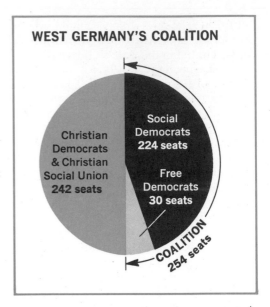

WEST GERMANY'S COALITION

Christian Democrats & Christian Social Union 242 seats

Social Democrats 224 seats

Free Democrats 30 seats

COALITION 254 seats

The results of West German elections.

mann's election as president, and the National Democrats, led by Adolf von Thadden and accused of neo-nazi tendencies. These two small parties were fighting for the 5 per cent of the ballots that would secure them seats in the Bundestag (Parliament).

In polling on September 28, Kiesinger's Christian Democrats won 46.1 per cent of the vote and Brandt's Social Democrats 42.7 per cent. The National Democratic Party failed to gain enough votes to secure seats in the Bundestag. But the Free Democrats of Walter Scheel emerged holding the Bundestag balance of power, despite a loss of 19 of the 49 seats the party held in the previous Parliament.

Brandt, acting swiftly, aligned the Free Democrats with his Social Democrats to assure a total of 254 seats in the 496-seat house. On October 21, the Bundestag elected Brandt the first Social Democratic chancellor of Germany since 1930.

One of Brandt's first actions as chancellor was to revalue the German mark. On October 24, the mark was increased 9.29 per cent, from 25 cents U.S. currency to 27.3 cents.

▶ **GREECE**

Premier George Papadopoulos announced on April 19 the restoration of three of the 12 articles suspended from the new Greek constitution, which had been promulgated by the ruling colonels in 1968. The articles restored concerned "sanctity of the home," the right of association, and the right of assembly. The nine articles that remained suspended included the right to hold elections to choose a representative government.

The Government said that it had a timetable for restoring the remaining suspended articles. The Government also said that it had drafted a law that will allow political parties, now banned in Greece. These moves did not halt the criticism from the other nations of Western Europe. At a Council of Europe meeting in December, Greece was charged with violating human rights. Greece withdrew from the Council just as the Council was about to expel Greece.

▶ **ICELAND**

On January 23, Iceland formally applied for membership in the European Free

Trade Association (EFTA). This group of seven European nations is led by Great Britain. It accounts for 40 per cent of Icelandic trade.

▶ IRELAND

On May 21, President Eamon de Valera dissolved Ireland's lower house of Parliament, the Dail, and called a general election for June 18. Premier John Lynch said that the election had been called so that Irish voters could decide in an atmosphere of calm the future of their country on the eve of the 1970's, "a period of great challenge." Lynch's Fianna Fail Party was returned to power with 75 seats, an absolute majority over all other parties.

Ireland, linked by religion with the minority of Roman Catholics in Northern Ireland, was very concerned with the fighting there. It called for a UN force to keep peace in Northern Ireland, which, though internally self-governing, is under British rule.

▶ LUXEMBOURG

A cabinet crisis of three months ended on January 27 when the Christian Socialist Party and the Liberal Party agreed to form a coalition Government. The new Government was sworn into office on January 31 with Pierre Werner again heading it.

▶ MALTA

A joint statement on April 4 ended a rift of 10 years between the Malta Labor Party and the Roman Catholic Church, which had declared voting for Labor candidates a mortal sin and had withheld communion from Labor Party members.

▶ NETHERLANDS

An international uproar broke out when the Netherlands granted political refuge on January 24 to Liao Ho-shu, Chinese Communist charge d'affaires in The Hague. An announcement in Washington on February 4 said that Liao had arrived in the United States to seek political asylum. Peking charged that Liao had been "incited to

betray his country and [was] carried off . . . by the Central Intelligence Agency." As a result of the incident, Communist China called off the 135th meeting of Chinese and United States ambassadors, which had been scheduled for Warsaw, Poland, on February 20.

▶ NORWAY

A four-party coalition of anti-socialists was returned to power in September general elections by the narrowest majority in the history of Norway. The alliance of Conservative, Liberal, Center, and Christian People's parties won only 76 seats in the Storting (Parliament), while the opposition won 74.

▶ PORTUGAL

Even though opposition parties took part, the ruling National Union Party won all 130 seats in National Assembly elections held on October 26. Nearly 2,000,-000 Portuguese voted in the first elections since strong man Antonio de Oliveira Salazar suffered a stroke in September 1968 and was removed from power. Marcelo Caetano, who succeeded Salazar as premier, cautiously tested limited measures of liberalization in 1969.

▶ SPAIN

Generalissimo Francisco Franco, 76, announced to the Spanish Cortes (Parliament) on July 22 that he had decided to name as his successor Prince Juan Carlos de Borbon y Borbon. The 31-year-old Prince was chosen over his father and rival pretender to the throne, Don Juan de Borbon y Battenberg. The father denounced Franco's action.

In October, Franco announced major cabinet changes that left only four of 18 ministerial posts unaffected. Younger men replaced all three military service ministers. In one of the most significant changes, Foreign Minister Fernando Castiella y Maiz was replaced by Gregorio Lopez Bravo. Castiella had been the architect of repeated confrontations with Great Britain

Olof Palme, new prime minister of Sweden (above). Sweden offered aid to Hanoi and gave refuge to U.S. servicemen who refused to fight in Vietnam. Below, U.S. sailors who jumped ship.

over Gibraltar. Lopez Bravo, on the other hand, is pro-European and pro-American. He is expected to negotiate reasonably with Britain on Gibraltar and with the United States on military bases in Spain. The Opus Dei, a powerful Roman Catholic lay organization, emerged strongly represented in the new Cabinet by young technocrats.

▶ **SWEDEN**

Tage Erlander, Social Democratic premier of Sweden for 23 years, retired in October. He was replaced by Olof Palme, one of the country's most radical politicians. Mr. Palme opposes America's role in Vietnam. In 1968 he had marched side by side with a North Vietnamese diplomat in a torchlight parade protesting the Vietnam war. The succession of Palme sharpened the differences between Stockholm and Washington. These differences caused the withdrawal of the United States ambassador from the Swedish capital in 1968.

During 1969, Sweden announced it would grant a loan of $45,000,000 to North Vietnam, despite pressure from the United States that Sweden wait until the war was over. The aid program begins in 1970. Sweden continued to offer asylum to United States servicemen who refused to fight in Vietnam. By late 1969 they numbered about 300.

▶ **SWITZERLAND**

On February 18, Arab guerrillas attacked a Boeing 720 jetliner of the El Al Airline as it was about to take off from Zurich International Airport for Tel Aviv, Israel. Three crewmen and three passengers were wounded by machine-gun fire. An Israeli security guard aboard the plane slipped down an emergency chute and shot one of the attackers dead. Airport personnel captured the three other Arabs.

J. J. Meehan
United Press International

See also Charles, Prince of Wales; France; Great Britain; Italy; Pompidou, Georges.

EVERS, CHARLES

CROWDS of Negroes gathered in the plaza of a shopping center named after Medgar Evers, an official of the National Association for the Advancement of Colored People (NAACP) who had been murdered in 1963. They were congratulating each other and laughing and crying with joy. They rejoiced because on May 13, 1969, Charles Evers, brother of the late Medgar, won the Democratic nomination for mayor of Fayette, their poverty-stricken town in southwestern Mississippi. Although it was a primary, Evers was assured the mayorship because he would run unopposed in the June general elections. He thus became the first black mayor of a biracial Mississippi town since Reconstruction days. To the Negroes of Fayette, who compose about three quarters of the population, his elec-

tion meant promise and hope for the future.

Charles Evers is a direct, warmhearted man. He is known for his backwoodsy way of speaking and his ability to inspire people to work together for the Negro cause. He was a strong leader of the highly successful campaign to get blacks to run and vote in municipal elections throughout the state. He was helped by hundreds of students, lawyers, labor-union men, and politicians. His determination resulted in more than 175 Negro candidates' running for offices in the 1969 Mississippi primaries. It also resulted in his defeating R. J. Allen, the white mayor of Fayette for the last twenty years.

James Charles Evers was born in Decatur, Mississippi, on September 11, 1922. He served in the Army, first in the Pacific as a volunteer during World War II, and then as a reservist during the Korean war. He received a B.A. degree from Alcorn A. & M. College in Lorman, Mississippi, in 1950.

In 1951, Charles moved to Philadelphia, Mississippi. There he and his brother, Medgar, began an NAACP membership drive. This work continued until 1957. At the same time, he worked as a disc jockey and opened a few small businesses. However, he was harassed by segregationists because of his association with the NAACP. He left the state and moved to Chicago in 1957.

On June 12, 1963, the name of Evers gained nationwide fame. On that day, Medgar Evers was shot and killed in Jackson, Mississippi, by a sniper. A few days later Charles took over his brother's job as NAACP field director in Mississippi. He held that position until he became mayor.

Evers is married to the former Manie Laura Magee. They have four daughters.

On July 7 white control passed on to black as Charles Evers was sworn in as mayor. Blacks and whites alike hoped that he could, as he put it, "make Fayette the best little town in the whole world."

See also CIVIL RIGHTS.

FASHION

EVERYONE was busy doing his or her own thing in fashion in 1969. In fact, your own thing was the only fashion there was. What met the eye was sometimes beautiful, sometimes weird. Young people on the street put themselves together like works of art. They suited fashion to themselves, rather than themselves to fashion. The Woodstock rock-music festival in August set a new standard for physical casualness. Frayed blue jeans, tied-and-dyed shirts, tattered undershirts, floppy-brimmed hats, and beads were uniform. Different ethnic

Embroidery was part of 1969's fashion message for the young. A teen-ager, left, in an embroidered shirt and vest. Above, the maxicoat swept onto the scene with the arrival of fall.

decorations ranged from Hungarian embroidered shirts to fringed leathers in the American Indian style. Young girls scorned bras and made the natural-looking bosom, outlined by tight body shirts or clinging T-shirts, the fashion. The minis were the shortest ever.

In the meantime the over-thirty generation carried on as best it could. It was not an easy job for the older woman to keep up the shape of the young. But with a record interest in exercise salons and physical fitness, she tried.

▶ BLACK DESIGNERS AND MODELS

For the first time, black designers were getting solid recognition for their fashion creativity in an integrated world.

Bill Smith got a top job at Richelieu, Inc. Bill said that he was proving "creativity can make money" with his futuristic designs. He spearheaded a group of costume-jewelry designers who were making huge bibs and vests of chains, pearls, and semiprecious stones.

Stephen Burrows created not only a look of his own but a group of followers. Stephen's group assumed the silhouette of fashion drawings: long-legged bodies in colorful, short-waisted, skintight tops, and long, droopy, 1930's-style cuffed pants—boys and girls alike. The group also led the way in fringes, applying them in beaded profusion on pants, shirts, bags, belts, and other leather garments.

Jon Haggins and Scott Barrie worked for their own wholesale houses. Haggins was a specialist in bias cut, a technique most often associated with Paris' famed Mme. Gres. Haggins updated the bias cut by combining it with a lot of bare skin, and black models paraded his clothes with unequaled cool. Barrie became a specialist in cutting pants, and Seventh Avenue models flocked to his showroom for perfectionist fit. Haggins and Barrie designed clothes that could be worn interchangeably by either sex, with the emphasis on 1930's-style T-shirt tops and wide-legged, cuffed pants.

Black mannequins blossomed. An all-black model agency called Black Beauty got under way, with 39 male and female models on call. It was a big leap forward from the dozen or so black models maintained by integrated agencies the year before. Naomi Sims had "top black model" covers on both *Ladies' Home Journal* and *Life,* as well as fashion magazines.

▶ MAXIS, MIDIS, AND PONCHOS

With the arrival of fall came the falling of hemlines. Maxicoats swept into the street—mostly on young schoolgirls. Young girls struggled along in long coats, boots, pants, long scarves, and crocheted berets.

Fashion leaders predicted more of a future for the "midi" length—ten inches off the ground. The stores that were importing fashions from Europe went to great lengths to explain to their customers that any length skirt was O.K. This left up to the public the problem of whether to wear a mini, knee-length, midi, or maxi skirt. This confusion was certainly reflected in slow fall sales in most areas, with the exception of the flying maxi.

Another fashion adopted by the young crept into high fashion. Ponchos, capes, and shawls turned up in the couture collections of Valentino in Rome and St. Laurent in Paris.

▶ FROM PANTS TO CLOGS

Pants were everywhere. Floppy pants that grazed the ground had the proper "cool." Pleated-top pants that looked like Fred Astaire's were definitely 1969. Bell-bottoms endured.

For the beach, crocheted bikinis were the most popular. Do-it-yourself tied-and-dyeds were the rage with high-school boys and girls, who dipped cutoff blue jeans and T-shirts in their own color combinations.

The Establishment and the young also widened the gap in accessories. The youthful bag was a fringed suede pouch hung loosely from a shoulder strap. Establishment types were still involved with signature pieces: Vuitton handbags and luggage

Children's clothes mirrored every cut and curve of adult fashions.

from Paris; Gucci shoes, bags, skirts, and vests from Italy; and scarves with Bill Blass, Geoffrey [Beene], Chester [Weinberg], [Jacques] Tiffeau, and the like boldly printed on them.

Swedish clogs were heard clumping to school and office all over the land. As fall moved into winter, more platform shoes with clunky heels emerged as the proper shoe to wear with long, droopy pants. Boys' shoes starred two-tone color combinations, such as red and green, or blue and yellow.

▶ MAKEUP AND HAIRDOS

In makeup the look ranged from ultra-natural to the look of chorus girls in Ruby Keeler movies. An off-Broadway musical called *Dames at Sea* illustrated the new makeup. The two female stars had colored eyelids, scarlet lips, and frizzy hair. Colored eye makeup became the new focal point for beauty-company promotions. Just as most women had learned how to apply a battery of false eyelashes, the look was changing to spiky lashes which had to be clipped and glued to the eyelid one by one.

The concierge hairdo—hair piled up on the head with wispy tendrils escaping—swept across the fashion scene.

MEN'S FASHIONS

Men's fashions followed the ladies'. Young people had given the older men courage to dress more colorfully. Sideburns, mustaches, beards, and collar-covering hair among the middle-aged became popular. So too did fitted Edwardian suits, acceptance of wool jersey as a suitable, comfortable fabric for men's clothing, and long topcoats six inches from the ground. Jump suits were introduced by designers new to the men's field. The day of the astronaut had dawned, and barriers to fashion for men seemed out of date.

For the boys in the street, it was still the fringed buckskin jacket, the Arlo Guthrie hat, with worn blue jeans, and touches of motorcycle-black leathers with nailheads.

CHILDREN'S CLOTHES

Children's clothes seemed to be returning to the nineteenth century, when they

The jump suit for spacemen and earthlings.

Little girl's coat is styled like an adult's.

were more or less imitations of grown-up clothing. Even fur coats became realities for children, and a six-year-old blonde could easily have a wardrobe of four fur coats. Fifteen years was still a realistic discovery age for models. Considering that young people were going to determine fashions for the years ahead, it was clear that the earlier one starts, the better. Nineteen may soon be over-the-hill.

JO AHERN SEGAL
Look Magazine

FINLAND. See EUROPE, WEST.

FOOD

Cyclamate-free sodas were rushed to stores after the ban on cyclamates in beverages.

IN 1969, there was great concern with hunger and malnutrition in the United States. Previously, the emphasis had been mainly on hunger and malnutrition in the developing countries.

▶ MALNUTRITION IN THE UNITED STATES

A 1968 report of Household Food Consumption conducted by the United States Department of Agriculture showed that 20 per cent of United States households had "poor" diets. A "poor" diet is one that provides less than two thirds of the recommended amount of one or more nutrients. In 1955 only 15 per cent of diets were classified "poor."

A study, called the National Nutrition Survey, was started by the Department of Health, Education, and Welfare to determine the extent of malnutrition among people in low-income groups.

One outcome of the present concern with hunger and malnutrition was the appointment of a special adviser to the President. The adviser is Jean Mayer, professor of Nutrition at Harvard University. Dr. Mayer organized the December White House Conference on Food, Nutrition and Health. The purpose of the conference was to attempt to work out a national nutrition policy. The conference declared a national hunger emergency. It urged a guaranteed annual income of $5,500 for a family of four, free breakfast and lunch for all school children, and expansion of all food programs. The conference also asked that food programs be directed by the Department of Health, Education, and Welfare, instead of the Department of Agriculture, and that the poor administer the programs.

▶ NUTRITION EDUCATION

It is becoming more and more evident that nutrition is a social science, as well as a biological science. This recognition is providing a much-needed spur to nutrition education programs.

A practical nutrition program was introduced by the Cooperative Extension Service of the Department of Agriculture. The program involves the use of non-professional persons, or "nutrition aides," who are trained by professional nutritionists. The aides work with homemakers in the areas of food buying, meal planning, food preparation, child nutrition, and other family food problems. Low-income families are encouraged to buy food stamps which enable them to buy more food than their limited resources would buy on the market. The food stamp program is one of the Federal programs designed to help feed the poor.

▶ THE SEARCH FOR PROTEIN

The results of recent research have heightened concern about worldwide malnutrition. The research links mental retardation with malnutrition. Lack of enough protein, particularly in the early years of life, is strongly suspected as a cause of permanent mental damage.

One proposal is put forth frequently as a partial solution to the problem of protein needs in developing countries. The proposal is the fortification, or enriching, of cereal grains with lysine. Lysine is an amino acid the body needs. Lysine is also one of the amino acids of which protein is made. In corn, wheat, rice, and other grain products, lysine is present in limited amounts. In many countries, a single cereal grain is the mainstay of the diet. Recent research has shown that cereal foods may provide a reasonably adequate diet for adults. But because of their low total protein content, as well as their low lysine content, cereal foods are unsatisfactory as the only source of protein for young children.

In September, scientists from around the world gathered at Massachusetts Institute of Technology to discuss the pros and cons of fortifying cereals with lysine. The scientists reached a general agreement. Governments of countries needing protein improvement should be encouraged to support lysine enrichment of the main cereal products.

Another approach is genetic improvement, or the development of improved strains, of cereal grains. Opaque-2 is a genetically improved grain. It has a much higher lysine content than ordinary corn. In protein quality, Opaque-2 corn compares favorably with milk as food for young children. In some Latin American countries, where corn is a staple in the diet, efforts are under way to introduce this nutritionally superior corn. Often people refuse a nutritional improvement of their diet if it requires a change in their food habits. But the adoption of Opaque-2 does not require such a change.

Scientists continue to search for new sources of protein. One of these sources is fish protein concentrate, a tasteless, odorless powder made from whole fish. The powder can be added to food without changing the flavor or texture noticeably.

Algae are simple plants, of which seaweed is one example. These are another source of protein. Unfortunately, the un-desirable flavor of algae discourages their food uses at the present time.

Bacteria, a source of high-quality protein, can be grown on petroleum. Once freed of the petroleum, these bacteria may be a possible source of food.

Soybeans, long known to contain high-quality protein, are being processed to resemble meat and other popular food items. The soybean protein is isolated and later spun into fibers. These can be processed so that they look like meat, poultry, cheese, or nuts. Soybean products can be manufactured at a much lower cost than meat. Thus, they hold the promise of improving the diet of low-income groups in industrial nations, like the United States, where such foods as meat and poultry are very much a part of people's lives.

▶ **GOVERNMENT SAFETY MOVES**

Late in the year, Robert H. Finch, Secretary of Health, Education, and Welfare, banned the use of the artificial sweeteners known as cyclamates in beverages and most drugs, but not in foods. He gave September 1, 1970, as the deadline for removing from the market all beverages and drugs containing the artificial sweeteners. The Secretary's action was based on the discovery that large amounts of cyclamates caused cancer of the bladder in experiments with rats.

The safety of monosodium glutamate, a chemical often added to foods to heighten their flavor, was also questioned. The question of safety arose as the result of research done at the Washington University School of Medicine in St. Louis. Large doses of monosodium glutamate fed to infant mice caused damage to a part of the brain. Several makers of baby foods announced that they would stop using the chemical. The Food and Drug Administration planned to review monosodium glutamate and three other chemicals commonly added to foods. All had been considered safe.

HAZEL METZ FOX
University of Nebraska

4-H CLUBS. See YOUTH ORGANIZATIONS.

Charles de Gaulle, with his wife, vacations in Ireland after resigning French presidency.

FRANCE

ON April 28, 1969, at 11 minutes past midnight, the following message from President Charles de Gaulle flashed across France and around the world: "I cease to exercise my functions as President of the Republic. This decision takes effect today at noon."

So ended De Gaulle's reign of more than 10 years as president of France. Immediately politicians who had stood in his shadow began campaigns to replace the towering figure who had stamped on Europe the image of his Gaullist "grand design."

▶ DE GAULLE'S CAREER

Early in World War II, De Gaulle established himself as leader of the exiled Free French forces. The General returned in triumph to Paris at the Liberation. Elected president of the provisional Government of France in 1944, De Gaulle was credited during his first term in office with averting civil war. He disarmed rival Resistance groups, gambled on appointing Commu-

nists to key government posts, and introduced economic reforms. In 1946 he quit the Government, however, over the rejection of his wish that strong presidential powers be written into the new constitution.

De Gaulle was called out of retirement in 1958 by a nation again threatened with civil war—this time over the issue of Algerian independence. Given wide emergency powers, De Gaulle ended the war and "decolonized" Algeria and other French possessions in Africa. In September 1958 a new constitution providing for a presidential form of government was adopted by the voters of France.

The constitution De Gaulle secured gave him powers greater than those of any other democratically elected chief of state. He interpreted them as he saw fit. He withdrew French military forces from the North Atlantic Treaty Organization (NATO); he made France a nuclear power; and he personally explored diplomatic *détente* with the Soviet Union and with China.

De Gaulle repeatedly barred British attempts to enter the European Common Market. After the 1967 Six-Day War between Israel and the Arab states, De Gaulle cut off shipments of fighter planes to Israel and tried to gain influence among the Arabs. His policies angered Washington. And he infuriated Ottawa (Canada) by his attempts to woo French nationalists in Quebec.

On the home front, in the spring of 1968 massive student and worker demonstrations erupted. The workers were discontent with low wages, and the students sought better facilities and overall reforms. Although the demonstrations threatened to bring down the Government, De Gaulle announced his firm stand for "legitimacy" in the face of disorder, and called for a general election. When this was held late in June, De Gaulle's prestige won his supporters control of the National Assembly by the largest majority in French history.

In 1969 came anticlimax. De Gaulle threatened to quit unless a referendum on a Yes or No ballot approved his proposals to cut the powers of the Senate and grant greater autonomy to the French provinces. The prospect of a France without De Gaulle failed this time to rally the same support as in the past, and nearly 53 per cent of the voters rejected the reforms. Following this rebuff, De Gaulle, true to his word, resigned.

▶ FRANCE AFTER DE GAULLE

First to announce his candidacy to succeed De Gaulle was Georges Pompidou. Pompidou, age 57, had served as premier for 6 years, only to be dismissed by De Gaulle shortly after the 1968 "revolution." Pompidou swiftly aligned the support of a potential rival, former Finance Minister Valéry Giscard d'Estaing, whose influential Independent Republican Party often supported Gaullists in the National Assembly.

Gaston Defferre, 58, socialist mayor of Marseilles, also announced he would seek office. Communist Jacques Duclos, 72, declared his candidacy, and lesser candidates also entered the race. But the candidate who posed the greatest surprise threat to Pompidou was Alain Poher, 60. As president of the Senate, Poher became interim president of the Republic following De Gaulle's resignation.

In the first round of balloting, on June 1, Pompidou won 44.46 per cent of the votes, Poher 23.31 per cent. Duclos, who staged a final rally despite Leftist squabbling, emerged a close third. He promptly ordered his supporters not to vote in the runoff election between Pompidou and Poher. The decision by Duclos, which eliminated any anti-Pompidou sentiment Poher might have tapped among the Communists, helped lose the election for Poher. Pompidou became president with 58.2 per cent of the votes cast in the second round of balloting, on June 15.

Pompidou's choice as premier was Jacques Chaban-Delmas, an outspoken critic of De Gaulle's disregard of the legislature. Nevertheless, Pompidou spent two days after his inauguration forming, with Chaban-Delmas, a Cabinet designed to repair unity as well as the Gaullist image French voters had rejected. Pompidou appointed Maurice Schumann as foreign minister in place of Michel Debré, who had been cool toward Common Market policies and a hard-line Gaullist. In a series of appointments indicating a renewed willingness to co-operate with the other nations of Europe, he named Giscard d'Estaing finance minister, Jacques Duhamel as minister of agriculture, René Pleven as minister of justice, and Joseph Fontanet as minister of labor. Debré was named defense minister with the title of minister of state. At a meeting in Brussels in July, Schumann promptly indicated to Common Market ministers that Pompidou had dropped De Gaulle's policy of automatic veto of British attempts to join.

▶ ECONOMY

After a sudden surprise cabinet meeting August 8, the Government announced devaluation of the franc by 11.1 per cent, effective August 10. The decision reversed De Gaulle's refusal to devalue 9 months earlier, and cut the value of the franc from 20 cents to 18. Devaluation caused a Common Market crisis by lowering the prices of exported French farm products. Ministers in Brussels exempted French agricultural products from Common Market price structures for a year.

In September, simmering unrest at rising costs erupted in a series of railway, bus, and subway strikes. Wage demands threatened to undermine austerity measures imposed by Pompidou to avert runaway inflation resulting from the devaluation of the franc.

J. J. MEEHAN
United Press International
See also EUROPE, WEST.

FUTURE FARMERS OF AMERICA. See YOUTH ORGANIZATIONS.

GABON. See AFRICA.

GAMBIA. See AFRICA.

GAMES AND TOYS

A family plays Toss Across, a kind of ticktacktoe played with beanbags.

WHEN we go to a toy shop today, we find many more kinds of toys to choose from than we would have found in the same shop ten years ago. And the toys of today often seem to be more grown-up and more complicated than toys were in the past. One major reason for this change is that parents are more aware of the ways in which good toys and games help their children grow up. Another is that youngsters want their toys to be more and more like the objects in adult life they are meant to imitate. Toys of this sort that were especially popular in 1969 included miniature cars (about 2 to 6 inches long), powered by gravity or springs, which drive along plastic roadways; spaceman figures and equipment inspired by the moon landings; and novelty-action dolls and games.

▶ GAMES

Years ago a game was thought of as something to do indoors, sitting on the floor or around a table, on a rainy day. Today's games are frequently of this type. But many others require more action or mental skills than do the traditional kinds.

Several new action games for toddlers as well as for slightly older boys and girls made their debuts in 1969. One is a version of ticktacktoe in which beanbags are tossed into a box in an attempt to line up a trio of X's or O's. Another new action game is a grab-bag contest in which the bag grabs the player's hand if he does not remove some of the contents quickly enough. In another game, players attempt to shoot marbles through a maze full of obstacles that may take a player's marbles out of circulation.

In 1969 several new versions of the classic "strategy and capture" games were introduced. One makes it possible for four people to play checkers at the same time. A second combines many of the procedures of chess, regular checkers, and Chinese

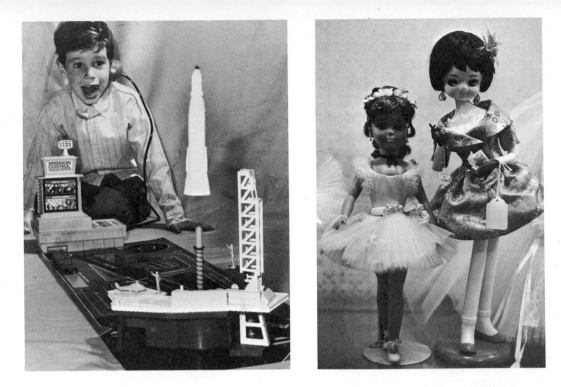

New toys for 1969 mirrored the year's happenings and trends. Toy moon rocket (above left) soars aloft from mini launching pad. Ethnic dolls (above right) were a welcome idea. And toy rock-polishing sets (below) tuned in on the great interest in the rocks brought back from the moon.

checkers. And a third provides a numbered playing board for chess beginners.

Other popular games were those that emphasize one or more of the three R's. These often employ flash cards. They are made for preschool youngsters and children in the early grades at school. Older children graduate naturally to anagrams and other traditional word-building games. A variation brought out in 1969 calls for the players to construct words while playing a rummy-style card game.

Pursuit-to-a-goal board games were great favorites during 1969 as always. A newcomer—for girls only—requires the players to go on a shopping spree, as directed by the results of a dice toss, to find something "just right" to wear for special occasions.

Board games with sports themes and tabletop mechanical- or electric-action sports games following the rules and play of baseball, football, hockey, basketball, or bowling continued to be popular. A newcomer to this family of games in 1969 was a mechanical hockey game in which the goalies are able to vacate their nets to block goals. Tabletop shuffleboard was another important addition.

▶ DOLLS

All through history the doll has been the most important and best-loved of toys. Recent additions to the traditional kinds of baby dolls and toddler dolls are fashion-model dolls, sometimes as much as 18 inches high, for which dresses and suits can be bought separately. Another new idea in dolls is the very large toddler doll, 31 inches high. Also in 1969, battery-powered or sound-wave-powered dolls became available. These dolls can play catch with a ball, play an accordian, or giggle at their own jokes.

The "ethnic doll" is a very important newcomer to the doll world. The first accurately made Negro doll was produced in 1968. And in 1969 a new all-Negro toy company in Los Angeles, the first of its kind, went into high gear, producing several models of black dolls.

▶ OTHER TOYS

Many other interesting toys apart from games and dolls made their appearance in 1969. Motorless vehicles for children in the form of cars, tractors, roadwork vehicles, and even airplanes to ride in and steer were great favorites. Dune buggies, inspired by the new sport of sand-dune driving, were popular—either in small-scale or big enough to ride in. Among small-scale vehicular toys, the most amusing in their mock realism were the ten-inch diesel trucks that give off "real" air pollution in the form of "real" smoke.

All kinds of other delights await today's browser or shopper in the toy store. Miniature power tools can be purchased, and so can plush toy animals in psychedelic colors. For the domestically inclined child there are dessert-making devices for easily turning out cakes, popcorn, cookies, cotton candy, or ice cream. But very likely none of these amusements thrilled the really up-to-date child any more than the space toys inspired by the Apollo 11 and 12 moon landings.

The toy astronauts themselves are either very like the real ones or are more fanciful, in the spirit of science fiction. Their vehicles and equipment also span a broad range from the real to the imaginative. They include such items as a space bubble, a space station, a space crawler, and a space sled. Some of the robot astronauts take off from a space base in a saucer that bounces off anything in its way. Others ride in a rocket ship that can be steered. To make these toys even more fun to play with, a copy of the lumpy moonscape can be made at home, either out of plaster of Paris or from rocks and sandy soil collected at the beach or in the yard. This will provide an interesting terrain for the space dolls and vehicles to scramble over.

LIONEL WEINTRAUB
President, Toy Manufacturers
of America, Inc.

A breccia moon rock shows glass-lined pits on its surface.

GEOLOGY, LUNAR

THE mission of Apollo 11 expanded man's knowledge of the geology of the moon. The astronauts brought moon samples from the Sea of Tranquility back to earth. These samples were examined and analyzed at NASA's Lunar Receiving Laboratory at the Manned Spacecraft Center in Houston, Texas. From these samples, scientists obtained new information about the moon's age and composition.

The lunar samples contained rocks and fine-grained material, or fines. Generally, fragments larger than one centimeter are called rocks. Fragments smaller than one centimeter are called fines.

▶ FINES

Fines make up about 28 of the 47 pounds of lunar material returned by the Apollo 11 astronauts. The fines consist of glass, rock fragments, and individual mineral grains. The fine-grained material is slightly brownish charcoal gray in color and averages about 0.1 millimeter in size.

About half of the fine-grained material is glass. Most of the glass fragments are angular. Some of the fragments, though, are round, oval, dumbbell-shaped, and teardrop-shaped.

▶ ROCKS

There were two kinds of rock found on the moon by Apollo 11. One is a crystalline rock. The other is an aggregate rock called a breccia.

Breccia

The breccias are gray to dark gray in color. They also have specks of white, light gray, and brownish gray. Breccias are a fused mixture of fine-grained material and fragments of mineral, rocks, and glass. The breccias were formed from crystalline rocks that were broken into small pieces by impact blasting on the surface of the moon. Many of these small pieces melted under the impact and were fused together with fine material to form a rock.

Crystalline Rocks

The crystalline rocks are igneous, or volcanic. That is, these rocks were once in a molten state.

The lunar crystalline rocks look very much like earth volcanic rocks. They range in size from fine-grained (0.1 millimeters) to medium-grained (1 to 2 millimeters). There are many spherical cavities or pits, called vesicles, throughout the rock. The pits are lined with glass.

The crystalline rocks are made up mostly of the minerals plagioclase feldspar ($CaAl_2Si_2O_8$), pyroxene ($Fe_{1/2}Mg_{1/2}$-$CaSi_2O_6$) and opaque minerals, mostly ilmenite ($FeTiO_3$). In addition, the fine-grained rocks contain some olivine ($FeMgSiO_4$). The medium-grained rocks contain some late-stage cristobalite (SiO_2). These minerals found in the moon rocks are the same minerals that are found in basalt, which is a common igneous rock in the earth's crust.

▶ GLASS

Glass occurs on the lunar surface in three manners. First there is the glass in the fine-grained material that was described above. Second there are glass splashes on the surface of some rocks. The third type of glass occurs as blebs in the center of small (about one-foot diameter) craters. These blebs look like glassy blisters or drops of solder. All of this glass probably formed during a meteorite impact. The impact caused the rocks to heat up enough to melt and the liquid rock to be thrown out forming a crater. The liquid rock then cooled into a glass.

▶ SHAPE OF THE LUNAR MATERIAL

Most rocks returned by Apollo 11 are rounded. This rounding was probably caused by solar radiation or micrometeorites hitting the rocks at high speeds and chipping the sharp edges off. The fine material is angular not rounded. This may be the result of repeated meteorite impact.

The lunar material shows small, glass-lined pits. There are also blemishes on the surface of many rocks, especially surrounding the pits. The blemishes are crushed feldspar crystals. Both the pits and the blemishes are the result of microparticle impacts at very high speeds.

▶ CHEMISTRY

The chemical makeup of both the lunar fines and rocks is basically similar to earth basalt. But lunar material is different from earth and meteorite material in the high content of refractory elements. Lunar material has more titanium, chromium, and zirconium than earth materials. Lunar material has a low content of the low-melting-point elements: sodium, potassium, lead, and rubidium. Also, the rocks lack minerals that contain water. Three new minerals were found in the lunar samples. For the time being, they have been named ferropseudobrookite pyroxmangite, and chromium-titanium spinel.

▶ DATING

Only some preliminary age dates of the lunar material were known by the end of 1969. The moon rocks that were returned by Apollo 11 were formed at least 3,500,000,000 years ago. This is not, however, the age of the moon. The earth, moon, and solar system are thought to be 4,500,000,000 years old.

▶ APOLLO 12 FINDINGS

While scientists continued to study the material described above, work began on the 75 pounds of lunar rock and soil brought back from the Ocean of Storms by Apollo 12. Early findings indicate that these rocks are perhaps a billion years younger than the material in the Sea of Tranquility.

JEFFREY WARNER
Associate Curator
Lunar Receiving Laboratory
Manned Spacecraft Center, NASA

See also ASTRONOMY; SPACE.

GERMANY. See EUROPE.

GHANA. See AFRICA.

GIRL SCOUTS. See YOUTH ORGANIZATIONS.

GOVERNORS

ONLY two gubernatorial elections were held in 1969. They generated national interest because President Richard Nixon gave campaign speeches in behalf of the Republican nominees, and both of them won.

In New Jersey, Congressman William T. Cahill defeated former Democratic Governor Robert Meyner, who was attempting a comeback. And in Virginia, for the first time in 84 years, Republicans took over the governorship with Linwood Holton, a personal friend of President Nixon. The losing Democratic candidate was William C. Battle. A Democrat, however, won the lieutenant governorship of Virginia.

With gubernatorial contests in 36 states, including California, New York, and Ohio, 1970 will be a most eventful election year. Governor Nelson Rockefeller of New York announced his candidacy for a fourth term. As of 1969, Republicans controlled the chief-executive position in nearly all Northern industrial states. They will want to hold these seats to strengthen the Republican position for the presidential election of 1972.

Since 1908 the governors have met in annual conferences. The 1969 National Governors Conference was held in Colorado Springs, Colorado, September 1–3. At the meeting, the governors called upon the Federal Government to finance all welfare costs. Governor John A. Love of Colorado was chosen chairman of the National Governors Conference for 1969–70.

There were also several regional gubernatorial conferences. At these conferences, governors meet in groups to discuss common problems. Crime control was one of the topics at the Midwestern Governors Conference held in Wichita, Kansas, June 30–July 2. Environmental problems and campus unrest were discussed at the Western Governors Conference in Seattle, Washington, July 28–31. And the bussing of students to achieve racial balance in schools was a major topic at the Southern Governors Conference in Williamsburg, Virginia, September 15–17.

HUGH A. BONE
University of Washington

GOVERNORS OF THE UNITED STATES

ALABAMA	Albert P. Brewer (D)	**MONTANA**	Forrest H. Anderson (D)
ALASKA	Keith H. Miller (R)	**NEBRASKA**	Norbert T. Tiemann (R)
ARIZONA	John R. Williams (R)	**NEVADA**	Paul Laxalt (R)
ARKANSAS	Winthrop Rockefeller (R)	**NEW HAMPSHIRE**	Walter R. Peterson (R)
CALIFORNIA	Ronald Reagan (R)	**NEW JERSEY**	William T. Cahill (R)*
COLORADO	John A. Love (R)	**NEW MEXICO**	David F. Cargo (R)
CONNECTICUT	John N. Dempsey (D)	**NEW YORK**	Nelson A. Rockefeller (R)
DELAWARE	Russell W. Peterson (R)	**NORTH CAROLINA**	Robert W. Scott (D)
FLORIDA	Claude R. Kirk, Jr. (R)	**NORTH DAKOTA**	William L. Guy (D)
GEORGIA	Lester G. Maddox (D)	**OHIO**	James A. Rhodes (R)
HAWAII	John A. Burns (D)	**OKLAHOMA**	Dewey Bartlett (R)
IDAHO	Donald Samuelson (R)	**OREGON**	Tom McCall (R)
ILLINOIS	Richard B. Ogilvie (R)	**PENNSYLVANIA**	Raymond P. Shafer (R)
INDIANA	Edgar D. Whitcomb (R)	**RHODE ISLAND**	Frank Licht (D)
IOWA	Robert D. Ray (R)	**SOUTH CAROLINA**	Robert E. McNair (D)
KANSAS	Robert B. Docking (D)	**SOUTH DAKOTA**	Frank Farrar (R)
KENTUCKY	Louie B. Nunn (R)	**TENNESSEE**	Buford Ellington (D)
LOUISIANA	John J. McKeithen (D)	**TEXAS**	Preston Smith (D)
MAINE	Kenneth M. Curtis (D)	**UTAH**	Calvin L. Rampton (D)
MARYLAND	Marvin Mandel (D)	**VERMONT**	Deane C. Davis (R)
MASSACHUSETTS	Francis W. Sargent (R)	**VIRGINIA**	Linwood Holton (R)*
MICHIGAN	William G. Milliken (R)	**WASHINGTON**	Daniel J. Evans (R)
MINNESOTA	Harold LeVander (R)	**WEST VIRGINIA**	Arch A. Moore, Jr. (R)
MISSISSIPPI	John Bell Williams (D)	**WISCONSIN**	Warren P. Knowles (R)
MISSOURI	Warren E. Hearnes (D)	**WYOMING**	Stanley K. Hathaway (R)

* Elected November 4, 1969

After the investiture of the Prince of Wales, the Royal procession leaves Caernarvon Castle.

GREAT BRITAIN

ON July 1, 1969, at Caernarvon Castle, Wales, a young man of 20 recited a feudal vow of fealty to his mother, Queen Elizabeth II: "I, Charles, Prince of Wales, do become your liege man of life and limb and of earthly worship, and faith and trust I will bear unto you to live and die against all manner of folks." With this vow came the climax of the investiture of Charles Philip Arthur George Windsor as Prince of Wales. The ancient pageantry of this ceremony cheered the hearts of the people of the United Kingdom of Great Britain and Northern Ireland during a time of crisis.

▶RELIGIOUS STRIFE IN NORTHERN IRELAND

The Government of Prime Minister Harold Wilson faced its gravest problem in Northern Ireland. Northern Ireland, which is often called Ulster, is part of the United Kingdom of Great Britain and Northern Ireland. It has its own domestic government, with a parliament and a prime minister, even though final authority rests with the British Government in London.

During much of 1969, Roman Catholics, demanding equality, and Protestant extremists fought street battles. Lives were lost, and great destruction was caused. The Catholics were supported by a young girl, Bernadette Devlin, who was elected to the British House of Commons on April 18.

Under pressure from both factions, Terence O'Neill, prime minister of Northern Ireland, called a general election February 24. Reverend Ian Paisley, a militant Protestant leader, campaigned against O'Neill for his parliamentary seat. O'Neill and his Unionist Party won 36 seats in the 52-seat House. But pressures continued on the Prime Minister, whose moderate policies sought equality for the Catholic minority in local elections, employment, and housing.

In April, violence exploded in the streets of Londonderry, Northern Ireland's second largest city. A group of about 1,000 Catholic civil-rights demonstrators clashed with followers of Paisley. Street fighting continued until the Royal Ulster Constabulary, the strongly pro-Protestant police force, drove Catholics back into their home neighborhood, the Bogside district. Catholics put barricades across streets leading to Bogside, but not before many Catholic homes had been hit by fire bombs hurled by Protestants. News of the rioting touched off Catholic-Protestant clashes in other cities. Saboteurs set fire to nine post offices in Belfast and blew up a vital water main. Prime Minister O'Neill then called for help from Britain, which retains final authority for the region.

Wilson agreed to let British troops stationed in Ulster guard power stations and

British Prime Minister Harold Wilson faced many problems during 1969, chief among them the religious strife in Northern Ireland.

other public utilities. But he told O'Neill that unless Ulster's Parliament legislated "one-man-one-vote" equality for Catholics in local elections, the British Government would order the reform. O'Neill made local-election rights an issue of personal confidence among Unionist members of the Ulster Parliament. He won their support for legislation by a narrow vote of 28 to 22.

O'Neill's opponents then forced a meeting of the 800-member Unionist Party council to review his action, which for the first time would enable thousands of Catholics to vote in local elections. Faced with a rejection of his policies by the council, O'Neill resigned. He gave his support to middle-of-the-road Unionist James Chichester-Clark. Chichester-Clark was approved by a single vote.

In July, Londonderry exploded again. When rioting subsided, one man lay dead. More than 100 were injured, including 50 policemen.

In August, the worst Catholic-Protestant riots in over 30 years raged through Londonderry and Belfast. Police had to use tear gas to quell crowds. The toll in destruction, dead, and injured rose above that of July. Chichester-Clark appealed for direct use of British troops to restore order. London responded by sending 300 soldiers to Londonderry. A force of 600 British troops marched into Belfast. Eight persons were killed and nearly 800 wounded.

Chichester-Clark then flew to London for talks with Prime Minister Wilson. The two agreed to grant Lieutenant General Sir Ian Freeland, British commander, full authority over the Northern Ireland police. The Catholics welcomed this move, seeing the British troops as the only body that could possibly protect their rights and their lives.

A bitter peace, maintained only by the presence of the British troops, collapsed in October. Battles raged more viciously than ever, and British troops were ordered to shoot to kill snipers. One policeman and 2 civilians died; 56 persons were injured; and 22 British soldiers were hospitalized with gunshot wounds. At year's end, the number of British troops in Northern Ireland had risen to 9,000.

▶ **LABOR PARTY TROUBLES**

As the fighting in Northern Ireland continued, Prime Minister Wilson faced other problems. In May, his ruling Labor Party lost heavily in local elections in England, Scotland, and Wales. Voters swept Labor members from hundreds of seats on local councils all over Britain.

Disillusion with Wilson's leadership sharpened into a party revolt. As many as 100 Labor members of the 104 in the House of Commons pledged to oppose government plans to increase the low individual charges for Britain's National Health Service by 25 per cent. Nearly as many Labor M. P.'s rallied against legislation drafted to curb widespread wildcat strikes. Opposition to the antistrike legislation cut deep into the trade-union movement, the foundation of Labor Party political and financial strength.

Prime Minister Wilson had given up an earlier plan to control wages by decree. Chancellor of the Exchequer Roy Jenkins disclosed Wilson's retreat and announced government backing for the antistrike bill, called the Industrial Relations Act, in his annual House of Commons budget address in April. The budget imposed $816,000,000 in new taxes. The Government, aware that Labor had fallen as much as 20 per cent behind Conservatives in popularity polls, tailored the new taxes to fall most heavily on wealthy Britons and on businessmen. But the union chiefs still told Wilson that they would mass their forces against the antistrike bill.

Trade statistics published in the wake of Labor's May election losses added to Wilson's woes. The figures disclosed that the gap between what Britain sold and bought abroad in April had widened to a $141,600,000 deficit. Continued refusals by union leaders to drop their opposition to antistrike legislation forced Wilson to delay the bill and finally to drop it in June. In return the Trades Union Congress promised to avert or settle strikes it considered unreasonable.

In spite of the troubles in Northern Ireland, his earlier popularity plunge, and internal Labor Party quarrels, Wilson's fortunes rose markedly toward the end of 1969. Exports reached record levels, and a $115,000,000 trade surplus was registered in August. The annual autumn Labor Party conference voted complete confidence in Wilson's leadership. Labor cut the Conservative lead in some public-opinion polls to less than 10 per cent.

J. J. MEEHAN
United Press International

See also CHARLES, PRINCE OF WALES; DEVLIN, BERNADETTE.

GREECE. See EUROPE, WEST.

GUATEMALA. See LATIN AMERICA.

GUINEA. See AFRICA.

GUYANA. See LATIN AMERICA.

HAITI. See LATIN AMERICA.

A model-rocket enthusiast installs descent parachutes in his miniature spacecraft.

HOBBIES

THE sight of astronauts walking about on the moon's surface created new interest in many hobbies as well as in real space activities. Model rockets, many of them scale models of the real thing, and stamps honoring the Apollo moon missions were added to collections all over the world. Even coin collectors got into the space act, as private mints issued special coins to honor American astronauts.

▶ CRAFT AND MODEL HOBBIES

During 1969, creative hobbies attracted many more thousands of fans. Creative hobbies are those which offer the hobbyist the opportunity to put something together. Generally, creative hobbies include model-kit building, or putting together plastic or wooden pieces to construct a scale model of an airplane, vehicle, ship, or boat; science items, such as microscopes, human- or animal-anatomy kits; and model-railroad scenic layouts. They also include hundreds of different handicraft projects.

Model Rocketry

New safety elements in launching model rockets, and the tremendous interest in the 1969 moon landings, attracted many young hobbyists to model rocketry.

A junior space technician prepares his model rocket for lift-off. At right, the rocket reaches its highest point, and the descent parachutes are deployed.

For some years following World War II, many states did not allow model rockets. They were considered dangerous. In 1969, only a few states still restricted model-rocket sales and launchings. When approved equipment is used, and safety procedures are followed, statistics show that model rocketry is even less dangerous than gas-model-airplane activity.

Model rocketry is a highly technical scientific hobby. It appears to be an ideal father-and-son hobby because adult supervision is recommended. And adult interest in model rockets is at least as high as that of younger people.

Narrow-Gage Railroading

Most young people today have never seen a locomotive train. It may be possible therefore that about a decade from now model railroading will be of only historical interest. The average age of today's model-railroad enthusiast is 34 years. Only about 20 per cent are in the 8-to-19 age group.

The tiny "N"-gage trains and accessories in such demand during 1969 were popular with hobbyists in Europe twenty years ago. However, it has not been until recently that the micro-miniature-scale mechanisms have been perfected enough to permit little chance of mechanical failure. Today these

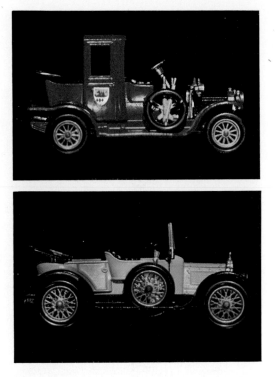

"Models of Yesteryear" miniature automobiles: a fire-engine-red 1912 Packard Landaulet and a 1911 Daimler.

tiny trains can run around the track many hours without mechanical problems.

Crafts

Stained-glass art craft was popular among handicraft enthusiasts. Handicrafters used kits to make Tiffany-type lampshades, jewelry pins, mobiles, candleholders, table ornaments, and even "cathedral" stained-glass windows. The kits include preshaped colored-glass pieces, high-gloss channel lead, wire, and solder.

The best-selling craft and art was painting by numbers. Other popular crafts were liquid-plastic-resin projects, decoupage, bead flowers, gold-leafing, and feather flowers.

Miniature Cars

Die-cast scale-model cars continued to be the most popular collectors' hobby in 1969. The number of such hobbyists was estimated to be about 6,000,000 throughout the world. They spent about $65,000,-000 for miniature cars at an average cost of 65 cents each. Most collectors were in the 8-to-12-year-old group. From the age of 14 on, interest in the miniature cars tends to vanish and be replaced by a more direct interest in owning and driving the real thing.

The newest trend in collectors' miniature vehicles was the addition of extremely free-rolling wheels which allows for extra play value.

WILLIAM H. VAN PRECHT
Consultant, Hobby Industry
Association of America

▶ **STAMPS**

On July 20, 1969, artronaut Neil Armstrong became the first man to set foot on the moon. To commemorate this event the U.S. Post Office issued a stamp that was 50 per cent larger than any other U.S. commemorative stamp. In fact, it was the largest stamp ever issued in the United States.

The initial printing of this stamp was 120,000,000. But the demand was so great that more printings were made. A record number of first-day covers were also sold.

The die, from which plates for printing the stamps were made, was taken to the moon by the Apollo 11 astronauts. When the astronauts returned to earth they were kept in quarantine for almost three weeks. The die was also quarantined. This was one of the reasons for the delay in issuing the stamp. The 10¢ airmail stamp did not appear at post-office windows until September 9.

Many other new stamps were issued in 1969. Most of these were commemoratives. In January, four stamps were issued for the "Beautification of America." These stamps had an unusual feature. The sheets were in the usual fifty-stamp size. But each block of four in the sheet consisted of four different stamps. The same feature

New stamps of 1969. Among the major events commemorated are the Apollo 11 moon walk, the Pope's African visit, and the investiture of the Prince of Wales.

had been used as long ago as 1936 to commemorate the Third International Philatelic Exhibition held in New York.

Other commemorative stamps that appeared during 1969 were:

Fiftieth Anniversary of the American Legion.

Grandma Moses.

Apollo 8 Mission.

Two Hundredth Anniversary of California's Settlement.

John Wesley Powell.

Alabama Statehood Anniversary.

Botanical Congress.

Daniel Webster (Dartmouth College Case).

One Hundredth Anniversary of Baseball.

General Eisenhower.

Christmas Commemorative.

Crippled Children and Adults Rehabilitation.

Other than these commemoratives, two interesting items were issued during 1969. One of these was a stamped envelope with the unusual denomination of 1.6¢. These envelopes will be used by charitable and nonprofit organizations. Such organizations have special, lower rates for bulk mailing. The second item was the first U.S. issued, multicolored 6¢ stamp in coil form. It shows the American flag and White House.

Canada issued about 15 stamps in 1969. One stamp commemorated the 200th anniversary of Charlottetown, Prince Edward Island. Another commemorated the 50th anniversary of the first nonstop crossing of the Atlantic Ocean by air.

HERMAN HERST, JR.
Columnist, *Hobbies Magazine*

Coins from the Lilly collection, left to right: Transylvania, 1657; Hildesheim, 1528; Roman Empire, A.D. 134–8; Byzantine Empire, 1028–34; Nuremberg, 1680.

▶ COINS AND COIN COLLECTING

The portrait of Abraham Lincoln first appeared on the U.S. one-cent piece in 1909. This fine portrait was sculptured by Victor D. Brenner. Over the years, some of the details in Lincoln's features were lost. Because of this, Mint engravers made a redesigned master die. Thus the 1969 cents came out of the Mint with much more detail than the 1968 cents. This was a small but important move for those who appreciate the beauty of coinage.

On May 26 the Smithsonian Institution put on display the Josiah K. Lilly gold collection. The Smithsonian had acquired the 6,125-piece collection in 1968.

The new United States Mint in Philadelphia was dedicated on August 14. It is the largest and most automated mint in the world. It cost $39,400,000.

The new Mint can produce 8,000,000,-000 coins a year. This is at least twice the number any other mint can produce. This can be done because of many new processes. A revolutionary new coin roller, for example, can produce 10,000 coins a minute.

The coin shortages that began in the mid-1960's ended in 1969. One reason for this was that the Nixon administration ended the ban against the melting and exporting of silver coins. The Government also eased gold-coin import regulations. Foreign coins minted before 1934 can now be brought into the United States without restriction.

In January 1969, David M. Kennedy became secretary of the Treasury. Mrs. Dorothy Andrews Elston became treasurer. When they took office a new series of currency, dated 1969, was launched.

Before these appointments, in the closing days of the Johnson administration, Joseph W. Barr was named secretary of the Treasury. He served for only four weeks. But during that time a surprise $1 1963 B currency series was issued. Over 470,000,-000 were printed during the next five months.

The issue of high-denomination notes was halted during 1969. This included issue of $500, $1,000, $5,000, and $10,000 notes. Actually none had been printed for almost 25 years. Now only $1, $5, $10, $20, $50, and $100 notes are in circulation.

In 1969, Congress considered legislation that would restore the $1 coin to circulation. This move was supported by the vending industry as well as by the Treasury and Mint people. The old silver dollar was last produced in 1935. Advocates of the $1 coin want a coin of the same size as the old silver dollar. It would, however, have little or no silver. It would have a portrait of Dwight D. Eisenhower.

In 1969, coin prices continued their upward trend. This rise in prices was particularly strong in the case of common U.S. coins. These have become tied to the world gold markets.

A Roman-numeral-dated, high-relief, plain-edge, wire-rim variety of the 1907 Saint-Gaudens double eagle ($20 gold) was uncovered in 1969. It had gone unlisted for some sixty years.

CLIFFORD MISHLER
Numismatic Editor
Coins Magazine and *Numismatic News*

HOUSING

IN the field of housing, 1969 started on a note of optimism, with outgoing President Johnson calling for a total housing and community-development budget of about $2,772,000,000, or $459,000,000 more than in 1968. He saw the money as going to strengthen programs begun under the landmark Housing and Urban Development Act, passed August 1, 1968.

The programs to receive funds in 1969 included public housing, rent supplements, Model Cities plans (programs aimed at improving the total environment, social as well as physical), and urban renewal. President Johnson placed the number of "dwelling units" (houses or apartments) to be built or revamped in the year at 503,000.

▶ HOUSING STARTS

In January the "housing starts" rate was 1,878,000. ("Housing starts" is the term used for the beginning of construction of one dwelling unit and the rate applies to the number of housing starts in a year.) Starts on private homes were particularly good in January, having increased 22 per cent over December 1968. By the end of the year, however, the rate of starts was down to 1,336,000.

▶ CONSTRUCTION-INDUSTRY PROBLEMS

After February the United States construction industry faced many problems that resulted in falling rates in housing starts through the rest of the year. Chief among the difficulties were higher interest rates and a shrinking supply of Federal monies available for mortgages.

Labor problems and the pattern of their settlement created the second obstacle to health in the housing field in 1969. Labor Secretary George P. Shultz revealed that of all construction-industry labor negotiations between January 1 and mid-September, 31 per cent had resulted in strikes (as com-

pared with the overall U.S.-industry figure of 13 per cent). As a result of negotiations, construction workers gained a median 15.1 per cent increase in wage and fringe benefits in 1969. This was more than double the size of median wage-benefit increases in U.S. industry viewed as a whole. These gains for workers, coupled with high land costs and high interest rates, had the overall effect of slowing the growth of the industry.

Another problem facing the housing industry in 1969 was discrimination. In Pittsburgh and other cities, Negro workers held demonstrations to emphasize their demands that they be given more jobs in the construction industry. To help overcome this problem, President Nixon established a new Construction Industry Collective Bargaining Commission, which might help solve the problems affecting labor unions, minority groups, and the building industry. Labor Secretary Shultz ordered into effect the "Philadelphia Plan," stipulating "goals" for hiring of minority groups in six skilled craft unions working on Federally assisted housing.

▶ GOVERNMENT ACTIONS

On May 8, George Romney, secretary of housing and urban development, put forward a new plan to increase greatly the number of low-cost housing units. The plan, Operation Breakthrough, is essentially one to gain volume production. This would be done through the use of more prefabricated homes and parts of homes and less on-site construction. Under this new approach to solving the housing problem, much more of the work of providing housing would take place in the factory. Mobile homes as well as prefab housing played a part in Secretary Romney's vision of the future.

In mid-September, Mr. Eugene Gulledge, president of the National Association of Home Builders, was chosen by President Nixon to head the Federal Housing Administration (FHA). His post carries the titles of assistant secretary of housing and urban development and Federal housing commissioner.

▶ **OUTLOOK FOR THE FUTURE**

Two major events of the fall seemed signposts for the future. In mid-September, Preston Martin, Federal Home Loan Bank board chairman, announced that local savings and loan associations will henceforth be allowed to borrow on ten-year terms for investment in "inner city" housing (the traditional borrowing period had been one year). This action was taken to encourage local savings and loan associations to use advances from their District Home Loan banks to fund Government-approved and -insured projects. The aim of the Nixon administration was to give the local savings and loan groups experience with large-scale risk-free lending so that they will later move on to fully private lending to low- and moderate-income housing.

Then, on October 1, President Nixon announced a cutback of $215,000,000 in funds for the Model Cities program scheduled for the fiscal year July 1969-June 1970. Whether this cut only reflects a postponement in spending, as the Department of Housing and Urban Development claims, was not absolutely clear. But a government tendency to favor private-enterprise solutions and to hold down on direct infusions of Federal funds—even into Federally-inspired programs in the field of housing—seemed in late 1969 to be taking shape.

HUSAK, GUSTAV

AFTER the August 1968 Soviet invasion and occupation of Czechoslovakia, the world waited for major political changes. The first of many changes came on April 17, 1969. On that day, Alexander Dubcek, first secretary of the Czechoslovak Communist Party and leader of the country's liberalization program, was forced to resign. He was replaced by Gustav Husak, first secretary of the Slovak Communist Party.

Husak was drawn from the ranks of the "centrists." Centrist politicians are liberal in theory, but they believe that co-operation with the Soviet Union is the only realistic road for Czechoslovakia to follow. In office, Husak promised that he would not return to the repressive policies of the past. He warned, however, that he would not tolerate anti-Soviet riots that could bring more Russian troops into the country.

The selection of Husak pleased the Soviet Union. But Czechoslovaks viewed him with mixed emotions. They believed he would tighten political controls to please the Soviets. But they also felt he would be more effective in dealing with the Soviets than Dubcek had been.

Gustav Husak was born on January 10, 1913, in Bratislava, in the Slovak part of the country. He became a member of the Communist Party in 1933, but during the Stalinist purges he was imprisoned for nine years. He was released in 1960 and allowed to rejoin the Communist Party three years later.

Husak was named a deputy premier of Czechoslovakia in April 1968. After the Soviet occupation later that year, he became first secretary of the Slovak Communist Party and a member of the Czechoslovak Communist Party Central Committee and Presidium. In November he was elected a member of the Executive Committee of the Presidium. His 1969 appointment to the post of first secretary of the national Communist Party climaxed his fast rise to power.

See also CZECHOSLOVAKIA.

ICELAND. See EUROPE, WEST.

Indians show their support of Prime Minister Indira Gandhi.

INDIA

INDIA celebrated the 100th anniversary of the birth of Mahatma Gandhi in 1969. Gandhi, the apostle of nonviolence, led India to independence from British rule. But the year-long celebrations were marred by outbreaks of civil disorder and violence.

▶ CIVIL DISORDERS

Hindus and Muslims clashed violently in September in Gujurat, Gandhi's home state. It was the most serious outbreak of Hindu-Muslim communal strife since the British withdrew in 1947. The Indian Army was called to restore order, and a curfew was imposed. More than 400 people, mostly Muslims, were killed. The incident began in the city of Ahmedabad, the capital of Gujurat. It was touched off when cows, which the Hindus worship, strayed onto the grounds of a Muslim mosque. Angry Muslims drove off the herd, and a riot ensued. It quickly engulfed the region. Arson, looting, and mob violence continued for six days before order was restored.

The strife coincided with the climax of the Gandhi centenary, October 2, 1969. Ironically, throughout his life, Gandhi preached tolerance and nonviolence. "Intolerance is a special species of violence and therefore against our creed," he cautioned his followers.

Earlier in the year, civil disorder swept the cities of Bombay and Hyderabad. The violence in Bombay began when right-wing militants demanded settlement of a border dispute between the states of Maharashtra and Mysore. The demonstrators also demanded full autonomy for the Marathi-speaking people of Maharashtra. By the time the riots were over, 43 persons had been killed, hundreds had been injured, and more than 1,000 had been arrested.

Violence swept Hyderabad, the capital of Andhra Pradesh State, in June. Demonstrators there demanded a separate Telengana state within Andhra Pradesh. Prime Minister Gandhi visited the city to try to quiet the mobs. Troops were brought in to restore order.

▶ **POWER STRUGGLE IN THE CONGRESS PARTY**

During the year there was an intense struggle for power in the Congress Party. The party has governed India since independence. The struggle unfolded between a left-wing faction led by Prime Minister Indira Gandhi and a faction called the "Syndicate." This group represents conservative industrialist interests and has long controlled the Congress Party.

Prime Minister Gandhi sought to gain control of the Congress Party. She forced her Syndicate rival, Deputy Prime Minister Moraji Desai, from the Cabinet. And, over the strong objections of the Syndicate, she endorsed the election of V. V. Giri as the fourth president of India. (India's third president, Zakir Husain, died on May 3.) The Prime Minister also introduced a series of economic measures which the Syndicate opposed. One was the nationalization of India's 14 largest banks.

In November the Syndicate expelled the Prime Minister from the Congress Party. Mrs. Gandhi called the move illegal. Immediately a majority of Congress Party members in Parliament gave her a vote of confidence. The Syndicate then tried to censure her Government. But a motion to censure for the "humiliation" of being left out of a meeting of Islamic nations in Morocco was defeated. The Prime Minister had won her first battle in Parliament with the Syndicate.

However, to retain power Prime Minister Gandhi will have to form an alliance with Leftist and independent parties. Or she will have to call a general election in 1970.

▶ **FOREIGN RELATIONS**

Prime Minister Gandhi visited Japan in June to meet with Japanese Prime Minister Eisaku Sato. The two leaders discussed Asian security. On July 31 and August 1, President Richard Nixon of the United States met with Prime Minister Gandhi in New Delhi.

India has generally pursued a policy of nonalignment in foreign affairs. However, in 1969, India's Foreign Minister Dinesh Singh said that India supported the Soviet Union in its border dispute with Communist China. India was particularly concerned about followers of Communist Chinese leader Mao Tse-tung setting up bases in remote Indian villages. Pictures and slogans of Mao Tse-tung were seen during the year in rural areas of some states.

▶ **THE ECONOMY**

The year saw a general improvement in India's economic outlook. Overall exports were up and imports were down. By the start of 1969 the trade deficit had decreased. In 1968 the deficit was $735,000,000; in 1967 it had been $1,180,000,000.

India's best gains were made in agricultural production. The food situation was no longer critical. However, the United States continued its massive food-grain shipments to bolster India's reserves.

The production of wheat was particularly successful. Improved fertilizers, better irrigation, and high-yield strains of wheat were being used to increase production. In 1968 and 1969, India did not have to import as much wheat as in previous years. By the mid-1970's, India is expected to become an exporter of wheat.

In 1969, India's first nuclear-power station began operations. The station is at Tarapur, near Bombay. In Bihar State, India's first uranium mine and mill began producing uranium concentrates.

ARNOLD C. BRACKMAN

INDONESIA. See ASIA.

Upholstered foam seating units, which can be pulled apart and rearranged.

INTERIOR DESIGN

HISTORY shows clearly that broad social change has always been a factor in design and in the creation of environment. But perhaps only with time will we be able to pinpoint such changes in the remarkable year of 1969 when man enbarked on the interplanetary age. When you read history, change seems sharp and significant. It is pinned down to definite dates. But when you are living through such periods, change seems to go more slowly. Social changes that are now developed have been years in the making.

In 1969 many social problems and factors influenced interior design. Overpopulation, the housing shortage and less living space influenced interior design. So, too, did population mobility, especially the continuing trend toward cities. Other influencing factors were the increasing demands by the disadvantaged minorities for better living standards, and the continuing youth explosion.

Technological progress, too, continued to provide new approaches to interior design in 1969. Advances by industries dealing in plastics, man-made fibers, and paper proved so readily acceptable that they were quickly taken for granted in interior design.

Fads and fashions in interior design are given too much space by the press. It is therefore necessary to discount much that is reported as being new or trend-setting. Fads are, after all, short-lived. It is not until a fashion has become an accepted style that it becomes important. This rarely happens unless the fashion has definite new advantages.

Op, pop, and supergraphics, for example, are fashions even though they were reported as trends. Motifs with harsh, psychedelic colors, designed to exemplify youth, and unconventional lighting effects were also reported as trends. These trends dominated model rooms, photographed interiors, and other displays in 1969. But most young people who were actually planning rooms to live in were far more conservative in their tastes.

Similarly, a return to the 1930's theme was called a trend in 1969. The 1930's theme was a re-creation of the cinematic dreams of set designers from old Jean Harlow films and Busby Berkeley spectaculars. This design used fantasies of white, silver, and crystal with low, squashy furniture and deep, pale carpets. Such furnishings are not practical in a servantless society. And the 1930's theme did not take hold.

Innovations in 1969 which show evidence of survival power are listed below.

▶ WALLS

A great variety of original wallpapers were produced in 1969, and wall treatments became important. Metallic wallpapers were very popular. The polished, lacquered, or "wet," look gave walls a new dimension. And there were many experiments in vinyl and coated wall coverings. Two wallpaper designs were especially popular. One was a small, allover geometric design. The other was a large design with stylized flowers and symbols. Among the new wall coverings was a light, carpet-like material, which gives the effect of running the floor carpet up the walls. It is long-lasting and costs little to maintain.

▶ FLOORS

Wall-to-wall carpeting continued to appeal to most people. There was also a marked interest in new, tough "outdoor" carpets. These were used for indoor heavy-duty areas such as kitchens. However, there was a declining interest in hard-surface flooring such as vinyl tile.

Wood flooring became important again. Innovators bleached wood floors and rubbed them with white paint, stained them with colors or painted them in brilliant shades. There was more interest in wood floor patterns. Old wood parquets, herring-bones and checkerboards, narrow- and wide-board flooring were widely reproduced.

Pattern-on-pattern—different, sometimes dazzling and often jarring—was a popular fad in 1969.

There were two extremes in carpet textures: very flat and tightly woven, and very shaggy and loose. Rugs reflected this carpet trend. But the outstanding rug of 1969 was the animal skin. Flat, silky, smooth-haired skins such as pony and steer were much in demand. Zebra, however, was the most popular of the animal skins. The appeal of the black-and-white zebra hide gave conservationists concern about the survival of this species. Such animal-skin patterns were also copied in fur fabrics, straw, and other types of material.

▶ PATTERN

Patterns played an important role in home decorating in 1969. Many of these patterns were geometric. There was a vogue for mixing patterns of several scales, styles, and colors in one room. Pattern-on-pattern was stressed. That is, walls might have one pattern, the ceiling another, upholstery another, and rugs another. The effect, often dazzling, could also be confusing. Pattern-on-pattern resulted in restless rooms. This will not become a permanent part of the decorating world.

Selenite (left) and septarium are among the more expensive minerals available for decorative purposes. This selenite sample sells for $125, the septarium for $89.

▶ WINDOW TREATMENT

More and more people extended wall treatments to the window areas. Blinds or shades were covered, or laminated, with the same material used on the walls. Roman shades, for example, were made of fabric-matching wall coverings. Curtaining depended on fabric interest rather than elaborate styling. Experiments were made with ropes of hanging beads for window coverings. These were designed to rid the homemaker of maintaining curtains.

▶ FURNITURE

Interest in oiled or waxed wood in furniture declined in 1969. Instead pale woods, such as blond ash or oak, were popular for furniture. Much new furniture was made of polished chrome, stainless steel, and heavy plate glass. Chrome and steel were used instead of brass in furniture hardware. Thick plate glass replaced marble, for example, as tabletops. Lacquered and high-gloss surfaces were chosen instead of conventional wood finishes.

Many people mixed richly upholstered and tufted furniture pieces with the steel and glass elements in rooms. Linen, velvet, and needlepoint were in demand as upholstery fabrics. These soft, sheenless surfaces acted as counterpoint to the high shine of the steel and glass.

Innovations in plastic furniture were see-through-plastic pieces and inflatables. Chairs and even sofas were made of sausagelike rolls of high-colored plastic. These could be blown up with a vacuum cleaner or a bicycle pump. Such furniture remained conversation pieces at best. However, they indicate the future use of plastic as a material of its own and not as imitation of something else.

▶ ACCESSORIES

The large, often overpowering abstraction, or hard-edge oil painting, was a continuing choice as an accessory in 1969. But such art often seemed to represent status more than genuine taste. Spectacular graphics as well as colorful designs in silk were framed for walls. Posters were widely used and beloved by the young.

Plate-glass surface renewed interest in crystal and glass accessories. Decorative obelisks, eggs, paperweights, goblets, and other objects of varying shapes made of clear crystal and glass, plain or faceted, were unusually displayed in groups.

The accessory of the year, however, was definitely the rock. Every variety of mineral

Multipurpose "machine for living" is used for storage, studying, and sleeping.

was used as decoration. Some were polished, some left in their crude state. Others were arranged randomly or mounted on bases of plastic or brass. Rock hunters swarmed over the countryside, and dealers who sold rocks were kept very busy. The nearest contender to the rock was the seashell.

▶ **COLORS**

The main color choices in 1969 were in the citrus family. These colors went from pale lemon yellow through the yellow-green spectrum to brilliant parrot green. In midyear there was an emergence of a new pastel called Canton pink. Also, lilac and lavender, long ignored in decoration, came on strong. These colors made an impression on people weary of the clashing psychedelic colors.

▶ **MULTIPURPOSE ROOMS AND FURNITURE**

There was more interest in dual, triple, and all-purpose rooms. Rooms were planned for many uses at all hours of the day and night: sitting room-bedrooms, bedroom-living rooms, library-dining rooms,

home office-library-guest rooms, living-dining-kitchens, bar-television-library-cardrooms. Furniture reflected this trend by being suitable for any room. And there was more interest in concealed beds, sofa beds, and other types of furniture capable of leading a double life.

Many of the achievements in 1969 were the result of trends that began several years ago. New ideas seen in 1969 may indicate a future trend. One pioneering effort was the "furniture landscape," in which modules, or units, of upholstered foam rubber are fitted together to form one large furnishing or separated to create several small furnishings. Another was a "machine for living," a compact furniture unit which can be moved into almost any sort of space. One such unit contains drawers, shelves, desk, seats, bed, and lighting.

WILLIAM PAHLMANN
Fellow, American Institute
of Interior Designers

ITALY

Prisoners rioting in Milan—one of the many problems that plagued Italy during 1969.

DURING 1969, Italy was torn by domestic turmoil. Strikes, riots, student unrest, and the collapse of the Government all created an atmosphere of crisis.

▶ PREMIER RUMOR RESIGNS

The coalition of center and left-wing parties that governed Italy under Premier Mariano Rumor collapsed in July. It was the 29th Government to fall since the end of World War II. The collapse came about when the Socialist Party, coalition partner of Rumor's Christian Democratic Party, split over the question of co-operation with the Communist Party.

▶ RUMOR FORMS A NEW GOVERNMENT

President Saragat immediately asked Rumor to try to form another coalition Government of center and left-wing parties. Rumor's early efforts failed, as did efforts by Senate President Amintore Fanfani. Rumor explored the possibilities of forming a coalition with one or the other of the two socialist parties, but right-wingers in his own party rejected collaboration with the left-wing Socialists. Rumor was thus forced to form a minority Christian Democratic Government whose shaky survival depended on approval of its actions by both squabbling socialist factions. The new Government was sworn in on August 6.

▶ DOMESTIC STRIFE

The emergence of the thirtieth Government from the worst crisis in the country since World War II scarcely brightened the grim outlook in Italy. During this year, strikes and violence were widespread. Prisoners rioted; opposing student factions clashed in the streets; and there were crippling strikes by civil servants, railroad workers, farm workers, and others. Italy urgently needed reforms to cut red tape and inefficiency and to narrow the gap between the rich and the poor. Yet Premier Rumor and his minority Government stood no chance of legislating these reforms because the opposing factions in Parliament were constantly squabbling. No solutions appeared possible short of general elections in 1970. Politicians predicted that the Communists, who already controlled more than 25 per cent of the electorate, would score large gains at that time.

J. J. MEEHAN
United Press International

IVORY COAST. See AFRICA.
JAMAICA. See WEST INDIES.

President Nixon welcomes Prime Minister Eisaku Sato to Washington.

JAPAN

FOR the first time since the end of World War II, Japan showed signs of changing its foreign policy. "Regarding the problem of Asian security," Prime Minister Eisaku Sato observed after the United States withdrew the first of its combat troops from Vietnam, "it is Japan that is gradually going to play the leading role while the United States will be co-operating from the sidelines."

Japan's Finance Minister Takeo Fukuda enlarged on this theme. He said that the time is approaching for Japan to assume the burden of its own defense.

▶ JAPAN'S NEW ROLE IN ASIA

Japan's gradual emergence in Asia as a power factor stems from four basic developments: increasing Soviet naval activity in the Indian Ocean, through which 90 per cent of Japan's oil requirements are shipped; Communist China's development of a nuclear arsenal; the British withdrawal from east of Suez, which will be completed by 1971; and the moves by the United States to disengage from Vietnam.

Japan plans to increase its foreign aid to the poorer nations of Asia. Japanese aid to Asia will double in the next 5 years. By the mid-1970's, aid is expected to reach $700,000,000 a year. By 1980, Japan's aid to Asia could be $5,000,000,000 a year.

Japan, which has depended upon the United States for its defense, spends about $12 per person per year on defense. (The United States spends about $370 per person on its own defense.) Accordingly, the United States wants Japan to pick up more of the costs of Japanese defense. If the Japanese economy continues to expand at its present pace, Japan is expected to spend $2,400,000,000 on weapons by 1975. At this rate, it will have a formidable military establishment by 1980.

In 1969, Japan's Defense Agency called for strengthening the armed forces. One area in which defense will be bolstered is in Japan's northern sea frontier with the Soviet Union. A small naval force will be installed at Yoichi, a port on the northern island of Hokkaido. With this, for the first time since World War II, Japan will have a permanent naval establishment patrolling the Hokkaido waters.

▶ RETURN OF OKINAWA

Japan's interest in assuming responsibility for its own defense was whetted as a result of the Okinawa issue. The status of Okinawa, which the United States captured during World War II, had become a central issue in Japan's relations with the United States. The problem was complicated by the fact that Okinawa had become an important part of the United States defense system in the Pacific.

Premier Sato visited the United States at the end of November to negotiate a final agreement with President Nixon for the return of Okinawa. At the meeting, the United States agreed to return Okinawa to Japan in 1972. In exchange the United States will have wider use of its military bases in Japan.

▶ JAPANESE-U.S. DEFENSE TREATY

Japan's defense treaty with the United States comes up for review in June 1970. Both nations favor automatic extension of the treaty. This would provide for United States bases in Japan for another ten years.

The treaty is opposed by Premier Sato's major political opposition, the Socialist Party. It is also opposed by Japan's left-wing student groups. In 1969 the students staged a series of demonstrations against the treaty. They also demonstrated for the return of Okinawa.

The most violent demonstration took place on October 21. It was called "international antiwar day." Tokyo was nearly paralyzed by bands of roaming students who hurled gasoline bombs and smashed windows in downtown areas. But the demonstrations were short-lived, and most Japanese expressed dismay with the behavior of the militants.

▶ UNIVERSITIES UNDER SIEGE

Japan's problems with student demonstrations and strikes at universities led to a new law. As of August 17, in universities where there has been student strife for more than nine months, university departments may be suspended. If the disputes are not settled within one year after they arise, the university may be closed.

More than 65 universities were troubled by student disputes in 1969. The students claim that the universities are out of date and need reform. They have been pressing their demands by striking and by barricading the schools. Japan's Education Ministry hopes to bar such tactics under the new law. The law defines a university dispute as a situation under which education is blocked by actions of students. These actions include abandonment of classes, and occupation of university buildings. By the end of 1969, the law had not been tested. Many universities remained under siege.

▶ THE ECONOMY

The Japanese economy in 1969 continued to expand at an astonishing rate of better than 10 per cent a year. Japan emerged not only as Asia's industrial giant but also verged on becoming the third leading industrial power in the world.

The economic statistics were impressive. In 1969 the gross national product was more than $150,000,000,000. This is the second highest in the noncommunist world and third in the entire world. Japan continued to be the leading shipbuilder in the world, building more than half of the world's new ships. Another area of industrial success was automobile production. Japan exported 700,000 cars in 1969.

ARNOLD C. BRACKMAN

See also ASIA.

JORDAN. See MIDDLE EAST.
KENYA. See AFRICA.

Prince Juan Carlos with his wife, Princess Sophia of Greece, and three children.

JUAN CARLOS, PRINCE OF SPAIN

IN Spain no question has received more attention than who will succeed Generalissimo Francisco Franco, 76. Franco has been ruler of Spain since 1939.

On July 22, 1969, Franco named Prince Juan Carlos of Bourbon as the future chief of state and next king of Spain. Juan Carlos was given the title Prince of Spain until he becomes king. Franco personally proclaimed his successor to the Spanish Cortes (Parliament). His choice was overwhelmingly approved. This was one of the most important political events in Spain since the end of the Civil War in 1939.

If Franco dies or leaves office, Juan Carlos will become Spain's first king since 1931. In that year his grandfather, Alfonso XIII, vacated the throne and went into exile with his family. Don Juan, Juan Carlos' father, still claims his right to the throne. He is now living in Portugal in exile. Don Juan would legally be the next king if the regular order of succession were followed. But Franco rejected Don Juan because their political beliefs are so different. Also, he has often criticized Franco. Don Juan believes that Spain should be a democracy. If he were king he would institute many reforms. His son Juan Carlos was raised and trained by Franco. He probably would not be so liberal as his father.

Juan Carlos was born on January 5, 1938, in Rome, Italy. His parents were living there in exile with his grandfather, King Alfonso.

Juan Carlos first went to Spain in 1948. From that time on he was carefully educated and supervised by Franco. He attended military academies and then held a lieutenant's commission in all three of the country's armed forces. He studied at the University of Madrid and served apprenticeships in government ministries. He also traveled a great deal.

In 1962 Juan Carlos married Princess Sophia of Greece. They have two daughters and a son.

See also EUROPE, WEST.

KENYA. See AFRICA.

KOREA

IN Korea the communist North continued to apply military pressure along the demilitarized zone of the 38th parallel in 1969. Attacks against South Korean and U.S. troops continued, though on a reduced scale. In the South, meanwhile, the Government faced a constitutional crisis.

▶ SOUTH KOREA

The crisis in South Korea was generated by President Chung Hee Park's decision to seek a third presidential term in 1971. The constitution of South Korea limits a president to two terms. President Park's decision set off student demonstrations during the summer. He was also criticized by the political Opposition, the New Democratic Party.

President Park had the help of the ruling Democratic Republican Party and its allies. He arranged for the passage of a special bill through the National Assembly at a secret, predawn session on September 14. The bill set up a national referendum to amend the constitution to permit Park to seek a third term.

In October, South Korea went to the polls and approved the amendment. It was a two-to-one landslide victory for Park. He cited North Korean belligerence as a reason for his seeking a third term. However, his critics charged that by doing so he set back the development of Korean democracy.

Park's move followed three successive years in which the North Koreans had mounted an increasing number of armed raids into the South. In 1966 there were 50 incidents; in 1967, 546 incidents; and in 1968, 629 incidents, including an attempt to assassinate Park. But with the rise in political instability in the South in 1969, the North Korean attacks tapered off. It was thought that North Korea had decided to rob Park of his argument and therefore sharpen political tensions between Park and his opponents.

▶ NORTH KOREA

In North Korea, Premier Kim Il Sung reported in March that the top military leadership had been changed in December 1968. It was thought that the military command had been purged because of the failure of the raids into South Korea. Nonetheless, during the year, military pressure was kept up on United States forces in South Korea.

On April 14, North Korea shot down an unarmed United States Air Force EC-121 reconnaissance plane. The plane was downed over the Sea of Japan, 90 miles from the North Korean coastline. The 31 men aboard perished. In October the North Koreans ambushed and killed four American soldiers near the southern boundary of the demilitarized zone along the 38th parallel. This was the 60th communist infiltration attempt along the cease-fire line in 12 months.

In August a U.S. Army helicopter was shot down over North Korean territory and the three crew members captured. They were finally released in December after the United States, at North Korea's insistence, issued a formal apology for the accidental intrusion.

The harsh treatment by North Korea of the crew of the USS *Pueblo* was revealed during a U.S. Naval court of inquiry. The *Pueblo,* a Navy intelligence ship, had been captured in January 1968. North Korea had released the ship's 82 surviving crew members late in December 1968. In May 1969 the court of inquiry recommended that Commander Lloyd M. Bucher, captain of the *Pueblo,* be court-martialed for permitting the ship to surrender without firing a shot. However, U.S. Secretary of the Navy John H. Chafee overruled the court of inquiry. He barred any disciplinary action, on the ground that the crew had "suffered enough" during 11 months of mistreatment in captivity.

ARNOLD C. BRACKMAN

KUWAIT. See MIDDLE EAST.

LABOR. See ECONOMY, U.S.

LAOS. See ASIA.

LATIN AMERICA

Rockefeller's visit to Latin America: anti-U.S. demonstration in Argentina; armed guard in Brazil.

IN 1969 the Latin American nations showed a unity of purpose seldom seen before. In part, the unity was directed against the United States. These nations demanded, for example, that Washington give them better treatment on the economic front.

On the part of the United States, the new Nixon administration sought to recast the United States role in hemisphere affairs. The Alliance for Progress, the broad umbrella covering mutual aid and self-help efforts to improve conditions in Latin America, was still a cardinal factor in U.S.– Latin American relations. But President Nixon in his October speech stressed the concept of "partnership" as the factor which ought to dominate relations between Washington and its neighbors to the south.

President Nixon wanted to have a fresh report on the state of conditions in Latin America, and so he asked New York Governor Nelson A. Rockefeller to undertake a "listen and learn" mission. During the late spring and early summer of 1969, the Rockefeller mission visited 20 of Latin America's 24 nations. While there, Governor Rockefeller encountered hostility that frequently forced him to cut short his visits. Chile, Peru, and Venezuela asked him to cancel his visits entirely.

At the same time, the Latin American nations met at the Chilean beach resort of Viña del Mar where they prepared a document highly critical of the United States. This "Latin American Consensus of Viña del Mar," delivered to Mr. Nixon in June, called on Washington to change its trade and aid policies in Latin America. It demanded that the United States accept more Latin American goods and that tariff barriers be lowered. It also demanded that aid be increased and that strings not be attached to the aid money (the custom has been to require 90 per cent of aid money to be spent on U.S.–made goods).

Rockefeller's report called for many of the same items demanded by the Latins, including lower U.S. tariffs and repeal of the Hickenlooper amendment (which cuts aid to countries seizing U.S. companies).

Rockefeller also asked for the creation of a secretary of Western Hemisphere affairs. The most controversial proposal was one for stepped-up U.S. military aid.

In his policy speech in late October, based in part on the Rockefeller report, President Nixon said that Washington henceforth would not try to influence Latin Americans to have democratic governments. Instead, it would adopt a policy of working with whatever government is in power. He did not put much stress on the economic and social goals of reform contained in the Alliance for Progress started under President Kennedy. But he did call for economic growth in the hemisphere during the 1970's. To this end, he announced the removal of the requirement that aid money be spent on U.S.–made goods. The loan money, he said, would be free for use anywhere in North or South America. Moreover "non-tariff barriers to trade" would be reduced and "generalized tariff preferences" for all developing nations would be sought.

The following events occurred in individual countries throughout Latin America in 1969.

C. Burke Elbrick, U.S. ambassador to Brazil, shows how kidnapers blindfolded him.

ARGENTINA

Economic progress was registered in Argentina by a cutback in the cost of living and an increase in the gross national product. However, personal freedoms were reduced by new measures curbing freedom of speech and press. A number of magazines were closed during the year because of anti-government articles. The military leader, General Juan Carlos Ongania, also faced problems within the army between officers favoring heavier military control of the country and those favoring relaxation of controls.

BOLIVIA

President Rene Barrientos Ortuño, who with General Alfredo Ovando Candia had seized power in 1964, died in a helicopter crash in April. During the next five months, a weak civilian government under Barrientos' Vice-President, Luis Adolfo Siles Salinas, held power. But late in September, General Ovando seized power and adopted a sharply nationalistic tone for his government. He took over the Bolivian subsidiary of Gulf Oil Company in October, saying that Gulf was not leaving enough profit in Bolivia. General Ovando's policy appeared to parallel that of neighboring Peru's military leadership.

BRAZIL

The struggle between hard-line and soft-line officers on how to run South America's biggest nation continued through the year. The struggle was intensified by the sudden stroke suffered by military President Artur da Costa e Silva in August. When it became evident that Costa e Silva would not quickly recover from his stroke, the military chose General Emilio Garrastazu Medici to succeed him. (Costa e Silva died in December.)

The government continued its policy of removing hundreds of civilians from public life. New lists included politicians, writers, and educators, none of whom will now be able to hold their jobs for ten years.

Terrorism in Rio de Janeiro and São Paulo reached alarming proportions during the year. In early September, United States Ambassador C. Burke Elbrick was abducted. He was released after 15 political prisoners held by the government were freed and allowed to go into exile.

Thirteen of 15 political prisoners set free by Brazil in exchange for Elbrick's release.

CHILE

Early skirmishing for the 1970 presidential race got underway during the latter half of 1969. Also during 1969, Leftist pressure forced President Eduardo Frei Montalva to adopt new economic measures with a distinct nationalist tone. Some of the pressure even came from within Frei's own Christian Democratic Party. He forced the Anaconda Copper Company to agree to a Chileanization of its copper holdings. The eventual outcome is likely to be nationalization.

A mutiny of Chile's usually docile military in mid-October shocked the nation and led to pay and benefit concessions for the underpaid officers and soldiers in Chile's army.

COLOMBIA

Quiet economic progress continued in Colombia under President Carlos Lleras Restrepo. Although various guerrilla bands fought skirmishes with army troops several times in 1969, they suffered important setbacks, for the military won the upper hand in most engagements.

Lleras Restrepo visited Washington in June and told President Nixon of his country's support for the "Consensus of Viña del Mar."

COSTA RICA

A lively presidential campaign was underway in Costa Rica. The election will be in February 1970. Former President Jose Figueres is expected to win again. Economic progress was registered with a sizable increase in foreign investment, a 5.1 per cent increase in the gross national product, and the start of a new campaign to attract tourists.

CUBA

The trend toward the Sovietization of Cuba continued during the year. Prime Minister Fidel Castro spoke favorably of the Soviet Union on several occasions, reversing the three-year era of poor relations with his chief ally.

The dominant theme in the economy was the effort to make the goal of 10,000,000 tons of sugar for the 1970 harvest.

A number of key people defected from Cuba in 1969. Half a dozen of them were intelligence and military specialists who defected to the United States.

The skyjacking of U.S. and Latin American airliners by people wanting to go to Cuba reached an all-time high in 1969 as 59 planes were diverted to the island.

DOMINICAN REPUBLIC

President Joaquin Balaguer began an active campaign for re-election. In the process, he placed a variety of curbs on the Leftist opposition, particularly the Dominican Revolutionary Party of former president Juan Bosch. There were a number of clashes between police and supporters of Mr. Bosch, who is in exile. The economic growth of the past several years slackened somewhat in 1969.

ECUADOR

Surprising economic growth was made during the year. President Jose Maria Velasco Ibarra held onto the presidency despite predictions that Ecuador's military would overthrow him as they have done on three other occasions. New industry was largely responsible for the economic growth.

EL SALVADOR

This tiny Central American country faced economic problems in 1969 as a result of the so-called "soccer war" with Honduras, which erupted in July. Salvadorian troops pressed deep into Honduras before Organization of American States (OAS) peacemakers arrived to separate the combatants.

The basic cause of the war was El Salvador's population explosion. In recent years this has led to a sizable emigration of Salvadorians to sparsely populated Honduras. A recent Honduran land-reform program, however, took over many of the small plots farmed by Salvadorians. As a

Honduran troops advance against the forces of El Salvador during the brief "soccer war" in July.

result, the Salvadorians flocked back to their homeland in large numbers.

GUATEMALA

Guatemala was in the economic doldrums throughout the year. This was caused by the El Salvador-Honduras war, which disrupted the Central American Common Market, and by low prices for agricultural products. President Julio Cesar Mendez Montenegro weathered a variety of political storms, but the military hovered in the wings.

In the weeks just before Christmas, terrorism increased. At least eight political figures were killed, and the President imposed a form of martial law.

GUYANA

Prime Minister Forbes Burnham pressed on with his program of trying to win the allegiance of the nation's dominant East Indians. The East Indians are traditionally loyal to one of their own, former Prime Minister Cheddi B. Jagan. Burnham seemed to be making some headway, naming a number of East Indians to his cabinet. But he was beset with border disputes with both Venezuela on the west and Surinam on the east.

HAITI

Rumors spread through the island in May and June that "President for Life" François Duvalier was ill. And indeed he failed to appear at receptions and other events during those two months. But when Governor Rockefeller visited Haiti in July, Duvalier appeared quite fit.

During the year a number of opposition leaders termed communist by the government were executed without trial. In reprisal, Haitian exiles and anti-Duvalier Americans flew over Port-au-Prince spraying parts of the city with machine-gun bullets and dropping make-shift fire bombs.

Economic progress on a limited scale was noted in this poorest country of the hemisphere, particularly as half a dozen United States firms opened factories in 1969 to carry on assembly operations.

HONDURAS

Hard pressed during the war with El Salvador in the summer, Honduras' economy lagged badly in 1969. It was not expected to recover quickly. But the resolve of the Honduran people to fend off the Salvadorians lessened the effect of the economic lag. Supplies coming to Honduras from neighboring Nicaragua were of help.

HEADS OF GOVERNMENT

Argentina	JUAN CARLOS ONGANIA, president
Bolivia	ALFREDO OVANDO CANDIA, president
Brazil	EMILIO GARRASTAZU MEDICI, president
Chile	EDUARDO FREI MONTALVA, president
Colombia	CARLOS LLERAS RESTREPO, president
Costa Rica	JOSE JOAQUIN TREJOS FERNANDEZ, president
Cuba	OSVALDO DORTICOS TORRADO, president
	FIDEL CASTRO, prime minister
Dominican Rep.	JOAQUIN BALAGUER, president
Ecuador	JOSE MARIA VELASCO IBARRA, president
El Salvador	FIDEL SANCHEZ HERNANDEZ, president
Guatemala	JULIO CESAR MENDEZ MONTENEGRO, president
Guyana	L. F. S. BURNHAM, prime minister
Haiti	FRANCOIS DUVALIER, president
Honduras	OSWALDO LOPEZ ARELLANO, president
Mexico	GUSTAVO DIAZ ORDAZ, president
Nicaragua	ANASTASIO SOMOZA DEBAYLE, president
Panama	D. LAKAS BAHAS, president
Paraguay	ALFREDO STROESSNER, president
Peru	JUAN VELASCO ALVARADO, president
Uruguay	JORGE PACHECO ARECO, president
Venezuela	RAFAEL CALDERA RODRIQUEZ, president

	POPULATION	CURRENCY*	LAFTA	CACM
Argentina	24,360,000	3.5 new pesos = $1.00	X	
Bolivia	4,608,000	12 pesos = $1.00		
Brazil	93,137,000	4.3 new cruzeiros = $1.00	X	
Chile	9,821,000	11.2 escudos = $1.00	X	
Colombia	22,127,600	17.6 pesos = $1.00	X	
Costa Rica	1,764,600	6.6 colons = $1.00		X
Cuba	8,364,000	1 peso = $1.00		
Dominican Rep.	4,343,000	1 peso = $1.00		
Ecuador	5,997,000	21.4 sucres = $1.00	X	
El Salvador	3,400,000	2.5 colons = $1.00		X
Guatemala	5,140,000	1 quetzal = $1.00		X
Guyana	719,000	2 dollars = $1.00		
Haiti	5,222,400	5 gourdes = $1.00		
Honduras	2,585,000	2 lempiras = $1.00		X
Mexico	50,666,000	12.5 pesos = $1.00	X	
Nicaragua	2,060,000	7 cordobas = $1.00		X
Panama	1,445,000	1 balboa = $1.00		
Paraguay	2,378,000	126 guaranies = $1.00	X	
Peru	13,609,000	38.7 sols = $1.00	X	
Uruguay	2,935,000	250 pesos = $1.00	X	
Venezuela	10,743,000	4.5 bolivars = $1.00	X	

* US $; 1969 exchange rates
LAFTA—Latin American Free Trade Association
CACM—Central American Common Market

DEPENDENT LATIN AMERICA

	STATUS	HEADS OF GOVERNMENT	POPULATION
BR. HONDURAS	Self-governing British colony	SIR JOHN PAUL, governor	127,000
		G. C. PRICE, premier	
FR. GUIANA	French overseas department	PAUL BOUTEILLER, prefect	46,800
SURINAM	Netherlands overseas constituent	JOHAN H. E. FERRIER, governor	401,600
		J. SEDNEY, minister-president	

MEXICO

The ruling Partido Revolucionario Institucional named Luis Echeverria, the secretary of government, as its candidate for the 1970 presidential elections. This is tantamount to election, but in the tradition of all PRI candidates, Echeverria began a campaign in earnest.

Student protests continued throughout the year, but on a much-reduced basis. Population growth worked against economic growth during 1969.

NICARAGUA

Some economic lag was registered as a result of the El Salvador-Honduras war. But the Somoza family dictatorship weathered the storm fairly well as new industries, sparked by European investment, were set up. There was evidence also of a slackening in the birth rate—a factor which could help improve the economic picture.

PANAMA

President Jose M. Pinalla was hospitalized in June. Colonel Bolivar Urrutia was named acting president. The military, however, under General Omar Torrijos, remained the power behind the Government. In December, Torrijos' opponents in the National Guard tried to unseat him while he was visiting Mexico City. Torrijos quickly returned and re-established his control over Panama. Demetrios Lakas Bahas replaced Urrutia as president.

PARAGUAY

General Afredo Stroessner's dictatorship relaxed its political hold on the nation a little to allow more political opposition to organize and operate. The economic growth of the nation under Stroessner registered 5.7 per cent during 1969—a record.

PERU

The military leaders under General Juan Velasco Alvarado completed the take-over of the International Petroleum Company, the Peruvian subsidiary of Standard Oil of New Jersey. They demanded that the company pay nearly a billion dollars in back taxes and other duties. Long negotiations with the United States over this issue resulted in a stalemate. However, Washington did not impose the so-called Hickenlooper amendment, which calls for suspension of aid and other assistance to a nation which fails to enter into negotiations on compensation of seized U.S.-owned property within six months after the seizure. Washington clearly wanted to sidestep such a confrontation. Peru also adopted a land-reform law in June. It resulted in the take-over of large U.S.-owned holdings. In October, Peru negotiated the take-over of the U.S.-owned telephone company.

URUGUAY

Urban terrorism continued to bedevil the government of President Jorge Pacheco Areco. But for the first time in five years there was moderate economic growth, and some payments on international debts were made. However, freedom of the press to report the urban terrorism was curtailed during the year.

VENEZUELA

Rafael Caldera Rodriguez, who was inaugurated as the president of this oil-rich country in March, quickly established his Christian Democratic Party (COPE) as a political force with which to reckon. He obtained support from many groups and began talks toward receiving more oil revenue from United States and other foreign oil companies, which carry on 93 per cent of Venezuela's export trade.

Caldera's plan to pacify the Leftist guerrillas in the countryside was balked despite broad offers of amnesty. Later, the military carried out a number of campaigns to clear the hills of guerrilla forces. They were only partly successful, and terrorism in the countryside continued to be a disruptive factor in Venezuela.

JAMES NELSON GOODSELL
The Christian Science Monitor

Chief Justice Warren Earl Burger.

Former Chief Justice Earl Warren.

LAW

THE major events of general public interest in law in 1969 concerned members of the U.S. Supreme Court as individuals rather than as a tribunal.

▶ WARREN BURGER REPLACES EARL WARREN

Chief Justice Earl Warren stepped down in June at the age of 78 after serving on the bench for 16 years. To succeed him, President Nixon appointed Warren Earl Burger, a 61-year-old Minnesotan. Justice Burger had been sitting since 1956 on the U.S. Court of Appeals for the District of Columbia. He is considered a "strict constructionist" [interpreter] of the Constitution. Burger was sworn in on June 23 as the 15th chief justice of the United States.

▶ CLEMENT HAYNSWORTH REJECTED

President Nixon's second Supreme Court appointment was that of Clement F. Haynsworth, Jr., 56, chief judge of the United States Fourth Circuit Court in South Carolina. On August 18, Haynsworth was named to fill the seat vacated by Associate Justice Abe Fortas in May. With these two appointments, President Nixon moved to reshape the Supreme Court to one that, in his words, might be more inclined to "strictly interpret the Constitution, give Congress a leeway to write law, and be less willing to overturn laws passed by elected representatives."

While there was little opposition to the confirmation of Burger as chief justice, Judge Haynsworth ran into opposition. His nomination was opposed, as expected, by many liberals in Congress and by civil-rights groups such as the National Association for the Advancement of Colored People. He was also opposed by organized labor. The AFL-CIO was very unhappy about his deciding vote in a ruling that

Resigned: Justice Abe Fortas

Rejected: Judge Clement Haynsworth

went against labor in a textile workers' case. But the major factor influencing the Senate's rejection was the question of ethics. Haynsworth had ruled on cases while owning stock in companies involved in the cases. The Senate turned him down by a vote of 55–45. At year's end, President Nixon had not yet submitted another name to the Senate.

▶ **THE FORTAS AFFAIR AND JUDICIAL ETHICS**

The Haynsworth rejection came about because many Republican senators had previously criticized Justice Fortas, and could not then ignore what might have been a breach of judicial ethics on the part of Judge Haynsworth.

Associate Justice Abe Fortas' resignation from the Supreme Court came after public disclosure that while serving on the court he had agreed to accept a $20,000 yearly retainer for non-legal advice to the family foundation of a financier who at the time was under Federal indictment and was later imprisoned. Fortas' action violated no law. But it showed such great

insensitivity to the proper role of a judge that he placed his otherwise distinguished career in jeopardy. He also lowered public respect for the court, at least for the time being.

There were other results of the "Fortas affair." The Supreme Court took steps to establish guidelines for the outside activities of its members. Also, the Judicial Conference of the United States, at the prodding of Chief Justice Earl Warren, issued directives restricting outside activities of all Federal judges below the level of the Supreme Court. In September, the American Bar Association (ABA) set up a panel of nine judges, lawyers, and law professors to rewrite its code of ethics for judges.

Coincidentally, at its August annual meeting, the ABA adopted a complete revision of its code of ethical standards for lawyers. The new code, called the Code of Professional Responsibility, replaced a code that had scarcely undergone any changes since 1908. The revision was not a repercussion of the Fortas affair.

MAJOR DECISIONS OF THE SUPREME COURT IN 1969

CIVIL RIGHTS

Tinker v. Des Moines Independent Community School District (February 24) ruled 7–2 that students have a right to wear black armbands in protest against war and that to deny this protest is in violation of freedom of speech.

Shapiro v. Thompson; Washington v. Legrant; Reynolds v. Smith (April 21) ruled 6–3 that one-year residency requirements for welfare in Connecticut, Pennsylvania, and the District of Columbia were unconstitutional. The Court stated that such a rule was an unconstitutional barrier to travel.

CRIMINAL LAW AND PROCEDURE

Benton v. Maryland (June 23) overruled 6–2 a 1937 opinion that the double jeopardy (the concept that someone cannot be tried twice for the same crime) clause of the Fifth Amendment does not apply to states.

North Carolina v. Pearce; Simpson v. Rice (June 23) ruled 6–2 that a person who has a conviction set aside and has a retrial and then is convicted once again may not be given a longer sentence at the retrial unless the trial judge can show reasons for a longer sentence. The Court made the point that a person should not be punished (with a longer sentence) because he has sought a new trial.

Chimel v. California (June 23) ruled 6–2 that police may search only an arrested suspect's person and immediate surroundings without a search warrant. If a suspect's premises are to be searched, a search warrant is needed.

EXCLUSION OF A CONGRESSMAN

Powell v. McCormack (June 16) ruled 7–1 that the House of Representatives could not exclude a member-elect (New York Congressman Adam Clayton Powell) on the basis of his past misconduct, but must seat him if he has been duly elected in a regular election and meets the Constitution's requirements as to age, citizenship, and residence.

SCHOOL DESEGREGATION

Beatrice Alexander, et al v. Holmes County, Mississippi, Board of Education (October 29) ruled unanimously that school districts must end segregation "at once" and conduct integrated school systems "now and hereafter."

SERVICEMEN AND SELECTIVE SERVICE

McKart v. United States (May 26) ruled unanimously that a man may be exempt from the draft as a "sole surviving son" even after his parents have died.

O'Callahan v. Parker (June 2) ruled 5–3 that the U.S. Army cannot court-martial a soldier in peacetime for a crime committed away from his post while he is on leave and out of uniform. The Court ruled that the military had jurisdiction only if the civilian offense is service-connected.

THE SUPREME COURT

Chief Justice: WARREN E. BURGER

Associate Justices: HUGO L. BLACK, WILLIAM J. BRENNAN, WILLIAM O. DOUGLAS, JOHN M. HARLAN, THURGOOD MARSHALL, POTTER STEWART, BYRON WHITE

The two major trials of the year were those of James Earl Ray (above, right), assassin of Dr. Martin Luther King, Jr.; and Sirhan Sirhan (below, center), assassin of Robert F. Kennedy.

In December, Chief Justice Burger appointed a panel of ten Federal judges to oversee the financial and out-of-court activities of all judges except those on the Supreme Court. The panel will review their outside income until the ABA completes the rewriting of its code of ethics for judges.

▶ TRIALS

The two biggest criminal cases of 1968 were settled in 1969. These were the assassinations of Senator Robert F. Kennedy in Los Angeles and Dr. Martin Luther King, Jr., in Memphis.

In March, James Earl Ray, an ex-convict, pleaded guilty before trial to the sniper-slaying of Dr. Martin Luther King on April 4, 1968. Ray's defense counsel was Percy Foreman, one of the leading criminal lawyers in the United States. Only two month's before Ray's sentencing, Foreman had said that he "believed someone other than Ray" had murdered Dr. King. But later he reportedly persuaded his client to plead guilty to enhance his chances of escaping execution. Ray did escape the death penalty. He was sentenced to 99 years of imprisonment at the Tennessee State Penitentiary.

In Los Angeles, Sirhan Bishara Sirhan, a Jordanian Arab and a resident alien in the United States, stood trial for the June 5, 1968, murder of Senator Kennedy. As in Ray's case, Sirhan had eminent criminal lawyers to defend him. Unlike Ray's case, there was no question that Sirhan was the assassin, and the defense was primarily one of insanity. But the jury was not convinced of Sirhan's insanity and quickly convicted him. Under California law, the jury is then called upon to pass sentence. It ignored pleas for leniency and sentenced Sirhan to death.

Another trial that attracted a great deal of attention in 1969 was that of New Orleans businessman Clay Shaw. District Attorney Jim Garrison had charged Shaw with conspiracy to assassinate President John F. Kennedy in 1963. Shaw was quickly acquitted, and Garrison's case was so weak that the trial judge expressed wonder that he was even able to obtain an indictment.

CHARLES F. KILEY
Editor, *New York Law Journal*

LEBANON. See MIDDLE EAST.

LESOTHO. See AFRICA.

LIBERIA. See AFRICA.

LIBRARIES

IN 1969 the underlying theme of library plans and programs throughout the United States and Canada was "libraries and people." This theme was reflected in the American Library Association's lively annual convention held in June in Atlantic City and in the activities of individual libraries.

Since World War II three basic problems have preoccupied library planners: resources (the actual collections in the libraries); organization; and methods of operation. But recently the needs of present and potential library users have taken center stage. The previous concerns remain, of course. But people have become the central focus of attention, because the collections, organization, and methods always were meant to serve them.

▶ RESOURCES

During 1969 the number of different kinds of publications available to libraries continued to grow. Hard-cover books came from the publishers at an increased rate of about 5 per cent. But other kinds of publications and materials increased even more. New magazines appeared constantly, both the traditional kinds and the "alternative" press, produced by groups and organizations critical of American society. Libraries tried to keep up with a growing variety of governmental and technical reports. Newer media—films, tape and disc recordings, visual aids (charts, maps, globes), models, and programed-learning materials —are now fully accepted as resources in a well-equipped library.

The new audiovisual aids are highly approved by librarians and educators. They are so firmly accepted that in 1969 the American Library Association and the National Educational Association published a booklet called *Standards for School Media Programs* advising schools on how best to select, set up, and maintain these exciting new educational tools.

▶ INTERLIBRARY CO-OPERATION

In 1969, library reorganization stressed relations between libraries. The purpose is to mobilize the resources of all libraries together to serve the user better. Systems under which public libraries co-operate, co-ordinating services of local libraries in counties and regions, are now well started in most states and provinces. Attention during 1969 was given to so-called "metropolitan networks" which would pool the resources of scholarly, academic, and public libraries in such distant metropolitan centers as Toronto and Chicago, or Minneapolis and New York. Statewide networks are growing in Pennsylvania, Illinois, Maryland, and other states.

▶ REDUCTION IN FEDERAL FUNDS

The movement toward co-ordinated interlibrary service was given an at least temporary setback by reductions in Federal funds for libraries in 1968 and 1969. The Johnson administration proposed a cut in Federal money for schools and libraries. Then, early in 1969, the Nixon administration made drastic further cuts in the proposed library appropriations. Congress, however, restored part of the cuts.

The Federal Government did not act during 1969 on the 1968 report of the President's National Advisory Commission on Libraries, which called for a permanent National Commission on Libraries and Information Science.

▶ AUTOMATION

Automation, in the form of computer services and new communications tools, has come to the library. In 1969 the MARC (machine-readable cataloging) system started national operation. Based on the Library of Congress catalog, this system provides centrally prepared cataloging data on magnetic tape for local production of card catalogs and book catalogs.

A group of young people pay a visit to a Brooklyn [New York] Public Library bookmobile on a neighborhood street.

▶ LIBRARIES TO PEOPLE

The renewed interests of librarians in bringing library service close to people, so that it can become part of the fabric of their lives, are shown by new projects set up in urban ghettos. Books, often in paperback form, are brought right into the slums. They are made available on the street corners, in housing projects, and in places where poor people must wait for services, such as welfare offices and medical clinics. The books often contain practical information—about jobs, problems of the shopper, and welfare rights—drawn from library sources. Collections presenting the history and culture of black citizens are provided. For children, bookmobiles go into the streets, brightly decorated, playing music, showing films, bringing storytellers.

The interest in the people who use libraries is also showing itself in freshened concern about censorship of libraries and violations of the principle of freedom to read. While restrictions on intellectual freedom and expression are not so prevalent and organized as they were a decade or more ago, attempts to apply pressure to libraries regularly occur. Particular attention was given during 1969 to ways and means to help individual librarians who stand up to restrictions on freedom to read.

Indeed, the theme of relating libraries to users runs through programs in various kinds of libraries. School libraries are working more closely with the educational process. College libraries are experimenting with the concept of a "library college," centered on student and faculty use of library resources rather than on the lecture hall. University and scholarly libraries seek to learn more about how researchers use resources. And libraries in business and industry seek new ways to extract, condense, and disseminate information throughout their companies.

Groups within the American Library Association are pushing in the same direction. Among these is the new Round Table on Social Responsibilities. The Congress for Change is a forward-looking organization existing outside the ALA but made up primarily of ALA members. The ALA itself in 1969 officially appointed a Committee on New Directions to identify priorities for the period ahead.

Young people who respond to these prospects are entering library schools and the profession. The voices of the younger professionals were prominent among those calling in 1969 for change. But the search for new roles and increased effectiveness was not confined to the younger generation. While no marked changes occurred in established libraries in 1969, responsive chords were touched among administrators and practitioners. Indeed, the year 1969 was one marked by the growth of new attitudes and outlooks in preparation for fresh patterns of library service in the 1970's.

LOWELL A. MARTIN
Professor of Library Service
Columbia University

LIBYA. See MIDDLE EAST.

LITERATURE

Illustration showing scene on board ship is from "Darwin and The Beagle."

SATIRE, criticism, and relentless observation of American life and customs were characteristic of the best American literature in 1969.

▶NOVELS

One novel that won both critical and popular acclaim was Philip Roth's *Portnoy's Complaint*. Here was a funny, moving, and sexually frank portrait of a boy growing up in a middle-class Jewish family. Another novel that won acclaim was Evan Connell, Jr.'s *Mr. Bridge*. It was a quiet and exactly described view of a solid Kansas City paterfamilias, the husband of the celebrated *Mrs. Bridge*. In *Them* the prolific Joyce Carol Oates turned the chronicle of a poor-white family in Detroit into a parable of urban violence.

Violence was defined with unusual imagination and skill in Kurt Vonnegut, Jr.'s latest fable, *Slaughterhouse-Five: Or the Children's Crusade*. The violence was in the form of the Allied air raid on Dresden in 1945, in which 135,000 civilians were killed. Notable works of two classic European authors, Louis-Ferdinand Céline and Vladimir Nabokov, appeared. Céline's posthumous *Castle to Castle* was a pungent and blackly humorous autobiographical novel about French wartime collaborators in defeat. Nabokov's *Ada, or Ardor: A Family Chronicle* was a love story and an investigation of time, rich as usual with puns, tricks, and literary ambushes. In another exploration of time, the Victorian novel was radically modernized by John Fowles in his romance, *The French Lieu-*

tenant's Woman. Fowles is known for his earlier novel, *The Collector.*

▶ POETRY

Of the poets, Robert Lowell wrote *Notebook 1967–68,* a long poem that was the author's personal political history of a dramatic 18 months of dissent. *The Complete Poems* of two other poets, Elizabeth Bishop and the late Randall Jarrell, also appeared.

▶ MEMOIRS

Memoirs were prominent in 1969's nonfiction. Political memoirists represented three administrations. In *Present at the Creation,* Dean Acheson, secretary of state under President Harry S. Truman, gave a crisp account of the bold part he played in the State Department from 1941 to 1953. These were the epic years of World War II and the cold war. John Kenneth Galbraith's *Ambassador's Journal: A Personal Account of the Kennedy Years* was personal indeed. It was written in the form of a diary and letters to President John F. Kennedy while the author served as United States representative in India. The late Senator Robert F. Kennedy's *Thirteen Days: A Memoir of the Cuban Missile Crisis* was his inside story of the dramatic 1962 crisis. It was controversial because it named names. The first major inside story to emerge from the Johnson administration was Eric F. Goldman's *The Tragedy of Lyndon Johnson.*

▶ AUTOBIOGRAPHIES AND BIOGRAPHIES

Frank O'Connor, the late Irish master of the short story, continued his autobiography in *My Father's Son,* notable for the depiction of literary Dublin in his youth. The playwright and novelist Lillian Hellman wrote her autobiography, *An Unfinished Woman.*

The major biographies of 1969 dealt with legendary figures. In *Ernest Hemingway: A Life Story,* Carlos Baker examined every available detail of the writer's life and works for the most encyclopedic biography of Hemingway yet. T. Harry Williams wrote *Huey Long,* the first authoritative study of the 1920's and 1930's Louisiana Governor and Senator. Williams interviewed Long's friends, relatives, and enemies, and with this book established Long as a major figure in American political history. John Womack, Jr., put a famous revolutionary in definitive perspective in his *Zapata and the Mexican Revolution.* A biography as challenging and original as the subject was Erik H. Erikson's *Gandhi's Truth: On the Origins of Militant Nonviolence.* Erikson offered a psychohistorical analysis of the character and politics of the great Indian leader.

A much-visited subject was successfully confronted by Antonia Fraser in her *Mary Queen of Scots.* The sympathetic biography carefully dismissed many of the wilder legends. R. M. Hatton's *Charles XII of Sweden* brought to life in lively detail a generally forgotten 18th-century military genius. Alan Moorehead's *Darwin and the Beagle* told the story of the great naturalist's discovery of evolution, and used many contemporary illustrations to great effect. Commodore Matthew C. Perry's personal journal of *The Japan Expedition 1852–1854* appeared for the first time, illustrated by artists who were with him on his historic mission.

▶ FACSIMILE EDITIONS

Facsimile editions—exact reproductions of famous books and manuscripts—increased in number and quality. One of the most beautiful was the reproduction of *The Très Riches Heures of Jean, Duke of Berry,* a famous illuminated French manuscript. An eyewitness account of the first circumnavigation of the world, *Magellan's Voyage,* was published in a facsimile of the original and was accompanied by a translation by R. A. Sketton.

▶ HISTORICAL WRITING

The origins and consequences of nazi Germany continued to be a source of historical writing. Richard Watt's *The Kings*

Depart: The Tragedy of Germany; Versailles and the German Revolution was a popular history that won praise from the professional historians. Harrison E. Salisbury drew on interviews with many survivors for *The 900 Days: The Siege of Leningrad.* This was the first large account of one of the longest and fiercest sieges in history.

▶ POLITICS

The presidential election year of 1968 provided plenty of material for contemporary American history. The campaign itself was first described by a team of English journalists, Lewis Chester, Godfrey Hodgson, and Bruce Page, in *An American Melodrama,* a massive piece of reportage. This was followed by Theodore H. White's *The Making of the President 1968,* the third in his series.

The Vietnam war continued to dominate American politics. Senator Eugene J. McCarthy of Minnesota told the story of his antiwar presidential attempt in *The Year of the People.* Jack Newfield wrote *Robert Kennedy: A Memoir,* an account of the New York Senator's campaign that ended with his assassination in California. Noam Chomsky, a leading critic of the war, argued in *American Power and the New Mandarins* that scholars and experts have been too concerned with methodology. Chomsky felt they have compromised their critical independence by their participation in government policy-making. From within the Johnson administration came a revealing memoir of dissent. It was *The Limits of Intervention: An Inside Account of How the Johnson Policy of Escalation in Vietnam Was Reversed,* by Townsend Hoopes, President Lyndon B. Johnson's undersecretary of the Air Force.

▶ SOCIAL COMMENT

The anger and disaffection of American blacks were expressed by Julius Lester in his autobiographical *Search for the New Land.* The student rebellion at Columbia was described by Jerry L. Avorn and others in *Up against the Ivy Wall.* The Presidential Commission on the Causes and Prevention of Violence produced a number of reports: on the history of violence in America, on assassination, on civil rights and violence, and others. The quality and fairness of news coverage of controversial events were questioned. Some insight was available in *The Kingdom and the Power,* Gay Talese's account of the personal struggles for power on *The New York Times.* The method and meaning of success in the corporate jungle were wittily and wisely clarified by Laurence J. Peter and Raymond Hull in *The Peter Principle.*

Traditional life-styles and the perils to the natural environment figured prominently in 1969. Josephine Johnson's *The Inland Island* vividly described effects of the encroachment of industry on an Ohio farm. In *Akenfield: Portrait of an English Village,* Ronald Blythe gave an impressionistic social history of an English village through the monologues of its inhabitants. Jane Jacobs' *The Economy of Cities* explored the function of economic growth in the life of cities. Bruno Bettelheim's *The Children of the Dream* described the communal upbringing of children in Israeli kibbutzim. An omnipresent social system was amusingly observed in *Life on Man* by Theodor Rosebury, a bacteriologist who described the behavior of microbes living on people.

▶ SPORTS BOOKS

Sports books, another growing category, went to extremes. *Levels of the Game* by John McPhee was an intense personal report on a tennis and character match between Clark Graebner and Arthur Ashe at Forest Hills. *The Baseball Encyclopedia: The Complete and Official Record of Major League Baseball* was compiled with the help of computers by Information Concepts, Inc., and presented a new generation of baseball statistics.

ROGER JELLINEK
The New York Times Book Review

See also PUBLISHING.

LITERATURE, CANADIAN

CANADA'S best-known writer is Marshall McLuhan. His newest book, *Through the Vanishing Point: Space in Poetry and Painting,* was published in 1969. It is an interesting addition to McLuhan's views. McLuhan's main point in his writings is that the invention of movable type changed man's view of the external world. In *Through the Vanishing Point* he extends this idea to painting as well as poetry. The book has many illustrations.

▶ EXPERIMENTAL NOVELS

One of the most significant developments in Canada has been the emergence of new publishing houses, which concentrate on the work of young writers. The House of Anansi is the most successful of these. One of its most interesting publications in 1969 was Graeme Gibson's *Five Legs.* It gives a remarkable view of a man's revolt against the puritan tradition of Ontario.

Anansi has also begun a new venture called the Spiderline Series. These are first novels in paperback form. Five have been published. The best of them is *The Telephone Pole* by Russell Marois. It is a real view of an alienated English Montrealer who has dropped out of everyday life. Most of the novel is visionary. Characters and settings blur and interchange in a confusing but exciting way.

▶ FRENCH-CANADIAN BOOKS

The most interesting experiment in the Spiderline Series is *A Perte de Temps* (With Loss of Time) by a French-Canadian author, Pierre Gravel. It is written in French. The more difficult words are translated at the bottom of the page so that anyone with some reading knowledge of the language can understand it. The subject of the novel is timely enough. It is the

Canadian author Marshall McLuhan.

reverie of a young French Separatist looking back on his life of bomb-planting and other revolutionary activities. He is about to be arrested by the police. The book tells us a good deal about the Separatist movement, its goals, and its grim methods.

Almost twice as many books are published in Quebec as in the rest of Canada. French-Canadian authors are prolific and versatile. One 25-year-old author, Noel Tremblay, in 1969 published a very good play, *Les Belles Soeurs* (The Sisters-in-law). It is about the envy of women for a neighbor who wins a heap of trading stamps. Tremblay also published a science-fiction fantasy, *La Cité dans les Oeufs* (The City in the Eggs), and an adaptation of the Greek play *Lysistrata* for the National Arts Centre that opened in Ottawa.

▶ POETS AND NOVELISTS

Some well-established Canadian authors published some good work during the year. Margaret Laurence, best known for her novel, *A Jest of God,* that was made into the movie *Rachel, Rachel,* brought out *The Fire-Dwellers*. A sensitive and powerful work, it is a study of the life and frustrations of a Vancouver housewife. Mordecai Richler published *The Street,* a nostalgic and affectionate look at St. Urbain Street in Montreal. Irving Layton brought out a new book, *The Whole Bloody Bird*. It contains the prose chronicle of his visit to Israel as well as a number of poems.

Another well-known Canadian poet, George Bowering, has written a fine book called *Rocky Mountain Foot*. He spent two years in Alberta, and the book is the result. It has observations, poems, and sketches of people: all precise and memorable. Gwendolyn MacEwen published another book of poems, *The Shadow-Maker*. Her style is both elegant and precise.

Another woman poet, Margaret Atwood, who won the Governor General's Award in 1967, produced her first novel, *The Edible Woman*. This is quite a funny fantasy about a woman with several neurotic symptoms, including a fixation about food. It is an imaginative book, but Miss Atwood does not as yet have a firm grasp of character.

Erich Koch published his second book. It is one that is sure to be widely read. Titled *The French Kiss,* it is a humorous novel which begins with General de Gaulle's "Quebec Libre" speech in Montreal in 1967. The novel is narrated by a French history professor who was a secret agent for De Gaulle in Quebec. The novel makes an ironic comment on the Separatist situation in Quebec. Koch's point is that De Gaulle's French kiss on the expectant lips of the Separatists was in effect the kiss of death for the movement.

▶ CANADIAN PROFILES

Clarke, Irwin & Company produced the second book in their New Canadian Writing series, with stories by John Metcalf, D. O. Spettigue, and C. J. Newman. They are ably written stories about people in Toronto, Montreal, the Canadian north, and the Ontario countryside.

A significant feature of publishing in Canada during the year was the appearance of a number of studies of Canadian authors. Forum House published Eli Mandel's study of Irving Layton, Phyllis Grosskurth's study of the French-Canadian writer Gabrielle Roy, and Peter Buitenhuis' study of Hugh MacLennan. Clarke, Irwin & Company came out with Victor Hoar's study of Margaret Laurence and Dennis Duffy's study of Marshall McLuhan. Several others are in the works. These studies should provide good introductions to those seeking to get to know Canada's major authors.

Finally, mention should be made of a book of particular interest to readers in the United States. This is Victor Ullman's *Look to the North Star*. It is an account of how William King released his slaves from a Southern plantation and took them to Elgin, Ontario. There he gave them land to farm, against the strong opposition of his fellow Southerners and Ontarians too. It makes a valuable addition to the books about Canada and slavery in the United States. Most of the books on this subject usually center on the Underground Railroad, which ended in Ontario with freedom for fugitive slaves.

PETER BUITENHUIS
McGill University

LITERATURE FOR CHILDREN

"BOOK POWER" was the theme for the celebration of the Golden Anniversary of Children's Book Week in 1969. Gwendolyn Brooks' poem emphasized the importance of books in a world that was becoming increasingly audio-visual oriented.

From "Apricot ABC" by Miska Miles. Illustrated by Peter Parnall.

BOOKS FEED AND CURE AND CHORTLE AND COLLIDE

In all this willful world
of thud and thump and thunder
man's relevance to books
continue to declare.

Books are meat and medicine
and flame and flight and flower,
steel, stitch, and cloud and clout,
and drumbeats on the air.

Young tree will flower, fruit will grow,
While crickets click and roosters crow
And sparrows cheep
And locusts leap.
Young fruit will ripen in the sun
And busy creatures, one by one,
Will hop or jump or creep to see
Yellow-ripe apricots fall from the tree.

POETRY, SONGS AND GAMES

Barbara Cooney's *A Garland of Games and Other Diversions* (Holt) are as much fun today as they were 200 years ago. Librarians welcomed Virginia Tashjian's *Juba This and Juba That: Story Hour Stretches for Large or Small Groups* (Little). Delightful songs and games were included in *Wake Up and Sing* by Beatrice Landeck (Morrow) and *Hi! Ho! The Rattlin' Bog: and Other Folk Songs for Group Singing* by John Langstaff (Harcourt). Of all the ABC books, *Apricot ABC* by Miska Miles with illustrations by Peter Parnall (Little) was the most creative and charming.

REFERENCE BOOKS

Many of the reference books published in 1969 were curriculum-oriented. Still,

several were welcomed for the home library. These included *In Other Words: A Beginning Thesaurus* by W. Cabell Greet and others (Lothrop); Day Perry's *Dictionary of Basic Words* (Childrens); and *The Picture Dictionary for Children* by Garnette Watters and S. A. Courtis (Grosset). The whole family could enjoy E. L. Jordan's *Animal Atlas of the World* (Hammond). Shirley Glubok's one-volume abridgement of two volumes published by Alice Morse Earle in 1899 and 1922, called *Home and Child Life in Colonial Days* (Macmillan), was useful for browsing and for school assignments.

CLASSICS

Five old favorites were re-issued: *Little Women* by Louisa May Alcott (World), with lovely illustrations by Tasha Tudor; *Alice's Adventures in Wonderland & Through the Looking Glass* by Lewis Carroll (Little); a facsimile of the 1925 deluxe edition of *The Adventures of Pinocchio,* translated from the Italian by Carol Della Chiesa (Macmillan); George MacDonald's *The Light Princess,* illustrated by Maurice Sendak (Farrar); and the charming story of *The Velveteen Rabbit* by Margery Williams (Doubleday).

"The Fool of the World and the Flying Ship" by Arthur Ransome. Illustrated by Uri Shulevitz.

BIOGRAPHY

Lady Queen Anne by Margaret Hodges (Farrar) was a well-written story of the last of the Stuarts. Judith Masefield's *Shepherdess of France: Remembrances of Jeanne d'Arc,* illustrated by Leonard Weisgard (Coward), was a beautifully designed, poetic version of the maid's thoughts and experiences told in the first person.

Books by and about the Negro continued to represent a high percentage of the biographical publications. Much of the writing was mediocre or poor. But two books were of particular interest because of the subjects involved. Jean Maddern Pitrone's *Trailblazer: Negro Nurse in the American Red Cross* (Harcourt) was the fascinating story of Frances Elliott Davis' struggle for recognition and status. Ruby Zagoren's *Venture for Freedom: the True Story of an African Yankee* (World) gave the world another Amos Fortune in the person of Venture Smith, a seven-year-old African prince who was captured and brought as a slave to Connecticut in 1736.

FOLKLORE, FANTASY AND FAIRY TALES

Children continued to request books of imagination and fantasy. There are few collections of Eskimo tales, so a welcome addition was Ramona Maher's *The Blind Boy and the Loon and Other Eskimo Myths* (John Day). Terry Berger's *Black Fairy Tales* (Atheneum), illustrated by David Omar White, told South African tales of long ago. Virginia Hamilton's *The Time-Ago Tales of Jahdu* (Macmillan), illustrated by Nonny Hogrogian, were ageless and black. And Joan Payne's *The Raven and Other Fairy Tales* (Hastings) showed black heroes and heroines through story and pictures. A colorful, gay book was *The Fair at Sorochintsi* by Nikolai Gogol, retold and illustrated by Deborah Ray (Macrae). A beautiful Indian fable of the mouse turned into a maiden by a holy man was Mehlli Gobhai's *Usha: The Mouse-Maiden* (Hawthorn). Aliki provided gay illustrations for her retelling of the Greek folktale of the sea captain and the four fried eggs in *The Eggs* (Pantheon). The boys and girls who enjoy Pinocchio loved Marie Halun Bloch's *Ivanko and the Dragon,* illustrated by Yaroslava (Atheneum). This is the story of a stick of wood which becomes a boy, is captured by a dragon, and finally escapes. One of the most delightful versions of *The Miller, the Boy and the Donkey* was illustrated by Brian Wildsmith (Watts).

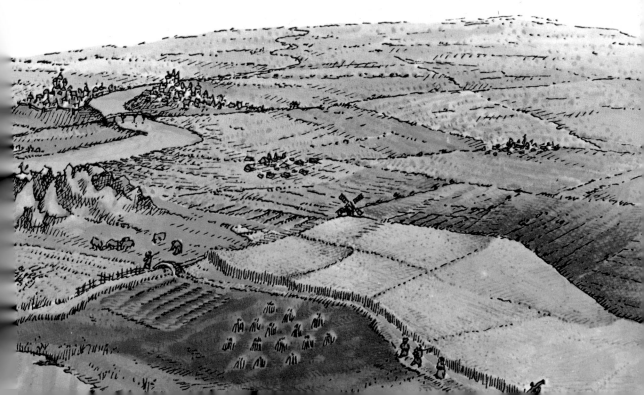

Cats were featured in folktales and fiction. A new edition of Charles Perrault's *Puss in Boots or "The Master Cat"* (World) was illustrated by Barry Wilkinson. *Mourka, the Mighty Cat* (Parents') illustrated by Charles Mikolaycak, was an amusing Russian folktale by Lee Wyndham.

▶ EASY-READING AND PICTURE BOOKS

There are always a few books that do not fit into the usual categories and appeal particularly to the preschool and primary-grade child. A controversial book was Louise Fitzhugh's *Bang Bang You're Dead* (Harper), a realistic story of children playing war. It should give parents food for thought. Ezra Jack Keats' *Goggles* (Macmillan) showed Peter and his friend Archie finding and fighting to keep a pair of motorcycle goggles. John Steptoe, a 19-year-old Negro, has written and illustrated a poignant story of a child in a foster home called *Stevie* (Harper).

An illustration from "Goggles," a delightful book by Ezra Jack Keats.

Two delightful picture books had rain as the central theme. *Rain Rain Rivers* by Uri Shulevitz (Farrar) was a mood book. *And It Rained* by Ellen Raskin (Atheneum) was the delightful tale of a tea party in the jungle with a pig, a parrot, and a potto.

▶ FICTION

Books for the Intermediates

The boys and girls who have just begun to read on their own continue to be "the forgotten child" in the book world. The best books are written year after year by the same authors, such as Carolyn Haywood and Beverly Cleary, and the books are often in a series. E. L. Konigsburg wrote an hysterically funny story of a Jewish mother and the local Little League baseball team in *About the B'Nai Bagels* (Atheneum). George Selden continued the adventure of Harry Cat, Tucker Mouse, and Chester Cricket, the heroes of *Cricket in Times Square,* in his *Tucker's Countryside* (Farrar). Both boys and girls enjoyed Marilyn Sach's *Peter and Veronica* (Doubleday), a sequel to her *Veronica Ganz* in which Veronica, the bully, gets her comeuppance, and *Danny Dunn and the Smallifying Machine* by Jay Williams and Raymond Abrashkin (McGraw).

Books for Boys

As usual, the quantity and quality of stories for boys far exceeded those for girls. Most of the boys' books had the central theme of "Who am I?" or "How do I relate to the world?"

Pistol by Adrienne Richards (Little) was a powerful story of a 14-year-old boy in Montana growing up in the midst of the Depression. A controversial book was John Donovan's *I'll Get There. It Better Be Worth the Trip* (Harper). It portrayed vividly yet subtly the growing pains and confusing emotional and physical responses of a 13-year-old boy. Books with modern settings were *Whose Town* by Lorenz Graham (Crowell), the third book about David Williams; *The Skating Rink* by Mildred Lee (Seabury), about a teen-age boy growing up in the rural South; and *Leashed Lightning* by Jo Sykes (Holt), the story of David Hollis and his desire to train show dogs against his parents' wishes. An excellent picture of the Gold Rush to the Klondike in 1897 was portrayed in Ruth Franchere's *Stampede North* (Macmillan). Janet McNeill's *Goodbye, Dove Square* (Little) was laid in England but spoke directly to American young people regarding urban redevelopment and the changing values of society.

Books for Girls

Of the many books written especially for the teen-age girl, four stood out. *In Spite of All Terror* by Hester Burton (World) re-created the bombing of London in World War II in the story of Liz, a London child evacuated to the country who returns to London to help. Kansas and Colorado in 1910 were the settings for the second story of a delightful family by Alberta Constant in *The Motoring Millers* (Crowell). Kitty Barne's *Barbie* (Little), the story of a child prodigy, appealed to all girls who love music. No punches were pulled in Florence Crannell Means' *Our Cup Is Broken* (Houghton), the powerful, unforgettable story of Sarah, a Hopi Indian girl. Sarah is torn between the two worlds of white and Indian and discovers that she fits into neither but must choose one.

It is fitting to close this resume of 1969 publications by mentioning *The High King* by Lloyd Alexander (Holt) because it was the Newbery Medal winner in 1969.

CAROLYN W. FIELD
Coordinator, Work with Children
Free Library of Philadelphia

MEDICINE AND HEALTH

MAJOR progress was made in many areas of the health sciences during 1969. But perhaps the most exciting medical work of the year took place during the moon landing by the Apollo 11 astronauts. Dr. Charles Berry, director of medical research at the Manned Spacecraft Center in Houston, Texas, and his associates were deeply involved during the flight and the actual moon walk. By means of telemetry (the technique of making measurements at a distance), the medical team measured the heart rate, oxygen use, and thermal (heat) output of the astronauts. The measurements gave the Houston team an idea of the amount of energy the astronauts were using. Then the doctors could decide whether the astronauts should slow down or rest. Other measurements were also taken and studied. Except for a small weight loss, the astronauts returned in excellent health.

▶ **TRANSPLANTS**

Heart transplants became the subject of increased debate during the year, and there was a considerable slowing of the rate of such transplants. The two men who had lived longest with transplanted hearts both died. Dr. Philip Blaiberg, who had survived 19 months and 15 days, died in August in South Africa. In October, Father Boulogne, a French Dominican priest, died in Paris 17 months and 5 days after his operation.

In the first year after Dr. Christiaan Barnard operated on Dr. Blaiberg, about

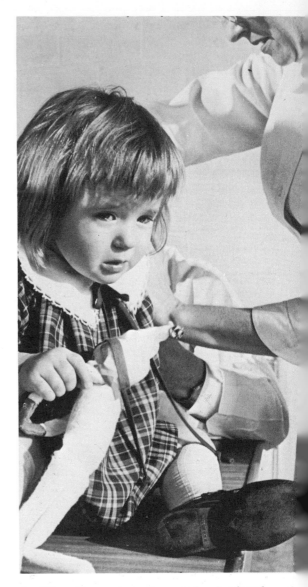

A little girl receives the newly developed German-measles vaccine during worldwide testing program.

100 heart transplants were performed. It was soon clear that from a technical standpoint, the operation was not difficult for a skilled surgical team. The major problem was the body's normal tendency to reject any outside substance. It is now fairly well recognized that it is unwise to continue to do vast numbers of heart

transplants until researchers solve the basic problem of rejection.

Other transplant techniques seem promising. Bone-marrow transplants have been successful in correcting immunologic defects. These are defects in the body's system of defenses against disease. Dr. Robert A. Good of the University of Minnesota and his associates were able to correct an immunologic defect in a child by transplanting bone marrow from his sister. (The transplant from a close relative is much more likely to take.)

Transplant of spleen cells from a dead person has produced marked improvement in patients with hemophilia and other bleeding diseases. The report by a team of Los Angeles researchers of this work is, however, an early one. In Belgium a patient with cancer of the esophagus became the first person in the world to receive a transplant of a larynx. Kidney transplants continued to be of lifesaving help to countless victims of kidney disease.

As a result of the activity in the field of transplants, the National Institutes of Health (NIH) asked the College of Surgeons to establish a transplant registry. This would be a computerized center listing all transplant information. Such information should help researchers and prevent repetition of errors. (Kidney transplants are already recorded in a separate registry.) In Europe, Eurotransplant, a five-nation organ-exchange program, is already under way.

▶ HEART DISEASE

New surgical approaches offered encouragement to people with diseased coronary arteries. (These are the small blood vessels that feed the heart muscle.) Surgeons implanted arteries taken from the chest wall directly into the heart muscle. The surgeons hoped the implanted arteries would take the place of the coronary arteries that had closed off or were narrowed by disease.

Another surgical development offered hope to heart-attack victims who suffer a

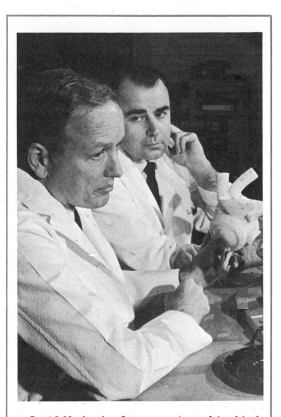

In 1969, in the first operation of its kind, Dr. Denton Cooley (left) replaced a patient's defective heart with a mechanical heart. Three days later a human heart was substituted for the mechanical one. Though the patient, Haskell Karp, died a day later, Dr. Cooley stated that the artificial heart had done its job: it had kept Karp alive until a donor could be found. At right is Dr. Domingo Liotta, designer of the mechanical heart.

rupture of the heart septum. This is a membrane separating the right side of the heart from the left. At Stanford University in California, Dr. Albert Iben reported sudden and great improvement in six patients who had surgery to repair the rupture.

▶ INFECTIOUS DISEASES

In 1969 there was a worldwide epidemic
continued column 2, page 241

WHY THE PACE OF HEART TRANSPLANTS HAS SLOWED

By DR. ADRIAN KANTROWITZ

IN December 1967, at the Groote Schuur Hospital in Capetown, South Africa, a patient's hopelessly damaged heart was replaced with a healthy one. The surgical team that performed this feat was led by Dr. Christiaan Barnard. A few days later, in Brooklyn, New York, a second team, led by Dr. Adrian Kantrowitz, completed the same operation on an infant born with a faulty heart. The surgical technique used in these operations had been developed by Drs. Norman Shumway and Richard Lower and their colleagues. By the end of February 1968 several other groups, all with strong backgrounds in animal studies, had successfully performed human heart transplants.

With these proofs that the surgical technique was practical, many other groups of surgeons attempted heart transplants. In November 1968 alone, 26 operations were done. By the end of 1968, 103 operations had been logged throughout the world.

The year 1969 saw a drop in the frequency with which heart transplants were performed. Since April 1969 no more than four transplants have been attempted in any one month. As of October 1969, only 45 operations had been recorded for 1969. The total up to that time was 148 transplants, performed in 146 recipients.

What has happened? Why has the pace of transplants slowed so dramatically?

Perhaps the main reason for the decline is the disappointingly low survival rate. In October 1969 only 31 of the 146 patients who had had transplants were still alive. (Dr. Philip Blaiberg, Dr. Barnard's second transplant patient, died 593 days after his operation, on August 17, 1969.)

The rejection process, in which the body tries to destroy substances foreign to itself, including another person's heart, is thought to have played a part in most of the deaths after transplants. Many surgeons and other doctors have become discouraged. They believe that methods for diagnosing and treating the "rejection phenomenon" are not yet good enough. Heart transplants should be halted or sharply reduced for the present, they think.

Other doctors continue to perform transplants and do not find reason for pessimism in the survival figures. They point out that

"Pirate" shows no sign of rejection three years after receiving a heart from an unrelated dog. The February 1967 operation was performed at Maimonides Medical Center, New York.

graft rejection had been observed for more than fifty years in animal experiments before the first human trials. Promising drugs that help the body tolerate a graft have been under study for a number of years. Since December 1967 much more has been learned, not only about how to do transplants but also about matching recipients with donors. Much has been learned also about the management of graft rejection and related problems. The death of Dr. Blaiberg, they point out, was probably not due so much to rejection as to damage of the heart's arteries from atherosclerosis, which had developed after the transplant.

Good progress is being made in the related field of artificial heart devices. During the past years, a number of devices to help certain functions of the heart have been used successfully in patients. The much more complex problem of making a mechanical device to totally replace the heart has also been studied. This is a spearhead of current research—the attempt to find a substance that can be implanted in the body without damaging or being damaged by the body's blood and other tissues.

of Hong Kong flu. The virus that caused this particular kind of flu was different from other flu viruses. Thus, the available vaccines were ineffective. Drug companies worked to prepare a vaccine in record time, and large numbers of people were vaccinated. But there were thousands of deaths because of the flu epidemic of 1969.

Rubella (German measles) is not a serious disease ordinarily, but when a woman is infected with it early in pregnancy, frequently the result is a deformed newborn. A rubella vaccine promises to overcome this risk. The vaccine has been carefully tested and is being used to vaccinate large groups of children. Since children are the ones who usually catch and spread the disease, the vaccination program should eliminate it.

Tuberculosis continues to be a major health problem, even in the developed countries of the world. Servicemen who are sent to countries with a high tuberculosis rate are exposed to the disease. The number of cases is on the upswing in this group. In addition to the drugs already used in treating tuberculosis, a new drug—ethambutol hydrochloride—has been used successfully.

In Trinity College, Dublin, Dr. C. V. Barry and his co-workers have developed a phenazine dye which they have found to be effective against leprosy.

▶ ADVANCES IN OTHER DISEASES

Parkinson's disease affects more than 1,000,000 Americans. It causes uncontrolled tremors and stiffness of muscles. In advanced cases the disease is almost completely disabling. In 1969, doctors continued their work with L-Dopa, a drug that has had dramatic effects in treating Parkinson's disease. The drug is still being tested in large groups of patients, but has not yet been released for general use by doctors for their patients.

Schistosomiasis is a disease caused by a parasite. In tropical countries the disease affects hundreds of thousands of people and requires lengthy treatment. A new drug has been found to cure schistosomiasis in 1 injection. The drug cured between 80 and 90 per cent of the patients to whom it was given in a trial.

A group of scientists has reported the first encouraging word in the treatment of Paget's disease, a chronic disease of bones. The group found that mithramycin, an antibiotic, antitumor agent, produced remarkable results.

Cancer research continued on many fronts. Researchers tested a number of new drugs to see their effect as anticancer drugs. Scientists also did much work to try to see if various viruses might cause some cancers in human beings.

Of particular interest is a discovery by Dr. Phil Gold and his co-workers at McGill University School of Medicine in Canada. They found in the blood of patients with cancer of the large bowel a particular substance, called a tumor-specific antigen. The discovery could be a breakthrough in developing a method of detecting cancer of the large bowel, and may even lead to a new method of treatment.

Another new test may make it possible to predict the likelihood of a person's developing cancer. Cells are taken from an individual and exposed to cancer-producing chemicals or viruses. The cells taken from some individuals and treated in this way show microscopic changes suggestive of cancer.

Late in 1969, Robert H. Finch, secretary of health, education, and welfare, banned the use in beverages of artificial sweeteners called cyclamates. They may be used in foods and drugs labeled to show cyclamate content. The government action followed the discovery of bladder cancers in laboratory rats that had been given huge amounts of the sugar substitute.

▶ OTHER HEALTH FIELDS

Football deaths reached a new high in the 1968–69 season, a study indicated. There has also been an increase in the number of injuries, particularly knee injuries. Officials have made new safety recommendations, and companies have developed equipment to give greater protection.

In 1969 the National Jogging Association was formed. Its purpose is to collect data on joggers over a three- to five-year period. The organization hopes to learn about the value of jogging in the prevention of heart attacks.

Cigarette sales continued to decline in 1969. A new government report confirmed that cigarette smoking is a serious health hazard. The report is the 1969 supplement to the 1967 Public Health Service review of the health consequences of smoking. The cigarette industry announced its willingness to give up broadcast advertising in the future.

The problem of drug abuse continues. Although young people tend to move away from the more addictive and dangerous drugs, the number of marijuana users seems to be on the increase. All of the government programs are being unified under a new Division of Narcotic Addiction and Drug Abuse, headed by Dr. Sidney Cohen. He recognizes that increased police action is not the solution. He feels we must begin to understand why young people turn to drugs. He also feels we must study these drugs, particularly marijuana, so that the physician has sound information about their effects to pass on.

The Department of Health, Education, and Welfare undertook in 1968 the first Federal survey of the state of nutrition in the United States. A first report indicated shocking evidence of malnutrition in children. The signs of malnutrition are as serious as they are in children in countries with a much lower standard of living.

The Food and Drug Administration (FDA) reported on the birth-control pills now being taken by 8,500,000 American women. The FDA termed the pills safe. It found, however, that the risk of death from blood-clotting disorders is 4.4 per cent higher in women who use the pills than it is in women who do not.

LEONARD I. GORDON, M.D.
Internist, New York City

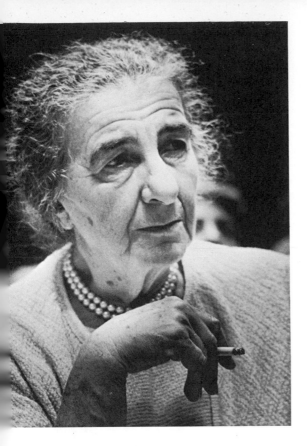

MEIR, GOLDA

WHEN Levi Eshkol, Israeli premier since 1963, died in February 1969, a power struggle seemed to be in the making. The two contenders for the premiership were Defense Minister Moshe Dayan and Deputy Premier Yigal Allon. To avoid a damaging party split, the ruling Labor Party, on March 7, nominated Golda Meir, a seventy-year-old grandmother. Ten days later Mrs. Meir, a pragmatic, strong-willed woman, was sworn in as the fourth premier of Israel.

Mrs. Meir was born Golda Mabovitz on May 3, 1898, in Kiev, the Ukraine. Her family settled in Milwaukee, Wisconsin, when she was eight years old. Although she had been trained to teach, she became an active Zionist. Zionists sought to create a Jewish nation in Palestine. In 1921 she emigrated to Palestine with her husband, Morris Myerson, and worked on a kibbutz, or communal farm (in 1956 she changed her name to Meir, the Hebrew spelling of Myerson). Three years later they moved to Jerusalem, where their two children were born. Today their son, Menachem, is a cello teacher in Connecticut. Their daughter, Sara, is a member of a Negev kibbutz. Mrs. Meir and her husband later separated, and he returned to the United States. He later moved back to Tel Aviv, where he died in 1951.

Mrs. Meir became an active member of Histadrut, the Jewish labor federation. She quickly rose to its executive committee. She also played a prominent part in the Jewish Agency. This organization helped establish the state of Israel. When the male leaders of that organization were arrested by the British, she became its political director for two years. In 1948 she signed the Israeli declaration of independence. A year later she became a representative in the first Israeli Knesset (Parliament).

In 1948 the first Arab-Israeli war broke out, and Mrs. Meir went on her first major diplomatic mission. She crossed the Jordanian border disguised as an Arab woman to meet with Jordan's King Abdullah. The same year, she was appointed ambassador to Moscow. She gave up this post in 1949 to become labor minister. Appointed foreign minister in 1956, she had at least one major disagreement with Premier Ben-Gurion. This was over recognition of West Germany, which Mrs. Meir opposed.

To win allies for Israel, Mrs. Meir led a very successful program among the new African nations. She presented them with "friends" instead of "experts" and "shared goods" instead of "aid." In 1966 she gave up the post of foreign minister and became secretary-general of the Mapai (Labor Party). Two years later she resigned because of her health. She returned to public life in 1969 as Israel's prime minister.

See also MIDDLE EAST.

METEOROLOGY. See WEATHER.
MEXICO. See LATIN AMERICA.

MIDDLE EAST

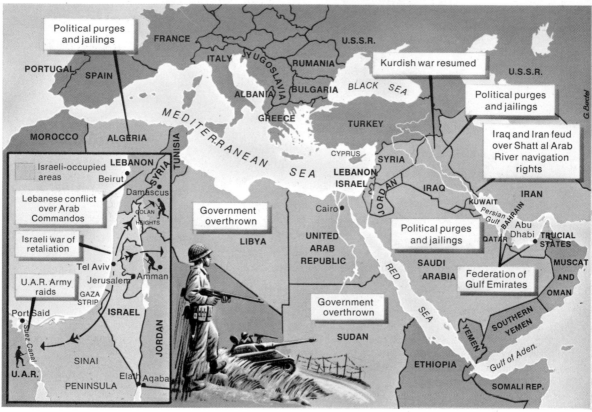

During 1969, the Middle East continued to be the area of greatest turmoil.

THE twin sources of instability in the Middle East—nationalism and revolution—were clearly visible in 1969. The governments of Libya and Southern Yemen were overthrown. The governments of Lebanon and Syria were forced to change their foreign policies by the threat of force and internal violence. Dissatisfaction with the rule of ailing President Habib Bourguiba of Tunisia was voiced publicly for the first time. There were jailings and purges in Algeria, Saudi Arabia, and Iraq. In Iraq, too, the Kurdish wars were renewed. The Arab-Israeli conflict, the rapid growth of the Palestine liberation movements, and the inability of the Great Powers to find a peaceful solution, all contributed to the instability of the region.

▶ **THE ARAB-ISRAELI DISPUTE**

In 1969, the Arabs and Israelis made no serious effort to reach a political settlement. On the contrary, border clashes, raids, counterraids, sabotage, and terrorism increased. Israeli forces retaliated on all four fronts: the United Arab Republic, Jordan, Lebanon, and Syria. Casualties on both sides reached their highest peak since the June 1967 war. It seemed unlikely that an agreement would be reached on the Palestinian refugee problem or that Israel would give up any of its conquered territory. The

Arabs settled for a "war of attrition" and the Israelis for a "war of retaliation."

The United Nations as well as the Great Powers tried to move the antagonists toward the peace table. Their efforts proved futile. The United States and the Soviet Union had an interest in defusing the conflict and in avoiding a direct confrontation. Still, they were unable to agree in their many discussions on a Middle East peace formula. American influence in the Arab world continued to decline. Indeed, in November at the meeting of the Arab League's Defense Council, the United States was called the Arabs' "Enemy No. 1."

The most active participants in the Arab-Israeli conflict continued to be Israel and the four states that border it: Jordan, Lebanon, Syria, and the United Arab Republic.

Israel

In February, Prime Minister Levi Eshkol died of a heart attack. This opened the possibility of a struggle for succession between Deputy Premier Yigal Allon and Defense Minister Moshe Dayan. To fill the post and avoid a split in the Labor Party, the top post was given to Golda Meir, the one person around whom most politicians could rally.

An able and astute party leader, Prime Minister Meir continued the policies of Eshkol. She pushed ahead with plans for economic development, despite heavy military costs, and forcefully met the Arab threat.

In an attempt to rule the country with the widest possible consensus, Mrs. Meir led the Labor Party in the October national elections in alignment with the left-wing Mapam Party. The results of the election were somewhat disappointing. The alignment won only 56 of the 120 seats in the Knesset (Parliament), 5 seats less than a majority.

The United States delivered the first of fifty Phantom jets to Israel in 1969, further drawing the wrath of the Arab states. Israel continued to respond to guerrilla attacks, artillery bombardment, and Egyptian forays across the Suez Canal with air strikes.

When a religious fanatic set fire to the Al Aksa Mosque in Arab Jerusalem, the Arabs accused Israel of arson. The mosque is the third holiest in the Muslim world, and the unfortunate event further increased tensions and hatred in the Middle East. The arsonist, an Australian, admitted setting the fire; he was tried in Jerusalem.

Jordan

King Hussein wanted to reach a settlement with Israel during 1969. He was, however, thwarted by Israel and by the Palestine Liberation Organization (PLO). Israel refused to negotiate the disposition of Arab Jerusalem. And the PLO sabotaged all efforts at reconciliation with Israel. Jordan was unable to stop the Palestine guerrillas from infiltrating into Israel or from shelling Israeli settlements from Jordanian territory. As a result, Jordan felt the full force of Israeli retaliation.

Lebanon

Half-Christian, half-Muslim Lebanon was torn over the issue of the limited operations of Palestinian guerrillas in southern Lebanon. The Christians of Lebanon tended to support a policy that would keep their country out of direct conflict with Israel. But the real division in Lebanon crossed confessional lines. It emerged as one between the left wing and the right wing, between the impatient young and their prudent fathers.

The issue was brought to the fore in October by the Palestinian commandos. Those commandos based in Lebanon and Syria refused to take orders from the Lebanese Government and tried to step up the conflict with Israel. Lebanon wanted to control the commandos, fearing that increased activity would invite retaliation by Israel. This conflict erupted into bitter fighting that lasted for 13 days. It threatened to destroy the fabric of the Arab world's only democracy. An agreement was reached, however, thanks to the mediation of Presi-

dent Nasser of the United Arab Republic.

The Lebanese Army's commander in chief, General Emile Bustani, and the chief of the Al Fatah commando group, Yasir Arafat, met in Cairo. They agreed that the commandos would restrict their activities to certain regions of Lebanon. From their strongholds in Lebanon, the guerrillas would be allowed to operate against Israel provided they "co-operate" with the Lebanese Army.

Guerrilla attacks from Lebanon resulted in Israeli air attacks and commando raids. To strengthen its hand, with Israel as well as with the Palestinian guerrillas, Lebanon replaced Army chief Bustani with a more militant general.

Syria

Syria remained among the most vocally militant of the Arab states with regard to the Arab-Israeli dispute. It continued to field a force of guerrillas—Al Saiqah—against Israel and gave strong support to these and other guerrillas in their struggle with the government of Lebanon.

A major shake-up took place in the ruling Baath Party in February and March. Defense Minister Hafez al-Assad, by a show of force in Damascus, the capital, strengthened his position within the party. This modest victory for the more-nationalist wing of the Baath Party helped end the isolation of the country. Steps were taken to improve relations with the Baathist rulers in Iraq as well as to re-establish the defunct Arab Eastern Military Command (Iraq, Syria, Jordan).

Progress was made with the giant Euphrates dam scheme, which the Soviet Union supports with large amounts of economic and technical assistance.

The Arab-Israeli conflict was no nearer to a solution in 1969. Indeed, as positions hardened, fighting and destruction increased. Al Fatah commandos, led by Yasir Arafat, left, set up bases in Lebanon and increased their sabotage activities in Israel. Most Arab commandos are Palestinians and are recruited from refugee camps, such as the one at right in Jordan. Many Arab youngsters begin commando training when they are 12 years old. For its part, Israel retaliated with air strikes against commando training bases in Jordan, Lebanon, and Syria. It also adopted sterner methods of retaliating against Arabs who live in Israel or Israeli-occupied territory and who give aid to the commandos.

United Arab Republic

Some of the heaviest fighting of the year took place along the Suez Canal. Artillery duels, air battles, and commando raids occurred almost daily between Egypt and Israel.

President Nasser continued as the most influential leader of the Arab world. He regained much of his popularity by escalating the struggle against Israel. In November he said that a political solution would be impossible, and that war is the only way to regain lost Arab lands. Nasser's voice in intra-Arab councils was strengthened by the new pro-UAR governments in Libya, Sudan, and Southern Yemen. His growing influence among the Baathists in Iraq and Syria and his successful mediation of the Lebanese crisis also increased his prestige.

Work on the Aswan Dam appeared to be on schedule. And there was an increase in revenues from oil production and cotton exports. Nevertheless, the Egyptian economy suffered because of high military costs. The failure to reopen the Suez Canal and a rapidly increasing population added to the country's economic problems.

▶ ALGERIA

President Houari Boumedienne continued to consolidate his power. He purged many former heroes of the struggle against France who questioned his dictatorial rule.

In 1969, Algeria increased its trade with the Soviet Union and was dependent on that country for much of its military equipment. Still, there remained a marked preference for Western goods and technology.

▶ CYPRUS

In Nicosia, the capital of Cyprus, negotiations continued with the aim of ending the rift between Greek and Turkish Cypriots. There was, however, little hope for an early settlement. Turkey and the Turkish Cypriots stuck to what appeared to be an inflexible position. On the other side, the Greek Cypriot extremists believed that Cypriot President Makarios had gone too far in seeking an accord with the Turkish Cypriots.

▶ FEDERATION OF GULF EMIRATES

After many delays, the Federation of Gulf Emirates was launched in October. The rulers of Bahrain, Qatar, and the seven Trucial Coast emirates elected Sheik Zayed bin Sultan al-Mihayan of Abu Dhabi as the federation's first president. The sheik is the wealthiest and most powerful of the nine rulers. Abu Dhabi was selected as the provisional capital. It was also agreed that the National Assembly should be composed of equal numbers of representatives from each of the autonomous sheikdoms along the Persian Gulf. However, the powers of the president remain to be determined by a constitution still under study.

▶ IRAN

Iran's fourth five-year development plan continued to be buttressed by economic and technical assistance from the Soviet Union and the United States as well as from oil revenues. In May, the Shah won concessions from the international oil consortium. The 15 oil companies linked in the consortium agreed to hand over $1,-000,000,000, or $100,000,000 more than they had paid in 1968.

In 1969 Iran turned its full attention to the Persian Gulf. From the Shah's point of view, this was made necessary by Arab claims to Khuzistan, the plain situated at the northern coast of the Persian Gulf; by Arab plans to dominate the Persian Gulf; and because access to Iran's main commercial and oil ports continued to lie through Iraqi waters.

On April 19, the Iranian Government canceled its 1937 agreement with Iraq which regulated navigation in the Shatt al Arab River forming Iraq's southern border with Iran. The pact gave Iraq almost complete control of the river. The Shah's timing to pick a quarrel with Iraq and for a show of force was well chosen. With troops in Jordan and Syria, and a division fighting the Kurds, Iraq could ill afford to meet the Shah's challenge. On April 22, an Iranian freighter, escorted by planes and naval ships, defied Iraqi warnings by sailing out of the Iranian port of Khorramshahr. It was unmolested and showed that Iran is ready to go very far to get the frontier changed to the middle of the river.

In October, the Shah visited Washington to discuss the implications of the forthcoming British withdrawal from the Persian Gulf. He also asked for military equipment. Without question, Iran is determined to play a leading role in the Persian Gulf, a role it is apparently willing to share with conservative Saudi Arabia. Iran is also determined to prevent the Arabian coast of the Persian Gulf from falling into the hands of Arab revolutionary forces.

▶ IRAQ

The year was marked by purges, arrests, and violence. The Revolutionary Council headed by Ahmed Hassan al-Bakr began a campaign of terror against everyone from the extreme right wing to the Communists. The campaign, including a series of political trials and hangings, was aimed at "purging the country of foreign imperialist influence."

The Kurdish war started again early in the year. The Baathist regime committed 60,000 troops to disarm and pacify the Kurds. Later in the year, while the fighting continued, the regime offered to set up a new Kurdish province, called Dohuk, within Iraq.

In May, Iraq became the first Arab and noncommunist state to extend full diplomatic recognition to the East German regime. During the year, Iraq developed closer economic ties with Eastern Europe and the Soviet Union. In July, in return for a long-term loan from the Soviet Union,

Moscow was given permission to exploit the oil fields in southern Iraq.

KUWAIT

The oil-rich state of Kuwait worked toward stability in the Persian Gulf. Fearful of the revolutionary Arab states, it is on good terms with Iran and Saudi Arabia.

Kuwait also continued its program of using oil money to buy independence, or at least time. A number of revolutionary Arab governments, particularly the U.A.R., received Kuwaiti money. Kuwait acknowledged in June that it is a major financial supporter of the Palestine commandos.

LIBYA

In September, Leftist army officers seized the oil-rich kingdom of Libya. King Idris formally abdicated and accepted exile in Cairo. With the military hovering in the background, a civilian cabinet was formed. Mahmoud al-Maghreby was named premier. But the strong man was Mohammad al-Qadhafi, head of the Revolutionary Command Council.

With its oil revenues, the new regime tried to speed up economic and social reforms. It also supported a more-nationalist policy, particularly in the struggle against Israel. A fifth of its oil resources were pledged to aid other Arab countries. Libya became one of the top three of the world's oil-exporting nations in 1969.

MOROCCO

The Islamic Summit Conference met in September in Rabat, capital of Morocco. The leaders of most of the Islamic world met to discuss the burning, in August, of the Al Aksa Mosque, the third most holy shrine of Islam, in Arab Jerusalem.

The conference ended with a condemnation of Israel, which was held responsible for the fire at the Al Aksa Mosque. But on the Palestine question, it was a case of Islamic disunity.

An Arab summit conference was also held in Rabat, in December. But the refusal of oil-rich Saudi Arabia and Kuwait to pledge more money to the nations actively involved in fighting Israel caused the conference to fall apart. This was considered a major blow to Arab unity and to the prestige of the conference sponsor, President Nasser of the United Arab Republic.

MUSCAT AND OMAN

The Sultanate of Oman, sometimes called Muscat and Oman, remained at odds with all of its neighbors except Abu Dhabi. Undefined frontiers, particularly with Saudi Arabia, and the ideological threat posed by Southern Yemen were its main concerns in 1969. The Dhofari Liberation Movement in Dhofar Province continued to be contained by the British-backed forces of the Sultan. Wealth from recent oil production created a desire of the Omanis to enter

The Shah of Iran arrives at the White House in October for a state dinner given in his honor. He is greeted by Mrs. Nixon as the President watches.

HEADS OF GOVERNMENT

Algeria	HOUARI BOUMEDIENNE, premier	Libya	MAHMOUD SOLIMAN AL-MAGHREBY, premier
Cyprus	ARCHBISHOP MAKARIOS II, president	Morocco	HASSAN II, king
	SPYROS A. KYPRIANOU, prime minister	Muscat and Oman	SAID IBN TAIMUR, sultan
Federation of Gulf Emirates	ZAYED IBN SULTAN AL-MIHAYAN, president	Saudi Arabia	FAISAL IBN ABDUL AZIZ, king
		Southern Yemen	SALMIN RUBAYA, chairman of presidential council
Iran	MOHAMMAD RIZA PAHLEVI, shah		MOHAMMAD ALI HAITHAM, prime minister
	AMIR ABBAS HOVEIDA, premier		
Iraq	AHMED HASSAN AL-BAKR, president and premier	Syria	NUREDDIN AL-ATTASSI, president and premier
Israel	SCHNEOR ZALMAN SHAZAR, president	Tunisia	HABIB BOURGUIBA, president
	GOLDA MEIR, prime minister	Turkey	SULEYMAN DEMIREL, prime minister
Jordan	HUSSEIN I, king	United Arab Republic	GAMAL ABDEL NASSER, president
	BAHJAT AL-TALHOUNI, premier		
Kuwait	SABAH AL-SALEM AL-SABAH, sheik	Yemen	ABDUL RAHMAN AL-IRYANI, president
Lebanon	CHARLES HELOU, president		ABDULLAH AL-KARSHUMI, premier
	RASHID KARAMI, prime minister		
Libya	MOHAMMAD AL-QADHAFI, chief of state		

	POPULATION	ARMED FORCES	CURRENCY*	ARAB LEAGUE
Algeria	13,686,000	57,000	5 dinars = $1.00	X
Cyprus	611,000	. . . .	1 pound = $2.50	
Fed. of Gulf Emirates	460,000	. . . .		
Iran	28,765,000	221,000	75.8 rials = $1.00	
Iraq	9,122,000	78,000	1 dinar = $2.80	X
Israel	2,881,000	22,500**	3.5 pounds = $1.00	
Jordan	2,394,000	55,000	1 dinar = $2.80	X
Kuwait	646,000	. . . .	1 dinar = $2.80	X
Lebanon	2,665,000	13,000	3.2 pounds = $1.00	X
Libya	1,968,000	6,000	1 pound = $2.80	X
Morocco	15,450,000	54,000	5 dirhams = $1.00	X
Muscat and Oman	770,000	. . . .		
Saudi Arabia	7,340,000	34,000	4.5 rials = $1.00	X
Southern Yemen	1,330,000	10,000	1 dinar = $2.40	
Syria	6,174,000	70,500	3.8 pounds = $1.00	X
Tunisia	4,934,000	17,000	1 dinar = $1.90	X
Turkey	35,398,000	483,000	9.1 lires = $1.00	
United Arab Republic	32,792,000	207,000	1 pound = $2.30	X
Yemen	5,100,000	. . . .	1.1 rials = $1.00	X

* US $; 1969 exchange rates
** Can be mobilized to 290,000

the modern world. There was dissatisfaction with the feudal rule of Sultan Said ibn Taimur.

▶ **SAUDI ARABIA**

King Faisal increased efforts to push his desert kingdom into the modern world. A five-year development plan was drawn up and almost 50 per cent of the national budget was earmarked for development projects. Priority was given to communications with an emphasis on new roads and port facilities. There was also a major attempt to lessen the country's dependence on oil revenues by developing agriculture and exploiting mineral resources.

From June through September, Saudi Arabia was shaken by a series of arrests in the air force and civil administration. These arrests reflected, to some extent, the unrest created by encouraging economic and social reform but not political reform.

In November and December, Saudi Arabian and Southern Yemeni troops clashed over the frontier post of Al Wadeea, which both countries claim.

▶SOUTHERN YEMEN

The government of President Qahtan al-Shaabi was replaced in June by a five-man Presidential Council headed by Salmin Rubaya. Mohammad Ali Haitham was named prime minister. The political purge brought to the fore men committed to a hard left-wing ideology.

▶TUNISIA

In March, Tunisia became an associate member of the European Economic Community in an effort to bolster its economy. However, Tunisia received a major setback in October following calamitous floods in the southern part of the country. Over 500 people were killed, 100,000 made homeless, 50,000 homes destroyed, and many farm animals drowned. The rains also affected the market gardens and the phosphate industry which form the backbone of the Tunisian economy.

Although there was some discontent in the country, President Habib Bourguiba was elected to a third five-year term on November 2. He ran unopposed.

▶TURKEY

Anti-American militants in Turkey are small in number. Yet in 1969 they continued to find a ready response among the Turks in general. Several factors threatened to undermine the traditional pro-Western position of Turkey. Many Turks are dissatisfied with the Western position on the Cyprus issue. Others feel that Western economic aid is unsatisfactory. The presence of American servicemen and their families—some 25,000—and the growth of Leftists and ultraconservative Rightist movements have added to the friction.

However, Turkey's fragile democratic institutions, under the watchful eye of the military, received a major boost in the October national elections. Suleyman Demirel's ruling Justice Party won a vote of continued confidence from an apathetic electorate. The pro-American conservative Justice Party received an overall majority in the National Assembly, winning 259 of the 450 seats. The left-of-center Republican People's Party of Ismet Inönü obtained a small increase in its share of the vote and 142 seats. Thanks in part to a change in the electoral system, extremist and splinter parties were virtually barred from representation in the National Assembly.

▶YEMEN

The long war in Yemen between the Royalists and Republicans was considerably dampened in 1969. It was a year of urban peacefulness, thanks in part to the astute leadership of President Abdul Rahman al-Iryani and to the decision of Saudi Arabia to withdraw support from the Royalists. (There were reports late in 1969 that Saudi Arabia had decided to resume aid to the Royalists.)

The moderate Republican Government's emphasis on the economy reflected a new mood in the country. Heavily dependent on Chinese, Russian and other communist aid, the Government began to cultivate economic ties with the noncommunist world. In July it resumed diplomatic relations with the West German Government with the hope of getting economic aid from Bonn.

The antigovernment Royalist forces seemed to be scattered and ineffective. The threat to the regime seemed more and more to come from the extreme Leftists within Yemen and in exile in Cairo and Aden. These people feel that the Government has not gone far enough in its revolutionary aims.

HARRY J. PSOMIADES
Queens College of the
City University of New York

See also MEIR, GOLDA.

MONGOLIA. See ASIA.

MOROCCO. See MIDDLE EAST.

MOTION PICTURES

THE personal film proved to be the box-office and artistic success for 1969. This type of film was marked by the director's distinctive style. It dealt with anti-Establishment or human-frailty themes.

The Dennis Hopper and Peter Fonda film *Easy Rider* was of this type. It appealed to young audiences with its slashing attack against a society that destroys those who refuse to conform. Another was Arthur Penn's *Alice's Restaurant*. It featured the young folk singer Arlo Guthrie and was based on his recording of *Alice's Restaurant Massacree*. In it, the efforts of a group of young nonconformists to cope with the Establishment are shown with humor, compassion, and sadness. *Medium Cool* was made by cameraman-turned-director Haskell Wexler. The 1968 Chicago Democratic national convention is the background against which he tells the story of a television news cameraman struggling with the problems of involvement, both in terms of his job and his personal life. John Schlesinger's *Midnight Cowboy* featured Dustin Hoffman and an impressive new actor, Jon Voight. *Midnight Cowboy* deals with two modern-day derelicts who ultimately develop a touching relationship as a result of their mutual rejection by society.

Several offbeat and unusual films were praised by the critics. Bob Downey's somewhat crudely made but hard-hitting black comedy, *Putney Swope,* was a satire of Madison Avenue. It is about blacks who take over an advertising agency from the whites. They run into the same temptations and the same pitfalls and finally conclude that "money is evil" by burning a ton of it. *Last Summer* is a modern-day parable by Frank and Eleanor Perry. In *Last Summer* the theme "belong or get out" is viciously shown, first in the killing of a sea gull and later in a gang rape. Another offbeat motion picture, *If,* dealt with the problems of the modern generation. It was directed by Lindsay Anderson, and concerned rebellious schoolboys whose fantasies and problems lead to open revolt.

Newcomers scored well, notably Ali MacGraw, who was teamed with Richard Benjamin and Jack Klugman in *Goodbye, Columbus*. It was based on a novella by Philip Roth and dealt with the generation gap in a Jewish family. Two new faces, Barbara Hershey and Cathy Burns, were in *Last Summer*. Some old-timers fared well also. Patty Duke performed well in *Me, Natalie*. And Alan Arkin was singled out for his performance as *Popi*, a Puerto Rican widower harassed by the problems of ghetto life. But Katharine Hepburn did not please the critics in her role as *The Madwoman of Chaillot,* a film version of the Giraudoux play.

▶ **MUSICALS AND COMEDIES**

For the audience that prefers song-and-dance motion pictures, there were Peter O'Toole and Petula Clark in the remake of *Goodbye, Mr. Chips*. Shirley MacLaine starred in *Sweet Charity*. And Sir Carol

---

ACADEMY AWARDS

Motion Picture: OLIVER!
Actress (tie): KATHARINE HEPBURN (*The Lion in Winter*); BARBRA STREISAND (*Funny Girl*)
Actor: CLIFF ROBERTSON (*Charly*)
Supporting Actress: RUTH GORDON (*Rosemary's Baby*)
Supporting Actor: JACK ALBERTSON (*The Subject Was Roses*)
Director: SIR CAROL REED (*Oliver!*)
Foreign-Language Motion Picture: WAR AND PEACE
Song: THE WINDMILLS OF YOUR MIND
Documentary Short: WHY MAN CREATES
Cartoon: WINNIE THE POOH AND THE BLUSTERY DAY

Reed's production of *Oliver!* starred Ron Moody as Fagin and nine-year-old Mark Lester in the title role. Joshua Logan came out with *Paint Your Wagon,* a film version of an 18-year-old Broadway show, with Lee Marvin, Clint Eastwood, Jean Seberg, and Harve Presnell.

In the comic vein, Woody Allen stole the show with *Take the Money and Run,* a mad mixture of slapstick comedy and parody in a quasi-documentary style. Not so effective were *Some Kind of Nut* with Dick Van Dyke in the role of an oddball bank clerk; Rowan and Martin's *The Maltese Bippy,* a variation of their television laugh-in; and the team-up of Bob Hope and Jackie Gleason in a film that is not funny, *How to Commit Marriage.*

▶ WESTERNS AND SCIENCE FICTION

The old standby, the Western, was made as a big-scale epic or as a film with an un-usual look at absolute mayhem. For the epic, Carl Foreman, producer-writer, J. Lee Thompson, director, and Dimitri Tiomkin, producer-composer, turned out a 70mm. Super Panavision and Technicolor film, *Mackenna's Gold.* In it Gregory Peck portrays the stalwart lawman who is forced to lead a group on a search for treasure. Needless to say, members of the party become corrupted by their own greed. Real Western violence, however, was graphically depicted in Sam Peckinpah's *The Wild Bunch.* In this film a number of stars, William Holden, Ernest Borgnine, Robert Ryan, Edmond O'Brien, and Warren Oates, put on a blood-and-guts spectacle never before seen. *The Wild Bunch* apparently intended to break down the romantic Western myth by showing killing and death as it really is.

The indestructible John Wayne played a one-eyed, whiskey-soaked, paunchy mar-

Mark Lester stars in the title role of the award-winning musical "Oliver!"

Glen Campbell, John Wayne, and Kim Darby in the Western "True Grit."

shal in *True Grit,* a more traditional Western. Somewhat more up-to-date in mood was *Butch Cassidy and the Sundance Kid.* It featured Paul Newman and Robert Redford in a Western that mixed laughs with broad action and visual effects.

For the science-fiction and action-mystery fans, there were a number of films whose titles quite aptly summed up their plots: *The Green Slime, Valley of Gwangi, Destroy All Monsters, Spirits of the Dead, Journey to the Far Side of the Sun,* and *Krakatoa, East of Java.* Best that can be said about these films is that if you have seen one, you have seen them all.

▶FAMILY FILMS

For the very young, Disney Studios produced *The Love Bug.* In it a Volkswagen is given a personality and a name—Herbie—and trickily maneuvers through a sugary plot. United Artists competed with *Chitty Chitty Bang Bang* in which Dick Van Dyke,

in the role of Caractacus Potts, an out-of-this-world inventor, comes up with an auto that can fly through the air and sail on the water. Less fanciful was *Ring of Bright Water* featuring the stars of *Born Free,* Virginia McKenna and Bill Travers. The film, a sentimental story of love and nature, centered on an otter named Mij. Equally effective was *Run Wild, Run Free,* a story of a white colt and a young boy, named Philip, played by Mark Lester. However, *A Boy Named Charlie Brown* was successful. It brought the characters from the *Peanuts* comic strip to the screen in an animated, full-length film.

▶SEX IN FILMS

Although the year was marked by the absence of any critically acclaimed foreign films, there were many sex pictures beginning with the much-talked-about *I Am Curious (Yellow).* From Sweden, this film tried to combine political, social, and sexual problems in a meaningful relationship. The film was quite controversial. Its admirers were equaled by those who found it repugnant.

Mostly, however, sex films were dull and silly, aimed at capitalizing on the trend toward nudity and the drug scene. Among the foreign films of this type were *More, Camille 2000, The Girl on a Motorcycle, Birds in Peru, Inga, Michael and Helga, La Prisonnière,* and *Succubus.* Not to be outdone, American film makers came through with *Three in the Attic, The Best House in London, Three into Two Won't Go,* and *Finders Keepers, Losers Weepers.*

▶ **THE NEW YORK FILM FESTIVAL**

The Seventh New York Film Festival offered 23 different programs with repeat showings for a total of 44 performances. The best-received of these films was director Eric Rohmer's *Ma Nuit Chez Maud,* a deft, tightly woven comedy in which a 34-year-old man is trapped by his personal ethics.

At the close of the festival a number of films immediately went into commercial release. Among these were *Oh! What a Lovely War,* a film adaptation of Joan Littlewood's successful stage presentation, savagely attacking the ridiculousness of war; *Adalen '31,* which tries to combine social and political themes with a lyrical style; Susan Sontag's *Duet for Cannibals,* a kind of mumbo-jumbo sex film of great ambiguity which the viewer can interpret freely.

A tradition was broken at the New York Flm Festival when it presented a Hollywood entry. The film was *Bob & Carol & Ted & Alice* by Columbia Pictures and featuring Natalie Wood, Robert Culp, Elliott Gould, and Dyan Cannon. It was well received by the audience, but not by some critics.

▶ **AMERICAN FILM INSTITUTE**

The American Film Institute, in addition to assisting young independent and college film makers with production grants, ex-

An otter named Mij is the center of the story in "Ring of Bright Water," based on the novel by Maxwell Gavin.

panded further with the help of the Corporation for Public Broadcasting, in setting up the Television Filmmaker Competition. AFI Director George Stevens, Jr., announced seven winners of the competition with awards totaling $100,000. The completed films will be screened for television broadcast. In addition, AFI's advanced professional school got under way in Beverly Hills, the first 15 film makers being selected from independent film makers and film schools around the country.

HAIG P. MANOOGIAN
Institute of Film and Television
New York University

A scene from "Help! Help! The Globolinks," Gian-Carlo Menotti's delightful new opera.

MUSIC

THERE were a number of unusual musical developments in 1969. Gian-Carlo Menotti, the Italian-born American composer, surprised the musical world with *Help! Help! The Globolinks*. This is an opera for and about children that proved highly successful with adult audiences. In the area of symphonic music, Pierre Boulez was named to succeed Leonard Bernstein as conductor of the New York Philharmonic. And in electronic music, the Moog synthesizer added a new dimension to musical sound.

▶ OPERA

In opera, at least, 1969 may well go down as the year of the Globolinks. Gian-

Carlo Menotti, at the age of 58, is among the few moderns who have been able to write operas people will pay to hear. *Help! Help! The Globolinks* had its world premiere in Hamburg, Germany, during the winter of 1968–69. Its United States premiere was held during the summer of 1969 at Santa Fe, New Mexico. Not every critic admired *Help! Help! The Globolinks*. But audiences loved it. There seemed no doubt that it would become at least as popular as his well-known Christmas opera, *Amahl and the Night Visitors*.

Help! Help! The Globolinks is not only a funny and tuneful fantasy about space invaders and schoolchildren. It is also a story about electronic music. These are the new tape-produced sounds that continued to hold the attention of extremely modern composers and audiences during the year. In Menotti's fable a group of weirdly shaped spacemen from another planet are continually accompanied by electronic music. Children riding in a school bus and armed with ordinary musical instruments attempt to keep them off. Needless to say, music—*real* music—conquers all. By the end of the short opera, the Globolinks and their blipping, whirring, grunting sounds have been put to flight. All this is expressed with the greatest charm and good humor. The opera thus lives up to the basic requirement of a successful stage work: to provide good entertainment. The opera also shows that Menotti's talent for creating melody is far from used up.

Another opera premiere during the year proved less fortunate. The Santa Fe Opera also put on *The Devils of Loudun* by Krzysztof Penderecki, a modern Polish composer. But not even a strong mixture of extremely modern tonal effects lent much interest to this tale of medieval French witchcraft, based on a book by Aldous Huxley.

More-familiar operatic business occupied the Metropolitan Opera. In 1968 and 1969 it maintained its record of virtually full houses throughout the year by sticking mostly to standard operas. Exceptions were productions of two twentieth-century works, Alban Berg's *Wozzeck* and Benjamin Britten's *Peter Grimes*. Other highlights of the season were new productions of Richard Strauss' *Der Rosenkavalier* and Richard Wagner's *Das Rheingold*. *Das Rheingold* is the second in a new *Ring of the Nibelung* series planned and conducted by Herbert von Karajan.

The Met had to delay the start of its fall 1969 season until December 29. The three-month delay was caused by a labor dispute involving 14 unions representing performers and stage workers.

Elsewhere in the country, operatic activities flourished on a normal scale. One of the most welcome events was the return to action of the Chicago Lyric Opera Company. It had been silenced the previous season by labor problems. In Atlanta, Georgia, a new arts center all but ended operations because of financial problems after a much heralded beginning. In Washington, D.C., planning continued for the projected John F. Kennedy Performing Arts Center, designed as a national cultural showcase. But actual completion, once scheduled for 1970, seemed a long way off.

▶ **SYMPHONY ORCHESTRAS**

In the symphonic world, one big question was answered while an even bigger one was left unsettled. The New York Philharmonic ended guessing about Leonard Bernstein's successor by choosing one in advance. They chose Pierre Boulez, the French composer-conductor. Boulez was widely praised during his month as guest conductor with the Philharmonic during the spring. He was expected to breathe new life into the orchestra's repertory. He was also expected to appeal strongly to younger audiences when he takes over in the fall of 1971.

Other conductors were also on the move. Thomas Schippers will take over the Cincinnati Symphony Orchestra in 1970. William Steinberg succeeded Erich Leinsdorf in Boston, and at the same time kept his directorship of the Pittsburgh Symphony. Among the veterans, Eugene Ormandy of Philadelphia remained unmoved among the changes. He kept his podium for the 33d year. In October, the Philadelphia Symphony celebrated the seventieth anniversary of its founding.

But the major question facing the nation's symphony orchestras was not finding new conductors. It was finding new sources of income. Orchestras throughout the year felt the pressure of inflation keenly. New labor contracts raised the costs of operations to levels that could not be met by increases in ticket prices. The leaders of the "Big Five" orchestras—New York, Philadelphia, Cleveland, Chicago, and Boston—held a series of meetings, first secretly, then openly. The leaders explored ways of improving their finances. No formula was adopted. But all promised to continue their efforts to work one out. The Minneapolis Symphony, one of the nation's finest second-line orchestras, pointed a possible way. It changed its name to the Minnesota Orchestra. It thus took on a regional, rather than a local, character. By doing this the orchestra hoped to increase its audiences.

▶ **ELECTRONIC MUSIC**

Electronic music continued to make inroads in the field of new music. It even began to have its effects upon manufacturers of classical musical instruments. The Baldwin Piano Company, for example, devised an instrument capable of artificial enlargement of its tones without distortion. Lorin Hollander, one of the best young pianists, introduced this instrument. He played it at a concert held in the cavernous Fillmore East in New York's East Village, an arena usually reserved for rock groups. A large audience made up mostly of young men and women turned out for the event.

But the major development in electronic music during the year came in the rapid growth of an instrument called the Moog (rhymes with vogue) synthesizer. The Moog synthesizer is named after its maker, engineer Robert A. Moog. The Moog can reproduce almost any sound known to man, and some sounds up to now unknown. The Moog can copy the sounds of strings, woodwinds, brasses, and the like. It can also emit various screeches and bleeps. These are of great use to experimental composers in search of new tone combinations. The sounds are also of use to television and motion-picture audio experts looking for unusual sound effects.

The Moog's triumphs during 1969 included an appearance at a garden concert held at The Museum of Modern Art in New York in late August. But its most lasting impact came in the issuance by Columbia Records of a release entitled *Switched-On Bach*. In the release, composer Walter Carlos uses the Moog to perform the *Brandenburg Concerto No. 3,* the *Air on the G String,* several fugues from *The Well-Tempered Clavier,* and other compositions of Johann Sebastian Bach.

The recording brought a freshness of sound and outline to these familiar works. It was an immediate hit with music critics and the public. It quickly became one of the fastest-selling records in the history of the industry. *Switched-On Bach* rolled up more than $1,000,000 in sales. As a result, many authorities expected the Moog and other electronic music synthesizers to play a considerable role in the music of the immediate future.

HERBERT KUPFERBERG
Music Critic, *The Atlantic*

MUSIC, POPULAR

IN 1969, Bob Dylan's major album was *Nashville Skyline.* Dylan used an acoustic guitar on the album and was backed by a small country band. In 1969, too, there was a demand for the early records of Buddy Holly, Jerry Lee Lewis, and other rock 'n' rollers from the 1950's and early 1960's. B. B. King and other early rhythm-and-bluesmen had for years played only ghetto clubs. In 1969, however, they found open doors at youth concerts and white clubs. All of these items indicated a movement in 1969 toward simplicity and toward the roots of real white country sounds and black blues sounds. This movement was a reaction against the sophisticated, artistic level to which rock had risen in the wake of The Beatles.

▶ **ELECTRONIC MUSIC**

While The Who made a best-selling, two-album rock opera in *Tommy,* the interest in electronic music seemed to move from the young, who had first listened to it, to people over thirty years old. Older people bought and listened to *Switched-On Bach,* an electronically made album. Many other albums followed this one. The most successful was Dick Hyman's *Electric Eclectics of Moog.* The Moog is a synthesizer, or an electronic instrument used to make sounds. It looks like a combination of an electric organ and a telephone switchboard. It can be played like a keyboard instrument or programed like a computer. The Moog was the synthesizer that was first used by The Byrds, The Beach Boys, Simon & Garfunkel, and The Beatles.

▶ **ROCK FESTIVALS**

1969 was the year of monster rock festivals. The festivals were so important to young people that *Life* magazine put out a special issue on the Woodstock Festival, held at Bethel, New York, in August. More than 400,000 young people attended this three-day music festival. Some of the year's festivals, such as those at Newport and Denver, were disorderly. But at Wood-

stock, at the Isle of Wight, England, and at other places, the youths were well-behaved. All of the festivals, however, were marked by drug use, poor sanitation, little

Robert A. Moog, inventor of the Moog synthesizer, in his electronic-music studio.

or no housing, bad weather, and overcrowding.

▶ NEW GROUPS

The taste for black sound that caused the rebirth of urban, electrified rhythm and blues also led to the formation of many white blues bands. From England came Ten Years After, Moody Blues and Blind Faith. American combos, or bands, such as Canned Heat, Steve Miller Band, and Blood, Sweat and Tears, all had best-selling albums. The artists of the Detroit or Motown sound (The Miracles, The Supremes) and of the Memphis sound (Otis Redding) remained in demand. So too did Aretha Franklin and James Brown.

1969 was the year of "soul." *Billboard* magazine changed the listing of black recordings from "rhythm and blues" to "soul." In the 1940's it had changed "race" records to "rhythm and blues."

1969 was also the year of supergroups. That is, combos of rock stars that came together in new groups after the breakup of other groups. Among these were the Led Zeppelin, Blind Faith, and Crosby, Stills and Nash. David Crosby had been with The Byrds. Stephen Stills had been with Buffalo Springfield. And Graham Nash had been with the Hollies. The meaning of these new groups was that the many colors of the rock spectrum (blues, jazz, folk, country, and electronic) were, perhaps, coming to a blend.

▶ RADIO PROGRAMING

Radio programing underwent an important change because of young-listener interest in Indian, free-form, synthesizer, and other nonpop music. So-called "underground" stations sprang up around the country, first in FM and then in AM. The term "underground" was not correct, because it involved such major stations as KABC in Los Angeles and WNEW in New York City. Underground did mean a new kind of pop programing, whose earmarks were suggested by a WNEW advertisement: "We don't play a record . . . because it's No. 1 or No. 2 or No. 12. If a song takes twenty minutes to play we allow twenty minutes for it." WNEW also said: "Young people today are twice as educated as their parents. They're concerned with the implications of the new morality. . . . The new rock music . . . speaks of a new order. A world where people are real and values are just. . . . WNEW-FM plays this rock."

▶ POP PERSONALITIES AND HIT RECORDS

The over-thirty generation did not lack for a new pop-song idol. In Welsh-born Tom Jones it found a singer who was as appealing as Presley and Sinatra. Within a few months, Jones, who had a weekly television show, had four gold records.

Hair, the rock musical that started as an offbeat production in an off-Broadway theater, turned into one of the phenomena of musical theater in the United States and other countries. During the year, the original-cast album became the No. 1 best seller. A recording by The Fifth Dimension, *Aquarius/Let the Sun Shine In,* was the No. 1 single.

Two of the year's biggest songs were *Oh Happy Day,* a gospel tune recorded in a West Coast church on old equipment, and *2525 (Exordium and Terminus),* a ballad by two country-pickin' guitarists from Lincoln, Nebraska.

1969 will be remembered as the year that Judy Garland went to her resting-place *Over the Rainbow.* Elvis Presley came out of an eight-year retirement from personal appearances. He played Las Vegas' newest hotel, The International, and scored a hit. Flatt & Scruggs stopped picking bluegrass together. Johnny Cash not only played Folsom and San Quentin prisons, but had his own television show broadcast weekly from Nashville's Grand Ole Opry.

ARNOLD SHAW
Author, *The Rock Revolution*

NATIONAL DEFENSE. See UNITED STATES.
NAURU. See PACIFIC ISLANDS.
NETHERLANDS. See EUROPE, WEST.
NEWSPAPERS. See PUBLISHING.

NEW ZEALAND

ON November 29, 1969, Prime Minister Keith J. Holyoake led the National Party to victory in nationwide elections. A major reason for Holyoake's retention of power was New Zealand's remarkable economic recovery after the severe recession of 1967–68.

▶ ECONOMIC RECOVERY

New Zealand's export earnings for the year ended June 30, 1969, were over NZ $1,000,000,000 for the first time in the nation's history. The record figure was largely the result of two factors. The first was the devaluation of New Zealand currency by 20 per cent in November 1967. The second factor was the recovery of export prices, especially for wool.

The major export earners were meat ($316,000,000), wool ($226,000,000), dairy products ($211,000,000), and forest products ($37,400,000). The value of manufactured goods exported rose from $64,000,000 in the previous year to $95,-200,000.

New Zealand achieved a balance-of-payments surplus for the year of almost $50,-000,000. The cost of living continued to rise. Unemployment declined from about 9,000 in mid-1968 to about 3,000 in mid-1969.

The National Development Conference

In May, 500 of New Zealand's most prominent economists, politicians, farmers, businessmen, educators, and trade unionists met to consider over 650 recommendations from 17 expert committees which had been meeting since August 1968.

Three main targets for economic development over the next decade were set. First, it was decided to increase the gross national product (GNP) by 4½ per cent a year until 1978–79. Second, an export-growth rate of 6.6 per cent a year was set in order to reach an export target of $1,-690,000,000 by 1978–79. Third, the Conference recommended an increase from 25 to 27 per cent in the share of the GNP devoted to investment expenditure.

New Zealand's Prime Minister, Keith J. Holyoake.

The Government, which sponsored the N.D.C., undertook to carry out the recommendations wherever possible. A 14-man National Development Council was set up to keep the targets under review.

Forestry

This sector of the economy showed amazing growth. The value of forest production over the past year was $302,000,000. Exports of forest products rose 50 per cent over the previous year. By 1978–79, New Zealand hopes to export at least 150,000,-000 cubic feet of timber a year.

The Manapouri Power Scheme

The first stage of the giant Manapouri hydroelectric-power program was completed in September 1969. The program has already cost over $100,000,000. The first stage produces 400,000 kilowatts of electricity. When the remaining three generators come into use, the 700,000-kilowatt production will make Manapouri the largest hydroelectric power station in the Southern Hemisphere. Much of Manapouri's power will be used by the $100,000,000 aluminum plant which Comalco Industries is building nearby.

▶ THE SECURITY INTELLIGENCE ACT

Parliament placed New Zealand's 13-year-old Security Service under the control of a minister who can be questioned in Parliament. It made provision for the appointment of a commissioner to whom citizens may appeal against the activities of the Security Service.

Head of Government: KEITH J. HOLYOAKE, prime minister
Population: 2,853,000
Armed Forces: 13,135
Defense Budget: $98,000,000*
Imports: $910,000,000*
Exports: $1,000,000,000*
Currency: 1 New Zealand dollar = US $1.10

* US $

▶ GRANTING OF THE RIGHT TO VOTE TO 20-YEAR-OLDS

In August, Parliament passed a bill lowering the age for voting from 21 to 20 years. All political parties supported the move. Some Labor members of Parliament and the sole Social Credit member favored lowering the age to 18.

▶ FOREIGN POLICY AND DEFENSE

New Zealand continued to value its alliance with the United States and maintained its military commitment in Vietnam. However, in June, Prime Minister Keith J. Holyoake warned President Nixon that if the United States enacted quotas against New Zealand lamb imports, lasting damage could be done to the relations between the two countries. Prime Minister Holyoake also warned that New Zealand's ability to maintain its defense expenditure would be in danger.

New Zealand's Government decided to adopt one per cent of the nation's gross national product as its target for overseas aid. The amount of money for the Colombo Plan for the 1969–70 fiscal year was doubled to $4,000,000

▶ THE PRIME MINISTER'S TRAVELS

Prime Minister Holyoake, who is also minister of external affairs, attended the Commonwealth Conference in London in January. He then visited West Germany, France, Italy, India, Pakistan, and Singapore. In May he went to Bangkok for the SEATO and Vietnam Allies' meetings. In July he attended a conference in Australia to discuss the defense of Malaysia and Singapore after Britain leaves the region in 1971. In August he returned to Australia for the ANZUS Council meeting. In September he visited the United States for talks with President Nixon. Then Prime Minister Holyoake went on to visit Canada.

BARRY S. GUSTAFSON
Political Studies Lecturer
Auckland University

NICARAGUA. See LATIN AMERICA.
NIGER. See AFRICA.

NIGERIA

IN 1969, events in Africa continued to be overshadowed by the civil war between Nigeria and the breakaway state of Biafra. The aim of the Nigerian Federal Government, under Major General Yakubu Gowon, was still to "keep Nigeria one." Biafra still insisted that its Ibo people and their neighboring tribes must become a separate nation. By the end of 1969 the civil war had been raging for 2½ years in spite of many peace efforts. In January 1970, however, the Biafrans, short of food, supplies, and war material, surrendered, thus ending the civil war.

▶ **CONTINUED STRIFE**

During the early part of 1969, Federal troops continued their advance, but the Biafrans fought back and began to regain some of their lost land. Although Federal

Map of Biafra, which, with the end of the civil war, will be reincorporated into Nigeria. At right, a Biafran soldier in retreat.

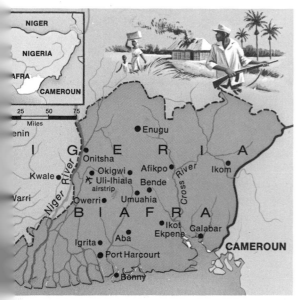

troops captured the Biafran provisional capital of Umuahia on April 22, the Biafrans claimed the recapture of Owerri two days later. By July the Biafrans were back in the suburbs of Umuahia, and by the end of August, Biafra claimed to have retaken 200 towns along the Owerri-Port Harcourt front.

As the year drew to a close, however, the Nigerians mounted a major offensive, which took a high toll of Biafran lives. Biafra found it increasingly difficult to obtain the arms necessary to carry on the fighting. In addition, the ever-present problem of too-little food and starving Biafran children added to the bleak outlook for Biafra. In January 1970, Nigerian troops once again captured Owerri, the last Biafran stronghold. They also captured Biafra's last major airstrip, cutting off all supplies to the Biafran Army. On January 12, with little food and ammunition left, Biafra surrendered.

In May 1969, General Odumegwu Ojukwu, leader of Biafra, said that more than 1,000,000 Biafrans had been killed in the preceding 3 years.

At the end of the war, it was estimated that as many as 2,000,000 Biafrans and Nigerians had been killed during the 30 months of fighting. Joint Church Aid officials said that Biafran children had been dying at the rate of 1,000 a day.

International observers reported that there was no evidence of a Nigerian policy of genocide against the Ibo people, and that the Nigerian treatment of prisoners of war was humane. The Federal Government was commended for efforts to normalize life in areas captured from the Biafran military.

With the surrender of Biafra in January 1970, once again there was the fear of genocide. It was feared that many Nigerian troops would not heed the order to end the fighting. Thus, Major General Gowon ordered Nigerian troops to protect surrendering Biafran soldiers. He also ordered the civilian police to ensure the safety of Biafran civilians.

▶ FOREIGN INVOLVEMENT

Most African nations had stayed out of the Nigerian conflict. But the OAU had managed to bring the two sides together several times, always to no avail. (The last such fruitless meeting was held April 18-20, 1969, in Monrovia, Liberia.) Four African nations—Ivory Coast, Gabon, Tanzania and Zambia—had recognized Biafra. South Africa was reportedly supplying Biafra with military aid. In March 1969, Haiti had recognized Biafra.

Of the major world powers, Britain and the Soviet Union had given aid to Nigeria, while France and Communist China had aided Biafra. The United States had officially remained neutral, but many U.S. citizens and humanitarian groups sympathized with Biafra and the plight of the civilians there.

▶ RELIEF EFFORTS

Attempts to bring relief to the victims of the civil war had caused much controversy. The Federal Government accused the ICRC of giving Biafra fuel and spare parts for military vehicles. The Federal Government asked the ICRC not to make flights to Biafra at night so that ICRC planes would not be mistaken for Biafran planes. Biafra asked that there be no day flights. In June an ICRC plane flying at night was shot down by Nigerian planes. A curtailment of ICRC flights following this chain of events caused a 50 per cent rise in the death rate from starvation.

Following the surrender of Biafra, the United States and other countries took steps to avert mass starvation there. President Nixon, after conferring with British Prime Minister Wilson, authorized an additional $10,000,000 in foodstuffs and medicine to be sent to Biafra. Several European governments also made plans to send food to Biafra.

MARGARET F. CASTAGNO and
ALPHONSO A. CASTAGNO
Director, African Studies Center
Boston University

See also AFRICA.

NOBEL PRIZES

Co-winners of the Nobel Prize for Medicine: Professor Max Delbruck of Cal Tech (top), Dr. Alfred Hershey of the Carnegie Institution (below), and Dr. Salvador Luria of MIT (bottom).

THE first Alfred Nobel Memorial Prize in Economic Science was awarded in 1969. The economics prize and the prizes in chemistry, literature, peace, physics, and physiology or medicine were worth $73,-000 each.

Chemistry: ODD HASSEL, Norway, former professor of physical chemistry, Oslo University; and DEREK H. R. BARTON, Britain, professor of organic chemistry, Imperial College of Science and Technology, London. They won the award for their work in describing the configurations of complex molecules and the importance of the configurations in the behavior of molecules in chemical reactions.

Economics: RAGNAR FRISCH, Norway, Oslo University; and JAN TINBERGEN, the Netherlands, of the Netherlands School of Economics in Rotterdam. They won the award for their work in econometrics, which is the use of mathematics to measure economic activity.

Literature: SAMUEL BECKETT, Irish-born avant-garde author who now lives and writes in France. His writings deal with human loneliness and despair. *Waiting for Godot*, a play published in 1952, is his best-known work.

Peace: UNITED NATIONS INTERNATIONAL LABOR ORGANIZATION for its fifty years of international service. The ILO was set up after World War I and became a specialized agency of the UN in 1946.

Physics: MURRAY GELL-MANN, U.S., professor of physics, California Institute of Technology, for his discoveries concerning subatomic particles.

Physiology or Medicine: MAX DELBRUCK, U.S., professor of biology, California Institute of Technology; ALFRED D. HERSHEY, U.S., director, Carnegie Institution's genetics-research unit; and SALVADOR E. LURIA, U.S., professor of microbiology, Massachusetts Institute of Technology. They were cited for having "set the solid foundation on which modern molecular biology rests."

NORTHERN IRELAND. See GREAT BRITAIN.
OBITUARIES. See DEATHS.
OPERA. See MUSIC.
OUTER MONGOLIA. See ASIA.

OCEANOGRAPHY

Drilling beneath the sea may unlock the secrets of the ocean basins.

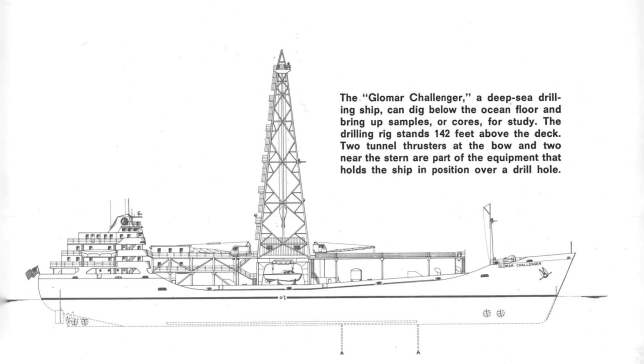

The "Glomar Challenger," a deep-sea drilling ship, can dig below the ocean floor and bring up samples, or cores, for study. The drilling rig stands 142 feet above the deck. Two tunnel thrusters at the bow and two near the stern are part of the equipment that holds the ship in position over a drill hole.

DURING 1969, man advanced his knowledge of the oceans and seas. He undertook many major projects and gained new insights into the history of the planet. At the same time, he learned more about methods of working in the ocean. He also turned his attention to the long-range problems of developing the riches of the seas.

▶ DEEP-SEA DRILLING PROJECT

Some of the year's most valuable findings can be credited to an 18-month Deep-Sea Drilling Project, which started in August 1968. The aim of the project is to try to determine the age of the ocean basins, the history of their formation, and the changes they have undergone. Scientists of Joint Oceanographic Institutions Deep-Earth Sampling (JOIDES) are conducting the research. They are from Scripps Institute of Oceanography, Columbia University, the University of Miami, the University of Washington, and Woods Hole Oceanographic Institution. The National Science Foundation is the sponsor of JOIDES.

The project centers on the *Glomar Challenger,* a ship equipped to bring up cores of rock and sediment. One of the ship's outstanding features is an automatic positioning system. This permits the vessel to remain stationary over the drill site.

During the first eight months of operation, the ship drilled and cored 54 holes at 31 sites, working in water from 4,000 to 18,000 feet deep. Nearly a mile of ocean-bottom cores were brought back for study.

Thus far, the most exciting finding of the project is physical evidence supporting the theory of sea-floor spreading. Over a period of millions of years, the continents have drifted apart, and scientists have come to believe that this drift is caused by spreading of the ocean floor.

Beneath the oceans there is a vast system of ridges in an almost continuous chain. The crests of the ridges are split by great rifts, or cracks. Magma, or molten rock, wells up through these rifts and spreads out along either side of the ridge to form new ocean bed. As the rock spreads, at the very slow rate of one centimeter a

The U.S. Navy's Sealab 3 (front) experiment in the Pacific Ocean in February was halted by tragedy: the death of aquanaut Berry L. Cannon.

year, sediment (silt and organic debris) is continuously deposited on it. Thus marine biologists believed that the farther away from the ridge they drilled, the older would be the sediment and the ocean bed beneath the sediment. This is exactly what scientists of the JOIDES project found.

In a line from New York to Dakar, Africa, which crosses the Mid-Atlantic Ridge, the scientists drilled several holes and brought up core samples. From core samples taken near the center of the ridge, they found that the layer of sediment was relatively thin. But as they moved away from the center, the sediment became thicker and older. This was determined by dating the fossils of tiny plants and animals found in the sediment.

A core sample taken 850 miles west of the ridge contained fossils that are 85,000,000 years old. Fossils found 100 miles from the ridge are only 18,000,000 years old. This discovery supports the theory that the ocean floor is younger near the central portions of the ridge and that the floor is older away from the ridge.

After its work in the Atlantic was completed, the *Glomar Challenger* moved into the Pacific Ocean. Early reports suggest that the findings here will be as exciting as those in the Atlantic. One core sample contained sediments that are more than 140,000,000 years old.

▶ PROJECT TEKTITE

The aims of Project Tektite were to learn more about man in the ocean environment, to conduct marine-science studies on the ocean floor, and to see how man functions in long periods of isolation. Four marine scientists lived 60 days under the sea—twice as long as anyone had ever lived there before.

On February 15, H. Edward Clifton, Richard A. Waller, Conrad V. W. Mahnken, and John G. Van Derwalker dove in scuba gear to an underwater habitat, or home. It rested 42 feet below the clear waters of Great Lameshur Bay in the Virgin Islands. The men lived in a habitat that was 2 connected upright cylinders, each one 18 feet high and 12.5 feet in diameter, mounted on a single rectangular base. Their habitat on the sea floor was connected to the surface with voice circuits, closed-circuit television, and power cables. The aquanauts swam from the habitat each day and carried out individual scientific studies.

During their 60-day stay, the scientists took blood samples from each other and sent them to a surface laboratory, along with the results of daily physical checkups. On the surface, the Navy and National Aeronautics and Space Administration

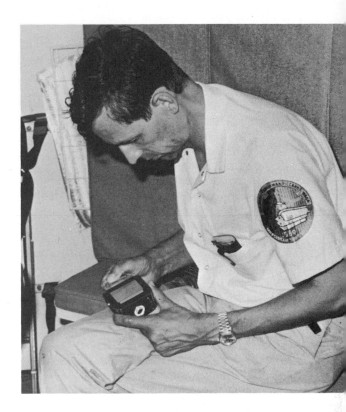

Dr. Jacques E. Piccard (above) led the Gulf Stream Drift mission in a yellow-and-white mini submarine, the "Ben Franklin" (right).

(NASA) teams observed the aquanauts continuously to measure how well they performed their tasks; how they reacted to one another; and how each man adjusted to his surroundings.

Sponsors of the project were the United States Navy, NASA, and the Department of the Interior.

Another project designed to test man's ability to live and work for long periods of time under the sea was the Navy's Project Sealab 3 off San Clemente Island, California. On February 17, the first day of the project, aquanaut Berry L. Cannon died of carbon-dioxide poisoning. The Navy stopped work on the program to investigate.

▶ GULF STREAM DRIFT MISSION

The Gulf Stream has interested scientists and seamen for centuries. It is a great current of water flowing up the east coast of North America. Benjamin Franklin made the first accurate chart of it in 1770.

For 30 days in July and August, Jacques Piccard, Swiss oceanographic engineer, and a crew of 5 carried out a research mission called Gulf Stream Drift. The men drifted from West Palm Beach, Florida, up the Gulf Stream to Halifax, Nova Scotia. They glided submerged in the *Ben Franklin,* a submarine 50 feet long.

The oceanographic objectives of their mission, sponsored by the Grumman Aerospace Corporation, were to investigate the Gulf Stream's currents, speeds, direction, turbulence, biological life, and physical and acoustical properties. (Acoustics is the science that deals with the behavior of sound.) Another objective was to measure the effects of long periods of isolation underwater.

▶ THE SS MANHATTAN

A major oceanographic-research project began in August with the SS *Manhattan.* The *Manhattan* is a tanker specially converted with an ice-breaking bow. She sailed from New York City in a successful attempt to open a Northwest Passage to Alaska. For the oil company sponsoring the project, its underlying purpose was commercial. The main interest of oceanographers, however, is the information the project will provide. They hope to gain new data on ice, oceanographic, and atmospheric conditions in the Arctic.

▶ THE PRESIDENTIAL COMMISSION

After two years of work, the Presidential Commission on Marine Science, Engineering and Resources submitted its report to the President and Congress early in January 1969. The far-reaching document will provide a basis on which Congress will legislate a national ocean program.

The Commission recommended the formation of a new Federal agency, the National Oceanic and Atmospheric Agency. It recommended that the agency have a 10-year, $8,000,000,000 program of ocean exploration and research.

▶ PLANNING FOR THE FUTURE

The seas offer vast resources for mankind: food, oil, and minerals. In the future the seas may also be a source of pure water for man and possibly a habitat.

The questions of the development and distribution of the ocean's resources are important ones. A 42-nation permanent committee of the United Nations General Assembly has been formed to study the peaceful uses of the ocean. A technical subcommittee reported during the year that in the near future, only a few countries will be able to take an active part in exploring the seabed. But the subcommittee stressed the idea that developments in the field should benefit everyone.

At the 17-Nation Geneva Disarmament Conference, in October, the United States and the Soviet Union offered a draft treaty to prevent the buildup of arms on the ocean floor. But no agreement on the seabed treaty was reached.

JOHN H. CLOTWORTHY
President, Oceans General, Inc.

OPERA. See Music, Classical.

OUTER MONGOLIA. See Asia.

A classroom scene at Rarotonga, capital of the Cook Islands. Aid from New Zealand has brought about free and compulsory education for all children up to the age of 16.

PACIFIC ISLANDS

THE march toward self-determination and economic progress continued to change society in the outwardly peaceful Pacific islands. Most of the islands and island groups of the Pacific remained to some degree under the control or protection of larger nations or were administered by them under United Nations trusteeships. The exceptions were Western Samoa and Nauru, independent island-states.

▶ COOK ISLANDS

The Cook Islands continued to get financial and technical help from New Zealand. In 1969, New Zealand announced that it will spend $10,000,000 to make the airport on Rarotonga into a jetport. In return

the Cook Islands' government has given New Zealand sole control of air-traffic rights into and out of the Cook Islands. New Zealand's subsidy to the Cook Islands was $2,000,000 in 1969.

▶ FIJI

Relations between the Fijian natives, who dominate the political system, and the Fijian East Indians, who control the economy, continued to be very strained. Talks took place over possible constitutional changes. These changes would increase Fiji's degree of independence from Britain. They would also change the system of voting to give the East Indians more of a voice in the government.

The University of the South Pacific at Laucala near Suva, the capital of Fiji, completed its first year of operation.

▶ FRENCH POLYNESIA

In February 1969 the territorial assembly on Tahiti voted 18 to 8 for more autonomy. In August the French Defense Ministry postponed hydrogen-bomb tests that were to have taken place in French Polynesia in 1969.

▶ NAURU

In March and April 1969, Nauru's Chief of State Hammer DeRoburt visited Australia and New Zealand to discuss the future of Nauru when its phosphate deposits are exhausted.

▶ TONGA

In August 1969, King Taufa'ahau Tupou IV announced that Tonga will become a fully sovereign nation sometime in 1970. Tonga will shed British protection in defense and foreign affairs when it becomes independent. The King's decision resulted from Britain's failure to back the building of a jet airport on Tonga.

▶ UNITED NATIONS TRUST TERRITORIES

The billion-dollar economic-development program for Papua-New Guinea begun by Australia in 1968 continued during 1969. This many-pronged effort should make Papua-New Guinea economically self-sufficient by 1980. It is viewed by Australia as the base for future self-government or independence for the territory.

Bougainville is part of the territory of Papua-New Guinea. On the island, the Conzinc Riotinto Corporation and the Australian Government in 1969 began to develop copper-ore deposits. The copper ore in the deposit is estimated at more than 500,000,000 tons. Within a short time the annual production could be 120,000 tons of copper and 600,000 ounces of gold. Conzinc will invest $300,000,000 in the venture. They will build a company town to house 10,000 people. Royalties and compensation will be paid to the territory. And there will be job training and jobs for 2,500 islanders.

The 10,000 acres where the copper deposits are located have been acquired by the company. But the local people refused to sell agricultural land for the company-town and construction-camp sites. When the Australian Government took the land by "compulsory acquisition" in August 1969, the police had to use batons and tear gas to disperse the demonstrators.

In the New Zealand-administered trust territory of Niue, elections were held in March 1969. A 5,000-foot airstrip is being built on the island.

A permanent air link has also been set up between New Zealand and the Tokelau Islands, another New Zealand trust territory.

Most of the small islands of Micronesia continued to be administered by the United States under a United Nations trusteeship. In November there was a poll in the Marianas, a part of Micronesia. It showed that most of the people preferred to have the Marianas join the territory of Guam.

The United States budget for Micronesia for 1969–70 was $41,600,000.

▶ UNITED STATES-ADMINISTERED PACIFIC TERRITORIES

In 1969, the United States agreed to return Okinawa, in the Ryukyus, to Japan. Okinawa has been the site of an important United States military base.

American Samoa was still administered by the United States Department of the Interior in 1969. But future self-determination was being discussed there.

▶ WESTERN SAMOA

As part of this independent country's drive for economic development, a fishing and freezing industry was started with Japanese assistance. In April 1969, the Legislative Assembly by a vote of 31 to 6 decided not to introduce voting for all adults.

BARRY S. GUSTAFSON
Auckland University

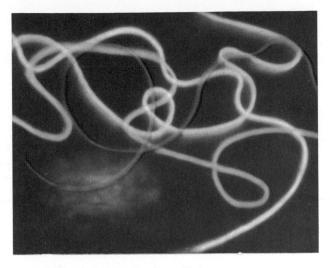

"Yellow Caterpillar" by Helen Frankenthaler, one of the abstract expressionists of the early 1950's. A show at New York's Museum of Modern Art revived interest in the group.

"Red Red" in acrylic by Dan Christensen, a member of the current group of soft-edge painters. The colors in Christensen's hazy painting were applied with a spray-can.

PAINTING

AMERICAN painting and sculpture in 1969 had no boundaries. No particular style or school dominated the scene. There was room for every point of view. One could see the open-mindedness of the general atmosphere as a stretch of calm water between waves. Or one could see it as a sign that artists would not work according to a set of hard-and-fast rules.

It was, on the whole, a year in which recent trends continued and became stronger. Once again artists explored familiar but fascinating ground, such as the meeting of art and technology.

In the matter of style, the most interesting event of 1969 was the rediscovery by a current generation of young talents of the leading American painters of the early 1950's. These painters were the so-called abstract expressionists or action painters. They included such well-known artists as Willem de Kooning, Mark Rothko, Adolph Gottlieb, and Helen Frankenthaler.

Attention centered on abstract expressionists largely as the result of an exhibition at New York's Museum of Modern Art. The exhibition was called "The New American Painting and Sculpture: The First Generation." In addition, De Kooning, Frankenthaler, and Barnett Newman received individual museum or gallery showings, as well. The black-and-white paintings and drawings of Jackson Pollock were exhibited in New York in March.

▶ SOFT-EDGE PAINTING

It is not surprising that many of the younger artists should feel a sense of kinship with these earlier painters. The return of the soft edge after years of ruled discipline, and the use of the material for its own sake struck the right chord for the present day. Dan Christensen's hazy paintings reveal levels of color applied with a spray-can. Lynda Benglis does "floor paintings" of liquid rubber, pigment, and wax.

"The Young Sabot Maker" by Henry O. Tanner (1859–1937), a black artist whose merits are receiving delayed recognition. Tanner, who painted in Paris, handled themes of everyday life with warmth.

A portrait of Tanner, painted by his teacher, the American artist Thomas Eakins.

Tom Holland, William Pettet, and Richard Tuttle were prominent at the Corcoran Gallery Biennial in Washington, D.C. All seem to have developed as heirs of the abstract-expressionist techniques, bringing with them a radiant freedom of attack.

▶ BLACK ART

The emergence—or possibly a more accurate term is the new visibility—of the American Negro artist was the third important trend of 1969. Individuals have been exhibited, but "1969: 12 Afro-American Artists" at the Nordness Galleries in New York is said to have been the first commercial-gallery grouping of its kind in this decade.

Plans were under way to bring back black artists whose merits have been overlooked. Toward midyear, Henry O. Tanner's paintings were being shown again. Tanner, who died in 1937, was a student of Thomas Eakins. He won a gold medal at the Paris Salon for his painting *The Raising of Lazarus*. His paintings on Negro themes have until now attracted little comment.

▶ COMPUTERS

Computers were a prominent theme—computers that could draw and switch

A helmet-mask from the New Hebrides is part of the Nelson Rockefeller collection of primitive art.

sound into light. A show called "Cybernetic Serendipity" was held at the Dupont Center of the Corcoran Gallery. The exhibits ranged from a computer portrait of President John F. Kennedy by Japanese engineers to Roger Dainton's *Simulated Synaesthesia,* which converted tapes and voices into colors.

▶CHALLENGES TO FORMAL ART

Disposable art was also prominent. Behind disposable art lay the idea that art works should not turn into sacred objects lasting through the centuries. Art works should be enjoyed as fleeting, vanishing fragments of time. The Canadian-born New York artist Les Levine performed actively in this area. His inventive treatment of gleaming plastics drew comment.

Related to the idea of disposable art were the ideas of "earthwork artists." Walter de Maria, one of this group, arranged great geometric patterns in the deserts of the world, bulldozed fields, and plowed tracts of empty soil with zigzag lines and symbols.

Formal art was indeed being challenged everywhere. At the Los Angeles County Museum, George Brecht showed 15 chairs stacked with unexpected objects. In New York, Richard Pettibone did a brilliant Andy Warhol parody, consisting of a "Warhol retrospective" of Campbell's Soup cans and Brillo boxes.

▶GALLERY EXHIBITIONS

In spite of these trends, the formal gallery exhibition was far from dead. One of the finest of the year's exhibitions was the summing-up of the career of the late American sculptor David Smith at New York's Guggenheim Museum. In the exhibition Smith emerged as a singular and superb artist whose earliest works declare his training as a painter. As the years went on, he progressed from rugged, welded-steel constructions to the powerful, polished-steel "Cubi" series. For lonely grandeur, there is nothing like it in United States art.

"The Gold of Ancient America" was a widely circulated exhibition of about 100 pieces of pre-Columbian gold dug from the graves of Indian aristocrats.

Other exhibitions of note included a show of sculpture of many styles at the Whitney Museum in New York. The National Gallery in Washington, D.C., showed Constable paintings. The works from the Nelson Rockefeller collection of twentieth-century and primitive art filled the galleries of three New York museums at once. The metal prints of Rolf Nesch, a 77-year-old Norwegian, were shown for the first time in the United States at the Detroit Institute of Art.

Shows at the Art Institute of Chicago, the Morgan Library in New York, the National Gallery, and the Art Gallery of Ontario marked the 300th anniversary of Rembrandt's death.

▶ THE LEHMAN COLLECTION

The Metropolitan Museum of Art received the largest gift in its history, the $100,000,000 art collection of the late Robert Lehman. The gift was announced in September as the museum prepared to start a year-long celebration of its 100th anniversary in 1970.

▶ THE CHANGING MUSEUM

"Harlem on My Mind," a much-discussed exhibition at New York's Metropolitan Museum of Art, illustrated the changing role of the city museum. The display was assembled by Allon Schoener, who had done a similar exhibition about the Jewish immigrant in New York; and two black co-workers, Donald Harper and Reginald McGhee. The exhibition consisted of 600 photomurals and audio-visual aids scattered throughout 13 galleries. It was intended to make people aware of black experience. But it was almost immediately condemned by Harlem leaders. They saw it as an overly sentimental white interpretation, playing up famous people instead of everyday things.

In an essay for the exhibition catalogue, Candice Van Ellison, a 17-year-old Harlem student, spoke bluntly of anti-Semitism among Harlem citizens. This caused further reaction. Thomas P. F. Hoving, the Metropolitan's director, finally made an apology and removed the statement from the catalogue.

As far as art is concerned, the incident was important because it answered some basic questions. Should a museum consist of a collection of art objects? Should it be a kind of bank or shrine? Or should it get actively involved with the "nerve-end" issues of community and state? "Harlem on My Mind" contained no "fine art" in the sense of painting or sculpture. And its attempt to enter the life around the museum, for better or for worse, represents the approach of many young curators and museum officials.

Of course, social involvement is but one kind of involvement. A more conventional method, perhaps, is involvement of the museum audience through the performing arts. Hartford's Wadsworth Atheneum has been a leader in such involvement, giving many experimental performances. In 1969 the museum added a new building. And it became the first museum in the United States to buy a sculpture by Tony Smith. The work is *Amaryllis*.

But whatever approach is used, social or artistic, it is certain that in 1969 the United States museum looked for a fresh identity as an institution.

ROBERT TAYLOR
Art Editor,
Boston Globe Magazine

PEACE CORPS

Peace Corps teachers at work in Botswana (left), the Philippines (above), and Liberia.

IN March, just after the Peace Corps celebrated its eighth anniversary, President Nixon announced that Joseph H. Blatchford would replace Jack Vaughn as director. (Vaughn, who had led the Peace Corps for three years, was later named ambassador to Colombia.)

During 1969 the rapid Peace Corps growth of earlier years leveled off. The number of volunteers throughout the world held steady at about ten thousand. By the end of the year, these volunteers were serving in 59 countries in Asia, Africa, and Latin America. In addition, a group of volunteers was in training for Guinea. In 1966, because of a dispute with the United States, this West African nation had expelled its first group of volunteers. Mauritius, a tiny island nation in the Indian Ocean, was also scheduled to receive volunteers, probably early in 1970.

During the year, the Peace Corps tried to involve citizens of host countries in the agency's operations. Many have already been employed by the Peace Corps as language and cross-cultural instructors. But in 1969 some joined the Peace Corps' overseas staff in permanent positions. In all, about two dozen host-country citizens are on the field staff. Twice that number have served in the United States as recruiters on college and university campuses.

Under its new Director, several changes were suggested for the Peace Corps in 1969. It was planned, for example, to broaden the base of participation. In the past, 80 per cent of the volunteers were college graduates in liberal arts. In 1969, it was hoped to involve more older people and non-college graduates, particularly those with technical skills needed in developing countries.

Another plan proposed in 1969 was that of a "reverse Peace Corps," in which foreign citizens would do volunteer work in the United States.

A third idea, changing the rules to permit volunteers to take their families overseas, was to be started on an experimental basis.

JOSEPH H. BLATCHFORD
Director, The Peace Corps

PEOPLE IN THE NEWS

ALDRIN, EDWARD E., JR., was the pilot of the lunar module on the Apollo 11 mission (July 16–24) and the second man to walk on the moon. "Buzz" Aldrin was born on January 20, 1930, in Montclair, New Jersey. He went to West Point and graduated third in a class of 475 in 1951. Aldrin was commissioned in the Air Force and flew 66 combat missions in the Korean war. He later entered an Air Force program at the Massachusetts Institute of Technology. In 1963 he earned his doctorate. His thesis was on orbital rendezvous. The Gemini and Apollo programs later adopted a system of rendezvous that Aldrin had suggested in his paper. Aldrin's first space flight was Gemini 12 in November 1966. On that mission he walked in space.

ARMSTRONG, NEIL A., commander of Apollo 11 (July 16–24), was the first man to walk on the moon. Armstrong, a civilian in the NASA program, was born on August 5, 1930, near Wapakoneta, Ohio. He first flew in an airplane when he was six years old. Armstrong entered Purdue University when he was 17. He left after his sophomore year to go on active duty in the Navy. He was a jet pilot in the Korean war. After Korea, Armstrong returned to Purdue. He graduated in 1955 with a degree in aeronautical engineering and went to work for the National Advisory Council on Aeronautics (NACA). At NACA's test center in California, he flew the X-15 plane as high as 200,000 feet. NACA became NASA and Armstrong became a civilian astronaut in 1962. He was command pilot of Gemini 8 in March 1966.

BEAN, ALAN LaVERN, Apollo 12 (November 14–24) astronaut, was the fourth man to walk on the moon. Bean was born on March 15, 1932, in Wheeler, Texas. He studied aeronautical engineering at the University of Texas on a Naval Reserve Officers Training Corps scholarship. Bean graduated in 1955. He was a Navy test pilot when he became an astronaut in 1963. Apollo 12 was his first space mission.

BLACK, SHIRLEY TEMPLE, was named by President Nixon on August 29 to the five-member United States delegation to the United Nations. Mrs. Black is a Republican Party campaigner and fund-raiser who once ran for office herself. In 1967 she was defeated for election to the House of Representatives from California. She was born on April 23, 1928, in Santa Monica, California, and became, as dimpled, curly-haired Shirley Temple, perhaps the most famous child motion-picture star. In the 1930's she starred in many musicals. She has three children.

BOULEZ, PIERRE, succeeded Leonard Bernstein as head of the New York Philharmonic. Boulez was born on March 26, 1925, near

Shirley Temple Black, U.S. delegate to the UN.

French conductor Pierre Boulez is the new head of the New York Philharmonic.

Montbrison, France. When he was a teen-ager he went to Paris to study at the Paris Conservatoire. In 1948 he was appointed music director of the Jean-Louis Barrault-Madeleine Renaud company at the Théâtre Marigny in Paris. In 1954 he began to use the theater to give avant-garde concerts that introduced contemporary music to young French audiences. A few years later Boulez moved to Baden-Baden, West Germany to become conductor of the South-West German Radio Orchestra.

CAHILL, WILLIAM T., was elected Republican governor of New Jersey on November 4. Cahill was born on June 25, 1912, in Philadelphia, Pennsylvania. He graduated from St. Joseph's College in Philadelphia in 1933, and four years later received a law degree from Rutgers. Cahill has been a teacher, special agent for the FBI, deputy attorney general, New Jersey state assemblyman, and since 1958, a member of the U.S. House of Representatives.

CERNAN, EUGENE ANDREW, was co-pilot of the Apollo 10 mission (May 18–26). He piloted the lunar module to 9 miles above the surface of the moon. Cernan was born on March 14, 1934, in Chicago, Illinois. He graduated from Purdue. He was a Navy pilot when he became an astronaut in 1963. On the Gemini 9 mission in June 1966, Cernan walked in space.

COLLINS, MICHAEL, was the Apollo 11 (July 16–24) command module pilot. Collins was

born on October 31, 1930, in Rome, Italy. His father was stationed there as a military attaché to the U.S. Embassy. Collins went to West Point. He graduated in 1952 and was commissioned in the Air Force. He was a test pilot when he became an astronaut in 1963. Collins' first space flight was Gemini 10.

CONRAD, CHARLES, JR., was the commander of the Apollo 12 mission (November 14–24) and the third man to walk on the moon. Conrad was born on June 2, 1930, in Philadelphia, Pennsylvania. He graduated from Princeton in 1953. "Pete," as he is nicknamed, was a Navy test pilot before becoming an astronaut in 1962. His other space missions were Gemini 5 in 1965 and Gemini 11 in 1966.

ELSTON, DOROTHY ANDREWS, was sworn in as treasurer of the United States on May 8. Within a few weeks, Mrs. Elston's signature began appearing on U.S. paper money. She had been appointed by President Nixon on March 28. Mrs. Elston, who was born on March 22, 1917, in Wilkes-Barre, Pennsylvania, has been an active Republican Party committeewoman and delegate to national conventions.

GORDON, RICHARD FRANCIS, Jr., was command module pilot on the Apollo 12 flight (November 14–24). Gordon was born on October 5, 1929, in Seattle, Washington. He studied chemistry at the University of Washington and graduated in 1951. Gordon was a Navy test pilot when in 1961 he won the Bendix Trophy Race, flying from Los Angeles to New York in record time—2 hours and 47 minutes. He became an astronaut in 1963 and was co-pilot of Gemini 11 in September 1966. On that mission he walked in space for 2 hours and 44 minutes.

HAYNSWORTH, CLEMENT F., Jr., U.S. Court of Appeals judge, was named by President Nixon on August 18 to be an associate justice of the Supreme Court. The Senate on November 21 voted against the nomination. Civil-rights and labor union groups opposed Haynsworth because of his conservative opinions. But the Senate, finally, rejected him because as a judge he had handed down decisions in cases where it was alleged he had a private interest. Haynsworth was born on October 30, 1912, in Greenville, South Carolina. He attended Furman University (founded by his great-great-grandfather) and Harvard University's School of Law. In 1957 President Eisenhower named him to the Court of Appeals for

Republican governors: right, William Cahill of New Jersey; below, Linwood Holton of Virginia.

the Fourth Circuit. After the Senate vote, Haynsworth returned to the Court of Appeals.

HOLTON, LINWOOD, was elected governor of Virginia on November 4. He is the first Republican governor of Virginia in 84 years. Holton was born in 1923. He is a graduate of Harvard University's Law School and was a member of the National Nixon for President Committee in 1968.

KNAUER, VIRGINIA HARRINGTON WRIGHT, was named by President Nixon on April 9 to be the President's special assistant for consumer affairs. Mrs. Knauer has been a Republican Party supporter. She founded a Republican Women's Council to sponsor political education. From 1960 to 1967 she was a member of the Philadelphia City Council. Mrs. Knauer was born in that city on March 28, 1915. She graduated from the University of Pennsylvania with a degree in fine arts.

LIN PIAO, was named Mao Tse-tung's future successor at the Congress of the Chinese Communist Party in April. Lin, defense minister since 1959, has been Mao's right-hand man since 1966. Lin was born in 1908. He graduated from Whampoa Military Academy in

1925. At that time Chiang Kai-shek (now president of Taiwan) was the commandant of the academy. Lin joined the Communist Party in 1927.

MANTLE, MICKEY, retired on March 1 after 18 years in baseball. All of those years were with the New York Yankees. Mantle acknowledged, "I can't hit any more." Mantle was born on October 20, 1931, in Spavinaw, Oklahoma. He spent 2 years in the minor leagues before joining the Yankees in 1951. His best years were 1956, 1957, and 1962. Those were Yankee pennant years and Mantle was Most Valuable Player 3 times. Plagued by leg injuries, Mantle played in fewer games during his last years in baseball. In 1967, he moved from center field to first base so that he would have less ground to cover on the field. That same year he surpassed Lou Gehrig's record (2,164 games) for most games played as a Yankee. By the end of his career Mantle had appeared in 2,401 games. His lifetime batting average is .298 and he hit 536 home runs.

McDIVITT, JAMES ALTON, commanded the Apollo 9 mission (March 3–13). On this mission the lunar module was flown for the first time. McDivitt was born on June 10, 1929, in Chicago, Illinois. During the Korean war, he was a fighter pilot. He flew 145 combat missions and won 9 decorations. After Korea, he remained in the Air Force and went to the University of Michigan and received a degree in aeronautical engineering in 1959. McDivitt commanded Gemini 4 in June 1965.

RHEAULT, ROBERT BRADLEY, was commander of the Fifth Special Forces (Green Berets) in Vietnam when he was relieved of his command. Eight Green Berets, including Rheault, were accused of killing a Vietnamese double agent. The charges were dropped when the Central Intelligence Agency refused to submit witnesses or evidence in the case. Rheault, a professional soldier, left the Army when the case was dropped. Out of uniform, he refused to offer further information about the case. Rheault was born on October 31, 1925, in Boston, Massachusetts. He attended West Point and graduated in 1946. His tours of duty before Vietnam included West Germany, Korea, and teaching at West Point. In his first tour of duty in Vietnam, Rheault won two Legions of Merit, five Air Medals, and a Combat Infantry Badge.

SCHWEICKART, RUSSELL LOUIS, was co-pilot of the lunar module and systems engineer on the Apollo 9 mission (March 3–13). Schweickart, a civilian in the NASA program, was born on October 25, 1935, in Neptune, New Jersey. He studied aeronautical engineering at the Massachusetts Institute of Technology. After graduation he spent four years in the Air Force. He then returned to MIT for a master's degree in aeronautics and astronautics. He became an astronaut in 1963 and Apollo 9 was his first space flight.

SCOTT, DAVID RANDOLPH, piloted the Apollo 9 command module. Scott was born on June 6, 1932, at Randolph Field in San Antonio, Texas. His father was then an Air Force pilot. Scott graduated fifth in a class of 633 at West Point in 1954. He was an Air Force pilot when he became an astronaut in 1963. Scott was co-pilot on the Gemini 8 flight in 1966.

SMITH, RALPH TYLER, Republican politician and lawyer, was named on September 17 by Illinois Governor Richard B. Ogilvie to take the U.S. Senate seat of the late Everett Dirksen. Smith was born in Illinois in 1915. At the time of his Senate appointment he was Speaker of the Illinois State House of Representatives.

STAFFORD, THOMAS PATTEN, was commander of the Apollo 10 mission (May 18–26). Stafford was born on September 17, 1930, in Weatherford, Oklahoma. He graduated from the U.S. Naval Academy in 1952. He helped to write two basic textbooks for test pilots. Stafford was an Air Force test pilot when he became an astronaut in 1962. Stafford's other space missions were Gemini 6 and 9.

YOUNG, JOHN WATTS, piloted the command module on the Apollo 10 mission (May 18–26). Young was born on September 24, 1930, in San Francisco, California. He graduated from the Georgia Institute of Technology in 1952 with a degree in aeronautical engineering. Young was a Navy fighter pilot and test pilot. He became an astronaut in 1962. Gemini 3 in March 1965 was his first space mission. He commanded the Gemini 10 flight.

Ralph Smith was appointed to the U.S. Senate.

Colonel Robert B. Rheault commanded the Fifth Special Forces (Green Berets) in Vietnam.

Mickey Mantle hangs up his No. 7 uniform for the last time. The Yankees officially retired Mantle's uniform in a special ceremony.

PHOTOGRAPHY

A FEW years ago it was unusual to see people carrying cameras except in parks and at vacation resorts. Today it is commonplace to see people carrying cameras with them everywhere they go. We have apparently entered an era in which nearly everyone either takes photographs or is interested in them.

One of today's unanswered questions is: What are all these people using photography for? In years past, people used photography to record family life or vacations. Some people centered their interests on the techniques of photography. This is no longer true. However, it is not fully known what new interests have replaced the old. An educated guess is that people are turning to photography as a way to express themselves. They hope it will give their lives more depth and meaning. In this search for meaning in life, they also look at photographs primarily in terms of what they mean. People no longer look at photos in terms of technique, surface prettiness, and composition.

▶ CAMERA MAGAZINES

Camera magazines for the general public have been technique oriented. Until recently the meaning of photographs has been paid very little attention. Writers and editors were not interested in the meaning of photographs. And they assumed that the public was also uninterested. Many of them had the idea that in a "good" photograph the meaning is always self-evident, and that there was no reason to write or talk about it. They insisted that the public was interested only in hard, technical facts.

This situation is changing. Today's most popular writers are those who write about photography's content, not its technique. Editors are telling writers to cut down on the amount of "boring technical material." The writers are being told to pay more attention to criticism and commentary.

An important indication of this change took place in *Modern Photography* magazine in 1968. In his column, Andreas Feininger declared that he had had his fill of writing about technical things. He added that he would thenceforth write about technique only as a means of creating meaning in photographs. Feininger is one of the world's great technical writers in photography. That he saw the need for a major change is very significant.

Another indication of the change is the apparent success of *Travel and Camera* magazine. The old *U.S. Camera,* it was bought by the American Express Company, which completely changed the magazine's old policies. *Travel and Camera* is no longer a technical magazine. Rather, its main concern is in the use of photography to help people see the world as meaningful. If a person uses his camera well on his travels, his trips will be much more meaningful to him.

Travel and Camera followed the course already set by the magazine *Camera 35*. In *Camera 35* the change of direction was heralded by Lou Bernstein. Mr. Bernstein writes on the relation of ethics, aesthetics, and philosophy to photography. The particular philosophy he talks about is called Aesthetic Realism. It was developed by the philosopher-poet Eli Siegel, who is Bernstein's teacher.

▶ PICTURE ANNUALS

Each year, the outstanding publishing events in photography are usually the picture annuals. Sometimes these annuals are good, sometimes not. In the United States, the Ziff-Davis annuals have been of high quality. These annuals include the *1970 Photography Annual, 1969 Color Photography, Woman 1970, 1970 35mm Photography,* and *1969 Invitation to Photography.* Their chief competitor is *U.S. Camera Annual,* which had been in the quality doldrums for several years. In 1969, however, this annual made a surprising comeback. The *U.S. Camera World Annual, 1970* is a well-designed book. It is filled with interesting and well-reproduced pictures. Insiders say that the presence of Mr. David Vestal on the annual staff largely accounts for the dramatic improvement. Mr. Vestal had previously worked for Ziff-Davis' *Popular Photography*.

In 1969 the Famous Photographers School moved into the annual field. It published a high-quality annual designed to sell for about $25. *Modern Photography* magazine also began publishing an annual.

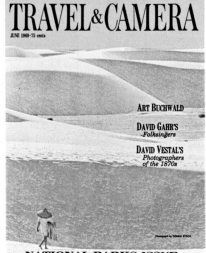

"TRAVEL & CAMERA": Cover photo and setting sun by Dennis Stock.

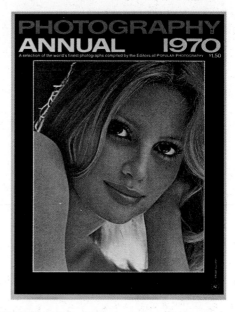

"U.S. CAMERA WORLD ANNUAL 1970": Cover photo by Len Steckler; young girl at window pane photographed by Richard Selby.

"PHOTOGRAPHY ANNUAL 1970": Cover photo by Jerome Ducrot; fish by Carl Purcell; the anhinga (or snakebird) by Pat Caulfield.

Many photographic books were published in 1969. For readers in their teens and early twenties, the outstanding ones were by Robert Frank, Nathan Lyons, and M. Richard Kirstel.

Frank's book, *The Americans,* is a re-issue by Grossman Publishing Company of an excellent book that had a strong influence on photographers now in their late twenties and early thirties. In it Frank gave his interpretations of Americans as he saw them while photographing the United States on a Guggenheim Fellowship. Some people have criticized the book, calling it a wickedly cynical put-down of Americans. Others have praised it, saying that it is full of indications of Frank's love for his fellowman.

Nathan Lyons' book is *Vision and Expression* (Horizon Press, in collaboration with the George Eastman House). It continues the series of Eastman House books intended to survey the work of the younger generation of photographers. The designation "younger" does not refer to the photographers' actual age. Rather, it refers to their attitudes—to those with a youthful viewpoint. The work of 154 photographers is represented in the book. Some are in their thirties and forties, but most are in their late teens and twenties. Their photographs represent the directions being taken by serious students of photography. Almost all of the photos are very personal. They show a strong interest in self-expression and self-discovery. Many of them tend toward surrealism, as if they were illustrations of dreams or nightmares. Some are bitter and very critical of today's society. They indicate that younger photographers are trying to express and confront those things that disturb them. Thus the photos represent a kind of therapy in which the artist uses his medium to heal himself.

The book *Pas de Deux* (Grove Press) by M. Richard Kirstel is an example of a

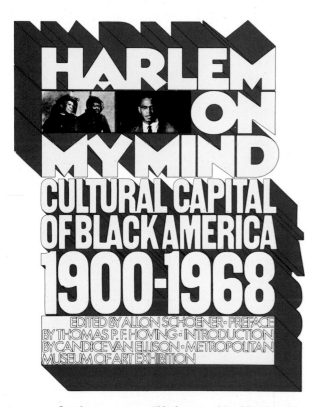

Catalogue cover, "Harlem on My Mind" exhibition, the Metropolitan Museum of Art.

The Museum of Modern Art, New York

"Dylan Thomas and his wife, Caitlin, in their room, Manresa Road, Chelsea" by Bill Brandt.

different kind of interest among the younger spirits in photography. They feel that sex is a legitimate subject for photography. The Kirstel book contains erotic but poetic photographs. They are powerful, beautiful, and in the very best of taste.

Kirstel is one of the leaders in photography among those who are trying to change the meaning of "pornography." They believe that if something contributes to the welfare and understanding of human beings, it should not be called pornography. This includes sexuality, so long as it is treated with respect and reverence.

On the other hand, the same people say that movies, books, or paintings that glorify violence and hatred should be labeled pornographic.

▶ **PHOTOGRAPHIC EXHIBITIONS**

The outstanding exhibition of the year was *"Pas de Deux."* This is the show that Grove Press translated into the book discussed above. The show was presented in the small, relatively unknown Exposure Gallery in New York's East Village. Yet it drew reviewers from all over the United States, Europe, and South America. Tiny as the gallery is, the show drew seven thousand viewers.

Among the large exhibitions, the most interesting and possibly most significant was "One Hundred Years of Photography —A History of Photographic Expression by Japanese." This show did not appear in the United States in 1969. However, a few photographs from it were printed in *Infinity* magazine. The exhibition is three times as large as the famous "Family of Man" show by Edward Steichen. It includes 1,640 prints.

From the viewpoint of photographic education, the significant show of the year was the 500-print exhibition in New York's Hallmark Gallery by students of Harry Callahan at the Rhode Island School of Design. Part of the show emphasized the Callahan teaching method. The rest of the photos reflected the current pictorial interests of the students. As a whole, they were well-crafted, well-designed, and very personal.

Roy De Carava's exhibition "Thru Black Eyes" was of great significance for young black photographers. These photographers are trying to use photography to help them establish their identities and build pride in their race. In this rapidly growing group, Roy De Carava is generally acknowledged as the "Old Master." His show, at the Studio Museum in New York's Harlem, represented 12 years of work by one of the most penetrating yet tender minds in photography.

The most-talked-about show of the year was "Harlem on My Mind," at the Metropolitan Museum of Art in New York City. According to many people, especially among the blacks, it was also the great blunder of the year. They thought it represented Harlem and the blacks very badly. They felt that at best the show was insulting to blacks. "Harlem on My Mind" was a very large show. Some prints were up to 15 or 20 feet long. It set the world's record for column inches of newspaper space devoted to it. Naturally it drew a record attendance at the museum.

A large retrospective exhibition by Great Britain's Bill Brandt was held at The Museum of Modern Art. English photography has been at a low ebb for many years. But Bill Brandt has long stood out as an important world figure in photography. His pictures are very powerful and have very negative overtones. He is the master of the "dirty" print. All of his pictures look as if they had been stored for ten years in an English coal mine. Oddly, with this coal-smoke quality there is sometimes (but seldom) a lyric kind of beauty. Brandt's pictures are largely concerned with commentary on the English culture. They suggest that the situation is nearly hopeless. People who wish to see life as very black indeed will find confirmation for their views in Brandt's work.

RALPH HATTERSLEY
Contributing Editor
Popular Photography Magazine

PHYSICS

THERE were three major developments in experimental physics during 1969. In the field of general relativity, a 50-year-old prediction made by Albert Einstein was verified. In particle physics, an Australian physicist claimed that he had discovered the quark, a theoretically predicted ultra-elementary particle. In plasma physics, the goal of electric power from controlled thermonuclear fusion seemed within reach.

▶ GRAVITY WAVES

As part of his theory of general relativity, Albert Einstein predicted that bodies whose motion is being accelerated will emit gravity waves. Such waves would be similar to the electromagnetic waves familiar as light, radio, and X rays. And like electromagnetic waves, gravity waves would carry energy from place to place.

For about forty years physicists ignored this prediction. They believed that gravity waves, if they did exist, would be too weak to detect. About ten years ago, however, Professor Joseph Weber of the University of Maryland began to work on the question. He believed that it should be possible to detect gravity waves if they are emitted by a very heavy object such as a star. Professor Weber and his team set up huge aluminum cylinders with special sensors. The sensors, he said, would measure any displacements, or motions, in the cylinders that might be caused by gravity waves. Professor Weber first reported his findings in 1968. He stated that his equipment had recorded vibrations, but he did not claim these were caused by gravity waves. In June 1969, however, after more study, Professor Weber reported in the journal *Physical Review Letters* that he was certain that some of the vibrations of his cylinders had been caused by gravity waves.

There is no way to focus or guide gravity waves. And so they are not likely to

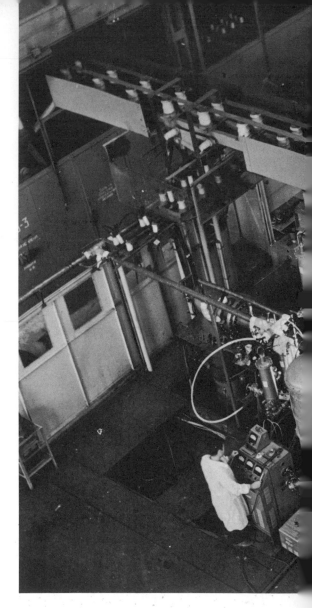

have any technological use. They will, however, be useful to astronomers, because many objects of interest to them, such as supernovae, are supposed to generate such waves.

▶ THE QUARK

The quark, according to physicist Murray Gell-Mann, is the most elementary subatomic particle. There are many other particles, such as the meson and the muon, which, for some time, physicists thought to be elementary. But when more than one

The Tokamak, the apparatus with which the Soviets hope to achieve controlled thermonuclear fusion.

hundred such particles were discovered, physicists began to wonder. Indeed, Gell-Mann and his associate, George Zweig, reasoned that this was altogether too many for them to be considered elementary. They thus theorized that there must be other, truly elementary particles. They called these particles quarks.

This theory set off a hunt for the quarks, and for some time an unrewarding search frustrated physicists at the world's largest laboratories. In 1969, however, Dr. Charles McCusker at Sydney University in Australia claimed that he had at last found quarks, in cosmic rays. Some physicists treated his claim with reserve, stating that they would like more evidence. Dr. McCusker continued to search for more quarks.

▶ CONTROLLING THERMONUCLEAR FUSION

Obtaining power from controlled thermonuclear fusion has been a dream of physicists and technologists for twenty years. In 1969 this dream moved closer to reality.

To achieve controlled fusion, hydrogen must first be heated to a temperature of 100,000,000 degrees. At this temperature hydrogen turns into a plasma (an electrically charged gas of ions and electrons). For sustained fusion, such a plasma must have a million billion ions per cubic centimeter. And it must be confined at that high temperature for one tenth of a second. Only if all these things take place will fusion occur to produce a useful amount of power.

The only practical way to contain such a hot substance is by using magnetic fields to hold the plasma in the middle of a vacuum chamber. For years attempts to design appropriate magnetic fields met with failure.

In 1969, however, American and Soviet scientists met with some success. In the Soviet Union, Lev A. Artsimovich reported holding a plasma of 70,000 billion ions per cubic centimeter for .02 seconds at 5,000,000 degrees. A British team of physicists, checking his findings, found that Artsimovich was even closer to controlled fusion than he thought. In the United States, Dr. Tihiro Ohkawa reported holding a plasma of about 1,000 billion ions per cubic centimeter at a temperature of 1,000,000 degrees for .07 seconds.

These results are much better than previous ones, and give hope that power from controlled thermonuclear fusion may be no more than a decade or two away.

DIETRICK E. THOMSEN
Physical Sciences and Astronomy Editor
Science News

POLAND. See EUROPE, EAST.

POMPIDOU, GEORGES

ON June 15, 1969, the people of France elected Georges Pompidou president of their country for the next seven years. On the second ballot, he defeated Alain Poher, the interim president since Charles de Gaulle had resigned on April 28. Pompidou was sworn in on June 20 at the Elysée Palace.

Georges Jean Raymond Pompidou was born on July 5, 1911, at Montboudif, a village in the Auvergne region of France. His father, a schoolmaster, taught Spanish. By the time he was 24, Pompidou had obtained degrees in both French literature and political science. He then began what could have been a lifelong career in teaching. In 1935 he married Claude Cahour. They have one son.

Pompidou served in the French Army from 1938 to 1940. During the German occupation of France, he taught in Paris. After World War II, when De Gaulle headed the provisional Government, he appointed Pompidou his personal aide, and

the two men became close friends. When De Gaulle resigned, Pompidou stayed on in several civil-service jobs. He then joined the Rothschild's banking firm, becoming its chief administrative director in 1956. But even during these years, Pompidou managed much of De Gaulle's personal affairs. De Gaulle returned to power in 1958, and four years later named Pompidou premier. This surprised many people, because Pompidou had never run for any office.

During his six years as premier, he served as De Gaulle's trusted confidant and adviser. Then, in July 1968, after Pompidou had successfully handled the student rioting and union strikes, De Gaulle shocked the country by asking Pompidou to resign. After Pompidou stepped down, he remained in the background, until January 1969, when he announced that he was interested in the presidency. Five months later, in the balloting that followed De Gaulle's resignation, Pompidou attained his goal.

POPULATION

THE Population Reference Bureau estimated that on July 1, 1969, there were 3,550,000,000 people in the world. This was a gain of about 70,000,000 over mid-1968. In 1969, world population increased by about 1,300,000 people each week.

World population is now doubling in 35 years. In many of the developing countries of Asia, Africa, and Latin America, the population is doubling in from 35 years to less than 20 years. This causes many economic and social problems in these countries. These problems are further complicated by the fact that in some of these countries, about 45 per cent of the people are under 15 years of age. This compares with 30 per cent in the United States and 25 per cent in northern Europe.

In some Latin-American countries the annual per capita income is between $200 and $600. In some African countries the situation is even worse: the annual per capita income is as little as $60. Thus, educating, feeding, and rearing so many young people on limited resources pose grave problems. This accent on youth also means that in no more than 15 years, the number of women between the ages of 20 and 30 will be nearly twice as large as it is today. And women in this age group have more children than any other age group.

The rate of world population growth is determined by the difference between births and deaths. Before 1800 there was little hope of controlling epidemics. Medical knowledge was not so advanced as it is today. Thus both death rates and birthrates were very high and nearly in balance. As modern medicine and public health became more effective, death rates began to decline. This happened first in the industrializing countries of Europe and North America. In these countries, about a generation after the death rate began to decline, the birthrate also began to go down.

The developing nations of the world have high birthrates, and population growth is tremendous.

Within a century, the birthrate was only a little higher than the modern death rate. This change has been called the "demographic transition."

Especially since the end of World War II, the decline in the death rate has gradually extended around the world. The decline in death rate has accelerated rapidly in the developing countries of Asia, Africa, and Latin America. But there has been no corresponding decline in the birthrate. The result has been a phenomenal acceleration in population growth.

In terms of population, the world can be divided into two sectors: the "have" nations and the "have-not" nations.

The have nations are the countries of Europe, the Soviet Union, Australia, New Zealand, Japan, Israel, and the countries of North America. These nations have a total population of about 1,000,000,000. Death rates and birthrates are low and roughly in balance. Population growth ranges from 0.5 per cent to over 1 per cent a year.

WORLD POPULATION
8000 B.C.—YEAR 2000

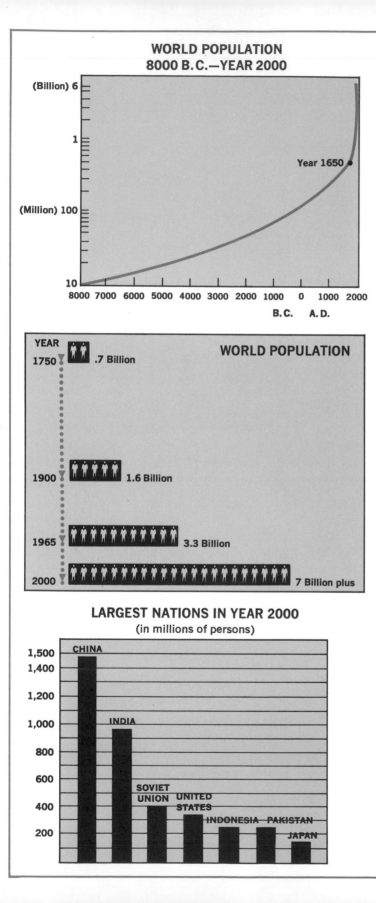

(Billion) 6

1

(Million) 100

Year 1650

10

8000 7000 6000 5000 4000 3000 2000 1000 0 1000 2000

B.C. A.D.

Before 1650, population increased 50 per cent every 1,000 years. Since 1650 the rate of increase has sky-rocketed to 2,000 per cent.

WORLD POPULATION

YEAR

1750 .7 Billion

1900 1.6 Billion

1965 3.3 Billion

2000 7 Billion plus

In the 150 years between 1750 and 1900, the population of the world doubled. World population is now doubling in 35 years.

LARGEST NATIONS IN YEAR 2000
(in millions of persons)

1,500 CHINA
1,400
1,200
1,000 INDIA
800
600
400 SOVIET UNION UNITED STATES
200 INDONESIA PAKISTAN
JAPAN

Seven nations are expected to account for almost 3,900,000,000 of the world's 7,000,000,000 people by the year 2000.

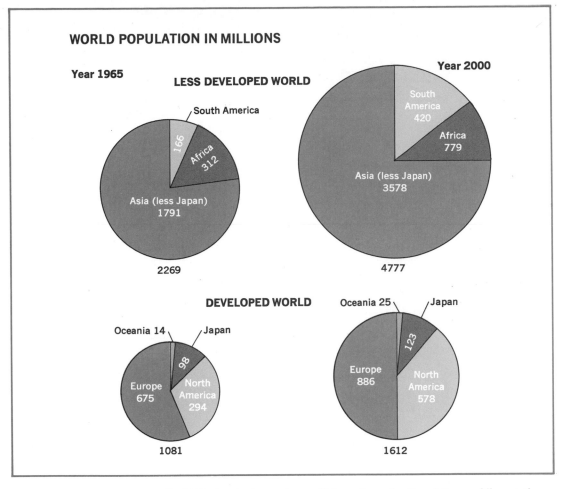

WORLD POPULATION IN MILLIONS

Year 1965

LESS DEVELOPED WORLD

Year 2000

South America

166
Africa 312
Asia (less Japan) 1791

2269

South America 420
Africa 779
Asia (less Japan) 3578

4777

DEVELOPED WORLD

Oceania 25 / Japan

Oceania 14 / Japan

98
Europe 675
North America 294

1081

123
Europe 886
North America 578

1612

By 2000, developing nations will have three fourths of the world's people.

These countries have high income, high levels of literacy, and adequate diets.

The have-not nations are the developing countries of Asia, Africa, and Latin America. These nations have a population of about 2,600,000,000, or about ⅔ of the world total. Birthrates have remained very high. They range from 35 to 50 births per 1,000 population every year. As a result, 86 per cent of all births in the world today take place in these countries.

The population crisis which continued to confront the world in 1969 is of enormous magnitude. There is no quick solution in sight.

In the past 10 years, urgent efforts have begun to be made to bring births into balance with deaths. The United States Gov-

ernment is now spending $50,000,000 in AID programs related to family planning and somewhat less than that amount to make family-planning programs available in the United States. Other governments and private foundations are spending additional millions for research and family-planning programs.

In order to halve the population-growth rate, it will be necessary to prevent a minimum of 35,000,000 births each year. The efforts made in 1969 were not on a scale to achieve even this limited objective.

ROBERT C. COOK
Population Consultant

See also individual countries and area review articles.

PORTUGAL. See EUROPE, WEST.

Of the 25,000,000 poor in the U.S., one third are Negroes.

POVERTY

THERE were about 25,000,000 poor people in the United States in 1969. The definition of "poor" was based on income: a family of four living on a yearly income of under $3,500 was considered to be poor. The number of poor and their problems continued to command the attention of the Federal Government.

▶ **GOVERNMENT POVERTY PROGRAMS**

The number of poor has decreased a little since 1964, when the Office of Economic Opportunity (OEO) was created as the Federal agency to deal with poverty. In some areas, the poverty agency has worked well, in some not as well as hoped for. Supporters of the poverty agency have argued that not enough money has been made available by the Federal Government to erase poverty in the United States.

In 1969 the OEO was reorganized. President Nixon said that the reorganization of OEO would free the agency to work harder on devising experimental programs to help the poor.

As of July 1, 1969, Head Start, the education program for preschoolers, was moved from OEO to the Department of Health, Education, and Welfare (HEW). Also into HEW went two smaller programs, Foster Grandparents Program and Comprehensive Health Centers. The Job Corps was moved to the Labor Department. OEO continued to administer the Community Action Program (under which the poor organize themselves for political action), Legal Services to the Poor, Neighborhood Health Centers, and VISTA (Volunteers in Service to America).

Congress in 1969 voted funds to support OEO for two more years.

The Nixon administration supported two other aids to the poor. One was part of the President's tax-reform program. The plan was to offer total exemption from income tax for persons below the poverty level. Tax credits aimed at encouraging investment in inner-city areas were also proposed.

The other type of effort supported by the Nixon administration was "self-help improvement projects." One such effort was being carried out in the Watts section of Los Angeles. In this, Negro and white businessmen have founded the Economic Resources Corporation. They have converted 45 acres of wasteland into an industrial park. Lockheed Aircraft Corporation has taken the lead in leasing a factory to make aircraft parts. The money to finance the project came from both the Federal Government and from private industry.

▶ HUNGER

Perhaps the most devastating effect of poverty is the chronic hunger it produces. In 1969, the number of hungry Americans was estimated at 10,000,000. The private sector—industry and organizations—has done little to deal with the problem. But the Federal Government has three food-assistance programs. They are Commodity Distribution, Food Stamps, and Child Nutrition.

Under the commodities program, the Federal Government distributes to needy families some of the food it buys to bolster the incomes of farmers. Persons receiving public assistance and others who fall below an income level determined by each state can get food each month. The program, however, has failed to gain much headway for several reasons. One is that many states and counties are not in the program. And the food that is provided is not adequate for a balanced diet.

The food-stamp program was intended to improve on the commodities program. It allows people to choose their own food and to pay for it with stamps. The stamps are more valuable than dollars. Also, the food-stamp program is not limited to people receiving public assistance. Still, some of its features put it out of reach of some hungry people. The monthly purchase of stamps requires a cash lump sum that very poor people find difficult to raise. Other drawbacks are a requirement to buy a minimum number of stamps or none at all and to buy the same number each month.

In 1969 the following remedies for the food-stamp plan were introduced in Congress: free stamps for people earning under $60 a month; food stamps for families of under four people with an income of less than $4,000 a year; and a limit of a family's expenditure on food stamps to 30 per cent of its annual income.

Only one third of the 6,000,000 poor children receive food and milk in school under the child nutrition programs.

The drawbacks of the food-assistance programs cause them to reach fewer than 6,000,000 of the 10,000,000 hungry people in the United States. And in more than one third of the nation's poorest counties there are no food programs.

The White House Conference on Food, Nutrition and Health was held in December. President Nixon, who had called the conference, said that it "sets the seal of urgency on our national commitment to put an end to hunger and malnutrition due to poverty in America." The 4,000 representatives of the poor at the meeting called for immediate action against hunger. They also asked for a guaranteed annual cash income of $5,500 for the poor.

GEORGE T. MARTIN, JR.
University of Chicago
JOANNA FOLEY MARTIN
Chicago Urban League
See also FOOD; SOCIAL WELFARE.

PROTESTANTISM. See RELIGION.

PUBLISHING

"The Saturday Evening Post," founded in 1728 by Benjamin Franklin, ceased publication with its February 8, 1969, issue (right). An issue from 1900 is shown at left.

PUBLISHING in 1969 saw the continuation of three major trends. Many new magazines appeared on the newsstands. "Underground" newspapers—those published primarily by dissident students—continued to proliferate. And book sales continued to soar, with 23,321 new titles published in 1968 and more than that number expected for 1969.

▶ MAGAZINES

On January 10, 1969, an era in magazine publishing came to an end. On that day *The Saturday Evening Post* announced it would publish no more. The last issue was dated February 8.

Another major publishing enterprise to disappear from the scene was the Sunday newspaper supplement *This Week* magazine. Its November 2 issue was its last. The reasons that these two magazines ceased to publish were complex. *This Week*'s managing editor, Campbell Geeslin, noted, however, that "like *The Saturday Evening Post* [in recent years] we were upsetting older readers faster than we could attract young ones." Specifically, the *Post* had tried to switch from a mass-circulation to a "class" publication. That is, it selected only upper-income readers from among its subscribers as a more effective lure to advertisers. In doing so, it cut its circulation from 6,800,000 to 3,000,000. But the move came too late to solve the magazine's financial problems.

This Week found itself in tough competition with local Sunday supplements, which took the local advertising dollar, and with television, which appealed to national advertisers.

Another magazine to end publication in 1969 was *Eye,* published by Hearst Magazines. This slick publication was aimed at the under-30 group. After only one year of publishing, the magazine decided that its 30,000 circulation was far short of a profitable enterprise.

New Magazines

In recent years some large-circulation magazines have disappeared. But hundreds of new ones have been established. The Magazine Publishers Association estimates that from 1965 to 1969 a total of 94 magazines were sold, merged, or discontinued, but 441 were begun.

Among the largest publications to be established in 1969 were *Family Health* (1,000,000), *Film Bill* (1,300,000), and *Homemaking with a Flair* (3,000,000). Three college publications also made their debuts: *Panorama* (annual, 3,400,000), *Class* (semiannual, 2,000,000), and *Equal Opportunity* (200,000). The last publication is for minority-group college students seeking a career.

In May, Bantam Books began distributing 130,000 copies of a "paperback magazine" aimed at the under-30 generation. This publication is called *US*. Planned for February 1970 by Random House was a semiannual paperback magazine for university black-studies programs. It will be called *Amistad,* after an 1839 slave ship on which the slaves mutinied and took over.

A British publisher of a men's magazine, *Penthouse,* introduced its first United States issue in September.

International Magazine Conference

The first International Magazine Conference was held May 25–28 at Williamsburg, Virginia. Publishers and editors from the United States heard speeches by their colleagues from Great Britain, France, Germany, Italy, Sweden, the Soviet Union, and Canada. Both French and German publishers reported moves on the part of their editors to obtain veto power in the choice of a new owner or the selection of a publisher when a publication is sold. The greater political emphasis in many European magazines accounted in part for the agitation by these "editors associations."

▶ **NEWSPAPERS**

Time Inc., the magazine publisher, moved into the newspaper field in 1969. It bought 21 Chicago suburban weekly newspapers and 10 tabloid semiweeklies in the North Shore area of Chicago.

In another acquisition, Scholastic Magazines bought *American Observer* and *Junior Review,* weekly 8-page newspapers on current events.

New Newspapers

On March 18 the Chicago Tribune Company announced the end of its evening newspaper, *The American.* Five weeks

The first issue of "Chicago Today," the tabloid that replaced "The [Chicago] American."

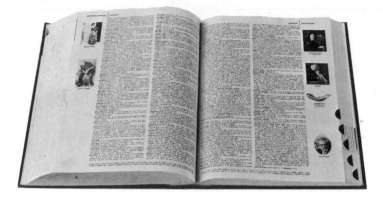

The American Heritage "Dictionary of the English Language."

later *The American* was replaced by "Chicago's first new newspaper in 28 years," a tabloid, *Chicago Today*. The tabloid format has often been associated in the past with sensational journalism. But many urban publishers say the public (especially commuters) prefers its compactness and convenience.

In May a new English edition of the French tabloid newspaper *Le Monde* appeared in the United States. Priced at 50 cents a copy, the newspaper had an initial circulation in the United States of 25,000.

Underground Newspapers

Additions in the newspaper field in 1969 included more "underground" papers. These were begun mostly on college campuses by dissident students. It was estimated in *Editor and Publisher,* the newspaper trade journal, that the "undergrounds" now number over 600, with distribution of more than 3,000,000.

▶ BOOKS

Publishers' Weekly estimated in March 1969 that 1968 gross book sales may approach $2,750,000,000. This is up $500,-000,000 from 1967. A Harper & Row book company estimate for coming years projected a 5.4 per cent annual growth rate in general trade books (not educational) for the next four years.

There were 30,387 books published in 1968. Of these, about 23,000 were new books. Some 7,000 were new editions of previously published books. Included among the 30,000 new books were 7,241 paperbacks. Similar proportionate ratios were expected for 1969.

Mergers and Sales

There were several major sales and mergers in the book-publishing field in 1969. Dell Publishing purchased Dial Press. Harper & Row acquired Basic Books and an affiliated book club. Crowell Collier and Macmillan acquired music publisher G. Schirmer. It then merged with C. G. Conn, Ltd., a musical-instrument manufacturer, and Gumps, Inc., a San Francisco department store.

Best Sellers

Best sellers during 1969 included these books with hard-cover copies in print of 100,000 or more:

Fiction: *The Godfather, The Love Machine, Portnoy's Complaint, The Andromeda Strain.*

Nonfiction: *The Peter Principle, Between Parent and Teenager, Miss Craig's 21-Day Shape-Up Program for Men and Women, The Money Game.*

Probably the most expensive single book produced was the American Heritage *Dictionary of the English Language.* Published on September 15, it cost more than $4,000,000 to produce.

KIRK POLKING
Editor, *Writer's Digest*

See also LITERATURE.

PULITZER PRIZES

AWARDS were made in 16 categories for the 1969 Pulitzer Prizes. Each winner received a $1,000 award.

Biography: BENJAMIN L. REID, professor of English, Mount Holyoke College, for *The Man from New York: John Quinn and His Friends.*

Drama: HOWARD SACKLER for *The Great White Hope,* a play based on the life of the first Negro heavyweight boxing champion, Jack Johnson.

Cartoons: JOHN FISCHETTI, political cartoonist, *The Chicago Daily News.*

Editorial Writing: PAUL GREENBERG, editorial page editor, *The Pine Bluff* (Arkansas) *Commercial.*

Feature Photography: MONETA SLEET, JR., staff photographer, *Ebony* Magazine, for his photograph of Mrs. Martin Luther King, Jr., at the funeral of Dr. King in Atlanta on April 9, 1968.

Fiction: N. SCOTT MOMADAY, professor of English, University of California in Santa Barbara, for *House Made of Dawn,* a novel about a young American Indian who leaves the reservation.

General Nonfiction: RENE JULES DUBOS, microbiologist, Rockefeller University, for *So Human an Animal: How We Are Shaped by Surroundings and Events;* and NORMAN MAILER for *The Armies of the Night,* a report of an anti-Vietnam war protest in Washington, D.C., in 1968.

Gold Medal: THE LOS ANGELES TIMES for public service in exposing "wrong-doing within the Los Angeles city government commissions."

History: LEONARD W. LEVY, chairman, department of history, Brandeis University, for *Origins of the Fifth Amendment.*

International Reporting: WILLIAM TUOHY, correspondent, *The Los Angeles Times,* for his reporting from Vietnam.

Local Reporting, General: JOHN FETTERMAN, *The Louisville* [Kentucky] *Courier-Journal,* for his article on the burial in rural Kentucky of an American soldier killed in Vietnam.

Local Reporting, Special: ALBERT L. DELUGACH, *The St. Louis Globe-Democrat,* and DENNY WALSH, *Life* magazine, for their series of

Norman Mailer (above) and microbiologist Rene Jules Dubos of Rockefeller University—co-winners of the Pulitzer Prize for General Nonfiction.

articles in *The St. Louis Globe-Democrat* exposing fraud within the St. Louis Steamfitters Union, Local 562. The series led to the court conviction of the offenders.

Music: KAREL HUSA, professor of music, Cornell University, for *String Quartet No. 3.*

National Reporting: ROBERT CAHN, correspondent, *The Christian Science Monitor,* for a series of articles on national parks in the United States.

Poetry: GEORGE OPPEN for *Of Being Numerous,* a book of poems describing contemporary America.

Spot News Photography: EDWARD T. ADAMS, Associated Press photographer, for his photograph of South Vietnam's national police chief shooting a Vietcong prisoner.

James Forman appears at a Protestant church to demand reparations for Negroes.

RELIGION

THE major religions in the United States faced the problems of social unrest, war, and ecumenism in 1969. Many of the events in Protestantism had to do with stewardship priorities. Protestants were taking a new look at the relationship between the money of the church and the mission of the church.

Within the Roman Catholic Church there continued to be sharp differences between reformers and traditionalists. Pope Paul VI warned against the changes sought by the reformers. In the Church hierarchy, the Pope elevated 35 churchmen to the rank of cardinal.

For Jews and Judaism, the continuing war in the Middle East was of major concern. In the interests of peace, Israel's Foreign Minister Abba Eban and Pope Paul held a historic meeting in the Vatican.

In Eastern Orthodoxy, Roman Catholic and Protestant clergy helped celebrate Patriarch Athenagoras' twenty years as honorary head of world Orthodoxy.

▶ PROTESTANTISM

Church members in 1969 were more aware of how church money was invested. It was thought wrong for churches to have money invested in certain kinds of places. Therefore, in New York the Union Theological Seminary sold holdings in Dow Chemical stock. Dow Chemical makes napalm, a jellied gasoline used in the Vietnam war. One Union professor called napalm "a specifically horrible sign of our national guilt." Some denominations withdrew money from banks giving credit to the Republic of South Africa. This was done because South Africa has a policy of apartheid, or racial separation.

Meanwhile, some church budgets were cut because less money was contributed. Some members donated less because they resented the social-action programs of the churches. In order to balance its budget, the Presbyterian, U.S. (Southern) Board of Christian Education said it would decrease its staff by 40 per cent and close its bookstores. And to save $1,000,000 a year the Christian Churches (Disciples of Christ) will hold its General Assemblies every two years instead of once a year.

At the same time, churches tried to make more than token gestures toward helping the poor. The United Methodist Board of Missions began work in rural economic development. The board believes that "rural poverty has been a factor in the explosive crisis now besetting the urban ghettos." The United Church of Christ approved funds for 12 test ministries designed to meet problems of rural and urban poor, and racism. One project was the planning of new rural towns for landless poor in southwestern Georgia.

Evangelical bodies also became involved in "financial evangelism." Campus Crusade for Christ began to buy rental houses in a ghetto in Miami, Florida. They will rebuild the houses and offer them for sale at low 3 per cent mortgages. The Walther League, youth auxiliary of the Lutheran Church-Missouri Synod, made world hunger its chief two-year concern. The three disaster

areas to which the churches responded through Church World Service, Joint Church Aid, and the World Relief Commission were Vietnam, Nigeria and Biafra, and the Middle East. The work of all religious faiths helped prevent total starvation in Biafra.

The most dramatic event of the year was the "Black Manifesto." Black militants led by James Forman demanded money "reparations" for past injustices suffered by American Negroes. Demonstrations were staged at many churches and at the headquarters building of the National Council of Churches. Religious executives generally agreed that valid issues were raised by the militants. But most did not agree with the militant methods. Some contributions were made to Mr. Forman's group.

The Manifesto set off major church rethinking on white-black relations. Several emergency programs for black economic development were begun.

Reparations were an important topic at the annual meeting of the Central Committee of the World Council of Churches, held at Canterbury, England. In the United States, the American Baptist Convention elected its first Negro president. He is Dr. Thomas Kilgore, Jr., a Los Angeles, California, pastor. In New Jersey the state office of the American Baptist churches said that it will no longer mention skin color when recommending ministers to local congregations. For the first time in the history of the Southern Baptist denomination, the largest American Protestant body, with 12,000,000 members, a Southern Baptist church voted to have dual membership with the Negro National Baptist Convention. The Negro Baptist group has 6,500,000 members.

There were setbacks and small gains in Protestant unity. In England, the Church of England rejected reunification with the Methodist Church. In the United States, the Reformed Church in America decided not to unite with the Presbyterian Church, U.S. (Southern). The conservative Lutheran Church-Missouri Synod approved

Pope Paul VI offers Mass at the opening of the Synod of Bishops in the Vatican. The bishops debated the issue of the sharing of Church powers.

"altar and pulpit fellowship" with the American Lutheran Church.

President Nixon, who has a Quaker-Methodist background, held Sunday services in the White House. The services, which were led by ministers, rabbis, and priests, drew the criticism of theologian Reinhold Niebuhr on grounds that the separation of church and state was being undermined.

KENNETH L. WILSON
Editor, *Christian Herald*

▶ ROMAN CATHOLICISM

Liberal reformers and conservative traditionalists in the Roman Catholic Church continued in 1969 to struggle over three issues. These are the birth-control question, celibacy of priests, and the governing of the Church. Reformers wanted greater sharing of papal authority. Traditionalists feared this kind of change more than any other. The issue is one that has been fought out many times in the past. But its long history does not make it less significant to the two sides in today's debate. Two of the issues drew the most attention.

Governing the Church

Pope Paul VI increasingly during 1969 cast his lot with the traditionalists. He believes that the demands of reformers threaten the Church with a loss of its identity. He warned almost weekly against what he saw as dangers to the purity of Catholic doctrine and the strength of the Church's discipline. The Pope did not, however, condemn those who seek reform. He acknowledged the worth of the movement for "authenticity" in religion and for "relevancy" on the part of the institutional Church. And by his visits to Uganda and to Geneva, Switzerland, he continued to present himself as a pilgrim pope open to the currents of the modern world.

Cardinal Leon-Joseph Suenens of Belgium, a reformer, gave an interview that was published in six languages. Suenens argued for changes to bring about the ideal of "collegial" government proposed by the Second Vatican Council. Essentially, Cardinal Suenens argued for decentralization, or the sharing of power among cardinals, bishops, priests, and even lay people of the Church. His program was strongly at-

Cardinal Dearden   Cardinal Wright   Cardinal Carberry   Cardinal Cooke

tacked by members of the Roman Curia (the Vatican's administrative body). However, at the October meeting of the world Synod of Bishops it became apparent that Suenen's views were widely shared. And the Pope accepted three Synod proposals aimed at strengthening the influence of the bishops on decisions affecting the whole Church.

Celibacy of Priests

The clearest evidence that the Church is in a state of crisis is seen in the increasing number of priests leaving the ministry for secular work and marriage. Reliable statistics on how many have left the Church were difficult to obtain. Discontent with the Church's unchanging stand on celibacy was one reason some have left. But many observers cited other reasons as more important. Among them was a loss of confidence in the usefulness of priestly work under present conditions. The single most important event of this kind was the resignation, followed by marriage, of Bishop James P. Shannon, formerly auxiliary bishop of St. Paul-Minneapolis. He had been a symbol and leader of the moderate reform movement.

New Cardinals

Four churchmen in the United States were among the 35 elevated to the rank of cardinal in 1969. They were Archbishops Dearden of Detroit, Cooke of New York, and Carberry of St. Louis, and Bishop Wright of Pittsburgh.

Another kind of leadership was offered by a small but determined band of Catholic priests, nuns, brothers, and lay persons who raided Selective Service offices. The raiders destroyed draft records to protest the Vietnam war. More-conservative Catholics were scandalized by such conduct. Conservatives also did not agree with liturgical experimentation, priests' resignations, open dissension, and criticism.

Thus, communication between the reform and traditionalist groups became more, rather than less, difficult during 1969. However, few predicted a schism either in the United States or elsewhere.

ROBERT G. HOYT
Editor, *The National Catholic Reporter*

▶ JEWS AND JUDAISM

For the Jews in Israel and the small Jewish communities in Iraq, Egypt, and Syria, the year brought more hostility and violence. And Israelis and their property were subjected to Arab terrorist attacks in England, the Netherlands, Germany, Switzerland, and Greece. These events were of concern to Jews throughout the world.

Israel's Prime Minister Golda Meir met with President Nixon in Washington, D.C., in September. The position of the Israeli Government remained that direct negotiations between Israel and its Arab neighbors were the only way to bring peace.

In October, Foreign Minister Abba Eban met with Pope Paul VI in Rome. It was the first official meeting between a pope and a member of the Israeli Government. The Pope again offered to help search for peace in the Middle East.

Jewish communities throughout the world continued to be Israel's chief source of moral and material support. In June, the Jerusalem Economic Conference brought

Israel's Foreign Minister Abba Eban meets with Pope Paul in the Vatican.

together 300 leading Jewish industrialists and businessmen from all parts of the world. The conference was held to get Jewish businessmen to invest in Israel. Israeli Government officials forecast a total of more than 30,000 new immigrants for the coming 3 years. And Israel will need an annual foreign investment of $200,000,000 in industry, agriculture, transportation, and tourism for the next 5 years.

American Jewry continued to seek solutions to its major problems of the late 1960's. There was growing uneasiness over anti-Semitism in ghetto areas. Jewish leaders also warned against three dangers to Jewish life. Two of these are inter-marriage and assimilation, and anti-Semitism. The third is the idea of Jewish "ir-relevance." This issue has been raised by young Jewish "activists" and revolution-aries. For example, some of the campus-revolt leaders are young Jews who say that Judaism has no meaning for their causes.

The American Jewish Committee published *Not Quite at Home: How an American Community Lives with Itself and Its Neighbors* in 1969. The book tries to give American Jews an understanding of how to preserve their culture and religion within the larger American community.

In the area of Jewish religion an important event was the creation of the Reconstructionist Rabbinical College in Philadelphia. The institution is sponsored by the Jewish Reconstructionist Foundation. It embodies the philosophy and theology of Professor Mordecai M. Kaplan. He defines Judaism as "the evolving religious civilization of the Jewish people." With the establishment of the Rabbinical College, Reconstructionism may be well on its way to emerging as the fourth major movement in American and world Jewry.

MEIR BEN-HORIN
Chairman, Division of Education
Dropsie University

▶EASTERN ORTHODOXY

The twentieth anniversary of Ecumenical Patriarch Athenagoras I on the throne of ancient Constantinople was celebrated in January 1969. Archbishop Iakovos, the primate of the Greek Orthodox Church of North and South America, held an ecumenical doxology in the Greek Orthodox Cathedral of the Holy Trinity in New York City. For the first time since the great schism of 1054, Roman Catholic and Protestant bishops took part. Archbishop Cooke of New York (later Cardinal) offered prayers for the Ecumenical Patriarch. Some extreme groups and some moderate Orthodox bishops, primarily Russian, protested the ecumenical prayer. Public opinion, however, favored this praying together for unity.

Ecumenical Patriarch Athenagoras I celebrated twenty years as spiritual leader of Orthodoxy.

Theological dialogue between the Orthodox Church and Roman Catholicism continued on all levels. On the parish level, the Roman Catholic Archdiocese of Boston in its *In Search of Unity* gave the Orthodox in Boston generous privileges. Roman Catholics will be able to attend the Orthodox liturgy. Also, Roman Catholics will be able ceremoniously to act as godparents and best men in Orthodox baptisms and weddings. And under certain circumstances, it provides for Roman Catholics to go to Orthodox priests for confession and communion. The Orthodox Church has not yet reciprocated in any way.

On the world level, Patriarch German of Serbia (Yugoslavia) was elected one of the presidents of the World Council of Churches. The representation of the Patriarchate of Moscow became more active in the World Council of Churches when Metropolitan Nikodim became head of the group in 1969. Membership in the World Council of Churches is taken very seriously by the Orthodox Churches. It is seen by Patriarch Athenagoras as an important tool to Christian unity.

In the United States, 1969 was a year of quiet but deep awakening of the many Orthodox ethnic jurisdictions to current religious, cultural, and youth movements. The ethnic groups include the Albanian, Bulgarian, Carpatho-Russian, Greek, Rumanian, Russian, Serbian, and Ukrainian churches. During the year, the Orthodox Churches of the Americas entered a period of re-examination. This is being undertaken as an attempt to meet present-day challenges in all areas of personal and communal living.

Archbishop Iakovos, the Orthodox spokesman on national and international levels, worked on the newly accredited Hellenic College in Brookline, Massachusetts, and its graduate school of divinity. The two schools are seen as the core of the envisioned Hellenic University.

NICON D. PATRINACOS
Editor, *The Orthodox Observer*

RHODESIA. See AFRICA.

RUMANIA

TWO trends reached high points in Rumania during 1969. From the outside world's point of view, the more spectacular of these trends was Rumania's increasing independence in foreign policy. This independence was most vividly shown on August 2-3. On that summer weekend, U.S. President Richard Nixon visited Bucharest, Rumania's capital. He received one of the most enthusiastic and most friendly welcome any American president has ever received abroad.

To most Rumanians, however, the more important trend was the continued consolidation of power by President Nicolae Ceausescu. Many people who had opposed him, or who, it was feared, might oppose him in the future, were purged from high positions in the Rumanian Communist Party.

▶ FOREIGN AFFAIRS

As 1969 began, there was still fear that Soviet forces might invade Rumania as they had invaded Czechoslovakia in August 1968. There were several reasons for this fear.

First, Rumania had strongly supported the liberal regime of Alexander Dubcek in Czechoslovakia. Second, Rumania had defied the Soviet Union by keeping diplomatic relations with West Germany and Israel. And, finally, Rumania had stayed neutral in the Chinese-Soviet controversy.

However, the Rumanians did not suffer the same fate as the Czechoslovaks. Indeed, at the end of 1969 it was clear that they had kept their national sovereignty. Also, they had extended their foreign-policy independence further than earlier.

Rumania had to make some concessions to the Soviet Union, of course. Rumanians did, for example, attend the international Communist Party Congress in Moscow in mid-1969. It was the first international meeting since 1960. But even there the Rumanians showed their independence. By so doing they helped prevent the Soviet

President Nixon, riding with Rumanian leader Nicolae Ceausescu, receives a very friendly welcome in Bucharest, capital of Rumania.

States concern for the continued independence of Rumania. It also increased the worldwide prestige of President Ceausescu and his Government.

Relations with Israel

Only slightly less daring than the warm welcome given Mr. Nixon was the Rumanian agreement with Israel to raise the diplomatic status of their respective envoys to ambassadorial rank. This move underlined the friendly relations between Rumania and Israel. It also further emphasized Rumania's role as the only communist nation not giving all-out support to the Arabs.

▶ DOMESTIC AFFAIRS

The 1969 Rumanian Communist Party Congress gave President Ceausescu a chance to achieve several important goals. At the Congress he denounced his predecessor, Gheorghe Gheorghiu-Dej. This was part of Ceausescu's plan for purging older leaders who had been party to Gheorghiu-Dej's political misdeeds, such as the repression of innocent Communists in the 1950's. The denunciation also created the framework for Ceausescu's policy of slow-but-steady liberalization in Rumania.

Rumania pushed ahead with its industrialization. The country continued to co-operate with the Council for Mutual Economic Assistance (Comecon), the Soviet bloc's economic co-ordination agency. But it placed far more stress on attempting to import the latest Western technology. Rumania also sought more and closer economic relations with Western nations such as France, West Germany, Britain, and the United States.

HARRY SCHWARTZ
The New York Times
See also EUROPE, EAST; UNION OF SOVIET SOCIALIST REPUBLICS.

RWANDA. See AFRICA.

SAUDI ARABIA. See MIDDLE EAST.

SCHOOLS. See EDUCATION.

Union from getting unified support for its anti-Chinese position.

In addition, the Rumanians played some role in arranging the September meeting in Peking, China, between Soviet Premier Kosygin and Chinese Premier Chou En-lai. Still, the Soviets continued to show their displeasure with Rumania. At the Rumanian Communist Party Congress in August, for example, the chief of the Soviet delegation denounced Rumanian independence as dangerous nationalism.

President Nixon's Visit

The decision to receive President Nixon was the most daring Rumanian move in 1969. It came at a time when the Vietnam war was still very active. From Nixon's visit, Rumania certainly hoped to get promises of greater economic and scientific co-operation with the United States. But this was not the major reason for Rumania's action. The major reason was that President Nixon's visit implied United

SOCIAL WELFARE

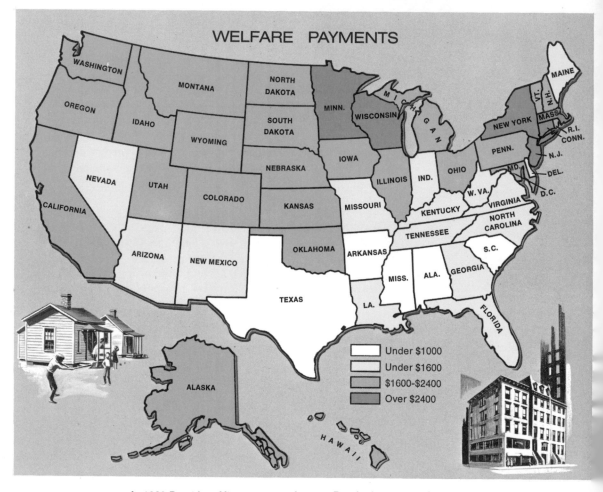

WELFARE PAYMENTS

☐	Under $1000
☐	Under $1600
☐	$1600-$2400
☐	Over $2400

In 1969 President Nixon proposed a new Family Assistance System, which would set a minimum payment of $1,600 a year for a family of four. Map shows current payments.

SOCIAL welfare programs in the United States fall into three broad categories—health, education, and welfare. Of the three, the most money is spent on welfare. Welfare is most directly involved with the problems of poverty. Most welfare programs are "income maintenance programs." They provide cash payments for certain categories of the population. These programs include social security, public income maintenance, unemployment insurance, and public assistance. Almost all welfare in the United States is funded and administered by Federal, state, and local government. Some welfare is provided by private groups such as labor unions, fraternal organizations, and some philanthropic groups.

In 1969, there were two trends for welfare programs. One was that more and more money would be needed for welfare. About 20 per cent of the Federal budget in 1969 went for retirement and social insurance and public assistance. In 1960, it was 16 per cent. And in 1950, it was just 13.5 per cent. The other trend was toward the Federal Government assuming the responsibility for welfare payments and programs.

In recent years, welfare programs have come under increasing criticism. It has been said that welfare does not reach most of the poor people and those who are covered by welfare do not receive adequate payments. Also, many people feel that welfare has destroyed the incentive to work.

Thus, in 1969, President Nixon proposed a new Family Assistance System. This was the first step in a planned sweeping reform of the welfare system in the United States.

▶ **PROPOSED WELFARE LEGISLATION**

The Family Assistance System would replace the Aid to Families with Dependent Children program. Its main purpose would be to help and encourage the poor who work. Before this, people who had jobs and were working usually could not receive public assistance money in addition to their earnings. However, under the new welfare program, people could work and still receive welfare payments.

One main feature of the new program would be to provide a minimum standard of Federal aid. This would be $1,600 a year for a family of four.

In addition, there would be a work requirement for those who can work, including mothers of school-age children. Public funds would be used for job training. The Department of Labor would create 150,000 new job-training opportunities for heads of families. And, day-care centers for 450,000 children would be set up.

Under the proposed Family Assistance System, payments would still be available

to the "working poor" as long as the family subsists below the poverty level. The payments end when the family reaches a certain level of income. Thus, when a family of four reaches an earned income of $3,920 a year, the payments stop. Also, should an able-bodied family head fail to apply for a job, only his share of the annual minimum payments would be withdrawn. The other family members would continue to receive their shares. The family security plan covers families only. It would not cover single persons or childless couples.

The final part of the President's plan combines three programs that now operate separately. These are Old-Age Assistance, Aid to the Blind, and Aid to the Partially and Totally Disabled. The programs cover about 3,000,000 people. Benefits would be increased. The Federal Government would assume a larger share of the cost of these programs, thus easing the burden on the cities and states.

▶ **SOCIAL SECURITY**

President Nixon in 1969 also proposed an increase of 10 per cent in social security payments. Some 25,000,000 people were receiving social security benefits in 1969. In addition to the increase, the President proposed that there be automatic increases in the future, to meet expected rises in the cost of living. Congress, however, passed a 15 per cent increase in social security benefits. Congress did not include automatic increases in the bill. And President Nixon signed the bill into law on December 30. The increase was effective for January 1, 1970. It raised monthly payments to an average-income couple, for example, from $170 to $195. The increase is to be financed by a rise in the social security tax rate on employees and employers.

GEORGE T. MARTIN, JR.
University of Chicago
JOANNA FOLEY MARTIN
Chicago Urban League

See also POVERTY.

SPACE EXPLORATION

"NO single space project in this period will be more impressive to mankind. . . ." Who among the 600,000,000 people around the world who watched astronaut Neil Armstrong place his foot on the moon would not now join the late President John F. Kennedy in that sentiment.

The thundering and beautiful launch of Apollo 11 on July 16. The heart-pounding tension of touchdown with the Eagle Lunar Module on July 20 in the Sea of Tranquility. Armstrong's foot-down with his declaration, "That's one small step for a man, one giant leap for mankind," and his reading with fellow astronaut Edwin Aldrin the plaque on Eagle's leg: "Here men from the planet earth first set foot upon the moon July 1969 A.D. We came in peace for all mankind." The tense lunar takeoff on July 21. The splashdown 950 miles southwest of Honolulu on July 24. This was an epic voyage.

▶ THE APOLLO MISSION

With their fellow astronaut, command-module pilot Michael Collins, these first men on the moon stepped out of the Lunar Receiving Laboratory August 10 at the NASA Manned Spacecraft Center in Houston after 18 days of isolation to receive a steady stream of praise and honors.

The precision of their eight-day flight perhaps impressed people as much as anything else about it. The command module splashed down only 42 seconds later than the planned time. It had traveled 952,700 miles.

Apollo 12, manned by Charles Conrad, Richard Gordon, and Alan Bean, repeated the Apollo 11 success. Launched November 14, it landed in the moon's Ocean of Storms exactly as planned. It set down only a few hundred feet from the Surveyor 3 spacecraft, which had landed on the moon on April 19, 1967. Conrad and Bean collected the TV camera from the Surveyor on the second of their two walks onto the moon. In addition, they set out many instruments. These included seismometer, solar-wind collecting sheet, magnetometer,

Apollo 12 Astronaut Alan Bean on the moon.

The Saturn 5 rocket, carrying the Apollo 11 astronauts, blasts off for the moon.

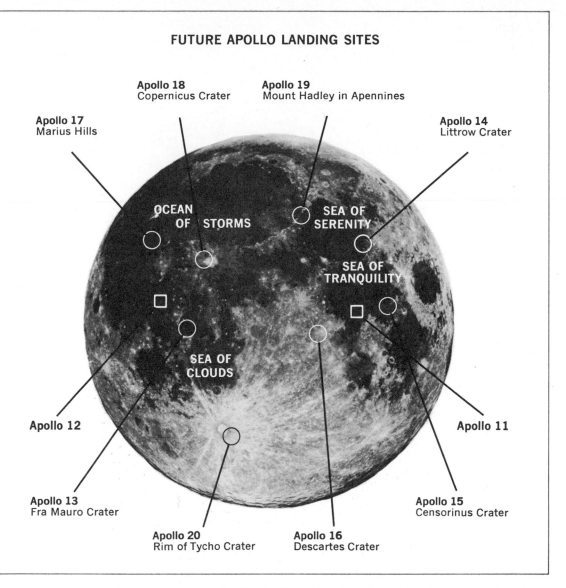

FUTURE APOLLO LANDING SITES

Apollo 18
Copernicus Crater

Apollo 19
Mount Hadley in Apennines

Apollo 17
Marius Hills

Apollo 14
Littrow Crater

OCEAN OF STORMS

SEA OF SERENITY

SEA OF TRANQUILITY

SEA OF CLOUDS

Apollo 12

Apollo 11

Apollo 13
Fra Mauro Crater

Apollo 15
Censorinus Crater

Apollo 20
Rim of Tycho Crater

Apollo 16
Descartes Crater

A map of the moon showing Apollo landing sites planned for 1970, 1971, and 1972.

solar-wind spectrometer, and ionosphere detector. The Apollo 11 astronauts had also set out a laser-beam reflector which showed that the moon is 131.2 feet farther from earth than previously measured. Both crews, of course, collected rock and soil samples.

A brief assessment of the initial experimental results from these flights is as follows: The moon shows no signs of life whatever. Its surface materials contain very, very little carbon, from which the life we know takes structure. There is no sign of water. There is, however, evidence of bombardment, including the somewhat surprising glassy beads.

As Anthony Turkevich and his associates at the University of Chicago predicted

Transportation for Apollo astronauts beginning in late 1971 or early 1972: a two-man lunar roving vehicle.

from information gathered by Surveyor 5, the moon rocks, at least near these spacecraft, contain a high percentage of titanium, between 7 and 8 per cent. On earth this would be considered a high-grade ore. The moon rocks differ in other chemical ways from earth rocks. This, and the fact that Apollo 11 igneous rocks show an age greater than 3,500,000 years, mean that the moon did not come from the earth. It more likely formed at the same time as earth, or was captured by it.

Apollo 12 had landed about 950 miles west of Apollo 11, in the Ocean of Storms. Early findings indicate that the rocks in this area are 1,000,000,000 years younger than the rocks found by the Apollo 11 astronauts in the Sea of Tranquility.

Prior to the moon landings, Apollo 9 had tested the lunar lander in earth orbit. In May, Apollo 10 had gone all the way to the moon in a dress rehearsal for Apollo 11, but no lunar landing was made.

The Apollo events and results have already filled books, and many more will follow as the astronauts undertake further landing missions.

NASA plans modifications of the Apollo equipment to increase mission time from 10 to 16 days and duration on the lunar surface from 36 hours to about three days. The later missions may make use of a roving vehicle. NASA issued a contract for its development following the Apollo 11 flight.

▶ SOVIET SPACE EFFORTS

The Soviet Union began 1969 with the rendezvous and docking of Soyuz 4 and Soyuz 5. These flights suggested that the Russians would be making an all-out effort to stay in the manned phase of exploration. They somewhat startlingly launched an unmanned spacecraft, Luna 15, on July 13, as a mysterious vanguard to Apollo 11. While the space flight was in progress,

M. V. Keldysh, president of the Soviet Academy of Sciences, told Colonel Frank Borman by phone that Luna 15 would not intersect the path of Apollo 11. This unmanned spacecraft crashed in the moon's Sea of Crises on July 21 during an attempted soft-landing of an instrument package designed to collect lunar soil and return it to earth.

Then, on October 11, 12, and 13 the Soviet Union launched Soyuz 6, 7, and 8, carrying in all seven astronauts. In space, these astronauts reportedly conducted welding experiments. This would have a direct operational use in setting up a large space station. It is very possible, in fact, that all three of these spacecraft were meant to dock with a space station weighing around 200,000 pounds, launched by the long-rumored new 10,000,000-pound-thrust Russian "super" space booster.

An indirect intelligence report in November claimed this booster blew up on the pad. Meanwhile, on November 4, Dr. Keldysh said the Soviet Union hoped to have a permanent space station orbiting the earth in the next five years. It is expected that the Soviet Union will be in space with a station much larger and more versatile than the planned Apollo space station.

▶ U.S. SPACE STATIONS

This coming U.S. space station would have a "workshop" and a telescope mount (ATM). These would be launched together by the first two stages of a Saturn 5 rocket into a circular orbit 220 miles high. First launch is scheduled for 1972. The workshop will test the ability of astronauts to work for long periods under relatively unconfined zero-gravity conditions.

A future U.S. space station. First launch is scheduled for 1972.

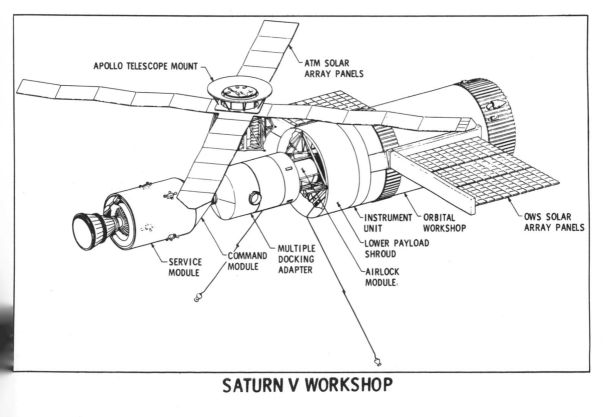

SATURN V WORKSHOP

An Apollo spacecraft launched by a Saturn 1B rocket will deliver a three-man crew to the space station. On the first trip they will stay for 28 days. Eventually a 56-day stay will be accomplished. The workshop will stay in orbit about eight months. It will have a 10,000-cu.-ft. hydrogen tank outfitted before the launch for living and working operations. An adapter will dock the Apollo spacecraft and hold the telescope mount. An airlock module will permit the crew to leave the workshop section without depressurizing it. Large solar panels will power the workshop and the ATM. The whole space station will weigh about 130,000 pounds.

The ATM will test the ability of astronauts to operate fairly exacting scientific equipment—an ensemble of astronomical instruments. These instruments will take measurements of radiations masked by the earth's atmosphere.

Although a modest system, this space station will home in on two key questions confronting the planners of long missions, such as to Mars.

First, can astronauts stand long periods of weightlessness without deteriorating physically? If they can not, the complexities of rotating the space station and creation of "artificial gravity" must be accepted.

Second, how well can astronauts work in space over long periods, in particular, conducting scientific experiments, such as observations in astronomy? Are they worth the trouble of putting up there, compared to automatic equipment?

▶ UNITED STATES–SOVIET CO-OPERATION

It is possible that the Russians and Americans will yet co-operate in space-station programs. After his flight, Colonel Borman, who is close to President Nixon, visited the Soviet Union. He was warmly received by Dr. Keldysh and others in the Russian space program. Before he went, on June 10, the U.S. Department of Defense canceled the Air Force's Manned Orbiting Laboratory, a secret spying system. Many considered the MOL provocative

and in the long run wasteful of engineering effort on manned spacecraft development. Then the Soviet Union sent two cosmonauts—Georgi Beregovoi (Soyuz 3) and Konstantin Feoktistov (Voskhod 1)—to the United States on October 20 for a two-week visit. Dr. Feoktistov met with Robert Gilruth, head of the NASA Manned Spacecraft Center, during the 6th Annual Meeting of the American Institute of Aeronautics and Astronautics in Anaheim, California.

Recently both sides have pushed for international co-operation in space. President Nixon, for example, expressed a desire for co-operation in an address to the 24th session of the UN General Assembly on September 18. And Wisconsin Senator William Proxmire introduced a resolution November 18 asking the Senate Foreign Relations Committee to explore means of bringing nations together in joint space enterprise. "It is time," Proxmire said, "we considered inviting other nations—indeed the entire world community—to participate in this venture, whose benefits are of such international character."

▶ SATELLITE APPLICATIONS

The Communications Satellite Corporation is manager for the international consortium of 68 countries known as Intelsat. In 1969, it put into operation the first truly global public communications-satellite network. Several Intelsat 3 launches were made in 1969. The launch scheduled for early 1970 will double the coverage over the Atlantic. These Intelsat 3's offer three times the capacity of the existing world cable network. Small nations as well as large can use this network without paying a penalty for being a small user. As to TV, Comsat has cut the cost of TV relay from an initial $8,100 per hour to $3,250 per hour with Intelsat 2, to $1,560 per hour with Intelsat 3. In short, the artificial satellite has just now plunged the world deep into a revolution in communications.

Intelsat 4, due in 1970, will increase the capacity of the world telephonic network five times. Transatlantic phone rates should then soon rival transcontinental U.S. rates.

The accord on a special TV satellite the United States will develop for India shows just how deep the communications revolution is. The two countries signed an agreement in September clearing the way for an Applications Technology Satellite (ATS) to be placed into synchronous orbit over the equator. The satellite will beam television to over 5,000 Indian villages. Any small city in the United States has more TV sets than all of India with its population of over half a billion people. Each village will have a receiving station costing about $500. A few years after the service begins in 1972, the cost of such stations should drop to about $100. Villagers will gather at the "town hall" to see programs agreed to by the Indian Government. These will include programs on improving agricultural practices, national culture, and family planning. It seems very likely that this system will start an enormous demand for direct TV services around the world. Brazil already has shown interest in such a system, which does not require the use of ground relay stations.

In short, by the mid-1970's, only political decisions will stand between the world community of nations and a vast unified public-information medium, with nations like Japan ready to fill the home-receiver market. In 1969, the United States also agreed to let U.S. companies sell Japan equipment and technical information that will permit it to develop communications satellites. Japan has scheduled launch of one of these by 1975.

A 1969 experiment conducted by General Electric with ATS 1 and 3 for NASA illustrates the trend of using satellites for practical purposes. The satellites served to locate automatically a ship, an aircraft, a truck, and an ocean buoy. A ground station transmitted a coded signal to the two satellites which then relayed them to the ground. The vehicle associated with that code then transmitted a coded reply to the satellites.

Tacomsat 1, largest communications satellite.

Both satellites then relayed it to the ground station. There a computer analyzed the time for the relay and, from the known position of the satellites, predicted the position of the vehicle—all in a few seconds. The computer placed the vehicles within 3–5 miles, as good a performance as navigation aids not using satellites now give. The system also relayed voice communications to the vehicles. Such a system could track any moving object, such as an iceberg or a sea buoy.

The most ambitious planners, however, foresee satellites that will combine services in communications, meteorology, geodesy, navigation, and earth-resource surveys.

The future: a space shuttle that carries a satellite into space and returns with men and cargo.

The spur to progress toward such a system will be the so-called Earth Resources Technology Satellite (ERTS). Operational models of this 1,600-pound vehicle will be launched in the early 1970's.

Concerning such satellites as ERTS, President Nixon made this statement in his UN address September 18:

"The journey of Apollo 11 to the moon and back was not an end but the beginning. There will be new journeys of discovery. And beyond this, we are just beginning to comprehend the benefits that space technology can yield here on earth, and the potential is enormous.

"For example, we now are developing earth-resource survey satellites, with the first experimental satellite to be launched sometime early in the decade of the seventies.

"Present indications are that these satellites should be capable of yielding data which could assist in as widely varied tasks as these: the location of schools of fish in the oceans; the location of mineral deposits on land; the health of agricultural crops.

"I feel it is only right that we should share both the adventures and the benefits of space, and as an example of our plans, we have determined to take actions with regard to earth-resource satellites as this program proceeds and fulfills its promise.

"The purpose of those actions is that this program will be dedicated to produce information not only for the United States but also for the world community. We shall be putting several proposals in this respect before the United Nations."

▶ MILITARY SATELLITES

During 1969 the United States military services launched many reconnaissance, communications, space-environment, and nuclear-detection satellites. Among these was the world's largest communication satellite, Tacomsat 1, launched February 9. This 1,600-pound satellite employs 10,000 circuits. It will conduct experiments in communications among aircraft, ships, and troops in the field. Its antennas can project signals strong enough to be picked up by a 1-ft.-diameter antenna on the ground. The Russians, of course, have not been idle with unmanned reconnaissance, environmental, and communication satellites. On September 23, they launched the 300th satellite in the Cosmos series.

▶ DIRECTIONS FOR THE FUTURE

In September, President Nixon's Space Task Group (STG) sent him a report entitled *The Post Apollo Space Program: Directions for the Future*. The report listed these goals:

"Increase man's knowledge of the universe by conduct of a continuing strong

The first pictures of Mars taken by Mariner 6, as seen on television sets.

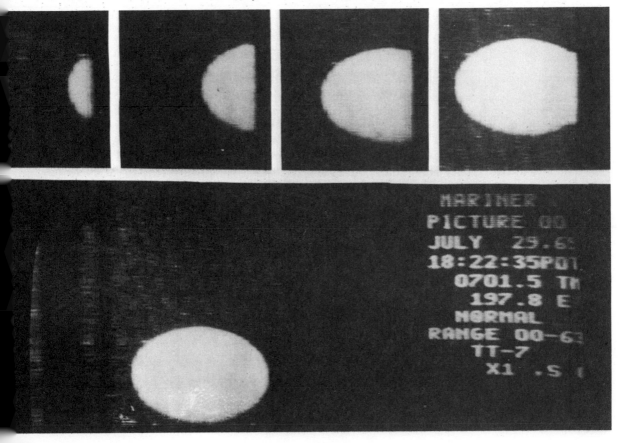

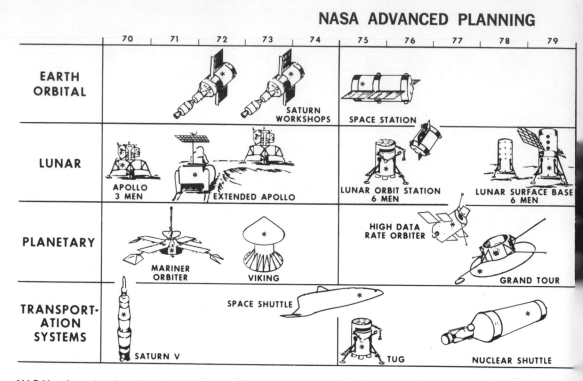

	70	71	72	73	74	75	76	77	78	79

EARTH ORBITAL — SATURN WORKSHOPS, SPACE STATION

LUNAR — APOLLO 3 MEN, EXTENDED APOLLO, LUNAR ORBIT STATION 6 MEN, LUNAR SURFACE BASE 6 MEN

PLANETARY — MARINER ORBITER, VIKING, HIGH DATA RATE ORBITER, GRAND TOUR

TRANSPORTATION SYSTEMS — SATURN V, SPACE SHUTTLE, TUG, NUCLEAR SHUTTLE

NASA's plans for the future include everything from space stations and extended stays on the moon, in the early 1970's, to a manned landing on Mars, in the 1980's.

program of lunar and planetary exploration, astronomy, physics, the earth and life sciences.

"Develop new systems and technology for space operations with emphasis upon the critical factors of: (1) commonality, (2) re-usability, and (3) economy, through a program directed initially toward development of new space transportation capability and space station modules which utilize this new capability.

"Promote a sense of world community through a program which provides opportunity for broad international participation and co-operation."

At the end of the list, but not part of it, the Space Task Group added this statement:

"As a focus for the development of new capability, we recommend the United States accept the long-range option or goal of manned planetary exploration with a manned Mars mission before the end of this century as the first target."

In effect, the STG recommendations invite debate over the future of the space program for a year. This left the President the option of holding a major commitment to the manned space effort open until mid-1971.

NASA submitted a report, in contrast, that put space exploration No. 1. As NASA sees it, "The decade of the 1970's can be the decade of U.S. pre-eminence in space exploration and applications . . ." serving "a broad range of national purposes: scientific, technical, economic, social, and political. . . ." The wedge in this program would be increasingly large space stations and a new re-usable launch vehicle called the "space shuttle." In its report to the new president, it was as though NASA leaders could still hear a young and vigorous JFK proclaim: "The exploration of space will go ahead, whether we join it or not, and it is one of the great adventures of all time and no nation which expects to be the leader of other nations

FOR MANNED SPACE VEHICLES

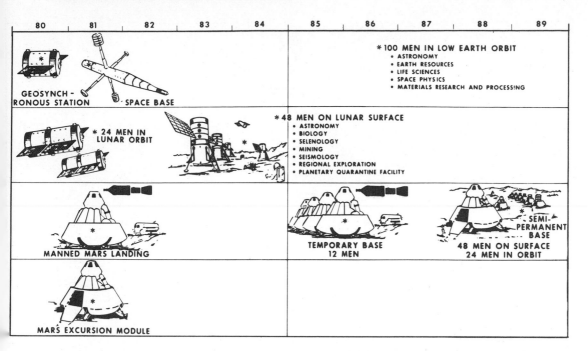

| 80 | 81 | 82 | 83 | 84 | 85 | 86 | 87 | 88 | 89 |

GEOSYNCH-RONOUS STATION   SPACE BASE

*100 MEN IN LOW EARTH ORBIT
- ASTRONOMY
- EARTH RESOURCES
- LIFE SCIENCES
- SPACE PHYSICS
- MATERIALS RESEARCH AND PROCESSING

*24 MEN IN LUNAR ORBIT

*48 MEN ON LUNAR SURFACE
- ASTRONOMY
- BIOLOGY
- SELENOLOGY
- MINING
- SEISMOLOGY
- REGIONAL EXPLORATION
- PLANETARY QUARANTINE FACILITY

MANNED MARS LANDING

TEMPORARY BASE
12 MEN

SEMI-PERMANENT BASE
48 MEN ON SURFACE
24 MEN IN ORBIT

MARS EXCURSION MODULE

Within two decades NASA hopes to have semi-permanent bases on Mars as well as the moon, with astronomers and other scientists traveling to the moon and beyond by space shuttle.

can expect to stay behind in this race for space. . . ."

As if to illustrate his meaning, the Apollos and the Mariners 6 and 7 unmanned spacecraft to Mars led the United States to an ever-broader and more commanding position in deep-space exploration during the year. Meanwhile, two Russian Venus probes failed to return data in May, and at least one Russian Mars probe failed on launch in March.

The Mariners, launched February 24 and March 27, flew by the planet July 31 and August 5. Mariner 6 returned 74 pictures of the planet; Mariner 7, 126, thirty-three of these close up. The several other instruments of the spacecraft revealed a planet lacking, as far as can be detected, nitrogen, water, or organic compounds in its atmosphere. Carbon dioxide and carbon monoxide swath the planet—a bleak picture indeed for life.

These Mariners really placed the U.S. unmanned spacecraft program on the way to the outer planets. For they confirmed the ability of the engineers to explore Mars or Jupiter now as well as the moon could be probed five years ago.

Now, however, except for Apollo, NASA runs out of attention-getting deep-space missions until Mars orbiters in 1971 and Mars landers in 1973. Without another Apollo and with the Vietnam war and inflation still on, it has become an open question whether the President and the public will take the high road of exploration the space agency would like to see, or simply play it safe with relatively inexpensive application satellites and limited military developments. So the vintage space year of 1969 ends on the odd note that more may mean less.

JOHN NEWBAUER
Editor in Chief
Astronautics & Aeronautics

See also MAN IN SPACE, the special article which begins on page 10.

SPAIN. See EUROPE, WEST.

SPORTS

The amazin' world champion Mets get a ticker-tape parade in New York City.

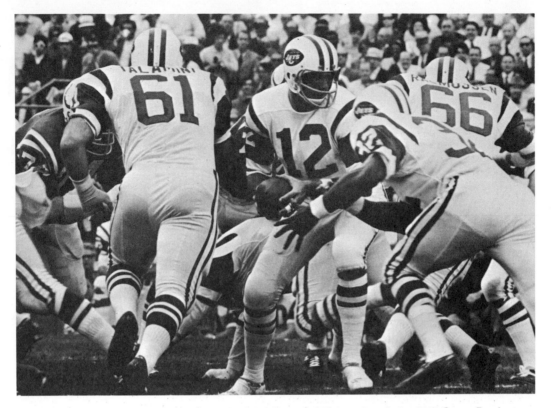

Jet quarterback Joe Namath (12) in action during 1969 Super Bowl game.

IN 1969, the year that man first walked on the moon, millions of sports fans witnessed two other events that were also out of this world. In fact, it may be light-years before two teams are underdogs quite as the New York Jets and Mets were underdogs in 1969. Any way you looked at it, the Jets did not have a chance against the Baltimore Colts in the January 1969 Super Bowl game because the Colts were National Football League champions, and everybody knew the only way to go in pro football was the NFL way.

The Mets? Well, the Mets had somehow won baseball's National League pennant. Nobody quite knew how, but of one thing they were sure: The Mets could not win the World Series against the Baltimore Orioles, for the Orioles were one of the best teams in baseball history.

So, in the year that man walked on the moon, the Jets beat the Colts, the Mets beat the Orioles, and Baltimore will never live it down.

▶ THE SUPER JETS

Broadway Joe Namath, the Jet quarterback, started it all the week before the Super Bowl game in January 1969 when he said a lot of things about the Colts, all of it bad. The Colts, tight-lipped, said they would do *their* talking on the field. But when the Colts then went out and blew two marvelous scoring opportunities in the first quarter, the Jets suddenly realized that they could indeed win the game. Behind Namath, New York drove 80 yards in 12 plays for the game's only touchdown, which was scored by fullback Matt Snell on a 5-yard run. The Jet defense then took over and forced the Colts into numerous errors, while Jim Turner's 3 field goals put New York in front 16–0. Baltimore did not get on the scoreboard until four minutes were left in the game, and by that time it was over. "Welcome to the AFL," jeered Namath following the 16–7 upset. All the Colts, their fans—and the NFL—could do was listen.

▶ SUPER BOWL 1970

In the January 1970 Super Bowl the AFL showed its strength once again. It was the fourth and final Super Bowl before the merger of the two leagues in 1970. The AFL's Kansas City Chiefs upset the NFL's Minnesota Vikings 23–7. The Vikings were helpless against the superb passing of the Chiefs' quarterback Len Dawson.

▶ THE AMAZIN' METS

That was in August, the month in which the Mets—even greater underdogs than the Jets—were whittling away at a Chicago Cub lead in the National League East that had once been 9½ games. (In an attempt to perk up sagging attendance, as well as give television an attractive play-off schedule each year, major-league baseball had broken its established leagues into divisions following the 1968 season.) Down the stretch, it seemed that the Cubs—so unbeatable early in the year—could do no right, the Mets no wrong. The night the Mets clinched the pennant in the East, fans swept out of the stands of Shea Stadium and onto the field, tearing up turf and grabbing the bases for souvenirs. When they were through, the field looked like the scarred surface of the moon itself. When the Mets went on to sweep the Atlanta Braves for the National League championship, the fans tore up the field again—and still again after the team stunned Baltimore in the World Series. (Before the football Jets could move back into Shea Stadium, the field had to be almost completely re-sodded.)

New York's pitching, led by Jerry Koosman, Tom Seaver, and Gary Gentry, stopped Baltimore's hitting with remarkable ease. After dropping the opening game in Baltimore, 4–1, the Mets came back behind Koosman to win the next day

Gil Hodges, happy manager of the Mets.

2–1. Back in Shea Stadium, they swept the next three games, with Koosman winning the last one, 5–3. Donn Clendenon, who hit three home runs in the series, was voted the Most Valuable Player in the Series. In defeat, it was manager Earl Weaver of the Orioles who summed up the New York victory as well as anyone: "They made the plays," he said, "and we didn't."

▶ CELTICS WIN NBA PLAY-OFFS

Springtime 1969 was, of course, play-off time in the world of pro basketball. The Boston Celtics, who had finished fourth in their division and prompted many a comment that age had finally caught up with them, came back to win the National Basketball Association play-offs in perhaps the team's most determined performance ever. After disposing of New York's young and determined Knickerbockers, the Celtics—

Montreal Canadiens' captain Jean Beliveau holds up the Stanley Cup. The Canadiens defeated the St. Louis Blues in four straight games to win the cup finals.

led by Bill Russell and John Havlicck—took on superstars Wilt Chamberlain, Jerry West, Elgin Baylor, and the rest of the Los Angeles Lakers for the championship. Their thrilling series went down to a dramatic seventh game in Los Angeles, where the Celtics grabbed the lead in the first quarter and never gave it up in a 108–106 win. It was Boston's 11th world title in 13 years, and easily one of their most satisfying. Several months later Russell, who had coached the team and played on it as well, retired from basketball and was replaced by Tommy Heinsohn.

College Basketball

The NCAA basketball tournament proved to be a rerun of the past year, with tall Lew Alcindor and the UCLA Bruins winning their third straight championship. The Bruins, who overcame a strong threat by Drake in the semifinals, won the championship by walloping Purduc, 92–72. Lew Alcindor, UCLA's star center, scored 37 points and dominated the game. After the tournament Alcindor signed the biggest contract in pro-basketball history: a reported $1,400,000, long-term arrangement with the NBA's Milwaukee Bucks.

▶ HOCKEY

In hockey, it was the big, bad Bruins from Boston challenging the swift, classy Canadiens from Montreal. The result was one of the most exciting Stanley Cup playoff series in years. As it turned out, however, the Bruins probably lost the series in the two opening games in Montreal, where twice they had led the Canadiens late in the game, only to have the home team charge back to tie, then win in overtime. Montreal then went on to easily sweep the West Division champion St. Louis Blues in four games. The new West

George Archer sinks a putt during the final round of the 1969 Masters Golf Tournament at Augusta, Georgia. It was Archer's first win in a major tournament.

Division, formed in late 1968, obviously has a way to go.

▶ GOLF

In golf an obscure fellow named Orville Moody captured the U.S. Open, while defending champion Lee Trevino wound up with a nightmarish card. And, in keeping with what has become tradition in recent years in Augusta, still another mystery man—George Archer—won the Masters. Like Gay Brewer in 1967 and Bob Goalby a year later, Archer was winning his first major championship. Still, almost as surprising as Archer's victory was the way Billy Casper, the three-day leader, blew the tournament on the front nine on Sunday.

▶ HORSE RACING

In horse racing, a superb thoroughbred by the name of Majestic Prince was indeed majestic for awhile. He became the first horse in racing history to remain undefeated through the first two events of the Triple Crown. Majestic Prince beat Arts and Letters in both the Kentucky Derby and the Preakness. But just when everyone wanted to see what would happen when they met in the Belmont, a longer race, trainer Johnny Longden said he was taking the Prince back to California for a rest. He would have, except owner Frank McMahon responded to his own desire—and that of millions—to see if the horse could win the Belmont and the Triple Crown. As it turned out, the Belmont was too long for the Prince—and just right for Arts and Letters—but the sport of kings had been treated to one of its most thrilling horses ever.

Arts and Letters, who won $555,604 in 1969, was named Horse of the Year.

GARY RONBERG
Sports Illustrated

WORLD DRIVING FORMULA 1 CHAMPIONSHIP

Race	Driver	Car
South African GP	Jackie Stewart, Scotland	Matra-Ford
GP of Spain	Jackie Stewart	Matra-Ford
Monte Carlo GP	Graham Hill, England	Lotus-Ford
Dutch GP	Jackie Stewart	Matra-Ford
French GP	Jackie Stewart	Matra-Ford
British GP	Jackie Stewart	Matra-Ford
West German GP	Jackie Ickx, Belgium	Brabham-Ford
GP of Canada	Jackie Ickx	Brabham-Ford
GP of Italy	Jackie Stewart	Matra-Ford
GP of United States	Jochen Rindt, Austria	Lotus-Ford
GP of Mexico	Denis Hulme, New Zealand	McLaren-Ford

World Road-Racing Champion: JACKIE STEWART

NASCAR Grand National Champion: DAVID PEARSON

USAC Stock-Car Champion: MARIO ANDRETTI

Indianapolis 500: MARIO ANDRETTI (Hawk-Ford)

SCCA Canadian-American Challenge Cup: BRUCE McLAREN

SCCA Trans-American Title: MARK DONOHUE

Mario Andretti holds his trophy after winning the Trenton 300-mile race. Andretti also won the Indianapolis 500.

BASEBALL

FINAL MAJOR LEAGUE STANDINGS

AMERICAN LEAGUE

Eastern Division

	W	L	Pct.	GB
Baltimore	109	53	.673	
Detroit	90	72	.556	19
Boston	87	75	.537	22
Washington	86	76	.531	23
New York	80	81	.497	28½
Cleveland	62	99	.385	46½

Western Division

	W	L	Pct.	GB
Minnesota	97	65	.599	
Oakland	88	74	.543	9
California	71	91	.438	26
Kansas City	69	93	.426	28
Chicago	68	94	.420	29
Seattle	64	98	.395	33

American League Pennant: Baltimore

NATIONAL LEAGUE

Eastern Division

	W	L	Pct.	GB
New York	100	62	.617	
Chicago	92	70	.568	8
Pittsburgh	88	74	.543	12
St. Louis	87	75	.537	13
Philadelphia	63	99	.389	37
Montreal	52	110	.321	48

Western Division

	W	L	Pct.	GB
Atlanta	93	69	.574	
San Francisco	90	72	.556	3
Cincinnati	89	73	.549	4
Los Angeles	85	77	.525	8
Houston	81	81	.500	12
San Diego	52	110	.321	41

National League Pennant: New York

LEADING BATTERS (400 or more at bats)

American League

	AB	H	RBI	Pct.
Carew, Minnesota	458	152	55	.332
Reese, Minnesota	420	136	69	.324
R. Smith, Boston	543	168	93	.309
Oliva, Minnesota	637	197	101	.309
F. Robinson, Baltimore	539	166	100	.308
Powell, Baltimore	533	162	121	.304
W. Williams, Chicago	471	143	32	.304
Petrocelli, Boston	535	159	96	.297
F. Howard, Washington	592	175	111	.296
Northrup, Detroit	543	160	66	.295
Andrews, Boston	464	136	60	.293
Buford, Baltimore	555	161	64	.290
Tovar, Minnesota	535	155	51	.290
White, New York	449	130	74	.290

National League

	AB	H	RBI	Pct.
Rose, Cincinnati	627	218	82	.348
Clemente, Pittsburgh	507	175	91	.345
C. Jones, New York	483	164	75	.340
M. Alou, Pittsburgh	698	231	49	.331
McCovey, San Francisco	491	157	126	.320
A. Johnson, Cincinnati	523	165	87	.315
W. Davis, Los Angeles	498	155	59	.311
Stargell, Pittsburgh	522	160	92	.307
Tolan, Cincinnati	637	195	93	.306
Sanguillen, Pittsburgh	459	139	56	.303
Staub, Montreal	550	166	79	.302
Hebner, Pittsburgh	459	138	47	.301
H. Aaron, Atlanta	545	163	96	.299
Brock, St. Louis	655	193	47	.295

WINNING PITCHERS (more than 20 wins)

	W	L	ERA
Seaver, New York, NL	25	7	2.21
McLain, Detroit, AL	24	9	2.77
Cuellar, Baltimore, AL	23	11	2.41
Niekro, Atlanta, NL	23	13	2.56
Marichal, San Francisco, NL	21	11	2.10
Jenkins, Chicago, NL	21	15	3.15

HOME RUN LEADERS (40 or more home runs)

Killebrew, Minnesota, AL	49
F. Howard, Washington, AL	48
R. Jackson, Oakland, AL	47
McCovey, San Francisco, NL	45
H. Aaron, Atlanta, NL	44
Petrocelli, Boston, AL	40
Yastrzemski, Boston, AL	40

1969 WORLD SERIES RESULTS

		R	H	E	Winning/Losing Pitcher
1.	Baltimore	4	6	0	Cuellar
	New York	1	6	1	Seaver
2.	New York	2	6	0	Koosman
	Baltimore	1	2	0	McNally
3.	New York	5	6	0	Gentry
	Baltimore	0	4	1	Palmer
4.	New York	2	10	1	Seaver
	Baltimore	1	6	1	Hall
5.	New York	5	7	0	Koosman
	Baltimore	3	5	2	Watt

BASKETBALL

FINAL NBA STANDINGS

Eastern Division

	W	L	Pct.
Baltimore	57	25	.695
Philadelphia	55	27	.671
New York	54	28	.659
Boston	48	34	.585
Cincinnati	41	41	.500
Detroit	32	50	.390
Milwaukee	27	55	.329

Western Division

	W	L	Pct.
Los Angeles	55	27	.671
Atlanta	48	34	.585
San Francisco	41	41	.500
San Diego	37	45	.451
Chicago	33	49	.402
Seattle	30	52	.366
Phoenix	16	66	.195

NBA Championship: Boston

FINAL ABA STANDINGS

Eastern Division

	W	L	Pct.
Indiana	44	34	.564
Miami	43	35	.551
Kentucky	42	36	.538
Minnesota	36	42	.462
New York	17	61	.218

Western Division

	W	L	Pct.
Oakland	60	18	.769
New Orleans	46	32	.590
Denver	44	34	.564
Dallas	41	37	.526
Los Angeles	33	45	.423
Houston	23	55	.295

ABA Championship: Oakland

During NBA play-off, Lakers' Wilt Chamberlain tries to block shot by Celtics' Bill Russell.

COLLEGE BASKETBALL

NCAA: UCLA
National Invitation: TEMPLE
Atlantic Coast Conference: NORTH CAROLINA
Big Eight: COLORADO
Big Sky: WEBER STATE
Big Ten: PURDUE
Ivy League: PRINCETON
Mid-American: MIAMI (Ohio)
Missouri Valley: DRAKE; LOUISVILLE
Pacific Eight: UCLA
Southeastern: KENTUCKY
Southern: DAVIDSON
Southwest: TEXAS A & M
West Coast Athletic: SANTA CLARA
Western Athletic: WYOMING; BRIGHAM YOUNG

BOATING

YACHTING

Distance Races

Annapolis-Newport: AMERICAN EAGLE (sloop)
Los Angeles-Hawaii: ARGONAUT (sloop)
Miami-Montego Bay: FLYWAY (yawl)
Newport-Cork, Ireland: KIALOA II (yawl)
Port Huron-Mackinac: DIAVOLO (sloop)
San Francisco-Tokyo: PEN DUICK V (sloop)

North American Yacht Racing Union Championships

Mallory Cup: GRAHAM HALL
Adams Cup: JAN O'MALLEY
Sears Cup: MANTON SCOTT
O'Day Cup: GORDON BOWERS

POWERBOATING

1969 Champion: MISS BUDWEISER (Bill Sterett, driver)
World Championship Race: MISS U.S. (Bill Muncey, driver)
Gold Cup: MISS BUDWEISER (Bill Sterett)

BOXING

WORLD BOXING ASSOCIATION CHAMPIONS

Flyweight: BERNABE VILLACAMPO, Philippines
Bantamweight: RUBEN OLIVARES, Mexico
Featherweight: SHOZO SAIJO, Japan
Jr. Lightweight: HIROSHI KOBAYASHI, Japan
Lightweight: MANDO RAMOS, U.S.
Welterweight: JOSE NAPOLES, Mexico
Jr. Middleweight: FREDDIE LITTLE, U.S.
Middleweight: NINO BENVENUTI, Italy
Light Heavyweight: BOB FOSTER, U.S.
Heavyweight *: JIMMY ELLIS, U.S.

* Joe Frazier recognized in New York, Maine, Massachusetts, Illinois, Pennsylvania, and Texas

BOWLING

AMERICAN BOWLING CONGRESS CHAMPIONS

Classic Division

All-Events: LARRY LICHSTEIN
Singles: NELSON BURTON, JR.
Doubles: DON McCUNE—JIM STEFANICH
Team: WEBER WRIST MASTERS (Santa Ana, California)

Regular Division

All-Events: EDDIE JACKSON
Singles: GREG CAMPBELL
Doubles: CHARLES GUEDEL—ROBERT MASCHMEYER
Team: P.A.C. ADVERTISING CO. (Lansing, Michigan)

WOMEN'S INTERNATIONAL BOWLING CONGRESS CHAMPIONS

Open Division

All-Events: HELEN DUVAL
Singles: JOAN BENDER
Doubles: GLORIA BOUVIA-JUDY COOK
Team: FITZPATRICK CHEVROLET (Concord, California)

DOG SHOWS

WESTMINSTER KENNEL CLUB

Best in Show: CH. GLAMOOR GOOD NEWS
Hound: CH. CROSSWYND'S CRACKERJACK, smooth dachshund
Nonsporting: CH. GOTSCHALL'S VAN VAN, Chow Chow
Sporting: CH. MAGILL'S PATRICK, English springer spaniel
Terrier: CH. GLAMOOR GOOD NEWS, Skye terrier
Toy: CH. RENREH LORELEI OF CHARMARON, Manchester toy terrier
Working: CH. PRINCE ANDREW OF SHERLINE, Old English sheepdog

INTERNATIONAL KENNEL CLUB

Best in Show: CH. ARRIBA'S PRIMA DONNA
Hound: CH. VAUGHT'S JOHN PAUL, American foxhound
Nonsporting: CH. ROUND TABLE LORAMAR YEOMAN, miniature poodle
Sporting: CH. ANCRAM'S SIMON, English cocker spaniel
Terrier: CH. GLAMOOR GO GO GO, Skye terrier
Toy: CONTINUATION OF GLENO, Yorkshire terrier
Working: CH. ARRIBA'S PRIMA DONNA, boxer

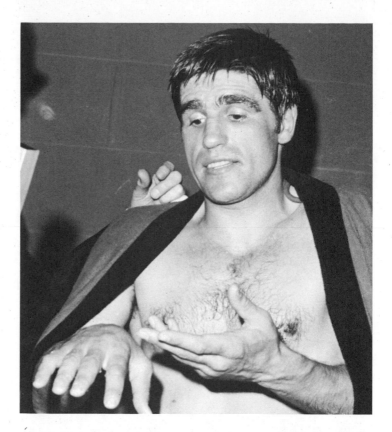

Right: Nino Benvenuti, middleweight boxing champion of the world. Below: Ch. Chumulari Ying Ying, a shih tzu. In 1969 this breed was recognized by the American Kennel Club.

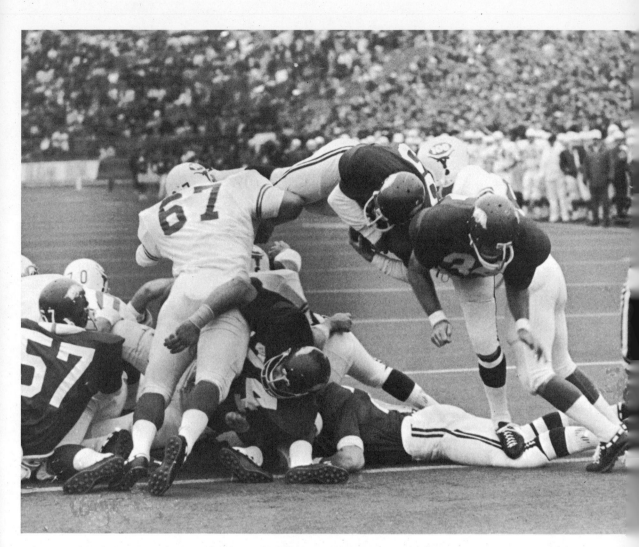

Arkansas' Bill Burnett (33) leaps over the Texas line to score a touchdown. Texas, the No. 1 college team, went on to win by the narrow score of 15–14.

COLLEGE FOOTBALL

Heisman Trophy: STEVE OWENS, Oklahoma
Lambert Trophy: PENN STATE
Atlantic Coast: SOUTH CAROLINA
Big Eight: MISSOURI; NEBRASKA (tied)
Big Ten: MICHIGAN; OHIO STATE (tied)
Ivy: DARTMOUTH; PRINCETON; YALE (tied)
Mid-American: TOLEDO
Pacific Eight: USC
Southeast: TENNESSEE
Southern: DAVIDSON & RICHMOND
Southwest: TEXAS
Western Athletic: ARIZONA STATE
Yankee: MASSACHUSETTS

FOOTBALL

FINAL NFL STANDINGS
EASTERN CONFERENCE
Century Division

	W	L	T	Pct.	PF	PA
Cleveland*	10	3	1	.769	351	300
New York	6	8	0	.429	264	298
St. Louis	4	9	1	.308	314	389
Pittsburgh	1	13	0	.071	218	404

Capitol Division

	W	L	T	Pct.	PF	PA
Dallas	11	2	1	.846	369	223
Washington	7	5	2	.583	307	319
New Orleans	5	9	0	.357	311	393
Philadelphia	4	9	1	.308	279	377

WESTERN CONFERENCE
Central Division

	W	L	T	Pct.	PF	PA
Minnesota *	12	2	0	.857	379	133
Detroit	9	4	1	.692	259	188
Green Bay	8	6	0	.571	269	221
Chicago	1	13	0	.071	210	339

Coastal Division

	W	L	T	Pct.	PF	PA
Los Angeles	11	3	0	.786	320	243
Baltimore	8	5	1	.615	279	268
Atlanta	6	8	0	.429	276	268
San Francisco	4	8	2	.333	277	319

NFL Championship: Minnesota

* Conference winners

FINAL AFL STANDINGS
EASTERN DIVISION

	W	L	T	Pct.	PF	PA
New York	10	4	0	.714	353	269
Houston	6	6	2	.500	278	279
Boston	4	10	0	.286	266	316
Buffalo	4	10	0	.286	230	359
Miami	3	10	1	.231	233	332

WESTERN DIVISION

	W	L	T	Pct.	PF	PA
Oakland *	12	1	1	.923	377	242
Kansas City *	11	3	0	.786	359	177
San Diego	8	6	0	.571	288	276
Denver	5	8	1	.385	297	344
Cincinnati	4	9	1	.308	280	367

AFL Championship: Kansas City

* Play-off winners

GOLF

PROFESSIONAL GOLF

U.S. Open: ORVILLE MOODY
Masters: GEORGE ARCHER
British Open: TONY JACKLIN, Britain
Canadian Open: TOMMY AARON, U.S.
PGA: RAY FLOYD
World Series: ORVILLE MOODY
Ladies PGA: BETSY RAWLS
U.S. Women's Open: DONNA CAPONI
Canadian Women's Open: SANDRA HAYNIE, U.S.

AMATEUR GOLF

U.S. Amateur: STEVEN MELNYK
U.S. Women's Amateur: CATHERINE LACOSTE, France
British Amateur: MICHAEL BONALLACK, Britain

COLLEGE GOLF

NCAA Team: UNIVERSITY OF HOUSTON
NCAA Title: BOB CLARK, California State
Women's Collegiate Title: JANE BASTANCHURY, Arizona State

HOCKEY

FINAL NHL STANDINGS
East Division

	W	L	T	Pts.	GF	GA
Montreal	46	19	11	103	271	220
Boston	42	18	16	100	303	221
New York	41	26	9	91	231	196
Toronto	35	26	15	85	234	217
Detroit	33	31	12	78	239	221
Chicago	34	33	9	77	280	246

West Division

	W	L	T	Pts.	GF	GA
St. Louis	37	25	14	88	204	157
Oakland	29	36	11	69	219	251
Philadelphia	20	35	21	61	174	225
Los Angeles	24	42	10	58	185	260
Pittsburgh	20	45	11	51	189	252
Minnesota	18	43	15	51	189	270

Stanley Cup: Montreal

Majestic Prince, center, races for the finish line during the 1969 Kentucky Derby.

Diane Crump, 20, female jockey.

HARNESS STAKES WINNERS

Race	Horse
Hambletonian	Lindy's Pride
Yonkers Futurity	Lindy's Pride
Kentucky Futurity	Lindy's Pride
Dexter Cup Trot	Lindy's Pride
International Trot	Une de Mai
United Nations Trot	Snow Speed
Little Brown Jug	Laverne Hanover
Messenger Stakes	Bye Bye Sam
International Pace	Overcall

THOROUGHBRED STAKES WINNERS

Race	Horse
Kentucky Derby	Majestic Prince
Preakness	Majestic Prince
Belmont Stakes	Arts and Letters
Wood Memorial	Dike
Woodward Stakes	Arts and Letters
Belmont Futurity	High Echelon
Matron Stakes	Cold Comfort
Spinaway Stakes	Meritus
United Nations Hdcp	Hawaii
Metropolitan Hdcp	Arts and Letters
Suburban Hdcp	Mr. Right
Brooklyn Hdcp	Nodouble
Jockey Club Gold Cup	Arts and Letters

ICE SKATING

Tim Wood, U.S. figure-skating champion.

FIGURE SKATING

United States Championships

Men: TIM WOOD
Women: JANET LYNN
Pairs: CYNTHIA and RON KAUFFMAN
Dance: JUDY SCHWOMEYER-JAMES SLADKY

World Championships

Men: TIM WOOD, U.S.
Women: GABRIELE SEYFERT, East Germany
Pairs: IRIN RODNINA-ALEXEI ULANOV, U.S.S.R.
Dance: DIANE TOWLER-BERNARD FORD, Britain

SPEED SKATING

United States Open Outdoor

Men: RICHARD WURSTER
Women: SUE BRADLE

World Championships

Men: DAG FORNAESS, Norway
Women: LASMA KAUNISTE, U.S.S.R.

1969 World Speed-Skating Records

Event	Holder	Time
1,000 meters	Ivar Eriksen, Norway	1:19.5
1,500 meters	Kees Verkerk, Netherlands	2:02.0
5,000 meters	Kees Verkerk	7:13.2
1,000 meters (women)	Elly Van de Brom, Netherlands	1:30.0
1,500 meters (women)	Johanna Schut, Netherlands	2:18.5
3,000 meters (women)	Johanna Schut	4:50.3

ROWING

COLLEGE ROWING

Intercollegiate Rowing Assn.: UNIVERSITY OF PENNSYLVANIA
Adams Cup: PENNSYLVANIA
Blackwell Cup: PENNSYLVANIA
Carnegie Cup: PRINCETON
Childs Cup: PENNSYLVANIA
Cochrane Cup: PENNSYLVANIA
Compton Cup: HARVARD
Dad Vail Trophy: GEORGETOWN
Goes Trophy: CORNELL
Madeira Cup: PENNSYLVANIA

BRITISH ROYAL HENLEY

Grand Challenge Cup (eights): EINHEIT SPORTS CLUB, East Germany
Thames Cup (lightweight eights): LEANDER CLUB, England
Princess Elizabeth Cup (schoolboy eights): WASHINGTON-LEE HIGH SCHOOL, Arlington, Virginia

SKIING

UNITED STATES ALPINE CHAMPIONSHIPS

Men

Slalom: BOBBY COCHRAN
Giant Slalom: HANK KASHIWA
Downhill: VLADIMIR SABICH
Combined: MALCOLM MILNE

Women

Slalom: BARBARA COCHRAN
Giant Slalom: BARBARA COCHRAN
Downhill: ANN BLACK

WORLD CUP

Men: KARL SCHRANZ, Austria
Women: GERTRUD GABL, Austria

NCAA CHAMPIONSHIPS

Slalom: PAUL RACHETTE, University of Denver
Downhill: MIKE LAFFERTY, University of Colorado
Cross-Country: CLARK MATIS, University of Colorado
Jumping: ODD HAMMERNESS, University of Denver
Team: UNIVERSITY OF DENVER

University of Pennsylvania rowing team.

SWIMMING

WORLD SWIMMING RECORDS SET IN 1969

Event	Holder	Time
	Men	
200-meter backstroke	Gary Hall, U.S.	2:06.6
100-meter breaststroke	Nikolai Pankin, U.S.S.R.	1:05.8
200-meter breaststroke	Nikolai Pankin	2:25.4
400-meter freestyle	Hans Fassnacht, West Germany	4:04.4
800-meter freestyle	Mike Burton, U.S.	8:28.8
1,500-meter freestyle	Mike Burton	16:04.5
200-meter indiv'l medley	Gary Hall	2:09.6
400-meter indiv'l medley	Gary Hall	4:33.9
	Women	
200-meter backstroke	Susie Atwood, U.S.	2:21.5
1,500-meter freestyle	Debbie Meyer, U.S.	17:19.9

Rod Laver, winner of the U.S. Open, Australian Open, French Open, and Wimbledon.

TENNIS

TOURNAMENT TENNIS

	U.S. Open	Wimbledon	Australian Open	French Open
Men's Singles	Rod Laver, Australia	Rod Laver	Rod Laver	Rod Laver
Women's Singles	Margaret Court, Australia	Ann Jones, Britain	Margaret Court	Margaret Court
Men's Doubles	Fred Stolle-Ken Rosewall, Australia	John Newcombe-Tony Roche Australia	Rod Laver-Roy Emerson, Australia	John Newcombe-Tony Roche
Women's Doubles	Françoise Durr, France-Darlene Hard, U.S.	Margaret Court-Judy Tegart, Australia	Margaret Court-Judy Tegart	Françoise Durr-Ann Jones

WORLD TRACK AND FIELD RECORDS SET IN 1969

Event	Holder	Time or Distance
Men		
440-yard dash	Curtis Mills, U.S.	0:44.7
3-mile run	George Young, U.S.	13:09.8
1-mile walk	Dave Romansky, U.S.	6:26.1
45-yard hurdles	Willie Davenport, U.S.	0:05.3
50-yard hurdles	Willie Davenport	0:05.8
70-yard hurdles	Willie Davenport	0:07.8
Pole vault	John Pennel, U.S.	17' 10¼"
16-lb. hammer throw	Anatoly Bondarchuk, U.S.S.R.	247' 7⅛"
Javelin throw	Jorma Kinnunen, Finland	304' 1½"
Women		
400-meter dash	Nicole Duclos, France	0:51.7
1,500-meter run	Jaroslava Jehlichova, Czechoslovakia	4:10.7
1-mile run	Maria Gommers, Netherlands	4:36.8
100-meter hurdles	Karin Balzer, East Germany	0:12.9
200-meter hurdles	Pamela Kilborn, Australia	0:26.1
Discus throw	Liesel Westermann, West Germany	209' 10"
Shot put	Nadezhda Chizhova, U.S.S.R.	67' ¼"

John Pennel, representing the Southern California Striders, sets a new world record for the pole vault: 17' 10¼".

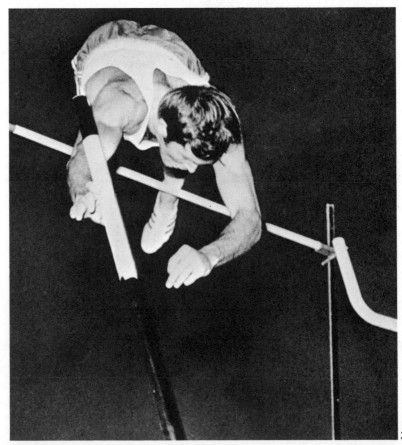

341

SPORTS FOR YOUTH

BEFORE sending his team onto the field against a much bigger, stronger opponent, the high-school football coach was doing everything he could to build up his players' confidence—and courage. In so doing, he tried every pep talk he could think of.

"Remember, boys," he said, "they pull on their pants just the same as you do—one leg at a time."

When he saw his 150-pound tackle shaking his head, however, the coach had to ask, "What's the matter, Timmy? They

Fishing and other individual sports, as well as team sports such as Little League baseball, attract thousands of youngsters each year.

do put their pants on the same as we do, don't they?"

"Oh sure, coach," the boy replied. "But their pants are five sizes bigger than ours."

Bigger, healthier, and brighter than ever before, more young people than ever before are pulling on athletic equipment today, be it a swimsuit or sweat shirt with football pads bulging beneath it. The youth of America has never been so athletically minded—and physically active—as it is now. Indeed youth participation in sports has become a fact of American life. Recent surveys show that roughly eight million youths of high-school age and under are taking part in some form of physical-fitness

More boys are playing in organized football games than ever before, but a pickup game, left, still has appeal. Right, a member of one of the fastest growing sports groups—young golfers.

activity each year. These sports include just about everything from badminton to bowling, and fishing to football.

It is impossible to determine how many young people take part in nonscheduled games and activities, such as pickup games on outdoor basketball courts, dives into the local swimming hole, and after-dinner fun over the basement tennis table. Of the scheduled and recorded events, however, swimming leads the way.

The Athletic Institute in Chicago estimates that about three million youths are taking part in organized swimming each year. The reason for the sport's popularity is obvious. Someday you may have to swim to save your life or someone else's. In addition, swimming opens the door to the wealth of outdoor water sports that captures the imagination of Americans from April through September—and, in places like Florida and the desert-resort areas of Nevada, California, and Arizona, the year around. Also, swimming is cheap. On a hot August afternoon, all you need to cool off is a suit, towel, and perhaps a noseclip.

For the same reason, basketball is one of the most popular sports among American youth. All a boy needs to play is a hoop and a ball, and if a friend is available a pickup game can go on for hours. (In pickup baseball, by contrast, everybody wants to bat. And since only one can bat at a time, everybody else winds up chasing the balls.)

About 2,000,000 boys under 12 and girls under 13 play a form of organized basketball each year. Even the smallest of schools find it relatively inexpensive to support a basketball program on league and sometimes intramural levels, since the equipment—trunks, shirts, socks, and balls—is so cheap. Some 700,000 youths play high-school basketball each year, one survey reports.

Still, no one would try to dispute the hold the national pastime, baseball, has upon American youth. A recent survey shows that some 2,000,000 boys between 8 and 12 years of age play Little League baseball each year and love it. Their parents do too. Some, in fact, are even lucky enough to get into the act, either as a manager or a coach. The popularity of Little League baseball was inevitable. After all, a father playing catch with his son in the backyard is all but an American institution. Television, too, has done its part, for there is not a locale in the United States where a major-league game is not beamed at least once a week. Not surprisingly, however, youth participation in baseball drops off sharply around age 16—when most become legally old enough to drive a car.

Television also spurred an interest in football. To get around the high cost of offering it on a competitive level, many schools started cutting the number of players on a team from the customary 11 to as few as 6. The result is that more boys are playing in organized football games today than ever before. Roughly 840,000 compete in 11-man high-school football teams; 2,000 play on 9-man teams; 30,000 on 8-man teams; and 15,000 on 6-man teams. And all this to the delight of the college-football coaches, who are marveling at the highly talented and well-coached youngsters coming onto their campuses. "A few years ago you couldn't trust one of them to throw a complete pass until he was a senior," says one college coach. "Now, they're throwing like pros as sophomores." The same is true in basketball.

The loneliest sport on the American scene is track and field—but you wouldn't know it by its number of young people who take part. Today, some 600,000 athletes of

A four-year-old may have trouble putting on his own boots, but he can still be taught to ski. Skiing is just one of the sports in which there is no age limit.

high-school age and under are dashing short distances and trotting long ones, jumping over some bars and vaulting over others, and throwing a heavy steel ball called the shot. Many athletes take up track and field simply to prepare themselves for other sports. But the major reason behind its popularity is that track and field is an individual sport. Whether an athlete wins or loses is important, of course. But regardless of what he did in his event, he did it himself—and for many, this is enough. Taking a page from its youth, middle-aged America is on its biggest jogging kick in history.

Among less-played sports like volleyball, softball, soccer, tennis, badminton, and wrestling, easily the fastest-growing among today's young is golf. In fact, the number of young people playing golf has doubled from the 81,900 reported by the National Federation of High School Athletic Associations in 1967. As in football, the increase is reflected in the glittering cast of new faces that has come upon the professional circuit in recent years.

And finally, a Canadian sport—hockey —has been all but adopted by young people in St. Louis, the Twin Cities of Minnesota, Chicago, Detroit, Boston, and the New York area. When the National Hockey League expanded in 1966, it brought the game into six new cities with a flair that inspired every boy old enough to skate. Leagues are now sprouting up all over the United States.

GARY RONBERG
Sports Illustrated

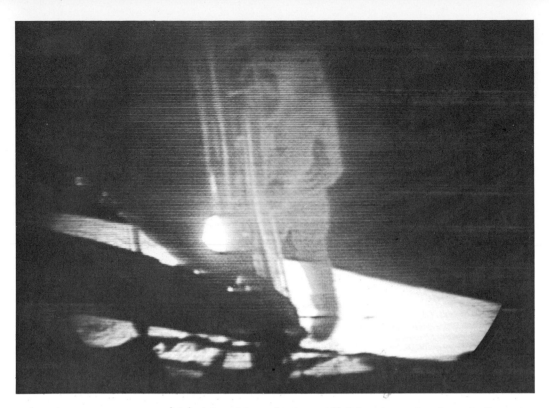

A television picture of astronaut Neil Armstrong stepping onto the moon.

TELEVISION

TELEVISION scored one of its most stunning achievements in 1969. Hundreds of millions of earthlings all around the globe watched Neil Armstrong become the first man to set foot on the moon. It was far and away the most significant television show ever. It gave ample support to television's claim that it is "a window on the world." Even viewers in such countries as Poland and Czechoslovakia were allowed the thrill of seeing Armstrong and Colonel Edwin "Buzz" Aldrin dancing in the lunar dust.

▶TELEVISION UNDER ATTACK

In 1969 the broadcasting industry was bitterly attacked by many people. Vice-President Spiro Agnew, in a nationally televised speech in November, said that television network news programs distorted the news. Even before this there was general unhappiness with television. It seemed to have been touched off by the widespread furor over network coverage of the 1968 Democratic convention in Chicago and the street riots during the convention.

Television officials more and more had to defend their programing—entertainment as well as news. Senator John O. Pastore of Rhode Island, chairman of the Senate communications subcommittee, criticized the networks for alleged excesses in "sex and violence." The Surgeon General of the United States looked into the impact of television programing on children. A National Commission on the Causes and Prevention of Violence said that television helped the growth of "moral and social values about violence which are inconsistent with the standards of a civilized society." President Nixon publicly endorsed Senator Pastore's crackdown.

Reacting to this outcry, the programers ordered television-series producers to cut down on violence. Not a single new Western was seen in the fall of 1969. Instead, the networks went heavily into situation comedies and variety shows. But one variety show, the *Smothers Brothers Comedy Hour*, was dropped. The Smothers brothers were taken off the air because their show needled the "Establishment." The networks also responded to the Washington pressures by changing the Saturday morning kiddie cartoons, which had been strongly laced with violent adventures.

On the news and public-affairs side, the public and politicians alike accused television journalists of bias. The journalists were said to be biased about such sensitive issues as the Vietnam war and race troubles. This left the broadcasters in a "who needs it?" mood. They eased up on hard-hitting documentaries. Their efforts concentrated instead on feature-type "magazine" series like CBS' *60 Minutes* and NBC's *First Tuesday*.

The reformers also hit television where it hurts most—in the pocketbook. Demands grew that the home screen be rid of cigarette advertising. Such advertising accounted for $200,000,000 a year of television revenues. Most in the industry resigned themselves to giving up the cigarette advertising.

▶ **CABLE TV**

Across the country, hundreds of communities were getting community-antenna-television (CATV) systems. Sometimes called cable TV, it is designed to end "ghosts" and other poor reception and to bring television into remote areas. It also gives viewers a wider choice of programming. Some of these cable systems can give subscribers (usually at a cost of about $5.00 a month) up to 24 channels. Some were beginning to originate their own programs as well as picking up and relaying every on-air signal within reach.

Not surprisingly, Congress, the Federal Communications Commission (FCC), the

---

EMMY AWARDS

Dramatic Series: N.E.T. PLAYHOUSE, National Education Television
Comedy Series: GET SMART, NBC
Variety Series: ROWAN AND MARTIN'S LAUGH-IN, NBC
Dramatic Program: TEACHER, TEACHER, NBC
Variety Special: THE BILL COSBY SPECIAL, NBC
Actor in a Drama: PAUL SCOFIELD (*Male of the Species*, NBC)
Actress in a Drama: GERALDINE PAGE (*The Thanksgiving Visitor*, ABC)
Actor in a Dramatic Series: CARL BETZ (*Judd for the Defense*, ABC)
Actress in a Dramatic Series: BARBARA BAIN (*Mission: Impossible*, CBS)
Actor in a Comedy Series: DON ADAMS (*Get Smart*, NBC)
Actress in a Comedy Series: HOPE LANGE (*The Ghost and Mrs. Muir*, NBC)
News: WALLACE WESTFELDT (report on hunger in the United States, *The Huntley-Brinkley Report*, NBC); CHARLES KURALT ("On the Road," *CBS Evening News with Walter Cronkite*); JOHN LAURENCE ("Police after Chicago," *CBS Evening News with Walter Cronkite*)
News Documentaries: CBS REPORTS: HUNGER IN AMERICA; LAW AND ORDER, PBL
Cultural Documentaries: DON'T COUNT THE CANDLES, CBS; JUSTICE BLACK AND THE BILL OF RIGHTS, CBS; MAN WHO DANCES: EDWARD VILLELLA, NBC; THE GREAT AMERICAN NOVEL, CBS
Daytime Programing: THE DICK CAVETT SHOW, ABC
Sports Programing: 19TH SUMMER OLYMPIC GAMES, ABC

---

broadcasting industry, and the swelling ranks of cable-casters were in a controversy over how fast CATV should be allowed to grow. For the speculation grew that the country someday would be completely wired through television cables for sight and sound. Advocates of this theory see domestic satellites as the vehicles for long-distance television. They see cable being used for local distribution.

More satellites continued to be lofted over various parts of the globe. And television actually achieved a worldwide ca-

"The Pink Panther" and "Here Comes the Grump" were among the new, less-violent children's cartoons to appear on TV screens in 1969.

pacity. But on the home front, the Government still had not decided on the ground rules for operating satellites.

Surprisingly, after years of debate, the FCC proposed to authorize pay-television systems. The move came even as the only experimental subscription service in the nation, at Hartford, Connecticut, was shut down. Meanwhile most of the motion-picture distributors in the United States were against pay television. In 1969 they waged an earnest, illogical battle to "save free TV" by getting filmgoers to protest pay television. However, few people thought that pay television would become big.

PUBLIC TV

Another potential competitor to commercial television also was having trouble getting a foothold. This was public television, an expanded, noncommercial version of educational television. The future of public television seemed bright when Congress created a semipublic corporation to foster high-quality "alternatives" to commercial-television fare. But Congress came up with only $5,000,000 for public television.

Under the Corporation for Public Broadcasting, a fourth national network actually was born during the year. The new network links over 180 noncommercial stations in the United States. But how much this network would be able to accomplish in quality programing depended heavily both on the mood of Congress and on how long the Ford Foundation, long educational television's chief backer ($180,000,000 so far), was willing to hand out grants.

TV PROGRAMS

For most viewers, all these concerns were less important immediately, of course, than what they had to choose from in entertainment. In this department, Rowan and Martin's innovative *Laugh-In* on NBC still was the big hit. Otherwise, most television fans seemed content to tune most often to old favorites like Lucy Ball, Ed Sullivan, Red Skelton, and Lawrence Welk.

A new children's program quickly became a favorite of preschoolers. The program, *Sesame Street,* is produced by the Children's Television Workshop which was set up by the Carnegie Corporation, the Ford Foundation, and the United States Office of Education at a cost of $8,000,000. The program is presented in five hour-long telecasts each week on educational stations.

Sesame Street teaches basic writing, reading, and arithmetic. It uses jingles, cartoons, and live action. And children were entranced by it.

RICHARD K. DOAN
Columnist, *TV Guide*

THAILAND. See ASIA.

THEATER

ON Broadway the highlight of the 1968–69 season was Howard Sackler's *The Great White Hope*. The play, which was brought in from a regional theater, Washington's Arena Stage, went on to win all the major awards. Off Broadway, the most noticeable development of the season was the blossoming of nudity onstage. *Oh, Calcutta!* was one highly publicized example. In this revue the entire cast appeared without clothing for a large part of the performance.

Financially, Broadway had a fairly good year. Nearly $58,000,000 worth of tickets were sold. This was $1,000,000 less than the season before, which had set the all-time record. Of the 67 shows that opened on Broadway during the season, 11 were considered financial successes.

▶ DRAMA

There was little question that *The Great White Hope* was the hit of the Broadway season. Directed by Edwin Sherin and starring James Earl Jones, it is a drama about the first Negro heavyweight boxing champion. It is based on the life of prizefighter Jack Johnson. Although its story involves boxing, its theme is the interaction of a black man and a white society. It was a critical success and a personal triumph for its lead, James Earl Jones. He was signed to play the role in the film version. *The Great White Hope* dominated the nonmusical plays. There were, however, several others of unusual interest. *We Bombed in New Haven* was an outlandish comedy with a serious comment on war. It was written by Joseph Heller, author of the novel *Catch–22*. The play's attitude toward war was much the same as that of the novel.

James Earl Jones as the first Negro heavyweight champion in "The Great White Hope."

Ben Franklin as portrayed by Howard Da Silva in "1776."

Hadrian VII, by Peter Luke, was taken from a novel by the eccentric writer Frederick Rolfe. In this play the British actor Alec McCowen gave one of the season's finest performances as a man who is unable to achieve priesthood—and suddenly finds himself pope.

Nicol Williamson, the superb young British actor, appeared in a production of *Hamlet.* Some critics thought it a landmark interpretation. Other critics considered the production overrated.

▶ MUSICALS AND COMEDIES

The surprise leader of the musicals was *1776.* This musical took on the unglamorous subject of the American Declaration of Independence, with such leading characters as John Adams, Benjamin Franklin, and Thomas Jefferson. Almost as unusual as its subject was the fact that *1776* had an original "book," or script. It was not taken from a novel, film, or dramatic play, as most Broadway musicals now are.

Chief contender with *1776* for consideration as the outstanding Broadway musical was *Promises, Promises*. It was taken from the popular film comedy *The Apartment* and made into a musical by Broadway's leading comedy writer, Neil Simon. Two of the nation's best-known popular-song writers, Burt Bacharach, Jr., and Hal David, wrote the songs.

Several other musicals during the season were noteworthy for many reasons. However, none was completely successful, either at the box office or in the opinion of the critics. *Zorba,* based on the novel *Zorba the Greek,* had songs by John Kander and Fred Ebb, who wrote *Cabaret.* *Dear World* was taken from a famous play, *The Madwoman of Chaillot.* Its star was Angela Lansbury, and its songs were written by the composer of *Hello, Dolly!,* Jerry Herman. *Canterbury Tales* was an English musical written by an Oxford professor, based on the stories by Chaucer. *Come Summer* employed the talents of two famous dance figures, Ray Bolger as star, and choreographer Agnes de Mille as director.

Dustin Hoffman in the theater as "Jimmy Shine."

Woody Allen stars in his own play, "Play It Again, Sam."

Three comedies were distinguished by their lead players. Dustin Hoffman, star of the film *The Graduate*, achieved a personal success in Murray Schisgal's *Jimmy Shine*. Comedian Woody Allen wrote and starred in *Play It Again, Sam*, which used material familiar to those who have seen Allen on television. And in a season notable for the absence of outstanding lead performances by women, Julie Harris was voted best actress for the light comedy *Forty Carats*.

▶ **OFF BROADWAY**

Off Broadway had another thriving season, one that will perhaps be remembered longest for its unclothed bodies. *Oh, Calcutta!* became the best-known of the shows with nudity. Others were *Geese, Sweet Eros*, and, off-off Broadway, *Che*, which attracted the attention of New York City authorities who closed it for a time.

One of the nation's great playwrights, Tennessee Williams, had his play *In the Bar of a Tokyo Hotel* presented off Broadway. Most critics thought that it was well below the standard of his best dramas.

The artistic successes off Broadway were *To Be Young, Gifted and Black, Adaptation* and *Next, Tea Party* and *The Basement, Big Time Buck White*, and three musicals, *Dames at Sea, Peace*, and *Promenade*.

▶ **REPERTORY**

For fans of repertory theater, there was a discouraging development in New York. The APA, one of the nation's best companies, played its last Broadway season, at least for the immediate future. The economics of Broadway, that is, the vast amount of money needed to put on plays, proved too much for the company. And for regional theater, a lack of money presaged trouble for the year ahead.

The New York theater season was distinguished by the work of several repertory-theater groups, some local, some visitors. It was generally felt that the Repertory Theater of Lincoln Center had one of its best seasons. Its outstanding production was *In the Matter of J. Robert Oppenheimer*.

The New York Shakespeare Festival's Public Theater came up with a biting, powerful play, *No Place to be Somebody*, by a Negro writer, Charles Gordone. Another successful drama by a Negro, Lonne Elder III, *Ceremonies in Dark Old Men*, was put on by the Negro Ensemble Company.

Among the visiting companies were the provocative Living Theater, returning from exile in Europe, the Minnesota Theater Company, The National Theater of the Deaf, Théâtre de la Cité (France), and Atelje 212 of Belgrade (Yugoslavia).

The Broadway season offered little promise of revitalization in the year ahead. But the activity off Broadway and by regional and repertory groups seemed to give assurance that American theater is not dead yet.

LEONARD HARRIS
Arts Editor, WCBS-TV News

TOGO. See AFRICA.
TOYS. See GAMES AND TOYS.

TRANSPORTATION

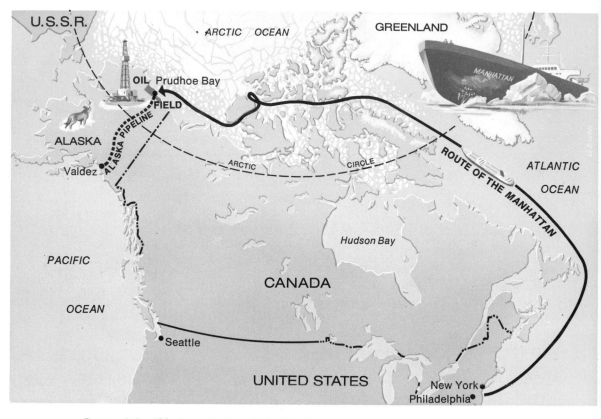

Route of the "Manhattan" through the Northwest Passage. Also shown is proposed pipeline.

AN experimental voyage by a tanker was the outstanding event of 1969 in transportation. The ship was the SS *Manhattan*. The trip was her historic voyage, August 24 to September 21, from the Delaware River to Prudhoe Bay, Alaska. This journey made reality out of what for almost 500 years had been an impossible dream: conquest by a commercial ship of the legendary Northwest Passage around the top of North America.

The 115,000-dwt *Manhattan* is the largest vessel in the United States merchant fleet. She is too big for the Gulf Coast-Delaware River trade where most United States tankers operate. Because her crews get higher wages than crews of foreign tankers, the *Manhattan* has been too expensive to compete with foreign-flag supertankers on foreign oil routes.

Then the discovery of vast oil deposits on the Arctic North Slope of Alaska opened new opportunities for the *Manhattan* and even bigger United States ships that might be built. Under United States law, all shipping between ports in the United States—which, of course, includes Alaskan as well as ports of the contiguous states—must be carried by United States ships.

The "Manhattan," largest vessel in the U.S. merchant fleet, plows through Arctic ice.

The oil companies hoping to exploit the Alaskan oil strike had only two reasonable ways of getting the oil to markets in the United States. One was to build an 800-mile pipeline from the Prudhoe Bay oil fields to Valdez, a port on the ice-free Gulf of Alaska. The cost of the pipeline alone is estimated at $900,000,000. Then the oil would have to be transported from Valdez to far-off refineries.

The Humble Oil Company thought another way would be worth exploring. Their engineers calculated that 20 or 30 supertankers of 250,000-dwt capacity—about twice that of the *Manhattan*—would be able to carry oil economically to markets on the east coast of the United States. They thought this would be commercially possible if the tankers could operate through the icebound Northwest Passage. It was necessary to test the idea.

The *Manhattan* has a 43,000-hp power plant. This is almost twice as powerful as other much larger tankers. She seemed like an ideal test vessel. The *Manhattan* was cut into sections and parceled out to several shipyards so that the extensive process of strengthening the hull and adding an icebreaking bow could be completed *continued on page 358*

HOW TO CURE TRAFFIC JAMS

By JOHN A. VOLPE

U.S. Secretary of Transportation

THE mathematics are simple. More than four fifths of the Americans commuting a quarter-mile or more to work travel by car. And two thirds of them travel alone—alone and usually bumper to bumper on the streets and highways of our urban areas.

Every day, through the simple process of growth, we add about 6,000 more people and 10,000 new cars to our potential traffic jam. Where will we put the people if we cover the cities with streets and parking lots for the cars?

We must improve public transportation so that more people want to use it. We must develop urban transit that is dependable, safe, comfortable, clean, and reasonably fast, inexpensive, and convenient. This is quite an order. Yet we must fill it—and soon—if our cities are to survive and prosper.

Our job at the Department of Transportation is to help the cities find the plan for public transportation that is best for their individual needs. We must then give them all the help we can to get it going. This plan must include transport for everyone—for commuters, for those who now have no way to get to jobs, and for those who are too handicapped, too poor, too old, or too young to drive.

How? In some cases, all that is needed is money to modernize an existing bus system. We are also testing steam- and turbine-powered buses, looking for a way to reduce air pollution while improving performance. In Boston we are helping to change an aged, grim subway into a bright, attractive one. Its services will be co-ordinated with a refurbished bus system. And early in the 1970's, the [San Francisco] Bay Area Rapid Transit District is scheduled to start service on the world's most modern rapid-transit system. Attractive, air-conditioned cars will cruise smoothly at up to 80 mph. Service is planned for every 90 seconds during rush hours.

What is right for San Francisco or New York may be wrong for Phoenix or Minneapolis. This is why the Department of Transportation's Center City Transportation Project is studying the public transportation in five sample cities. We hope to help these cities design and put into use comprehensive transportation systems for their urban centers. When the contract is completed, we should have various model transportation plans that can be adopted for other cities. These plans will consider existing technologies. They will also take into account plans on the drawing boards or in the experimental phase.

Under study are little cage-like vehicles that would be suspended from a rail several feet above the sidewalk curb. These would operate very much like a ski-lift. The Dashaveyor is another new idea. It would use fairly small, electric-powered, self-propelled units. The units would have wheels above and below an elevated track to insure stability. We are also studying monorails, moving sidewalks, Minicars, and other ideas.

Perhaps the biggest challenge is how to develop public transit that can operate well in suburban areas. One possible answer being studied is the computerized bus system, sometimes called Maxicab or Dial-a-Bus. The bus would arrive at the doorway shortly after a telephone call. It would then carry the rider to a connection with a rapid-transit system or to his destination if it is nearby. Another is the automated car-like vehicle. Here the driver would push a button to show his destination and then let the system do the work. We call this Personal Rapid Transit.

The tracked air-cushion vehicle (TACV) may some day soon move people from city center to airports at speeds up to 250 mph. Eventually, vehicles in tubes may reach speeds of 500 mph or higher. These could be put underground and thus conserve precious land space and avoid air pollution.

These are only some of the ideas for improved urban transportation. We are studying the possibility of new towns, with compatible land use and transportation carefully planned in advance. And we are looking at ways to get more good out of that old mass-transportation workhorse, the bus. Such ideas as bus expressways and special access ramps are being studied.

Of course, one way to cure traffic jams might be to tell people that they cannot drive their cars into the cities. We hope there is a better way. And we at the Department of Transportation, working with other Federal agencies, are doing our very best to find it.

in time to make the tests in 1969. By the end of summer, the ship was ready.

The *Manhattan* proved that the Northwest Passage is commercially passable. But passage alone did not mean that the route was economically feasible. That will await the answers to several questions now being considered by computer-assisted technicians studying the results of the *Manhattan*'s experimental data.

How large must icebreaking tankers be to be sure of forcing their way through the Arctic ice to the oil fields safely and profitably? How much power will they need? What is the best shape for the hull? What kind of propulsion system will be needed? What kind of terminals can be used?

When these questions are answered, the successful transit of the Northwest Passage by commercial freighters may be at hand. When this day comes, one of early explorers' fondest dreams will have been realized. More important, the mineral wealth of the Alaskan and Canadian northlands will have been opened to productive use.

▶ **CONTAINERIZED SHIPPING**

Containerization continued to grow in marine transport in 1969. A new type of container shipping gained in use. This was a modern adaptation of an ancient principle, the Ro-Ro (for roll-on, roll-off) design. The ancestry of this design can be traced at least as far back as the days of the pyramid builders in Egypt. They rolled enormous chunks of stone onto Nile barges for transport to the monument sites.

Ro-Ro containers differ from ordinary containers, which are simply boxes that are separated from truck cabs, lifted off their wheels, and stacked aboard ship. The Ro-Ro containers are open or closed trailers that are separated from truck cabs and are rolled aboard ship with the wheels intact. One special advantage of the Ro-Ro design is that it can handle certain cargo, such as circus animals, which cannot be transported in closed containers. Also, the rolling-on-and-off feature makes for fast loading and unloading.

On the North Atlantic, Atlantic Container Line since 1967 has been operating 4 ships that can carry both types of containers. The line in 1969 ordered 6 faster ships with the same design. In May the Moore-McCormack Lines began service with the first of 4 new 26-knot Ro-Ro containerships that can also handle conventional cargo. Another carrier, Transatlantic Steamship, is building 2 Ro-Ro ships in Sweden for use between the West Coast of the United States and Australia. Transamerican Trailer Transport has been operating a Ro-Ro ship on the 1,600-mile run between New York and San Juan, Puerto Rico, since 1968. Her owners say the ship, the *Ponce de Leon,* is the fastest freight ship in the world.

▶ **CRUISE SHIPS**

Passenger liners did not fare well in 1969 except for cruise ships. This year, however, saw the introduction of Cunard Lines' *Queen Elizabeth 2*. The *QE2* had problems on its break-in cruise. The turbines broke down and left the ship unable to navigate. But the problems were solved, and the ship performed brilliantly when it went into regular service early in the summer.

The *QE2* has been designed to recognize a new fact of life. It is a "floating resort hotel." The day of the passenger liner has ended. Future passenger queens like the *QE2* will spend most of their life carrying passengers on vacation cruises rather than transporting them from port to port.

▶ **THE RAILROADS**

In railroad-freight transportation, one of the most significant developments of the year was the opening of a new railroad to haul coal in Ohio. Not a common carrier and only 15 miles long, the new road is the Muskingum Electric Railroad. It is the first railroad in the United States to apply modern technology to railroad electrification. What is more, it is completely automated. It runs without human hands at the controls.

Unlike most railroads in the United States—long or short—the Muskingum Electric draws its power not from diesel engines but from overhead electric wires. It is the first railroad in North America to use a high-voltage, commercial-frequency-power system. This system has been used extensively in other parts of the world. The system makes it possible to use commercial electric power as generated without running it through costly frequency-changing equipment. Some railroad observers think the Muskingum Electric may foretell a rebirth of railroad electrification in the United States.

Passenger Railroads

The only good news in 1969 for railroad-passenger service in the United States was that Penn Central's Northeast Corridor Metroliners were a definite success. Beginning regular commercial service in January, the Metroliners make the 266-mile trip between New York City and Washington, D.C., in less than 3 hours. Rail travel between the 2 cities increased 49 per cent. By the end of the first 6 months, Metroliners were running 75 per cent full. This is high for almost any regularly scheduled railroad.

Railroad-passenger service in Canada has not proved profitable. The government-owned Canadian National Railways disclosed that it had failed in its attempt to make money by bringing passengers back to the rails. The Canadian National, from 1962 on, had cut fares, added new trains, and promoted service in an attempt to have people ride the railroad. As a result, revenue passenger-miles were doubled. But costs of operation rose even faster. Late in 1969, Canadian National announced it could no longer hope to make money on any of its intercity segments on the transcontinental run west of Ontario or in the Maritime Provinces. Trains to be operated

in these areas would need government subsidies.

In the United States, passengers carried by railroad dropped from 882,000,000 in 1943 to 295,000,000 by 1969. Passenger revenue for the same period fell from $1,700,000,000 to $444,000,000. By the end of 1969, at least 6 different bills and resolutions on railroad-passenger service were up for hearing before the Senate Commerce Committee's subcommittee on surface transportation. A bill favored by Senator Vance Hartke, subcommittee chairman, would provide for the Federal Government to repay the railroads for the money that is lost on passenger trains that are run for the public convenience.

▶ MASS TRANSPORTATION

In mass transit, the Nixon administration came up with a $10,000,000,000, 12-year program for Congress to consider. As proposed, the bill would authorize $3,100,000,000 during the next 5 years. It would improve and expand city and commuter bus, rail, and subway systems. Federal spending would rise from $300,000,000 in 1971 to $1,000,000,000 in 1975. The cities, however, did not greet the bill with unanimous approval. This is because Congress would have to appropriate funds each year. As the bill has been proposed, the cities cannot be sure that they will receive the money that has been promised.

One proposed amendment to the bill would permit the Transportation Secretary to authorize the entire $3,100,000,000 as soon as the bill is passed. The money, however, would still be spent over the 5-year period. But Congress has traditionally been reluctant to commit funds for a long advance period. At year's end, it looked as if the solution to the cities' transit problems might again be delayed.

RODERICK CRAIB
Contributing Editor, *Business Week*
See also AVIATION.

Soviet frontier guards on Damansky Island watch for Chinese troop movements.

UNION OF SOVIET SOCIALIST REPUBLICS

SOVIET leaders were concerned most with foreign-policy matters in 1969. Of greatest concern was their bitter, sometimes bloody, feud with Communist China. At home the Soviet leaders made great efforts to assure the loyalty of the Russian people. One way in which they did this was to step up their campaign to represent themselves as Lenin's heirs. Plans were made for the 1970 centennial of Lenin's birth. The Soviets hoped to make this celebration the greatest festival in Soviet history. Economically the

Soviets faced a slowdown in industrial growth. The many Soviet problems in 1969 caused a sense of unease in the country.

▶ FOREIGN AFFAIRS

On March 2 and 15, Soviet and Chinese troops fought over Damansky Island in the Ussuri River, which separates the Soviet Union from Manchuria. Both countries claim this island. The Damansky battles were followed by skirmishes in other areas. Some took place in the Far East. Others

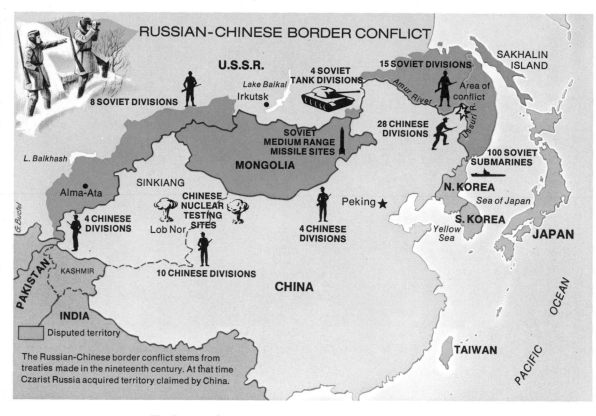

RUSSIAN-CHINESE BORDER CONFLICT

U.S.S.R.

8 SOVIET DIVISIONS

Lake Baikal

Irkutsk

4 SOVIET TANK DIVISIONS

15 SOVIET DIVISIONS

SAKHALIN ISLAND

Amur River

Area of conflict

Ussuri R.

28 CHINESE DIVISIONS

SOVIET MEDIUM RANGE MISSILE SITES

L. Balkhash

MONGOLIA

100 SOVIET SUBMARINES

N. KOREA

Sea of Japan

SINKIANG

Alma-Ata

CHINESE NUCLEAR TESTING SITES

Lob Nor

Peking ★

4 CHINESE DIVISIONS

S. KOREA

Yellow Sea

JAPAN

4 CHINESE DIVISIONS

PAKISTAN

KASHMIR

10 CHINESE DIVISIONS

CHINA

OCEAN

INDIA

☐ Disputed territory

TAIWAN

PACIFIC

The Russian-Chinese border conflict stems from treaties made in the nineteenth century. At that time Czarist Russia acquired territory claimed by China.

G.Buctaj

The Russian-Chinese border conflict in 1969 raised the specter of a full-scale war.

took place on the border between Soviet Central Asia and China's Sinkiang Province. These battles raised the specter of a full-scale war between the Soviet Union and China. Both countries reinforced defenses along their borders.

Pravda, the Soviet Communist Party newspaper, declared in September that such a war, if it came, would be a nuclear conflict and would involve much of the world. Further, there were some reports that the Soviets were considering a surprise attack against China's nuclear installations and were trying to find out the reaction of foreign communist parties to such a move.

Hundreds of soldiers were killed and wounded in the Chinese-Soviet fighting. Still, most of the fighting was verbal. Moscow called Mao Tse-tung and his support-

ers nationalist traitors. The Chinese responded by denouncing Soviet Communist Party Secretary-General Leonid I. Brezhnev and his associates. The Chinese called them "New Czars" who had betrayed communism and returned the Soviet Union to capitalism. They also accused the Soviets of entering into collusion with the United States.

The surprise Peking meeting in mid-September between Soviet Premier Aleksei N. Kosygin and Chinese Premier Chou En-lai provided the first break in the tension. This meeting, temporarily at least, put an end to the border fighting.

More-formal talks were held beginning in October. Attempts were made to reach an agreement on boundaries, but no apparent progress was made.

Following Soviet-Chinese fighting, Russians stage anti-Chinese demonstration.

The crisis over China affected many areas of Soviet foreign relations. At the time it began, a new Soviet-United States crisis over Berlin seemed to be building up. This tension quickly disappeared when the shooting began at Damansky Island.

Because of the possibility of war with China, the Soviets moved to safeguard their western flank in Europe. For one thing, they emphasized their desire for better relations with the West—including the United States and West Germany. They stepped up pressure on Czechoslovakia to become once again an obedient satellite. And the Soviet Union began pushing for a general collective-security agreement in Asia. This was an obvious attempt to build up a network of alliances with those countries bordering on China.

There were some areas where the China issue did not cause basic changes in Soviet policy. The Soviet Union, for example, continued to supply weapons to North Vietnam. And Soviet leaders made little effort to get the North Vietnamese to ease their demands on the United States and thus bring the Vietnam war to an end.

In the Middle East the Soviet Union continued to support the Arab states against Israel and to supply them with arms. At the same time, the Soviets continued to build up their Mediterranean fleet. But the Soviet Union did take part in four-power (United States, Great Britain, France, Soviet Union) talks that sought, without speedy success, to find some way to end the Middle East crisis. United States and Soviet officials also met privately.

There was evidence that some Soviet leaders did not want to limit missiles and other strategic arms while China was building up its supplies of modern weapons. Still, the Soviets agreed to begin talks on limiting strategic nuclear weapons. U.S. and Soviet representatives met in the fall.

Soviet efforts to mobilize forces against China were pressed most vigorously within the world communist movement. The climax to these efforts came in mid-1969 when an international congress of communist parties from all continents met in Moscow. This was the first such meeting since 1960. Moscow, against Chinese opposition, was able to get most communist parties to come to the meeting. This was considered a Soviet success. But the results of the congress must have disappointed the Soviets. This was because the Soviet leaders—despite a bitter anti-Chinese speech by Mr. Brezhnev—were unable to get the meeting to adopt an anti-Chinese resolution.

▶ DOMESTIC AFFAIRS

On January 22, 1969, a gunman seemingly tried to assassinate Soviet leaders traveling in a motorcade in Moscow. The shooting incident came in a period of severe political repression. Many dissenters had been put on trial, and some were sent to labor camps. Thus it was natural for the outside world to suspect that political dissidence was at the root of the incident. The Soviet Government, after briefly announcing what had happened, remained silent.

Later in 1969, there was another vivid expression of dissent. In July, Anatoly Kuznetsov, one of the Soviet Union's best-known young writers and the author of the world-famous novel *Babi Yar,* defected in London. Mr. Kuznetsov had gotten permission from the Soviet authorities to go to London to write a novel about Lenin's residence there. Once in England, the Soviet writer went to the authorities and asked for and received permission to stay there indefinitely. He denounced the Soviet regime in very strong terms.

The fact that Mr. Kuznetsov was able to get to London on the ground that he wanted to write about Lenin was not accidental. The Soviet regime has created a cult, even a worship, of Lenin. Lenin's birth centennial, to be held in 1970, has been the subject of an enormous propaganda campaign. It seems likely to be the greatest celebration in Soviet history. The object seems clearly to impress the Soviet people that the wisdom and virtue of Lenin are now possessed by the present rulers.

This propaganda campaign was accompanied by harsh measures directed at various dissident groups. These included Ukrainian and other minority nationalists; those who called for greater free speech; and those who protested the August 1968 invasion of Czechoslovakia.

During 1969, censorship was tightened. Almost the last bastion of liberalism officially permitted to operate was the magazine *Novy Mir* (New World). But even this magazine was publicly attacked by the Government in 1969. This raised questions about how long Alexander Tvardovsky, editor of *Novy Mir,* could continue running a magazine that took even a mildly unorthodox position at times.

Economy

Economically, 1969 was a disappointing year for the Soviet Union. The year began with a very harsh winter. This disrupted much industrial production and construction work. Hardest hit were the areas east of the Volga River. The disruption continued well beyond the winter. In addition, Soviet industry was hurt by a growing labor shortage.

Soviet economic reforms, begun in 1965, proved to be disappointing as they were extended to most of the Soviet economy. These reforms were designed to increase productivity by putting more emphasis on profits and profit sharing. However, the failure of the reform was caused in part by the opposition to the new ideas and new methods on the part of conservative managers used to the old ways.

Soviet production in 1969 increased, of course. But because of the problems listed above, the rate of growth over most of the year fell below 7 per cent. This was the lowest rate of improvement since 1964. This relatively slow industrial growth was combined with fears about agricultural output. In some key areas there were very poor weather conditions during the spring sowing season.

HARRY SCHWARTZ
The New York Times

UNITED NATIONS

IN the opinion of Secretary-General U Thant, the 24th birthday of the United Nations was not a happy one. In his anniversary message on October 24, 1969, Thant stated that "We have not done nearly enough to reach the goals solemnly proclaimed 24 years ago: universal peace, prosperity, social justice—a life worth living for every human being." Thant gave this list of outstanding problems in support of his charge: "The scourge of war is still with us. The armaments race continues under its own mad momentum. Human rights are being flagrantly violated. Most of the people of the world do not have enough to eat. There is poverty that can be alleviated. There is disease that can be prevented. There is ignorance that can be remedied. There is plain misery, unnecessarily marring the lives of so many of our fellow human beings. And now the very environment which must sustain a growing world population is becoming increasingly polluted."

With so many unsolved problems, there was surprisingly little initiative shown at the UN in 1969 to find solutions. Rather, too many people tried to find satisfaction in the simple adoption of resolutions. General Assembly President Angie Brooks said that this attitude had "helped to perpetuate the mythology of achievement, so that many . . . tend to go happily from one agenda item to the next without seriously considering the possibility or even probability that the resolution adopted will not be implemented."

In 1969, attention was focused on plans to celebrate the UN's 25th year in 1970. Many hoped that the forthcoming commemoration would attract fresh support for the UN from the public and from member governments. There were special efforts, also, to enlist the interest of young people in the anniversary. It was hoped that the young people's enthusiasm and commitment to peace could be brought to bear on an institution that gives the impression of having grown old and tired in the search for ways "to save succeeding generations from the scourge of war."

▶ GENERAL ASSEMBLY

The 24th regular session of the General Assembly convened on September 16. Its first action was to elect a woman president for the second time in UN history. She was Miss Angie Brooks, Liberia's assistant secretary of state. (The first woman President of the General Assembly was Madame V. L. Pandit of India. She served during the 8th regular session in 1953–54.)

During its opening days, the General Assembly attracted the usual large number of world statesmen. Eleven heads of state

UN observers along the Suez Canal, the scene of fighting between Israel and the U.A.R.

and prime ministers and 97 foreign ministers were among those in attendance. President Richard Nixon addressed the Assembly, and U.S. Secretary of State William P. Rogers held private conferences only with visiting officials from nations that have relations with the United States.

The United Arab Republic had broken its ties to the United States in 1967. But Rogers nevertheless conferred with U.A.R. Foreign Minister Mahmoud Riad. This exception emphasized the efforts of the big powers to try to find a peace formula for the Middle East. Mr. Rogers also met several times with Soviet Foreign Minister Andrei Gromyko in an effort to break the Middle East deadlock. But both men returned to their respective capitals without any evidence of substantial progress. Gunnar Jarring, U Thant's personal representative in an effort to bring about a peaceful settlement of the Middle East situation, resumed his diplomatic duties until there would be a further call on his services.

Mr. Jarring is the Swedish ambassador to Moscow.

As usual, there were more than one hundred items on the agenda of the General Assembly. Most of these were old issues: representation of Communist China; refugees in the Middle East and elsewhere; the racial policies of South Africa; Korea; Namibia (South-West Africa); and the budget. Among the new subjects on the agenda were: the problems of youth; the problems of the elderly and the aged; the hijacking of aircraft; and the observance of the UN's 25th birthday.

The General Assembly adopted a resolution expressing its desire to devise new methods "through which the enthusiasm and the energy of the young might be more effectively directed toward the spiritual and material advancement of all peoples." It called on young people to affirm their faith in international law and the principles of the United Nations Charter. The resolution also called on governments to promote the education of young people and to get young people involved in such UN programs as International Education Year, to be marked in 1970, and the Second Development Decade, which will start in 1970. In the resolution on the UN's 25th anniversary, the General Assembly suggested that a world youth assembly be held. It proposed that member states include young people in their delegations for the 25th regular session of the General Assembly.

In November the General Assembly began debate on the draft of an agreement that prohibits the placing of nuclear and other weapons of mass destruction on the ocean floor. The draft had been submitted to the 25-nation Disarmament Conference in Geneva by the United States and the Soviet Union.

Another major issue before the General Assembly was the problem of the use of chemical and bacteriological weapons. Secretary-General Thant submitted a complete report on this subject to the Assembly as well as to the Security Council and the Disarmament Committee. The report was prepared by experts who warned that "Advances in chemical and biological science, while contributing to the good of mankind, have also opened up the possibility of exploiting the idea of chemical and bacteriological (biological) warfare weapons, some of which could endanger man's future. . . ."

The General Assembly also received a report on what Secretary-General Thant called "the crisis of the human environment." It contained proposals to be taken up at a major UN conference in 1972 authorized by the 1968 Assembly. The report cited several causes of the crisis. These include a very rapid growth in population, increased urbanization, and technology—all associated with increased demands for space, food, and natural resources.

It was suggested that the 1972 conference consider these points in particular: joint efforts to meet environmental problems on national and international levels; preventive action that would reduce the need for corrective measures; and efficient use of current technological knowledge to cope with the problems.

With the aim of narrowing the gap between the rich nations and the poor, the 1968 General Assembly created a preparatory committee to plan for the Second United Nations Development Decade to begin in 1970. In 1969 the committee submitted to the General Assembly suggestions for promoting ways to increase standards of living, encourage full employment, and foster economic and social progress during the next ten years, especially in the developing countries.

▶ SECURITY COUNCIL

For another year, the Security Council spent much of its time dealing with mutual charges of cease-fire violations by Israel and the Arab states. Resolutions of censure were adopted without reducing the clashes in the Middle East. Secretary-General Thant warned that "an almost daily outbreak of violent events makes it ever more possible that we may be witnessing in the Middle East something like the early stages of a new Hundred Years' War."

Security Council resolutions against South Africa's control of Namibia and Rhodesia's white regime were ignored also.

The Security Council was once the UN's most powerful organ. Continued refusal to heed its resolutions led U Thant to warn that "If the world becomes accustomed to the decisions of the highest United Nations organ for peace and security going by default or being ignored, we shall have taken a dangerous step backward toward anarchy."

The United States obtained Security Council agreement for a committee to study a problem that Washington considers important: The growing number of ministates, or microstates, which join the UN, but which are unable to pay their way. The United States would like to limit such tiny countries to a kind of associate membership. Under this plan they would have some UN privileges but not the right to vote. Their financial responsibilities would also be reduced. Two such ministates that joined the UN in 1968—Swaziland and Equatorial Guinea—have a combined population of only about 600,000.

▶ ECONOMIC AND SOCIAL COUNCIL

The Economic and Social Council considered a wide range of issues in 1969. These included the proposals for the 1972 conference on the crisis of the environment and the Second Development Decade. In addition, the Council adopted a resolution calling on the Secretary-General and other UN officials to prepare a study for consideration in 1970 on the feasibility of creating an international corps of volunteers.

The Council offered several guidelines for such a corps. People would volunteer for the purpose of contributing to the development of a country and should thus

David A. Morse, director-general of the International Labor Organization. In 1969, the ILO celebrated its 50th birthday and was awarded the Nobel Peace Prize.

give their services without regard to financial benefit. Volunteers should be recruited on as wide a geographical basis as possible. The volunteer teams should be made up of people from several nations. No volunteer should enter a country without the request or approval of that country.

▶ SPECIALIZED AGENCIES

In 1969, the International Civil Aviation Organization discussed the increasing problem of international airplane hijacking. Nations were encouraged to adhere to the Convention on Offenses and Certain Other Acts Committed on Board Aircraft, which was agreed upon in Tokyo in 1963, and which came into force in 1969.

The International Labor Organization celebrated its fiftieth anniversary—and received its greatest reward. The ILO was named winner of the Nobel Peace Prize for 1969.

PAULINE FREDERICK
United Nations Correspondent, NBC News

THE UNITED NATIONS 24th SESSION

THE SECRETARIAT
Secretary-General: U Thant

THE GENERAL ASSEMBLY
President: Angie Brooks (Liberia)

MEMBER NATIONS AND CHIEF REPRESENTATIVES

Nation	Representative	Nation	Representative
Afghanistan	Abdul-Rahman Pazhwak	Kuwait	Muhalhel Mohamed Al-Mudhaf
Albania	Halim Budo	Laos	Khamking Souvanlasy
Algeria	Hadj Benabdelkader Azzout	Lebanon	Edouard A. Ghorra
Argentina	Jose Maria Ruda	Lesotho	M. T. Mashologu
Australia	Patrick Shaw	Liberia	Nathan Barnes
Austria	Heinrich Haymerle	Libya	Wahbi El-Bouri
Barbados	Oliver H. Jackman	Luxembourg	André Philippe
Belgium	Constant Schuurmans	Malagasy Republic	Blaise Rabetafika
Bolivia	Walter Guevara Arze	Malawi	Nyemba Mbekeani
Botswana	T. J. Molefhe	Malaysia	Tengku N. Mohamed
Brazil	João Augusto de Araujo Castro	Maldive Islands	Abdul Sattar
Britain	Lord Caradon	Mali	Mamadou Moctar Thiam
Bulgaria	Milko Tarabanov	Malta	Arvid Pardo
Burma	U Soe Tin	Mauritania	Abdallahi Ould Daddah
Burundi	Terence Nsanze	Mauritius	Radha Krishna Ramphul
Byelorussian S.S.R.	Vitaly S. Smirnov	Mexico	Francisco Cuevas Cancino
Cambodia	Huot Sambath	Mongolia	Mangalyn Dugersuren
Cameroun	Michel Njine	Morocco	Ahmed Taibi Benhima
Canada	Yvon Beaulne	Nepal	Padma Khatri
Central African Rep.	Michel Gallin-Douathe	Netherlands	D. G. E. Middelburg
Ceylon	Hamilton S. Amerasinghe	New Zealand	John V. Scott
Chad	Bruno Bohiadi	Nicaragua	Guillermo Sevilla-Sacasa
Chile	Jose Piñera	Niger	Adamou Mayaki
China	Liu Chieh	Nigeria	E. O. Ogbu
Colombia	Jose M. Morales-Suarez	Norway	Edvard Hambro
Congo (Brazzaville)	Adrien Bakala	Pakistan	Agha Shahi
Congo (Kinshasa)	Théodore Idzumbuir	Panama	Aquilino Boyd
Costa Rica	Luis Dobles Sanchez	Paraguay	Miguel Solano Lopez
Cuba	Ricardo Alarcon de Quesada	Peru	Manuel Felix Maurtua
Cyprus	Zenon Rossides	Philippines	Privado G. Jimenez
Czechoslovakia	Zdenek Cernik	Poland	Eugeniusz Kulaga
Dahomey	Maxime-Léopold Zollner	Portugal	Duarte Vaz Pinto
Denmark	Otto Borch	Rumania	Gheorghe Diaconescu
Dominican Republic	Horacio Julio Ornes Coiscou	Rwanda	Fidèle Nkundabagenzi
Ecuador	Leopoldo Benites	Saudi Arabia	Jamil M. Baroody
El Salvador	Reynaldo Galindo Pohl	Senegal	Ibrahima Boye
Equatorial Guinea	Gustavo B. Envela-Makongo	Sierra Leone	Davidson S. H. W. Nicol
Ethiopia	Kifle Wodajo	Singapore	T. T. B. Koh
Finland	Max Jakobson	Somalia	Abdulrahim Abby Farah
France	Armand Bérard	South Africa	Matthys I. Botha
Gabon	Jean Davin	Southern Yemen	Ismail Saeed Noaman
Gambia	A. D. Camara	Spain	Jaime de Pinies
Ghana	Richard M. Akwei	Sudan	Fakhreddine Mohamed
Greece	Dimitri S. Bitsios	Swaziland	S. T. Msindazwe Sukati
Guatemala	Maximiliano Kestler	Sweden	Sverker C. Aström
Guinea	El Hadj Abdoulaye Touré	Syria	George J. Tomeh
Guyana	P. A. Thompson	Tanzania	Stephen Mhando
Haiti	Marcel Antoine	Thailand	Anand Panyarachun
Honduras	Salomon Jimenez Munguia	Togo	Alexandre J. Ohin
Hungary	Károly Csatorday	Trinidad and Tobago	P. V. J. Solomon
Iceland	Hannes Kjartansson	Tunisia	Slaheddine El Goulli
India	Samar Sen	Turkey	Umit Haluk Bayulken
Indonesia	Hadji Roeslan Abdulgani	Uganda	Otema Allimadi
Iran	Mehdi Vakil	Ukrainian S.S.R.	M. D. Polyanichko
Iraq	Adnan Raouf	U.S.S.R.	Y. A. Malik
Ireland	Cornelius C. Cremin	United Arab Republic	Mohamed A. El Kony
Israel	Yosef Tekoah	United States	Charles W. Yost
Italy	Piero Vinci	Upper Volta	Paul Rouamba
Ivory Coast	Siméon Ake	Uruguay	Augusto Legnani
Jamaica	Keith Johnson	Venezuela	Andres Aguilar Mawdsley
Japan	Senjin Tsuruoka	Yemen	Mohamed Said Al-Attar
Jordan	Muhammad H. El-Farra	Yugoslavia	Lazar Mojsov
Kenya	Arthur E. Osanya-Nyyneque	Zambia	V. J. Mwaanga

THE GENERAL-ASSEMBLY COMMITTEES

Political and Security
Chairman: Agha Shahi, Pakistan

Special Political
Chairman: Eugeniusz Kulaga, Poland

Economic and Financial
Chairman: Costa P. Caranicas, Greece

Social, Humanitarian and Cultural
Chairman: Mrs. Abdallahi Ould Daddah Turkia, Mauritania

Trust and Non-Self-Governing Territories
Chairman: Théodore Idzumbuir, Congo (Kinshasa)

Administrative and Budgetary
Chairman: David Silveria da Mota, Jr., Brazil

Legal
Chairman: Gonzalo Alcivar, Ecuador

THE SECURITY COUNCIL

Britain *	Poland
Burundi	Sierra Leone
China *	Spain
Colombia	Syria
Finland	U.S.S.R. *
France *	United States *
Nepal	Zambia
Nicaragua	

* permanent

THE TRUSTEESHIP COUNCIL

Australia	France
Britain	U.S.S.R.
China	United States

Angie Brooks with Secretary-General U Thant.

THE ECONOMIC AND SOCIAL COUNCIL

Argentina	Jamaica
Brazil	Japan
Britain	Kenya
Bulgaria	Norway
Ceylon	Pakistan
Chad	Peru
Congo (Brazzaville)	Sudan
France	Tunisia
Ghana	U.S.S.R.
Greece	United States
India	Upper Volta
Indonesia	Uruguay
Ireland	Yugoslavia
Italy	

THE INTERNATIONAL COURT OF JUSTICE

Fouad Ammoun	Lebanon
Cesar Bengzon	Philippines
Federico de Castro	Spain
Hardy Cross Dillard	United States
Sir Gerald Fitzmaurice	Britain
Isaac Forster	Senegal
André Gross	France
Louis Ignacio-Pinto	Dahomey
Eduardo Jimenez de Arechaga	Uruguay
Manfred Lachs	Poland
Platon D. Morozov	U.S.S.R.
Charles D. Onyeama	Nigeria
Luis Padilla Nervo	Mexico
Sture Petran	Sweden
Muhammad Zafrulla Khan	Pakistan

UNITED STATES

THERE are a few years that stand out in history, when one age seems to end and another begin. Such a year is 1492, when Columbus discovered the New World. Another is 1776, the year of American independence. In all likelihood, 1969, the year man first set foot on another celestial body, will come to be so regarded.

But if 1969 was historic, indeed even revolutionary, in many ways it seemed much like the previous year. James Earl Ray, who had confessed to the 1968 murder of civil-rights leader Martin Luther King, Jr., was sentenced in 1969 to 99 years in prison. And Sirhan Sirhan was convicted of the 1968 assassination of Senator Robert F. Kennedy. These two legal proceedings recalled the tragedies of 1968 and underlined the continuing problem of violence in American life.

On the political scene, the Republican Party regained control of the presidency after eight years. But Richard M. Nixon, only the second Republican chief executive to take office since 1933, had to contend with a Congress controlled by the Democrats and with the fact that he had received a smaller percentage of the popular vote than any winning candidate in modern history.

President Nixon stressed his determination to try to bring the American people together again. He wanted, he said, to restore the national unity which had seemed to be so lacking in 1968. But to do this he had to find an acceptable way out of the Vietnam war. He had to restore domestic peace to the cities. And he had to deal with such major problems as a rapidly increasing population, increasing pollution of the environment, and a widening generation gap. Yet there was some reason to hope. The moon landing showed that enormous challenges could be met and overcome.

During his first year in office, President Nixon faced many of the same problems that had plagued his predecessor, Lyndon Johnson.

Left: Folk singer Pete Seeger during an antiwar rally. Right: A GI takes a much-needed rest. The Vietnam-war issue continued to divide the nation.

The successful Apollo moon landings indicated to many that domestic challenges, too, could be met and overcome by American technology.

Despite record wage settlements in 1969, rising prices brought despair to lower- and middle-income Americans already hurt by high taxes.

In 1969, as in the previous four years, the Vietnam war was the most vital foreign-policy issue. It was also the most controversial. Richard Nixon knew that if he were to have a successful administration he would have to end the war. And he would have to end it before it became a liability to him and his party as it had been for Lyndon Johnson and the Democrats.

The Vietnam War

For six or seven months President Nixon escaped severe criticism of his handling of the war. This was chiefly because he took some steps to reduce American involvement. He cut defense spending by several billion dollars. And he began to bring home some of the 540,000 American soldiers in Vietnam. The first troop withdrawals were announced in June, after President Nixon had talked with President Nguyen Van Thieu of South Vietnam at Midway Island. Twenty-five thousand troops left Vietnam by August 31. By the end of the year, with more reductions, the number of U.S. troops in Vietnam was below the 475,000 mark. In December the President announced that by April 1970 another 50,000 troops would be withdrawn.

The actual number of men to be withdrawn would depend upon how fast the South Vietnamese Army could take over responsibility for combat operations. Another factor would be the reaction of North Vietnam to the American peace gestures. The administration stated that it would be willing to withdraw all U.S. and allied forces over a 12-month period if North Vietnam forces also withdrew. The troop withdrawals, it was proposed, would then be followed by free elections under international supervision.

Even the most outspoken doves applauded Mr. Nixon's efforts to "de-Americanize" the war. But they still questioned his determination to continue to support the Thieu Government in South Vietnam.

Meanwhile, at the Paris peace negotiations, representatives of the United States,

South Vietnam, North Vietnam, and the Vietcong finally reached agreement on the procedural matters. But they failed to make any real progress. Chief U.S. negotiator Henry Cabot Lodge, who replaced W. Averell Harriman early in 1969, asked for mutual troop withdrawals. But North Vietnam and the National Liberation Front demanded that the United States withdraw all its troops unconditionally.

Lodge replied that the Communists were showing no real will to negotiate. Still, North Vietnam apparently did react to the troop withdrawals and to reduced American military action. Infiltration of North Vietnamese soldiers into the South declined. Secretary of State William Rogers stated in October that the enemy had "a net reduction in the last six or seven months of 25,000 to 30,000." The level of fighting in Vietnam fell off after September. Both sides seemed to be avoiding offensive operations.

Still, by the end of 1969, more than 40,000 Americans had been killed in battle in Vietnam. And with the peace talks at a standstill, Henry Cabot Lodge handed in his resignation. To many, this seemed to be evidence that President Nixon would be downgrading the peace talks and placing greater emphasis on Vietnamization of the war.

In December, President Nixon indicated that Vietnamization of the war was going better than expected. But many military leaders doubted that the South Vietnamese Army could match the Vietcong and the North Vietnamese. Heightening these fears was the report of increased infiltration from North Vietnam at year's end. Some military men expected a communist offensive early in 1970.

Antiwar Protests

Protests against the war had almost ended with Mr. Nixon's inauguration in January. It seemed that the protestors wanted to give the new president time to develop a peace policy. But as the summer ended, protests began anew. Republican

To counter antiwar protests, such as this one in New York, President Nixon called on the "silent majority" of Americans to support his Vietnam policy. The President insisted on a phased withdrawal of U.S. troops, not an immediate pullout.

Senator Charles Goodell of New York proposed that the President set the end of 1970 as the date for the removal of all U.S. forces from Vietnam. The military came in for renewed criticism when the Army arrested on charges of murder eight Special Forces, or Green Beret, officers and enlisted men. The Army alleged that the Green Berets had murdered a South Vietnamese double agent. It suddenly dropped the charges at the end of September. But the incident aroused a great deal of public resentment. This resentment grew in November, when word reached the United States about an alleged mass murder of 100 to 500 Vietnamese men, women, and children by a force of American soldiers.

A movement to observe a national Vietnam Moratorium Day on October 15 grew rapidly on the nation's campuses. It soon spread from the campuses to all segments of American life. Rallies were held in cities across the United States. President Nixon had stated that he would not be moved by such demonstrations. Still, its sponsors were certain that the moratorium had been effective. Among other things, they pointed to Nixon's removal of General Lewis B. Hershey as the director of Selective Service. For a long time he had been a target of youthful protestors.

At the time of the moratorium, public-opinion polls showed that 58 per cent of all Americans believed that the United States had made a mistake in getting involved in Vietnam. Nonetheless, in an address to the nation on November 3, President Nixon repeated that he would not be influenced by any demonstrations or moratoriums. He appealed to the "great silent majority" to support his Vietnam policy and give him time to carry out a plan for complete withdrawal of U.S. ground forces. Mr. Nixon's speech brought a deluge of mail to the White House in support of his position. At the same time, a second moratorium was held on November 15. It was even larger than the first. In Washington, D.C., 300,000 people massed in opposition to the war.

United States-Soviet Relations

There was a major breakthrough in United States-Soviet relations in October. It was announced that on November 17 the two countries would begin preliminary talks about limiting strategic arms. These first talks would be about procedural matters. Later, the talks, which were expected to last for months or even years, would focus on ways to limit missile systems.

The Strategic Arms Limitation Talks (SALT) began on schedule in Helsinki, Finland. Gerard C. Smith, director of the U.S. Arms Control and Disarmament Agency headed the U.S. delegation. First Deputy Foreign Minister Vladimir S. Semyonov led the Soviet delegation.

The decision to start talks came after two years of fencing between the two countries. President Lyndon Johnson had tried to achieve some sort of *détente* with the Russians. In fact this had been a major goal during the last year of his administration. But the Soviet invasion of Czechoslovakia in August 1968 temporarily ended these efforts. In March 1969, hopes for some type of understanding increased after the U.S. Senate approved the nuclear-nonproliferation treaty.

The Middle East

The Nixon administration in February said it would pursue "a new policy" in the Middle East. It gave no specific proposal to end the Arab-Israeli conflict. But it seemed to be favoring a policy that was less openly pro-Israel than had previously been the case. President Nixon endorsed four-power (U.S.S.R., U.S.A., Great Britain, France) discussions of the Middle East crisis. He believed that while the four powers could not dictate a settlement in the area, they could indicate those areas where the Arabs and Israelis could "have profitable discussions." Four-power talks were held, but little progress was made.

Latin America

President Nixon sent New York Governor Nelson Rockefeller on a series of four fact-finding tours to Latin America. The tours, completed in July, focused mainly on economic and trade problems. The reaction in Latin America to Rockefeller's visits was mixed. Some countries complained that Rockefeller's visit was too short: he spent only four hours in Guatemala. Also, anti-American feeling ran so high in Venezuela, Chile, and Peru that visits to these three countries had to be canceled.

The administration did not make public Rockefeller's recommendations. But in late October, President Nixon defined certain departures from the Alliance for Progress program of the Kennedy-Johnson years. He indicated that future United States aid would be designed to help Latin-American private business. Also, nations with representative governments would no longer get preferential consideration. Nixon, exempting only the case of Cuba, said "We must deal realistically with governments in the inter-American system as we find them." This was a reference to the military dictatorships of Brazil, Argentina, Peru, Bolivia, and several other Latin nations.

President Nixon's Trips

Soon after his inauguration, President Nixon announced that he would visit the United States' European allies. He did this in late February and early March. Upon his return, the President said that he felt he had established "a new relationship of trust and confidence that did not exist before." In a trip to Asia and Rumania in July and August, the President emphasized that the United States could no longer be a policeman for the world. He stressed that defense problems should be handled primarily by Asian nations themselves. The United States, however, would continue to provide aid against aggression.

▶ DOMESTIC AFFAIRS

"That's one small step for a man, one giant leap for mankind." These words were spoken by Apollo 11 astronaut Neil A. Armstrong, the first man to set foot on the moon. Armstrong took his fateful step at 10:56 P.M. Eastern daylight time on July 20, 1969. A few minutes later Edwin E. (Buzz) Aldrin joined Armstrong on the moon's surface.

Apollo 11 had blasted off on July 6, beginning the last leg of the American race for the moon. This race had begun in May 1961 when President John F. Kennedy declared in a special message to a joint session of Congress, "I believe that this nation should commit itself to achieving the goal, before this decade is out, of landing a man on the moon and returning him safely to earth." The decision, which Kennedy thought would be one of the most important of his presidency, met some opposition. Many people objected to spending so much money on the venture in space when so many problems remained on earth. Senator William Fulbright believed history would be more interested in how the United States dealt with unemployment rather than the unexplored. Kenneth Clark, a Negro psychologist, did not think "the moon is going to be an adequate substitute for the fact that we haven't addressed ourselves to clearing up the slums."

The defenders of the project based their arguments on national security, national prestige, and the unending quest of man to expand the frontiers of knowledge. Even with the triumphs of Apollo 11 and Apollo 12, some voices were raised against the expensive space program. But generally, national enthusiasm for space projects knew no bounds. And most agreed with Vice-President Spiro Agnew when he spoke of the United States' landing a man on Mars before the end of the century.

Politics

During the first half of 1969, Senator Edward F. Kennedy of Massachusetts was considered to be the front-runner for the Democratic presidential nomination in 1972. An automobile accident changed this. On July 18 the Senator drove a car off a bridge on Chappaquiddick Island, Massachusetts. A passenger in the car,

Quite often during the year, Vice-President Spiro Agnew dominated the news by attacking the press, television networks and commentators, and such "effete snobs" as Averell Harriman, who oppose President Nixon's handling of the Vietnam war. The Vice-President's raised voice, at a time when the President called for a quiet dialogue, was condemned by many, but according to polls, most "silent Americans" agreed with Mr. Agnew.

Mary Jo Kopechne, killed when Senator Edward Kennedy's car plunged off a bridge.

Mary Jo Kopechne, was drowned. A week after the accident, Senator Kennedy told of his efforts to save the girl's life. He admitted, however, that he had left the scene of the accident. He also admitted that he had failed to report it immediately to the police. For this, he later received a two-month suspended sentence. During the next few weeks there was a great deal of public comment on certain ambiguities in Senator Kennedy's statement. As a result, Massachusetts authorities ordered an inquest to determine if Senator Kennedy was guilty of any criminal charge.

Kennedy announced that he would not be a candidate for the presidency in 1972. He added that he had not intended to run for the office even before the accident. This led to speculation that Hubert Humphrey or Eugene McCarthy might again compete for the Democratic nomination in 1972. Others thought that Senator Edmund S. Muskie of Maine would also enter the race.

During his first year in office, President Nixon seemed determined to build his strength in the Midwest and the South by following a middle-of-the-road course in foreign and domestic affairs. He moved to

Senator Kennedy is surrounded by police and newsmen after pleading guilty to leaving the scene of an accident. He received a two-month suspended sentence.

fulfill a campaign pledge of "slowing down" the Supreme Court. He appointed Warren Earl Burger as chief justice of the United States to succeed the retiring Earl Warren. Burger is a conservative jurist with a record of long and distinguished judicial service. But Nixon ran into trouble when he chose Judge Clement F. Haynsworth, Jr., of South Carolina to succeed Associate Justice Abe Fortas. His choice drew fire from civil-rights and labor groups. Opponents of Haynsworth's nomination charged that, while serving on the lower levels of the Federal judiciary, he had made de-

cisions favorable to some companies in which he held stock. Justice Fortas had resigned after being charged with an alleged conflict of interest. The parallel was too close for comfort for many Republican senators. Nevertheless, Nixon disregarded all suggestions that he withdraw Haynsworth's name. He received a political setback when the Senate rejected Haynsworth's nomination, by a vote of 55 to 45.

The Vietnam war threatened to become a political liability for the Republicans. On September 30, Michael Harrington, a young Massachusetts Democrat, running

YES: DR. EDWARD TELLER

DEFENSE against incoming missiles is very difficult. The missiles approach at a speed faster than sound. They are a small target. And they must be hit with great force to put them out of action. To make matters worse, decoys can be sent over that are hard to tell from the missiles. And there are ways in which the observation of the missiles can be blocked. Finally, the defensive action must be taken within seconds.

Missile defense is needed because the aggressive missiles carry nuclear explosives that can devastate a country. The danger of an enemy attack can of course be reduced by our power to strike back. But it is better to avoid being hit by the aggressive missiles in the first place. Also, a good defense deters the enemy because he will not strike without being certain he can knock out nearly all U.S. missiles. After all, he does not want his own cities to be hit by those missiles that remain. And the aim of the first phase of U.S. missile defense is to protect a key part (not necessarily all) of our "retaliatory strike force."

There are many signs that the Russians started building missile-defense systems years ago. Because of Russian secrecy, we do not know just how effective this defense is. It may be poor or it may be excellent.

The real question is not whether the United States needs a missile defense: it does. The question is, Can a good missile-defense system be built? There are several reasons why it seems that it can.

One reason a missile-defense system can work is that nuclear explosives can be used to destroy the incoming missiles. These defensive explosives can be made powerful enough to destroy the incoming rocket while it is still far away. At the same time,

the power of the explosive can be so limited as to cause no damage on the ground and almost no radioactive fallout.

A second reason a missile-defense system can be successful is that several types of equipment are being designed for detecting and tracking incoming missiles. This equipment can probably be made to tell a heavy rocket from a light one (the light rockets will probably always be decoys).

Last but not least, missile defense appears possible because of the development of fast computers. With the help of this equipment, incoming rockets can be evaluated in less than a second.

It is important to know that little damage would be done if a defensive rocket were launched by a false alarm. If there is no invader to destroy, the defensive rocket itself will do no harm.

There is no doubt, however, that the need for rapid computations (mathematical calculations) is the most difficult problem in missile defense. But the hopeful part of this situation is that in the field of fast computers the United States is ahead. It is lucky that the United States has taken the lead in the computer field just as the U.S. lead in aggressive nuclear weapons is lessening.

Objectors to the deployment of missile defenses have said it would lead to a further escalation (increase) in the arms race. In view of the fact that Russian deployment has been going on for several years, this argument makes little sense.

In the long run the real importance of missile defense lies in the defense of our cities and of our people in general. If a reliable defense can be created, both the danger and the likelihood of nuclear war will be greatly reduced.

Dr. Edward Teller, associate director of the University of California's Lawrence Radiation Laboratory, helped develop the atom and hydrogen bombs.

DEPLOY AN ABM SYSTEM?

NO: DR. JEROME WIESNER

THE reasons the United States is unwise to build an anti-ballistic missile (ABM) system fall into five groups.

First, the ABM system is not needed: an attack on the United States by the largest missile force the Soviet Union can muster could not destroy enough U.S. missiles to prevent the United States from striking back. Second, even if the ABM system works, it will give little protection to the strategic forces it is supposed to help. Third, there are technical questions about whether this system can really work. Fourth, the building of an ABM system could escalate (step up) the arms race and thus reduce U.S. security. And finally, the ABM system will cost a great deal of money at a time when funds are sorely needed elsewhere in the economy.

In 1967 an ABM system called Sentinel was planned for placement near cities and missile stockpiles. It was foreseen as a protection against a small Chinese nuclear attack, a possibility for the 1970's.

The practicality of Sentinel came up for review early in 1969. Under the new Nixon administration, the system was renamed "Safeguard," and its purpose and deployment changed. Safeguard is not to be placed near U.S. cities. Its main purpose is now to protect the U.S. strategic force against Russian missile attack. It is meant also to guard against small, unsophisticated attacks by the Chinese.

When Safeguard came to a vote in the U.S. Senate, the debate was hot and lengthy, but the system passed—by one vote. In supporting Safeguard on its journey through Congress, Secretary of Defense Melvin Laird described the likely size of Soviet threat (unproven, due to Soviet secrecy) in such large terms he harmed his own argument. If the Soviet strike force is as big as he says, and if MIRV warheads are used (20 or 30 to a missile), it could quickly overwhelm the planned Safeguard. A Soviet attack could also use decoys. This would further reduce the value of the Safeguard system.

Also Secretary Laird did not take into account the fact that a great part of our deterrent force relies on the Polaris fleet and on several hundred bombers, some of which are always aloft. Several thousand planes of our tactical air force are available too, based on aircraft carriers and at airfields around the world. Part of this force could easily be used to retaliate.

The ABM system is the most intricate system man has ever tried to build. The computer program is the most sensitive part of the system. It is quite common for defects in large, complex computers to appear only when the system goes into real operation. The Safeguard computer programs are designed to handle millions of instructions. There are no other computers of this size in existence, but the difficulties met by smaller ones do not inspire confidence in this proposed giant. And there is no way of simulating a nuclear attack closely enough to be sure Safeguard will work when put to the test.

Some people supported the building of Safeguard even when told that it might not provide protection, saying that at least it could not do any harm. But it could do harm, for it could escalate the arms race and decrease U.S. security. If Safeguard is built, Soviet planners will have to overestimate its capabilities. They will respond by extending their ABM system or increasing their strike force. The United States will feel bound to respond again, and so on. The result of all this will be an increase in "damage capacity" by both sides. Then, if nuclear war occurs, both sides will suffer more.

Dr. Jerome Wiesner, provost of the Massachusetts Institute of Technology, was chairman of the President's Science Advisory Committee 1961–64.

Representative Alexander Pirnie (Rep., N.Y.) of the House Military Affairs Committee draws the first date in the draft lottery held at Selective Service Headquarters, Washington, D.C. Looking on is General Lewis B. Hershey (with glasses). Hershey, a favorite target of antiwar demonstrators, had been removed from the post of Selective Service director by President Nixon.

on an antiwar platform and exceedingly critical of the administration's handling of the conflict, won a special Congressional race for a House seat that the Republicans had held for over 90 years. This gave the Democrats five victories in seven Congressional elections during the year.

In addition to the Vietnam war, concern over violence and demands for "law and order" continued to be national issues during 1969. The President said that the law-abiding American was "fed up to here with violence." Indeed, the law-and-order question certainly dominated all others in municipal elections across the country. Civil-rights leaders and others protested, however, that "law and order" served as a respectable slogan to cover up racist attitudes. Samuel Yorty in Los Angeles and Charles Stenvig in Minneapolis won election as mayors of their cities after campaigns in which they took a hard line against "crime in the streets" and implied or openly stated that too many concessions had been made to minority groups. Similar law-and-order candidates won mayoralty contests across the nation. Apparently bucking the trend, however, Carl B. Stokes of Cleveland, the first Negro mayor of a major city, won re-election by a narrow margin.

The major test occurred in New York City. In the June primaries, conservative State Senator John J. Marchi defeated incumbent, nationally known John V. Lindsay for the Republican nomination. Mario Procaccino, running primarily on the law-and-order issue, defeated four liberal candidates for the Democratic nomination. In the November election, however, Lindsay, running as the candidate of the Liberal Party, was re-elected as the conservative vote divided between his two opponents.

President Nixon, who had campaigned in both states, hailed Republican victories in gubernatorial contests in New Jersey and Virginia. The Virginia election saw the first Republican take office in that state in 84 years.

National Defense

In March, President Nixon urged the Congress to approve his decision to deploy a revised anti-ballistic missile system (ABM). The revised system would consist of 12 sites employed to defend the United States' intercontinental missiles. Opponents warned that building an ABM system could escalate the arms race. They also said that the proposal would jeopardize arms-control talks with the Soviet Union. It was also contended that ABM

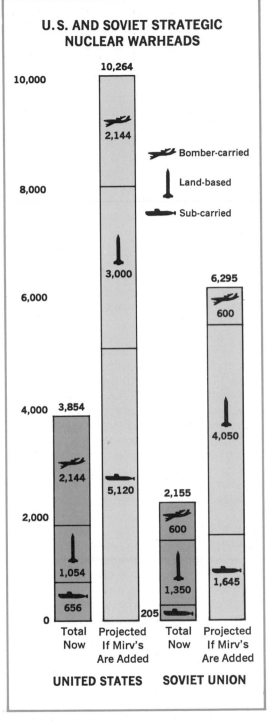

U.S. AND SOVIET STRATEGIC NUCLEAR WARHEADS

Bomber-carried

Land-based

Sub-carried

UNITED STATES

Total Now	Projected If Mirv's Are Added

SOVIET UNION

Total Now	Projected If Mirv's Are Added

Equipping missiles with multiple warheads (MIRV's), which both countries are developing, would triple warhead totals.

cost would eventually run into billions of dollars each year. Defenders of the Safeguard system described it as a minimal effort to guarantee American security and ensure the nation's ability to negotiate from strength. The ABM debate involved the political, scientific, and academic communities. And it spurred a rare turning out of all one hundred senators for the decisive vote in August. Opponents of ABM failed by one vote in their effort to block its deployment. The close vote and growing hostility toward huge defense spending indicated that future military appropriations would receive a closer and more critical scrutiny.

In another area related to national defense, President Nixon announced that he had banned the use of biological-warfare weapons by the United States. Some restrictions were placed on the use of chemical-warfare weapons.

In an effort to make the draft more equitable, a lottery system was instituted in December.

Race Relations

Negro leaders expressed resentment at the policies of the Nixon administration. The nomination of Judge Clement F. Haynsworth, Jr., of South Carolina for the Supreme Court was strongly criticized. So too was the willingness of the Justice Department to permit a year's delay in the desegregation of certain school districts in Mississippi. The Supreme Court unanimously reversed this decision in October. Negro leaders also attacked the decision to reduce Federal financing of several urban projects. Trouble erupted in Hartford, Connecticut, Omaha, Nebraska, and other cities during 1969. There was, however, much less urban violence and rioting to plague black ghettos than in the previous three years.

JOHN B. DUFF
Seton Hall University

UPPER VOLTA. See AFRICA.
URUGUAY. See LATIN AMERICA.
VENEZUELA. See LATIN AMERICA.

VIETNAM

THE tempo of the fighting in Vietnam slowed considerably during 1969. At the same time, the pace of political developments accelerated, although absolutely no progress was recorded at the Paris peace talks.

▶ MILITARY ACTIVITY

In February and March the Communists launched a general, though limited, offensive. First they shelled Saigon and 30 other cities with rockets and mortars. This was the first rocket attack on Saigon since former President Lyndon Johnson had ordered a halt to the bombing of the North on October 31, 1968.

By March the Communists had brought 115 cities under fire, including 25 provincial capitals and 30 district towns. Hundreds of Vietnamese civilians were killed, and more than 20,000 were made homeless. From then until almost the end of the year fighting continued to decline. Then in December there was an upsurge. The war cost to the United States and its allies, as well as to the communist forces, was high. By year's end, more than 40,000 American soldiers had been killed in combat.

Atrocities

Several reports of alleged atrocities came out of Vietnam during the year. The Army charge that several members of the U.S. Special Forces had murdered a Vietnamese double agent was quickly dropped in September. But in November the Army announced that it was investigating reports that members of C Company of the Americal Division's 11th Infantry Brigade had murdered 100 to 500 Vietnamese men, women, and children in the village of Songmy in March 1968. The village was re-

War casualties: civilian refugees.

ported to be a Vietcong stronghold. One platoon leader of C Company, First Lieutenant William L. Calley, Jr., was formally charged with the murders of at least 109 of these civilians.

From the American side came reports that during the 1968 Tet offensive, the Vietcong had murdered thousands of civilians in the city of Hue.

▶ POLITICAL DEVELOPMENTS

As the fighting eased, Hanoi, Saigon, and Washington maneuvered in the political arena. In June, President Nixon flew to Midway Island to confer with South Vietnamese President Nguyen Van Thieu. After the conference, Mr. Nixon announced plans to withdraw 25,000 U.S. troops from South Vietnam. By the end of the year, more than 60,000 troops were withdrawn, bringing the level below 500,-000 for the first time since 1967.

The President followed this announcement with several other decisions. He renounced an imposed military solution. He proposed free elections in South Vietnam under neutral, international supervision. He offered to withdraw all U.S. forces over a 12-month period. And he offered to negotiate a supervised cease-fire under international supervision. The President announced that the United States would accept "any political outcome [in South Vietnam] which is arrived at through free elections," including a coalition Government which includes Communists. "In short," the President declared, "the only item not negotiable is the right of the people of South Vietnam to determine their own future free of outside interference."

In an address to the people of the United States in November, Mr. Nixon said that he had worked out with South Vietnam "an orderly scheduled timetable" for the withdrawal of all U.S. combat forces. He said, however, that he could not make the timetable public. To do so, he stated, would remove the incentive for Hanoi to negotiate

A Vietcong soldier surrenders.

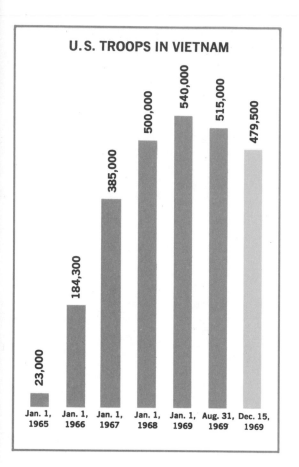

U.S. TROOPS IN VIETNAM

23,000	184,300	385,000	500,000	540,000	515,000	479,500
Jan. 1, 1965	Jan. 1, 1966	Jan. 1, 1967	Jan. 1, 1968	Jan. 1, 1969	Aug. 31, 1969	Dec. 15, 1969

The Vietnam war continued in 1969, though with reduced fighting. President Nixon cut back U.S. troop strength (top, left), but to a Special Forces soldier (bottom, left), the war remained a grim reality. One reason for U.S. troop reduction was the success of pacification, which brought more territory and people under

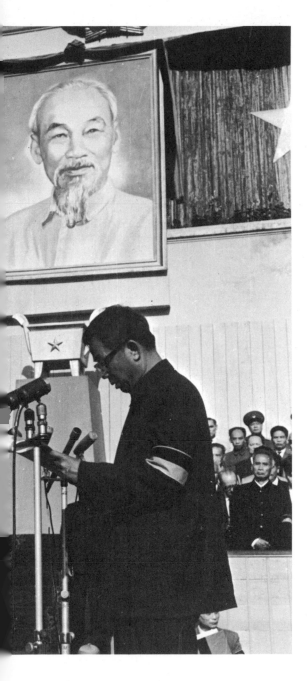

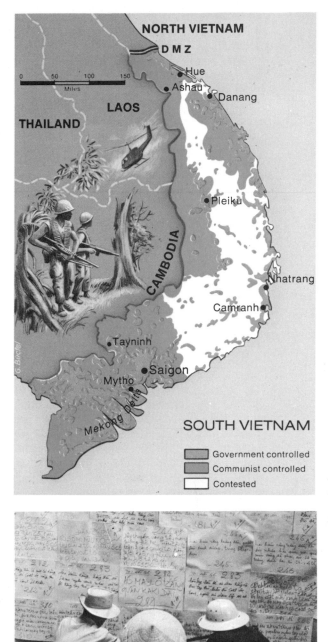

control of the South Vietnam Government (top, right). Bottom, right: Citizens of Hue read lists to determine if bodies found during 1969 were relatives murdered by the Communists during the 1968 Tet offensive. In Hanoi (center), Le Duan, new leader of North Vietnam, eulogizes Ho Chi Minh, who died in September.

NORTH VIETNAM

D M Z

Hue

Ashau

Danang

LAOS

THAILAND

Pleiku

CAMBODIA

Nhatrang

Camranh

Tayninh

Saigon

Mytho

Mekong Delta

SOUTH VIETNAM

Government controlled

Communist controlled

Contested

a peace settlement. In the same speech, Mr. Nixon appealed for support of his Vietnam policy.

Mr. Nixon made clear that he planned to "de-Americanize" the war. In the field, American troops would gradually be replaced by South Vietnamese troops. In December, Mr. Nixon reported that South Vietnamese troops were fighting well and that 50,000 more U.S. troops would return home early in 1970.

Mr. Nixon's plans to de-Americanize the war were implicit in the doctrine he outlined at Guam in July. The Guam Doctrine called on the noncommunist states of Asia to assume responsibility for their own defense.

South Vietnam

Against this background, President Thieu appealed to the people of South Vietnam to accept more sacrifices. We must "do everything we can do for ourselves before we turn to our friends to ask for more aid," he said. In large measure, the success or failure of South Vietnam to stand on its own may turn on long-overdue land reform. In South Vietnam, 60 per cent of the people are farmers, and 70 per cent of them are landless peasants who work largely for absentee landlords. In 1969 Thieu sent to the National Assembly a sweeping land-reform measure to correct this situation. But by year's end, the Assembly had failed to act.

North Vietnam

The Communists also tried to develop a new political strategy in 1969. In May the Vietcong, or National Liberation Front (NLF), issued a ten-point program which expressed "a desire to reach a political solution." The NLF also said it would be willing to enter into a coalition Government *before* free elections were held. The coalition Government would then supervise the withdrawal of U.S. troops. Shortly thereafter the Communists announced a "Provisional Revolutionary Government of the Republic of South Vietnam" as a successor to the National Liberation Front. It was a month later that President Nixon sent a secret letter to President Ho Chi Minh of North Vietnam. Ho's reply reached the White House on August 30. The communist leader said that "with goodwill on both sides a solution may be found." However, four days later Ho, who had been ailing, died.

To succeed Ho as president, the Communists chose 81-year-old Ton Duc Thang. But real power rested in the hands of Le Duan, first secretary of the Communist Party, and three other figures in the party hierarchy.

ARNOLD C. BRACKMAN

VITAL STATISTICS

FIGURES for the total births, deaths, marriages, and divorces that occur in particular places are called "vital statistics." (The word "vital" comes from the Latin word for "life.") In most countries these vital events are recorded by town or city officials. Such records, together with population counts from censuses and other surveys, enable births, deaths, marriages, and divorces to be counted and rates of increase or decrease to be figured. In 1969, the latest available statistics were for 1968.

▶ **DEATH RATES**

In 1968 there were about 1,923,000 deaths in the United States, 71,000 more than in 1967. The death rate was 9.6 per 1,000 population. The death rate has varied little since 1955, when a long downward trend of mortality leveled off. The increase in 1968 was due mainly to two epidemics of influenza, one in January and February and the other at the end of the year. This disease caused the deaths of many older people.

Heart disease was the leading cause of death in 1968. It was responsible for almost $\frac{2}{5}$ of the deaths in the United States. The rate was 372.9 per 100,000 population. Cancer ranked second, causing $\frac{1}{6}$ of the deaths. Next came cerebrovascular disease (strokes), responsible for more than $\frac{1}{10}$ of the deaths. Accidents, the cause of more than $\frac{1}{20}$ of the deaths in 1968, ranked fourth. The next ranking causes of death were, in order, influenza and pneumonia; disorders of early infancy; diabetes mellitus; arteriosclerosis; bronchitis, emphysema and asthma; and cirrhosis of the liver.

According to early counts, in 1968 the District of Columbia recorded the highest death rate in the United States, 13.2 per 1,000 people. Florida came next, with a rate of 11.6 per 1,000, and Missouri third, with a rate of 11.2. The death rates were lowest in Alaska (4.8) and Hawaii (5.5).

Death rates are affected by the age and sex of people living in different areas. For instance, if an area is inhabited by an unusually large number of old people, the death rate is bound to be higher—as in Florida. Death rates also vary according to whether or not people are married. The lowest mortality rates are among married people. The highest rates are among the divorced.

In the United States the life expectancy at birth in 1967 (the most recent year available) was 70.5 years. This broke down as follows: 67.9 years for white males, 75.0 for white females, 61.2 for nonwhite males, and 68.5 for nonwhite females.

There were 75,300 infant deaths in 1968, 2,900 fewer than in 1967. The infant death rate was 21.7 per 1,000 live births, a record low. The early count for the maternal death rate in 1968 was 27.4 per 100,000 live births.

BIRTH RATES

There were about 3,470,000 live births in 1968 in the United States. This was the smallest number since 1946. The birth rate was 17.4 per 1,000 population, continuing a steady decrease in the rate since 1957. The decline in births is due in part to changes in the timing of childbirth and to changes of fashion in family size.

In 1967 the white birth rate was 16.8, the nonwhite 25.0, and the plural birth rate (twins, triplets) per 1,000 live births was 19.7. Based on early data, the District of Columbia had the highest birth rate in the United States in 1968, 33.8. Utah and Alaska also had high rates, 23.4 and 23.3 respectively. The lowest birth rates were recorded in Kansas (14.8) and New Jersey (15.5). The ratio of males to females among births in the United States was 105 females born for every 100 males.

MARRIAGE AND DIVORCE RATES

In 1968 there were 2,059,000 marriages in the United States. This was the second highest total on record. The increase of 146,000 marriages (6.2 per cent over 1967) was the largest yearly increase since the end of World War II. The marriage rate per 1,000 population was 10.3. There were about 582,000 divorces and annulments in the United States in 1968, 48,000 more than in 1967. The divorce rate rose to 2.9 per 1,000 population in 1968. It had been 2.7 in 1967, and 2.5 in 1966 and 1965. Divorce figures are based upon reporting areas covering about 80 per cent of the population of the United States.

Early data shows that Nevada had the highest United States marriage rate in 1968, 202.2 per 1,000 resident population. The rate was 19.9 in South Carolina and 16.0 in Idaho. In 1965, Nevada had the highest divorce rate (23.0), followed by Arizona (5.4) and Oklahoma (4.8). The lowest divorce rates were in North Dakota (1.1) and South Carolina (1.2). The rates just mentioned are given according to the place where the marriage or divorce occurred, and not by the home state of the people involved.

FREDERIC SELTZER
Senior Actuarial Associate
Metropolitan Life Insurance Company

WEATHER

THE year 1969 had more than its share of dramatic weather. The winter of 1968–69 was one of the worst on record across the northern United States. The "year of the big snows" was followed by disastrous spring flooding in the Midwest. In California, destructive floods and mud slides followed winter rainfall that was eight times the normal in some areas.

On August 17, Hurricane Camille struck the Gulf coast. Camille brought winds up to 190 miles per hour and storm tides up to 30 feet. This was the most violent tropical storm ever recorded on the United States mainland. The remnants of this storm brought disastrous floods to the Appalachian Mountains near the Virginia-West Virginia border.

A photograph of Hurricane Camille taken by the weather satellite ESSA 9 as the storm struck the Gulf coast with winds of up to 190 mph.

▶**WEATHER EXPERIMENTS**

In this year of extreme weather, meteorological science took some giant strides. Man's most ambitious environmental experiment was conducted in the tropical Atlantic Ocean from May 1 to July 28. Called BOMEX (for Barbados Oceanographic and Meteorological Experiment), this investigation covered over 90,000 square miles of the atmosphere and ocean, from ocean depths of 18,000 feet to altitudes of 100,000 feet. Ships, aircraft, buoys, and satellites were used to gather data to see how the world's weather is shaped.

ESSA 9, the last of its type of weather satellite, was launched in February. The new TIROS M will be placed in polar orbit in 1970. It is the experimental prototype of a new system. The larger TIROS M satellite will do the work of ESSA satellites, and will provide infrared "photographs" of cloud cover over the dark side of the earth.

Several weather modification experiments were made during the year. Winter storm clouds over Lake Erie were seeded to determine whether snowfall might be modified.

Project Stormfury, a joint Navy, Air Force, and Environmental Science Services Administration experiment, seeded Hurricane Debbie in August with silver iodide crystals. This was done so that water would form around the crystals, turn into ice, and thus take away some of the heat from the storm. When heat is taken away, the hurricane loses energy. Debbie was the first storm to move into the atmospheric "laboratory" in several years. And it was the first to be seeded many times. It will be some time before the effects of seeding can be derived from Stormfury data. However, the experiment was termed an operational success.

Prepared by ENVIRONMENTAL SCIENCE
SERVICES ADMINISTRATION
Office of Public Information

See also OCEANOGRAPHY.

WELFARE. See SOCIAL WELFARE.

WEST GERMANY. See EUROPE, WEST.

A British paratrooper and a policeman play soccer with Anguillans.

WEST INDIES

THE islands of the Caribbean share a strong family likeness. They have, with the exception of a few low-lying coral islands like Barbados and Antigua, certain common features: sharply rising central mountain ridges; deep, narrow valleys; and a rim of coastal plain. The islands also have similar social and political contours, moulded by the same forces: slavery and the sugar plantation.

But there are differences that lie deep. These spring out of history, rather than geography. The region is one of search: search for economic security, search for a national identity.

▶ **FORCES AT WORK IN THE REGION**

In the Commonwealth Caribbean (formerly called the British West Indies), there are two seemingly contrary forces at work. One is a strong sense of belonging to a particular nation. The other is a growing feeling of belonging to a region.

Regional co-operation in at least three areas is now going on.

Higher Education

The university campus is one of the strongest unifying forces in the Commonwealth Caribbean. In 1946, 14 governments, acting in partnership with Great Britain, established the University of the West Indies. At first it was thought of as a small, select institution, with one campus at Mona in Jamaica. Today the university has 4,000 students, a campus in Trinidad, another in Barbados, and university centers in the other supporting countries.

Caribbean Free Trade Area

The marketplace is another point of growing contact. The Commonwealth Caribbean countries have set up a Caribbean Free Trade Area (CARIFTA), as a long step forward toward economic co-operation. The agreement provides for the removal of customs duties from items of trade between member nations.

A Caribbean Development Bank has been established, in which the Commonwealth Caribbean countries and Puerto Rico are involved. The Caribbean Development Bank and CARIFTA provide a structure for financing development in member countries.

Tourism

Throughout the region, tourism is transforming the economy and breaking down barriers. Present estimates suggest that at least 750,000 visitors from the United States and Latin America will visit the Caribbean in 1970.

Tourism also makes a neighborhood of the Caribbean, where once islands close to each other were rival outposts of empire. There was evidence that old attitudes were dying when Trinidad and Tobago, Barbados, and Jamaica were admitted to the Organization of American States and to the Inter-American Development Bank.

A plan is now under way to build a communications network linking all of Latin America. In July officials of the Inter-American Development Bank, of the United Nations Development Program, and of 15 Latin-American countries signed an agreement laying the groundwork for the project. The countries included Barbados, the Dominican Republic, Haiti, and Trinidad and Tobago.

These signs of communication and co-operation were matched by intensive efforts at development in each island.

▶THE INDEPENDENT NATIONS
Barbados

Barbados, with a population of more than 1,300 to the square mile, reported that its Family Planning Campaign has begun to show results. The population increase is being held down to 1 per cent per year.

Attempts continued to diversify the economy of the island, which depended too heavily on one crop: sugarcane. A Physical Development Plan for the island has been prepared. With the help of the United States Agency for International Development, a large housing development is under way. The island has a record of stability and good government. These attracted overseas investors, especially in the area of hotel development.

Jamaica

Jamaica's rapid population increase—2.9 per cent a year—was the nation's number one problem. Each week 1,000 more babies are born, and 20 per cent of the adult labor force is unemployed. The island has set up a Family Planning Council and started on a national campaign to check the population increase.

Efforts at economic development have produced real results. Bauxite is now the island's first money earner. Tourism is second. In order to lessen the drift to Kingston, the capital city, factories are being established in other cities and country towns.

During the year, Jamaica was admitted to the Organization of American States and changed its system of foreign currency exchange from the British pound to the dollar.

Trinidad and Tobago

With its supplies of oil and asphalt, Trinidad is the most highly industrialized country in the Commonwealth Caribbean. Tobago, with its sparkling blue water and sandy beaches, draws visitors from other countries. In both islands, the Government is promoting agricultural projects, in order to reduce the large amounts of food that must be imported. The projects include the development of dairy products and a pig industry. The hunt for more oil beneath the sea continues.

▶DEPENDENT COUNTRIES
Antigua

No island shows in more dramatic form the benefits of tourism than Antigua. Tour-

	HEADS OF GOVERNMENT	POPULATION
Barbados	ERROL W. BARROW	302,700
Jamaica	HUGH SHEARER	1,947,500
Trinidad and Tobago	ERIC E. WILLIAMS	1,126,400

	STATUS	POPULATION
Antigua	British associated state	63,400
Bahama Islands	Self-governing British colony	149,400
British Virgin Islands	British colony	9,350
Cayman Islands	British colony	10,000
Dominica	British associated state	71,700
Grenada	British associated state	100,000
Guadeloupe	French overseas department	330,500
Martinique	French overseas department	341,000
Montserrat	British colony	14,300
Netherlands Antilles	Netherlands overseas constituent	215,000
Puerto Rico	U.S. commonwealth	2,831,000
St. Kitts-Nevis-Anguilla	British associated state	63,500
St. Lucia	British associated state	108,700
St. Vincent	British associated state	94,000
Turks and Caicos Islands	British colony	6,500
U.S. Virgin Islands	U.S. unincorporated territory	53,000

ism in 1969 continued to give the island the highest per capita income among the Associated States. Dams have been built as a safeguard against droughts. The airport and runway are being extended to accommodate jumbo jets.

Bahama Islands

The Bahamas have the largest tourist industry of all the English-speaking islands. The total area of the islands in the group is just over four thousand square miles. Their size is about the same as Jamaica's, but the population density is only thirty to the square mile. Thus their problems are in many ways different from those of other countries of the Commonwealth Caribbean. There are more jobs than there are workers, with a shortage of skilled and professional people. The Government has placed education and communications first in its development planning. The construction of a number of airstrips throughout the islands has made communication easier. Labor flows into the Bahamas from Jamaica and Haiti. In 1969 the Government of the Bahamas deported numbers of Jamaicans and Haitians as illegal immigrants.

British Virgin Islands

The British Virgin Islands have been drawn into the "jet stream." The result is that not only Tortola and Virgin Gorda but more remote islands, like Anegada and Peters Island, attracted investors. The capital, called Road Town because it once had only one road, now has hotels, a marina for oceangoing yachts, and expanding public services.

Cayman Islands

The largest of the three Caymans, Grand Cayman, has some of the finest swimming and fishing in the region. Mosquito and sand-fly control work is ridding the island of its only two pests. The number of tourists increases each month, but the largest income is from offshore companies and trusts. Five years ago there was one bank. Now there are more than twenty banks and trust companies. In 1969 the Caymans began to earn money as a tax haven.

Dominica

The largest of the Associated States, Dominica began to develop its substantial forest resources through concessions to overseas companies. The wild terrain and heavy rainfall (from 100 to 250 inches a year) make communications difficult, but the Government has built roads linking every village in the island with the capital town, Roseau.

Grenada, St. Lucia, and St. Vincent

These three islands have a relatively close association. They were linked together and administered by Great Britain as the Windward Islands. In October, St. Vincent became an Associated State, the last of the group to achieve this status.

Guadeloupe and Martinique

Governed by France, these islands continued to enjoy the benefits of the European Common Market, and of a swiftly growing tourist industry. Guadeloupe obtained about 90 per cent of its income from sugar, rum, and bananas. Martinique produces the same crops, and in addition, has cattle, pigs, and sheep. The population is culturally French, with little interest in the rest of the Caribbean.

Montserrat

Montserrat turned its energies to improving its harbor and airport facilities. Unlike its neighbors, the island has a falling rather than an increasing population. Even by Caribbean standards Montserrat is poor. Its 39 square miles are for the most part too rugged for cultivation.

The Netherlands Antilles

The most stable and comfortably placed of the smaller islands appeared to be the Netherlands Antilles. But the calm was broken by a disastrous outbreak of violence in Willemstad, Curaçao, in May. The immediate cause was the laying-off of workers at the Shell Oil Company refinery. The attractive shopping center in the city was wrecked; Dutch troops were flown in; the Government resigned; and an interim Government was appointed.

Puerto Rico

Puerto Rico inaugurated a new Governor, Luis A. Ferre, who supports the idea of statehood for the island. He has said that he will respect the island's Commonwealth status while he is governor, however. Sugar was once the mainstay of the economy, but 1969 production was the lowest in history. A modernization plan is under way, aimed at bringing sugar production up to one million tons a year by 1974. Governor Ferre announced plans to develop the southwestern third of the island. The plans include the building of a new airport.

St. Kitts-Nevis-Anguilla

The Associated State of St. Kitts-Nevis-Anguilla enjoyed calm after a stormy period. In 1967, Anguilla broke away from the three-island federation, charging it did not receive a fair share of British aid. In 1969, British troops landed on Anguilla because of reports of gangster influence and control. Anguillans, led by their president, Ronald Webster, did not resist. The British promised Anguillans they would not be forced to return to a Government they did not want. The British were able to work out a compromise with the St. Kitts Government. A British official became responsible for Anguillan affairs, and Great Britain supplied money for the improvement of public services. The Government in St. Kitts went ahead with plans for hotels and better airport facilities. An outside commission is to examine the problem to help a long-term solution.

PHILIP SHERLOCK
Secretary-General
Association of Caribbean Universities

YEMEN. See MIDDLE EAST.

Boypower and teamwork both help to set up a Boy Scout camp.

YOUTH ORGANIZATIONS

MEMBERSHIP in youth organizations was high in 1969. The Boy Scouts of America, Boys' Clubs of America, Camp Fire Girls, 4-H Clubs, Future Farmers of America, and Girl Scouts of the U.S.A. all sought to involve even more youth—particularly minority-group members and youths living in the city—in their programs.

▶ BOY SCOUTS OF AMERICA

On January 1, 1969, the Boy Scouts of America began a plan called BOY-POWER '76. The plan aims to bring into Scouting one of every three boys in the United States. The plan will end in 1976, the 200th anniversary of the United States. By that year more than 6,500,000 boys will be Scouts.

A new look has been given to the Exploring program for boys 14 to 18. For the first time girls may take part in Exploring. More and more Explorer posts selected special-interest activities. This was often done with a desire to learn more about specific careers. Each Explorer post made doing things for its city, town or neighborhood a part of its scout program.

Scout programs were increased for poor neighborhoods and for people who have difficulty with the English language. More needy Scouts and boys who were not Scouts went camping in Scout camps. This was done through a special program of help set up by the Boy Scouts of America.

During 1969, nearly 2,500,000 Cub Scouts, boys 8 through 10 years of age, enjoyed work on monthly programs that centered on such subjects as ghosts and goblins, river showboats, and Indians.

In July 35,000 Scouts took part in the 7th National Jamboree in Farragut State Park, Idaho. The Scouts set up their own tents and cooked their own meals. They fished and took part in water sports. They went hiking and mountain climbing. Each boy, as a member of an 8-boy patrol, lived in this city of 18,000 tents for eight days. The theme of the jamboree was Building to Serve. Each Scout returning from the jamboree chose a project, based on this theme, to carry out in his own home community.

The membership of the Boy Scouts of America continued to grow in 1969. It reached an all-time high of nearly 5,000,-000 boys and 1,750,000 adults.

ALDEN G. BARBER
Chief Scout Executive
Boy Scouts of America

▶ BOYS' CLUBS OF AMERICA

In many neighborhoods, Boys' Club programs answered such street-corner complaints as "we have nothing to do." Indeed, during 1969, Boys' Clubs of America served more youths in more ways than ever before. By year's end, some 850 Boys' Clubs were in operation. These provided daily activities and guidance for over 850,000 young people in 46 states.

Activities placed especial emphasis on serving the inner-city youth, without neglecting his country cousin. Vocational training, education and cultural programs, and job counseling were just a few of the areas in which Boys' Clubs involved themselves. This is very much in line with the century-old Boys' Clubs philosophy of a positive approach to youth guidance.

At ceremonies in the White House, President Nixon congratulates 17-year-old Perry J. Ludy, Boys' Clubs of America "Boy of the Year."

On the average, one new Boys' Club was started each week. Still, the demand for more Boys' Club facilities was heard in hundreds of communities. Boys' Clubs spent more than $30,000,000 on new buildings, alterations, and camps.

The 63d annual convention of the Boys' Clubs of America was held in San Francisco from April 28 through May 1. Here some 1,000 professional Boys' Club workers sharpened their skills on such topics as drug abuse, inner-city problems, delinquency, and race relations.

Three days before the adult convention, teen-age members held their own convention. They discussed some of the same topics. More than 260 delegates from 50 cities in 22 states and Canada attended.

On March 19, in White House ceremonies, President Nixon named 17-year-old Perry J. Ludy of Oxnard, California, as the Boys' Club "Boy of the Year" for 1969. The President, honorary chairman of the Boys' Clubs of America, said that the tall scholar-athlete typified "juvenile decency in action." Young Ludy is the first Negro to win top national honors in the 23-year history of the event.

The start of the Nixon administration ended his Boys' Club administration. Mr. Nixon had served as board chairman for four years. During that time, membership and number of clubs had increased 30 per cent.

A. L. Cole, board president under Mr. Nixon, was elected to succeed him as board chairman. John L. Burns was named president. A. Boyd Hinds, a 40-year veteran of Boys' Club work, continued as national director.

E. J. STAPLETON
Director of Public Information
Boys' Clubs of America

▶CAMP FIRE GIRLS

In the summer of 1969 the Camp Fire Girls ran an exchange program in the United States for teen-age Horizon Club members. The girls visited and did volunteer community service in areas away from home. From Alaska to the east coast, the girls worked at day camps, on conservation projects, backpacked in national forests, developed primitive campsites, perfected outdoor skills, banded birds, and tagged butterflies.

The Camp Fire Girls ended its Metropolitan Critical Areas Project in 1969. The aim of the project was to test the programs of the Camp Fire Girls in highly crowded urban areas. As a result of the project, the Camp Fire Girls will offer programs to meet the needs of low-income girls living in crowded city neighborhoods.

Over 600,000 girls from age 7 through high-school age were in the Camp Fire Girls in 1969. And Camp Fire programs were carried out by over 400 chartered councils and associations throughout the United States.

AUDREY M. HUDSON
Camp Fire Girls, Inc.

▶4-H CLUBS

More than 3,500,000 4-H boys and girls spent a busy 1969. Most engaged in "learn by doing" projects in science, agriculture, home economics, personal development, community service, leadership, and citizenship.

The largest project enrollments were in animal science, plant science, clothing, foods and nutrition, health and fitness, recreation and crafts, engineering, safety, and community service. More than 500,000 9- to 19-year-olds took part in 4-H by television. A 4-H television educational series showed members how to do projects at home.

Nationwide, in 1969 the number of 4-H'ers in towns, cities, and suburbs grew rapidly. Nearly 32 per cent now live in urban and suburban areas. And more than 33 per cent are called "rural nonfarm" because although their homes are in the country, their families do not farm for a livelihood. About 35 per cent of 4-H'ers live on farms.

4-H members everywhere observed National 4-H Week in the fall. The October

5–11 theme was "4-H: Opportunity for All." During the 4-H Week, more youth were encouraged to join 4-H. And more men and women were urged to volunteer as 4-H local leaders.

The National 4-H Conference was held in Washington, D.C., for the 39th successive year. The conference was attended by about 225 delegates: 4 or 5 each from all the states, Puerto Rico, and the District of Columbia. The young people spent much of their time in groups. They discussed such topics as reaching the unreached, nutrition programs to feed hungry Americans, community needs, international relations and the impact on youth. Afterward the delegates made recommendations to their state and Federal professional 4-H leaders on how they felt 4-H could serve youth still more effectively.

About 1,650 high-ranking 4-H'ers attended the National 4-H Congress in Chicago in December. All were state, regional, or national winners of awards. More than 200 of these 4-H'ers received college scholarships valued at $500 to $1,600 each.

In 1969 about 200 young men and women were International Farm Youth Exchangees. About half were from 40 countries around the world. And about half were U.S. delegates from nearly 40 states. 4-H programs now reach around the world. The programs have been adapted to suit needs and conditions in about 85 countries.

E. Dean Vaughan
Director, 4-H Programs

▶ FUTURE FARMERS OF AMERICA

Future Farmers of America, the national organization of vocational agriculture students, had nearly 450,000 members in more than 8,500 local high-school chapters in 1969. The FFA is active in all states except Alaska. It also has chapters in Puerto Rico, the Virgin Islands, and Guam.

More than 12,600 FFA members and their guests attended the 42d National FFA Convention in Kansas City, Missouri, in October. The 115 official delegates, in a narrow vote, approved an amendment to the constitution which allows female membership. Until the vote, the FFA was an all-male organization. The delegates also approved an amendment creating an alumni category of membership.

In the election of national officers, Harry Wayne Birdwell, 20, of Fletcher, Oklahoma, was elected to serve as the 1969–70 National FFA president. His fellow officers are Dennis Joe Pharris, 19, of Hillsboro, Texas, secretary, and the four vice presidents, Steven E. Zumbach, 19, of Manchester, Iowa; Donald K. Shinn, 20, Columbus, New Jersey; David Dietz, 19, of Canby, Oregon; and C. W. St. John, 19, of Redfield, Arkansas. The new officers will serve through the 1970 National Convention.

Oscar J. Manbeck, a 21-year-old dairy farmer from Bethel, Pennsylvania, was named Star Farmer of America. This is the FFA's most coveted award. For the first time, the FFA presented the Star

Star Farmer of America Oscar J. Manbeck.

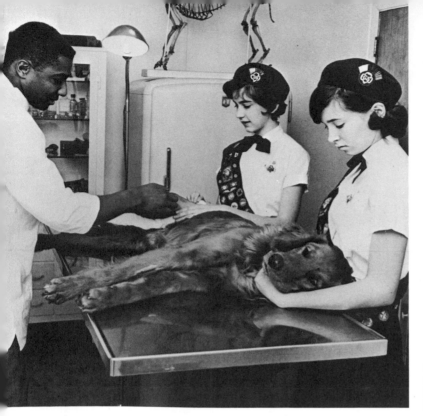

Scouts help care for a stray dog. This is one of the new Girl Scout community service programs.

Agri-Businessman of America award. This award recognizes outstanding work in agricultural-related professions. Ken Dunagan, 20, who operates a custom spraying and harvesting business near Willcox, Arizona, was the first vocational agricultural student to receive the Star Agri-Businessman award. Both Manbeck and Dunagan were presented $1,000 cash awards. Regional runners-up in the Star Farmer award were Walter T. Hudson, 21, Unadilla, Georgia; John D. Prahl, 22, Neoga, Illinois; and Gary A. Wollweber, 21, Edwall, Washington. Runners-up for the Star Agri-Businessman award were Charles S. Postles, Jr., 20, Milford, Delaware; Roger L. Phelps, 20, Marysville, Ohio; and Charlie Seidel, Jr., 19, New Braunfels, Texas.

Edward B. Hatchett, Jr., 18, of Glasgow, Kentucky, won the FFA's National Public Speaking Contest.

In 1969, the FFA began a "Work Experience Abroad" program to give students from the United States and abroad an opportunity to share in the farm life of a different country. Eight European countries provided homes for 31 FFA members. They lived for three summer months with host farm families. In the United States, 44 foreign students from nine countries lived and worked on farms.

A. D. Reuwee
Director of Information,
Future Farmers of America

▶ GIRL SCOUTS OF THE U.S.A.

In 1969 the Girl Scouts of the U.S.A. began a project called ACTION 70. Its goal is to fight prejudice and increase understanding among people. More than 3,750,000 Girl Scouts of all ages took part in this effort. Ideas for ACTION 70 were received from Senior Girl Scouts. Specific ways to carry out these goals were presented at the triennial National Council Meeting of Girl Scouts of the U.S.A. This meeting was held in Seattle, Washington, in October 1969.

In 1969 nearly 3,000 girls took part in international, national, and council-operated events in the United States and other countries.

During the year more than 250 Girl Scouts and Girl Guides took part in camps, conferences, and other international projects involving 38 countries. Of these girls, 183 were U.S.A. Cadette, Senior, and adult Girl Scouts. The rest were Girl Scouts from other countries. Some of these girls lived and worked with Girl Scouts in the United States. Others met with Girl Scouts abroad. Voluntary gifts to the Juliette Low World Friendship Fund from many thousands of U.S.A. Girl Scouts helped make these projects possible.

A major event for teen-age girls was an international conference held at the Girl Scout Cabana in Mexico. And five trips were made to Canada, France, Greece, Jamaica, and the Benelux countries. This gave many of the girls a chance to learn about these countries.

Nationally operated Girl Scout events in the summer of 1969 included a seminar for museum aides. This event was held in July at the Juliette Gordon Low Birthplace in Savannah, Georgia. There the 24 girls observed the workings of a museum. They also took part in arts workshops. These familiarized the girls in the architecture and crafts of the Victorian era, represented by the Birthplace and by historic restoration in Savannah.

In August, 416 older girls attended an All-States Rendezvous at the Girl Scout National Center West. This is the newest national property of the Girl Scouts of the U.S.A. It is in a magnificent setting of natural beauty in northern Wyoming. The girls had no imposed schedule. Rather, they made and carried out their own plans. Consultants skilled in natural sciences, geology, backpacking, music, archeology, and communications worked with the girls.

The Girl Scout Edith Macy Training Center in Westchester County, New York, was the scene of "Encounters by Dialogue" during July and August. Boys, girls, and young adults attended this three-week event. The sessions focused on the most relevant program for Girl Scouting in view of changing youth culture. Those attending discussed "What has Girl Scouting to do with racism, poverty, drug addiction, activism and dissent, family-life education, the arts, dress, and manners of young people today?"

Eleven council-operated events in 1969 were nationwide in scope. Among these events were six 12-day Canadian boundary canoe trips. Other gatherings took place in camp or university settings. These included a "World of People—Let's Talk" conference at Kent State University. Another was a "Reach Out" assemblage at Camp Innisfree, Michigan. "Heritage" excursions explored the Mississippi River area and points in Illinois and Missouri, as well as San Diego, California.

Early in 1969 a summary report was received on some 200 "Speakouts." These had been conducted by Senior Scouts all over the United States. In these forums girls from 15 to 17 discussed how to break down the walls of prejudice among people.

A drive was made to extend Girl Scouting to girls in isolated rural and inner-city areas. And there was a strong effort to develop leadership among minority-group members. As a result Girl Scout membership in some areas increased.

During the year, 24 Girl Scouts of the U.S.A. Life Saving Awards were presented. Four Girl Scouts were among those high-school seniors named as 1969 Presidential Scholars. They were honored by President Nixon in a June 20 ceremony on the White House lawn.

In June 1969, Tricia Nixon, a former Girl Scout, was honored by the Girl Scouts of the U.S.A. in a White House ceremony. She was given the press plate of her picture that appeared on the cover of the June issue of the Girl Scout publication, *American Girl.*

LOUISE A. WOOD
National Executive Director
Girl Scouts of the U.S.A.

YUGOSLAVIA. See EUROPE, EAST.

ZAMBIA. See AFRICA.

dictionary supplement

By Bruce Bohle

A

ABM *abbreviation.* Antiballistic missile. Often used in the phrase "ABM system." Such a system is designed to defend a country from the attacking missiles of another country. An ABM system usually has three parts: radar, a computer, and defensive missiles. Long-range and short-range radar detects enemy attacking missiles in flight. A computer directs and co-ordinates the system's overall operation. And defensive missiles intercept and destroy the enemy missiles before the enemy missiles reach their destination.

acquisition and tracking radar. Radar equipment used to search for and locate a spaceship in flight and then to trace the spaceship's course, or path, as it travels.

airbag *noun.* A safety appliance carried in an automobile as protection against injury to passengers. The bag is designed so that, in the event of an accident, the impact causes the interior of the bag to be filled with air quickly and automatically. The filled bag is intended to act as a cushion or buffer.

Al Fatah (also **Fatah**). The principal band of Palestinian guerrilla fighters active in the warfare between Arab states and Israel.

Alliance for Labor Action. An agreement between two leading U.S. labor unions, the Teamsters Union and the United Automobile Workers, reached in 1969. The unions pledged themselves to work together for the advancement of labor in general; especially to work for the passage of laws and the creation of programs, within the government or private industry, that seek to give working people as a class a better life.

AMSA *acronym.* Advanced manned strategic aircraft. A large U.S. bomber designed for long-range supersonic flight.

ao dai *noun.* A native dress worn by the women of South Vietnam. It is made of silk that permits the partial passage of light. It has a long, moderately full skirt that is slit on one side from the waist to the hemline at shoe level.

apocynthion *noun.* The highest point, or altitude, above the moon that is reached by a spaceship when it is traveling in orbit around the moon. (The term comes from Cynthia, one of the names for the goddess of the moon in ancient Greek religion.)

APS *abbreviation.* Ascent propulsion system. The equipment, especially the rocket engine, used by astronauts for a return trip to their spaceship while the spaceship is in a fixed orbit. For example, such equipment used by astronauts following a landing on the moon, when they seek to propel themselves back to the mother spaceship, which has been left to orbit the moon.

Arab Liberation Front. A Ba'athist (socialist) guerrilla organization in Iraq.

area defense. A method of protecting a country from the possibility of attack by enemy missiles. It uses an antiballistic-missile system (that is, anti-missile missiles, which seek and attempt to destroy enemy missiles in flight). It is planned to provide maximum protection for large areas, such as cities and their suburbs, rather than to protect isolated, or widely spaced, places that have direct military value. In this it differs from "point defense" (which see).

ARVN *abbreviation.* Army of the Republic of (South) Vietnam.

ascent stage. In space travel, the upper portion of the lunar module, housing the flight crew, ascent engine, and flight controls. See **lunar module**.

astromonk *noun.* A monkey sent on a flight into outer space to test the effects of a long space trip on a traveler's physical and mental well-being.

B

balanced fund. A mutual fund in which investments are made both in common stocks and in preferred stocks, and bonds.

ball control. Possession football (which see).

beautiful people. Hippies or young people like them, especially when in striking and colorful dress.

black capitalism. An economic system under which Negroes own and manage businesses or business undertakings, rather than serving only as employees.

black lung. *Informal.* Pneumoconiosis. A disease of the lungs known informally also as "miner's asthma." It is caused by breathing air filled with coal dust or similar mineral or metallic material. The disease is common among underground workers in soft-coal mines.

Black Panther party. An American organization with national headquarters in Oakland, Calif. It was founded to help Negroes secure full civil rights (those giving them legal, economic, and social equality with whites), by force if necessary, and to protect them from alleged police brutality. In 1969 the party broadened its goal by adopting a socialist program aimed at bettering the lot of all minority groups and the poor considered as a class, regardless of race.

broken play. A busted play (which see).

burn *verb tr.* To fire a rocket engine or engines of a spaceship while it is in flight. That is, to cause them to be ignited.

busted play (also **broken play**). In football a play, run by the team in possession of the ball, that differs from the one called by the quarterback. Such a makeshift play comes about, on the spur of the moment, when a fumble, a misunderstanding, or a similar blunder by one of the players makes it impossible to carry out the original plan of the quarterback.

buy in. To obtain an order or contract from the Federal Government, especially one from the Department of Defense, for the supplying of goods or services. Usually, to get such a contract by deliberately submitting a low bid, in the hope of getting extra payment before the contract is fulfilled. (Such contracts frequently have provided for extra payment where it could be justified.) See **overrun**.

C

cap com *acronym. Informal.* Capsule communicator. A person in a ground station who is assigned to communicate with astronauts in flight.

CBW *abbreviation.* Chemical and biological warfare. Warfare using agents such as poisonous gases and disease germs.

celestial guidance. In space travel the guidance that is provided for a craft in flight by relating its position to that of celestial bodies; guidance obtained by observing the position of visible planets.

China watcher. *Informal.* A specialist in Chinese affairs. Particularly a politician, student of politics, or diplomat who tries to forecast or explain the actions of the Communist Chinese as they affect the rest of the world.

clout *noun. Slang.* Power; influence; ability to accomplish something that one wants.

coloration *noun.* The sum of a person's beliefs, ideas, and ideals that sets a pattern for his behavior, that indicates how he thinks on matters affecting society as a whole and how he votes.

COMECON *acronym.* Council for Mutual Economic Assistance. The communist, Eastern European economic union similar in aim to the European Common Market. It was organized to integrate, or bring together under the direction of the Soviet Union, the economies of East Germany, Poland, Hungary, Bulgaria, Rumania, Czechoslovakia, Mongolia, and the Soviet Union. As such, it provides control over the affairs of those nations with respect to production of goods and services, distribution of such goods and services, trade, and development of natural resources.

command module. In space travel, that part of the spaceship in which the astronauts are housed during most of the flight. It serves as their living quarters, principal working quarters, and home base when they attempt space walks, descent to the moon's surface, or the like. See **CSM; service module.**

confrontation politics. An attempt to bring about quick and marked change, as in government, law, social institutions, or the way in which anything is run, by taking direct and forceful action rather than by relying on peaceful and gradual political means, such as petitioning and voting. This involves a head-on clash with those persons in authority and the refusal to accept their authority. The direct action often takes the form of mass protests or picketing, sit-in demonstrations, and the seizure of property.

conglomerate *noun.* A large corporation made up of companies in unrelated industries; thus a group of companies in completely different lines of business but owned or controlled by a single parent firm.

coop *verb intr. Slang.* To sleep while assigned to duty, instead of being on watch or patrol. (Said of a policeman.) —*noun.* A place where such a policeman sleeps, usually the interior of a parked patrol car or of a building located on his beat.

Corporation for Public Broadcasting (CPB). A federally chartered U.S. agency established by Congress "to encourage the growth and development of noncommercial educational radio and television." See **public television.**

cost overrun. An overrun (which see).

crash pad. *Slang.* Temporary lodgings or living quarters shared by hippies or other persons who lead a roving, unsettled life.

crazy *noun. Slang.* A youthful extremist; one who goes to extremes in demonstrating or protesting against something, such as the running of a university.

crunch *noun. Slang.* Something extremely difficult and usually demanding prompt action; a hard problem or task, or a period of crisis.

CSM *abbreviation.* Command and service module. This is the main component of a spaceship and consists of the command module and service module joined. See **command module; service module.**

cybernetic anthropomorphous machine (also **CAM, walking machine**). A machine, resembling a robot, or mechanical man, built to perform heavy work. It is 11 feet tall and has four jointed legs and a top structure for housing the man who operates it. The machine is capable of lifting objects weighing up to 500 pounds and of moving along the ground, with its front legs, objects twice this heavy. It was built by General Electric Co., under the supervision of Ralph S. Mosher, and first demonstrated publicly in April 1969.

D

delivery system. The way in which a branch of the government provides a service, such as medical care for the aged or poor; the machinery for carrying out programs intended to help people. Also the actual performance of such services, distinct from the laws that make them possible.

descent propulsion system. In space travel a system for controlling the descent, or downward flight, of a ship; especially, a rocket engine designed to brake, or slow, the descent of a lunar module as it nears the moon's surface. See **lunar module.**

descent stage. The lower portion of the lunar module, containing the descent engine and fuel tanks together with landing gear and storage sections. See **lunar module.**

destruct system. A means or method for destroying something intentionally and according to a plan or system worked out in advance. For example, a device for destroying a missile in flight, or a system for destroying secret military or scientific equipment or codes in danger of capture by an enemy.

diminished responsibility. In the eyes of the law, the condition of a person not fully responsible or answerable for what he does, yet legally sane. Such a person is said to act under diminished capacity; that is, without being fully aware of what he is doing at a given time and therefore not completely in control of his actions.

DMZ *abbreviation.* Demilitarized zone. An area separating two opposing sides in a war, where, by agreement of the two, no fighting or preparation for fighting is to take place. For example, the strip of land established to separate the forces of South Vietnam and North Vietnam and their allies at the border of those countries, or the similar truce area separating North Korean and South Korean armies.

doomsday clock. A clockface, pictured regularly in the *Bul-*

letin of the Atomic Scientists (published at the University of Chicago), that is intended to show how close the world is to nuclear war at a given time. As the hands of the clock approach midnight, the closeness to such war increases, and a reading of midnight would mean nuclear war itself. In March 1969, the clock read ten minutes before midnight. The last previous reading, in January 1968, was seven minutes to midnight.

doomsday machine. An imaginary machine built by one nation and able to destroy an enemy completely. The machine would be controlled by a computer that would trigger the machine automatically if the enemy did any act listed in advance as unfriendly and forbidden.

DPS *abbreviation.* Descent propulsion system (which see).

dragster *noun. Slang.* A drag racer.

DSRV *abbreviation.* Deep-sea rescue vessel. A U.S. Navy diving craft for rescuing crewmen of disabled submarines.

E

Electronic Video Recording (EVR). A television system that enables a viewer at home, or a group in a classroom, to watch selected material on film as it is played back through a conventional (home) television receiver. The system works much in the way a listener hears the content of a recording played back on a phonograph. Specially made miniature films are inserted, in the form of cartridges, into an electronic playback device attached to a television set. The playback device acts like a miniature television transmitter, changing what is on the film into electrical impulses and feeding them into the television receiver where they are seen on an unused channel. The film can be stopped at any point so that viewers may examine the content of a single picture.

emp *acronym. Informal.* Electromagnetic pulse. A strong, brief pulse of electricity that is generated, or brought about, by a nuclear explosion.

ESSA *acronym.* Environmental survey satellite. A U.S. unmanned spacecraft used in forecasting weather.

Euratom *acronym.* European Atomic Energy Community.

EVA *abbreviation.* Extravehicular activity (which see).

EVR *abbreviation.* Electronic Video Recording (which see).

extravehicular activity. Activity by an astronaut outside his spaceship during a flight. This includes a walk in space or a walk on the moon's surface.

extravehicular mobility unit (EMU). A space suit and other equipment worn by an astronaut during extravehicular activity. See entry above.

F

family *noun.* A division of the Cosa Nostra or Mafia; one of the groups of persons making up those organizations and having charge of gangland activities within a certain territory.

first-strike capability. The ability of a nation to make an attack on an enemy, with nuclear arms, from which the enemy could not recover; the ability to strike first and with such great force that the attacker need have no fear of being hit by return blows of any great force. See **second-strike capability.**

flap *noun. Slang.* Excitement; argument or quarreling; controversy.

flat-out *adjective.* All-out; with full effort or speed from the very beginning; not holding back a reserve of strength.

forthcoming *adjective. Informal.* Having an outgoing personality; easy to know or to speak to. (Often used by Secretary of State William P. Rogers to describe himself.)

four-point play. In basketball a play in which 4 points are scored: 3 as a result of a field goal, and 1 as a result of a successful free throw awarded because the player was fouled while making the field goal. Under the usual rules, such a play results in 3 points, including 2 from the field goal. Under experimental rules of the American Basketball Association, a professional league, 3 points were awarded for a field goal resulting from a shot made 25 feet or more from the basket.

G

G *abbreviation.* "Suggested for general audiences"; a motion picture considered suitable for children and adults alike. (A rating for movies, from the code of self-regulation of the Motion Picture Association of America.)

game ball. A football awarded by members of a winning team to one of their players chosen by them as the man who contributed most to the victory. The award is made shortly after the game is over.

game plan. In football the way in which a team intends to play in a given game; overall strategy; a plan of action considered by the coach as offering the best chance for victory.

gaposis *noun. Slang.* 1. Failure (of things) to match or be equal: *the gaposis between what we want and what we can afford.* 2. Lack of understanding or trust between persons: *Gaposis often affects parents and their children.*

G-forces *noun, usually plural.* Gravity forces, especially as they affect man's normal weight (what he weighs while on the ground) during travel in outer space.

golden slippers. *Slang.* In space exploration the gold-plated foot restraints, or supports, employed by an astronaut to keep him steady and in position as he works in space just outside his ship.

ground-elapsed time. In space travel, time calculated from the lift-off, or takeoff of a ship from earth; the number of days, hours, minutes, and seconds after the lift-off.

groupie *noun. Slang.* A girl who greatly admires rock'n'roll music, and who likes to gather round its star performers with others of her kind.

H

handgun *noun.* A gun intended to be operated with one hand of the person firing it; a pistol.

headend *noun.* In cable television the large master antenna that picks up broadcast signals and transmits, or sends, them, through a cable, into the television receiving sets of home viewers.

helicopter gunship (also **gunship helicopter**). A helicopter made for use in areas of heavy fighting. It is heavily armed for warfare and usually very maneuverable.

HEOS *acronym.* Highly Eccentric Orbit Satellite. An unmanned spacecraft developed by Western European industrialists. It is designed to orbit the earth and, in so doing, to measure radiation and study the earth's magnetic field.

Hold Me (also **Hold Me Darling, Tennessee Hold Me, Texas Hold 'Em**). A card game that uses most of the basic rules and techniques of poker. It differs in that up to 22 persons can play. Each player is dealt 2 cards for his hand, and each attempts to match these with 5 cards laid face up in the middle of the table to make the best 5-card hand.

House Committee on Internal Security. A committee of the U.S. House of Representatives, created to investigate organizations and persons that seek to overthrow the Federal Government "by force, violence, treachery, espionage, sabotage, insurrection, or any unlawful means." It has approximately the same duties as the former House Committee on Un-American Activities (HUAC), whose place it took in February 1969.

I

IMPACT *acronym.* Innovative Methods of Progressive Action for Community Tranquility. A program designed to fight poverty in the United States. It operates under agencies of the Federal, state, and local government and is intended to provide employment and cultural opportunities for the poor.

independent player. A player (which see).

instant replay. In television the showing again of an important part of live action, especially the action of a sports event, seconds after it has occurred, by means of the playback of a video tape.

Intelsat *acronym.* International Telecommunications Satellite Consortium. A union of more than sixty nations, including the United States, linked by communications satellites, or unmanned spacecraft used to relay television and telephone signals around the world to member nations. "Intelsat" is also used as the name of such satellites, which make possible the sending of telephone messages or television pictures from one nation to others far distant.

interface *noun.* Close communication between persons or groups, and co-ordination of their activities; liaison.

interrobang *noun.* A punctuation mark formed by superimposing (writing or printing) an exclamation point on a question mark. It is used, chiefly humorously, to express a sense of questioning or doubt mixed with surprise.

IUD *abbreviation.* Intra-uterine device. A contraceptive inserted in the female uterine cavity.

J

jawbone control. Control of wages and prices by the force of public opinion, especially by criticism of wage and price increases considered excessive or unreasonable by the public. This differs from wage and price controls laid down by law or by an agreement among workers, their employers, and (sometimes) the government.

jetport *noun.* An airport built for use by jet aircraft and thus capable of accommodating large jet airliners.

K

kurchatovium *noun.* Element No. 104 in the periodic table of chemical elements, according to Soviet Russian scientists. The Russians have claimed discovery and successful production of this heavy synthetic element, named for a leading Soviet physicist. Kurchatovium is in the same family of metals as titanium, zirconium, and hafnium.

L

Law Enforcement Assistance Administration. A U.S. governmental agency, part of the Department of Justice, created to fight crime. Its main job is to supervise the use of Federal money given to state and local governments to improve their systems of enforcing laws and bringing to justice persons accused of crime.

L-dopa (full name **Levo-dihydroxyphenylalanine**) *noun.* An amino acid present in the normal human brain and given in the treatment of Parkinson's disease, a disease of the central nervous system. In successful treatment, L-dopa is changed into dopamine through the body metabolism of the patient. The formation of dopamine, which is lacking in a Parkinson's patient, permits the normal working of his lower brain.

LEB *abbreviation.* Lower equipment bay of a spaceship.

lem *acronym.* See **lunar module.**

LGM *abbreviation.* Little green man. In some scientific writing and science fiction, an intelligent being somewhere in the universe besides earth and corresponding, on his own planet, to man on earth.

lip-sync *noun. Slang.* Lip synchronization. In television or motion pictures, the movement of the lips of a singer or speaker so that it appears he is producing the sound heard, when the sound is actually coming from a recording made by him or another person.

LLTV *abbreviation.* Lunar landing training vehicle (which see).

LM *abbreviation.* Lunar module (which see).

LOI *abbreviation.* Lunar orbit insertion. The act of bringing a spaceship into orbit around the moon.

looter-shooter *noun. Slang.* A public official, such as a governor, mayor, or police chief, who orders the shooting by police of persons who steal from shops and other business places during periods of racial rioting.

LTV *abbreviation.* Ling-Temco-Vought, Inc. One of the largest conglomerates in the United States, based in Dallas. By the late 1960's it had acquired more than thirty companies and was involved in more than eighty different lines of business. See **conglomerate.**

lunar landing training vehicle (**LLTV**). A U.S. craft, consisting of a wingless platform with a turbofan and thruster jet engines, used to train astronauts on earth for moon landings.

lunar module (also **LM, lunar exploratory module, lunar excursion module, lem, lunar landing craft**). The portion of a spaceship designed to land astronauts on the moon and then to take them from the moon back to the mother ship, to which the lunar module is linked during a moon flight.

M

M *abbreviation.* "Suggested for mature audiences (parental discretion advised)"; a motion picture considered suitable mostly for adults. (A rating for movies, from the code of self-regulation of the Motion Picture Association of America.)

Mailgram *noun.* A form of postal service provided by the U.S. Post Office Department and Western Union, as an experiment, beginning in 1969. It is a combination of service given to first-class mail and night letters. Mailgram messages are sent over Western Union lines to teleprinters located in post offices of those cities chosen to participate in the test; then they are delivered the following day by postmen on their regular mail routes.

Metroamerican *noun.* A young, adult, well-to-do and well-educated city dweller or suburbanite in the United States. He and others of his kind are thought of as a class having considerable influence in American political and social life.

Metroliner *noun.* A high-speed, all-electric train, one of a group that began operating between New York City and Washington, D.C., in January 1969, as a joint project of the U.S. Government and Penn Central Railroad.

minidress *noun.* A dress having a miniskirt, or very short skirt.

minority business enterprise. A business, usually small in size, that is owned or managed by members of a U.S. minority group, such as Negroes, Puerto Ricans, or persons of Mexican birth or parents.

MOBE (also **MOB**) *acronym.* National Mobilization Committee to End the War in Viet-

nam. A union of about one hundred American peace groups devoted to ending the war in Vietnam.

moonman *noun. Slang.* An astronaut on a flight to the moon or on one intended to orbit the moon.

MSR *abbreviation.* Missile-site radar. Part of an ABM system. This short-range radar directs defensive missiles (antimissile missiles) against incoming enemy attacking missiles, after being given the path of the enemy missiles in flight. See **ABM; PAR.**

mud *noun. Informal.* A mixture of clay, chemicals, and water that hardens like concrete and is used to stop the leaking of oil from oil wells running out of control.

N

New Canadians. Canadians whose parents or grandparents were neither English nor French.

New Democratic Coalition. A U.S. political organization of liberal Democrats made up chiefly of supporters of Eugene J. McCarthy, Robert F. Kennedy, and George McGovern in the presidential campaign of 1968.

nguoi thuong. The common man (of Vietnam), so called in the Vietnamese language.

Now generation. American youth of the late 1960's; especially, young people in revolt against rules of conduct laid down by older persons in authority, including their parents.

O

octopus *noun. Slang.* A hose, attached to an astronaut's space suit, that leads to his supply of oxygen.

overrun *noun.* Extra payment charged to the U.S. Government by a contractor, builder, or supplier of a service. The extra payment is the difference between the estimated cost of the job (what the builder or supplier thought the cost would be) and the amount he claims to have spent in providing goods or services because of rising prices of labor or material or extra work involved.

P

pacemaker *noun.* An electrically operated mechanical device inserted beneath the skin and connected to the heart of a person suffering from heart disease. Its purpose is to stimulate the heart and to set a new and desired pace for its beat, especially, a regular pulse rate.

PAR *abbreviation.* Perimeter acquisition radar. Part of an ABM system, whose job is to detect the approach of an enemy attacking missile at long range, to determine the path of the incoming enemy missile, and to send this information to the missile-site radar (MSR). See **ABM; MSR.**

peace dividend (also **peace-and-growth dividend**). The money that would be available to the U.S. Government to meet the needs of the country at home, and to permit the lowering of taxes, if a stable peace came to the world—especially with the end of fighting in South Vietnam.

peak *verb intr.* To reach a point of highest popularity or strength, as in a political campaign.

people's park. A public park, especially one created on privately owned land without necessarily getting permission of the owner.

pericynthion *noun.* The point of lowest altitude reached by a spaceship while flying in orbit around the moon.

player (also **independent player**) *noun.* An American nonprofessional tennis player who, unlike one classed as an amateur, can compete for prize money in open tournaments. The class or category of "player" was created in 1969 by the U.S. Lawn Tennis Association.

point defense. A method of defending a nation from attack by enemy missiles. It uses an ABM system and chiefly seeks to protect those areas that have direct military value, including military bases, command centers, and especially those areas where the nation stores its own offensive missiles (that is, missiles used not to destroy enemy missiles in flight but to strike at the enemy's own territory). See **ABM; area defense.**

possession football. A style of play in which a team seeks to control the action by keeping possession of the ball as much as possible; that is, by being the offensive (attacking) side and keeping the opposing team on the defensive. Such a style means taking few risks that could lead to fumbles or pass interceptions.

pressure point. In professional football the point after touchdown scored not by a placekick (conversion) but by a run or pass starting from the opponents' two-yard line.

preventive detention. The holding in jail of a person who has a criminal record, while he is awaiting trial on a new charge of breaking the law. Such a person is not granted temporary freedom, on bail, because it is feared he might break the law yet again before his trial and thus endanger society.

psych (also **psych up**) *verb tr.* To put a person, often oneself, in a desired frame of mind. To prepare psychologically.

PTV *abbreviation.* Public television (which see).

public television. Noncommercial television; programing not supported by the sale of advertising and not presented on a channel that sells commercials. Educational programs make up much of public television, which is often used interchangeably with the term "educational television" (ETV).

Q

QE2 *abbreviation.* The ship *Queen Elizabeth 2,* which entered service in 1969.

R

R *abbreviation.* "Restricted—persons under 16 not admitted unless accompanied by a parent or adult guardian." (A rating for movies, from the code of self-regulation of the Motion Picture Association of America.)

residual *noun.* In television an extra payment made to a performer, writer, or other contributor after the first showing of a program. Such payment is made for the right to show the program a second time or more.

Revitalization Corps. An American organization that resembles the Peace Corps but is privately operated. It was founded in Hartford, Conn., by Edward T. Coll to improve the life of slum dwellers in U.S. cities.

S

SCAD *acronym.* Subsonic cruise armed decoy. An American pilotless airborne weapon, a combination small bomber and decoy, designed for launching from a large bomber while many miles from its target. It is equipped with a warhead of more than twenty kilotons, together with a reflective radar device that causes it to appear the size of a large bomber on enemy radar screens.

schlepp *verb intr. Slang.* To walk slowly, ungracefully, and with marked effort; to plod.—*noun.* A dull, stupid person.

second-strike capability. The power of a nation to strike back with nuclear weapons in the event of a surprise enemy nuclear attack.

service module. That part of a spaceship containing engine, propellant tanks, and fuel cells. In operation, during most of the flight, it is joined with the command module to form the CSM. See **CSM.**

silo (also **launch facility**) *noun.* An underground storage place for an intercontinental ballistic missile.

Spartan missile. A defensive missile (that is, antimissile missile), part of the U.S. Safeguard antiballistic-missile system. It is a long-range missile designed to intercept enemy attacking missiles above the earth's atmosphere at altitudes between 200 and 400 miles. See **ABM.**

Sprint missile. A defensive missile, part of the U.S. Safeguard antiballistic-missile system. It is designed to intercept and destroy enemy attacking missiles at short range; that is, enemy missiles that have managed to approach their targets without being destroyed by Spartan missiles (see above).

SRAM *acronym.* Short-range attack missile. A U.S. nuclear missile that can be fired against an enemy target from a bombing plane in flight.

SS-9 *code name of U.S. intelligence.* A large and powerful intercontinental ballistic missile of the Soviet Union. It is said to be 120 feet in height and capable of hurling a warhead (the forward section containing the explosive) of from 8,000 to 12,500 pounds over a distance of 7,000 miles.

SST *abbreviation.* Supersonic transport (aircraft).

stack-up *noun. Informal.* Congestion or overcrowding at or over an airport, caused by air traffic that is too heavy to be handled in the space provided by the airport.

stovepipe pants (also, informally, **stoves**). Trousers, worn by young men or boys, with very thin, untapered, cylindrical coverings for the legs.

street people. Persons accustomed to gathering with their friends in or along public streets; especially, those without permanent or regular homes.

T

teach-in *noun.* A gathering of university students and faculty members for close study and examination of a topic of current interest, by means of lectures and discussions.

TEI *abbreviation.* Trans-earth injection. That point in a space flight when a ship breaks out of lunar orbit (that is, orbit of the moon), by means of the firing of a steering rocket, and heads back to earth.

telemetry *noun.* In space travel, coded information sent from a spaceship by radio to earth, where it is fed into computers for analysis.

Third World Liberation Front. An American civil-rights organization, active principally in student protest demonstrations at California universities.

TLI *abbreviation.* Trans-lunar injection. The point in a space flight when a ship breaks out of earth orbit and heads toward the moon.

turbotrain *noun.* A turbine-powered passenger train built for high-speed travel. The first such train began service in Canada in December 1968. It was driven by 4 gas-turbine engines using diesel fuel. It was about ⅓ the weight of a conventional train and built to travel around curves at high speeds. In April 1969 a group of Turboliners began regular service between Boston and New York. These employed modified aircraft (gas turbine) engines. They traveled faster than 170 miles per hour during test runs.

V

Vietnamize *verb tr.* To make Vietnamese in character and in fact; especially, to make the fighting of the war in South Vietnam the job and responsibility of the people of that country, rather than of the United States.

X

X *abbreviation.* Persons under age 16 not admitted; in some areas that have special laws in effect, the age limit is 18 or 21. (A rating for movies, from the code of self-regulation of the Motion Picture Association of America.)

XYY *adjective.* Having an XYY chromosome pattern instead of the usual XY of a man or boy. Normally the body cells of a male contain matched pairs of chromosomes, one labeled X and one Y. Some males have the usual matched pairs plus an extra Y chromosome, and as a result are said to be XYY. According to some doctors and scientists, an XYY man is likely to have problems of adjusting to his surroundings, arising from his personality, and may even become a criminal. Other scientists believe that a direct connection between the XYY pattern and crime has yet to be proved.

Index

A

Abernathy, Ralph, American civil rights leader 124
Ablation, in heat protection for spacecraft 13
ABM (anti-ballistic missile) system 129, 378–81
Abstract expressionism, art form 273, 275
Abu Dhabi, Trucial States 248
Academy Award winners 252
Accessories, things added to give style
  fashion 181–82
  interior design 208–09
Action games 188–90
Adolescence see Young people; Youth organizations
Advertising, cigarette 242
Afghanistan 88
Africa 60–71, 78–79, 243
  heads of government 70
  population in developing countries 293–95
  See also names of countries
Afro-American studies 165
Age, of rocks see Moon rocks
Agnew, Spiro, American vice-president 347, 375
Agriculture 72–75, picture 112–13
  See also names of countries
Air fares 103–04
Airlines, financial problems of 103–04
Airplanes, jet 104
Air pollution, picture 138–39
  automobiles 101
  government controls 140
Airport congestion 102, 140
Air traffic control 102
Alabama 84–85
  commemorative stamp 200
Alaska 354
  lemmings, research of mass suicide 137
Albania 169
Albert, Carl, U.S. congressman 126, picture 128
Alberta, Canada 232
Aldrin, Edwin E. ("Buzz"), Jr., American astronaut 26–29, 46, 94, 279, 375, picture 171
Alexander of Tunis, British viscount 150
Al Fatah, Arab guerrillas 36–37, 245–46, picture 247
Algae, as source of protein 185
Algeria 52, 247
Allen, Woody, American actor 353, picture 352
Alliance for Labor Action 162
Allon, Yigal, Israeli leader 245
American Bar Association 223, 225
American Heritage Dictionary 300
American Indians see Indians of North America; Indians of South America
American League standings, baseball 330

American Legion, commemorative stamp 200
American Library Association 226, 227
American Samoa 272
Amistad Dam, Mexico-United States 50
Anansi, House of, publishers 231
Ancient civilizations, archeological discoveries 79–80
Anguilla 38, 392, picture 389
Animals 105, 134–37
  high-protein feed from city wastes 73
  skins as floor coverings 207
  transplants of unborn 74
Ansermet, Ernest, Swiss conductor 150
Anthropology 76–77
Anti-ballistic missile system see ABM
Antifilibuster rule, Canada 113
Antigua 390–91
Anti-Semitism, in United States 306
ANZUS Pact, Australia with New Zealand and U.S. 98
Apartheid, racial separation 69, 303
Apollo, Project, space program 18–31
  Apollo 9 and 10 missions 38, 42
  Apollo 11, mission to moon 26–30, 46, 94–95, 374–75
  Apollo 12, mission to moon 30, 55, 313, 374–75
  commemorative stamps 199, 200
  farm crop data supplied by 75
  medical checks by telemetry 238
  rocks on moon found by 191–92
  Soviet Luna 15, mysterious vanguard 316
Applications Technology Satellites (ATS) 319
Aquanauts, marine science studies of 268–70
Arab-Israeli dispute 244–47, 362
  monthly incidents 34–57
Arab states see Middle East
Arafat, Yasir, Al Fatah commando 246, picture 247
Archeology 78–80
Architecture 81–86
Arctic, north polar region 115, 117
  lemmings and seal pups 137
Arctic North Slope, Alaska 50, 115, 270, 354
Arenales, Emilio, Guatemalan diplomat 150
Argentina 217
Arms limitation talks, in Helsinki 56, 175, 374
Arms races 378–79
Armstrong, Neil A., American astronaut 24, 26–29, 46, 94, 279, 374–75, picture 171, 347
Art 273–77
  interior design, use of art in 206–07
Artificial heart devices 241
Asia 87–93
  heads of government 92
  population in developing countries 293–95
  See also names of countries
Assassinations 46, 52, 363
Astronauts, men in space 14–31, 279–82, 313
  medical checks by telemetry 238
  space toys 190, picture 189
  See also names of astronauts
Astronomy 94–96
  space exploration 10–31, 312–23
Aswan Dam, United Arab Republic 247
Atlanta, Georgia 257
Atmosphere, of Mars and Venus 95
Atomic bomb, Communist China 120
ATS see Applications Technology Satellites
Audiovisual aids, in libraries 226
Australia 97–100, 272
Austria 175
Autobiography 229

G

N

Ireland concerned with strife in 177
violence between Catholics and Protestants 48
North Korea 40, 214
North Vietnam see Vietnam; Vietnam war
Northwest Passage 50, 115, 117, 270, 354, 355, 358
Norway 177
Novels 228–29, 231, 232
Nu, U, Burmese statesman 89
Nuclear energy 291–92
Nuclear fusion 291–92
Nuclear power plants
Finland 175
India 205
station on moon 30
Nuclear weapons
ABM, reasons for and against 378–81
China 120
use of ocean floor debated at UN 365
Nudity
motion pictures 255
theater 350, 353
Nutrition
Federal-assistance programs 297
first Federal survey for United States 242
malnutrition in United States 184

O

Oath of fealty 118, 194
Obits see Deaths
Observatories, advances in astronomy 95–96
Ocean liners 358
Oceanography 266–70
Off Broadway theater 350, 353
Office of Economic Opportunity 296–97
Official Languages Act, Canada 111
Oh, Calcutta! play 350, 353
Oil see Petroleum
Oil pollution, Santa Barbara, California 36, 139–40
Oil tankers 50, 115, 270, 354, 355, 358, picture 51
Ojukwu, General Odumegwu, Biafran leader 264
Okinawa, Pacific island 212, 272
Old-Age Assistance 311
Oliver, motion picture 253
Oman see Muscat and Oman
O'Neill, Terence, prime minister of Northern Ireland 195
Open admissions policy, for colleges and universities 164
Opera 256–57
Operation Breakthrough, housing plan 86
Orbiting Astronomical Observatory (OAO) 2 96
Orbiting Solar Observatory (OSO) 5 95–96
Organization of African Unity (OAU) 61, 67
peace efforts in Nigeria 263, 264
Orthodox Eastern churches 307
Osuna, Rafael, Mexican tennis star 154

P

Pacific islands and island groups 271–72
Painting 273–77
Paisley, Ian, Protestant minister in Northern Ireland 195
Pakistan 91
Palestine liberation movement 245, 249, picture 247
Palme, Olof, Swedish prime minister 178

Panama 221
Papadopoulos, George, Greek premier 176
Papen, Franz von, German statesman 154
Paperback books, Canadian 231
Papua-New Guinea 272
Paraguay 221
Paris peace negotiations, Vietnam war 54, 372
Park, Chung Hee, president of Korea 214
Parkinson's disease 241
Particle physics 290–91
Pas de Deux, book and exhibit 288–89
Passenger railroads 359
Pastore, John O. American politician 347
Pattern, in interior design 207
Paul VI, pope 304, picture 60
commemorative stamp, picture 200
peace efforts 71, 305, picture 306
Pay television 349
Peace, Nobel prize 265
Peace Corps 36, 71, 278
Pearson, Drew, American newspaper columnist 154
Pegler, Westbrook, American journalist 154
People's Revolutionary Movement, Congo (Kinshasa) 62
Peregrene falcon 137
Periodic table 118
Persian Gulf and Federation of Emirates 248
Peru 36, 44, 221
Pesticides 73
danger to birds 137
DDT, use banned in U.S. 48, 54, 138–39
Petroleum
Arctic Slope, Alaska 50, 115, 354
bacteria, as a source of protein 185
discoveries in Australia 99
Middle East, oil revenues 248, 249
Philadelphia Plan, for equal employment 124, 202
Philately see Stamps and stamp collecting
Philippines 91, 93, picture 278
Photography 284–89
Physical education 343–46
Physics 290–92
Nobel prize 265
Physiology see Medicine and health
Piccard, Jacques, Swiss oceanographer 270, picture 269
Picture annuals 284–85
Pigs, vaccination of 74
Pike, James Albert, American clergyman 154
Pill, The see Birth control
Pipeline, Arctic Slope, Alaska 355, map 354
Pire, Dominique, Belgian priest 155
Pirnie, Alexander, American official, picture 380
Pitchers, winning, in baseball 330
Planets
Mars 95, picture 94
Venus 95
Plants
cereal grains, search for protein 185
Plasma physics 291–92
Plastic furniture 208
Playhouse in the Park, Cincinnati, Ohio 82–83
Play It Again, Sam, comedy 353, picture 352
Pleiades, stars in the constellation Taurus 96
Podgorny, Nikolai, Soviet president, picture 168
Poetry 229
books for children 233–34
Canadian literature 232
Pogo effect, vibration 20

Q

R

Rural poverty 303
Rwanda 68

S

Safeguard, anti-ballistic missile system 379
Safety
  air traffic control 102
  food 185, picture 184
Saint Kitts, Caribbean island 392
Saint Lucia, Caribbean island 392
Saint Vincent, Caribbean island 392
Sardis, ancient city, Asia Minor, pictures 78, 79
Satellites, man-made 12–31, 318–23
  communications satellites 348–49
  weather satellites 388
Sato, Eisaku, Japanese statesman 211
Saturn, rocket 15, 20, picture 16, 314
Saud, Ibn Abdul, king of Saudi Arabia 155
Saudi Arabia 250–51
Savings and loan associations 203
School decentralization 167
School desegregation 107, 122–24, 167
Schultz, George P., American official 107, 162
Schweickart, Russell, American astronaut 23, 282
Science fiction, in motion pictures 254
Scott, David Randolph, American astronaut 23, 282
Scott, Hugh, U.S. senator 126, picture 127
Sculpture 273–77
SDS see Students for a Democratic Society
Sealab, Project 270, picture 268
Seale, Bobby, Black Panther leader 54, 123
Seals, animals 105, 137
Seeger, Pete, American folk singer, picture 371
Segregation see Desegregation
Seismometers, devices to detect vibrations
  moon seisms recorded 26, 94–95
Selby, Richard, American photographer 286
Selective Service System and servicemen 224
  Hershey removed as head 52, 373, picture 380
  lottery system 56, 381, picture 380
Semyonov, Vladimir S., Soviet official 374
Senate, United States see United States Congress
Senegal 68–69
Separatism, for blacks 124
Separatist movement, in Quebec, Canada 109–10, 115
  books about 231, 232
Sesame Street, children's TV program 349
Sex, in motion pictures 254–55
Shahn, Ben, American artist 155
Shah of Iran, ruler 248, picture 249
Shannon, James B., former Catholic bishop 305
Shaw, Clay, American businessman 38, 225
Shepard, Alan, American astronaut 14
Ships and shipping 354–55, 358
Shoes 182
Sierra Leone 69
Sihanouk, Norodom, Cambodian prince 89
Sikkim 93
Singapore 93
Sirhan, Sirhan Bishara, assassin of Robert Kennedy
  40, 225, 370
Skiing 339, picture 346
Skyjacking see Hijacking
Slavery, books about 232
Smith, Gerard C., American public official 374
Smith, Ian, Rhodesian prime minister 66, picture 67

Smith, Ralph Tyler, American politician 282
Smithsonian Institution 201
Smrkovsky, Josef, Czech leader 143, 144
Social problems
  books about 230
  violence, investigation of 56
Social sciences 184
Social security 311
Social welfare 310–11, map 310
  Australia and Canada 100, 110, 115
  malnutrition in United States 184, 242
  residency rules 125
  See also Civil rights; Poverty, war on
Somalia 52, 69
Songbooks, for children 234
Soul music 260
South Africa 69, 303
  Lesotho and Malawi, dependence on 66
South America see Latin America
Southeast Asia 89–91, 93
Southeast Asia Treaty Organization (SEATO) 98
Southern Yemen 251
South Korea 214
South Vietnam see Vietnam; Vietnam war
Soviet Union see Union of Soviet Socialist Republics
Soybeans 74, 185
Space communications 318–21, 347–49
  tracking stations in Australia 99
Spacecraft 12–31
Space exploration 46, 312–23
  Apollo 9, and 10 missions 38, 42
  astronomy, new findings in 94–96
  commemorative stamp 199, 200
  history of the space projects 10–31
  lunar geology 191–92
  medical checks by telemetry 238
  Post-Apollo space program 321–23
  See also Astronauts; Man in space
Space probes 95, picture 94
Space stations 317–18, 322
Space suits 20, picture 21
Space toys 190, pictures 189
Spain 177–78, 213
  Equatorial Guinea, Spanish citizens evacuated 62
Speleology, study of caves and caverns 77, 79
Sports 324–41
  books about 230
  young people 342–46
  See also names of sports
Sports cars 101
Sputnik I, Soviet satellite 12
Stafford, Thomas, American astronaut 42, 282
Stained-glass art craft 199
Stamps and stamp collecting 199–200
Star-Agri-Business of America award 396–97
Star Farmer of America award 396
Stars 95–96
State governments, United States 160
Steckler, Lou, American photographer 287
Stern, Otto, German-American physicist 155
Stock, Dennis, American photographer 285
Stock market 160–62
Stokes, Carl B., American official 125, 380
Stormfury, Project, hurricane seeding 388
Storms, Ocean of, Apollo 12 landing 313
Strategic Arms Limitation Talks (SALT) 56, 175, 374
Strikes 162
  Canada 52, 108, 113
  Europe 36, 196

United Automobile Workers 162
United Kingdom of Great Britain and Northern Ireland
    see Great Britain and Northern Ireland, United
    Kingdom of
United Nations 364–67
    human environment, concern over 141
    member nations and chief representatives 368–69
    trust territories 272
United Nations Development Decade 366
United States 370–81
    Arab-Israeli dispute 244–45
    China's relations with 120–21
    Congress, membership list 131–33
    economic conditions 157–62
    Latin American relations 215–16, 374
    strategic nuclear warheads, chart 381
    trust territories in Pacific 272
United States Armed Forces 214, 321
United States Congress 126–30
    conservation legislation 140–41
    Haynesworth rejected for Supreme Court 222–23
    membership list 131–33
    pollution legislation 140
United States Mint, in Philadelphia 201
Universities and colleges
    basketball 327, 331
    Canada 115, picture 114
    student disorders 36, 163–65, 212
    underground newspapers 300
    University of the West Indies 389
    See also Student unrest
Unmanned spacecraft program, U.S. 323
Upper Volta 71
Uranium 205
Urban renewal programs 86
Uruguay 221
U.S. Camera World Annual 285, picture 287

V

Vaccination and inoculation 241, picture 238
    testing and treatment for animal diseases 74
Vanguard, Project, space program 12
Venezuela 38, 44, 221
Venus, planet 95
Venus space probes 95
Vietcong, Vietnamese Communists 386
Vietnam 382–86
Vietnam war 382–86
    alleged massacre at Songmy 56
    anti-war demonstrations, 53, 54, 372–73
    Australia 97
    Green Berets 50
    Paris peace negotiations 372
    Soviet weapons to North Vietnam 362
    troop withdrawals 44, 56, 87, 372, 383, 386
    war cost and inflation 129–30, 157–59
Villella, Edward, American dancer, picture 145
Violence
    civil rights, harm to the cause of 124–25
    commission on causes and prevention of 56
    in literature 228, 230
    motion pictures and TV 253–54, 347–48
Virgin Islands, British 391
Vital statistics, population 386–87
Vocabulary 399–406
Volpe, John A., American official, picture 356
Vostok, Soviet rocket 14, picture 15

Voting
    age reduction proposals 175, 262
    one-man-one-vote for North Ireland 195

W

Wadsworth Atheneum, museum 277
Wages and salaries 113, 159, 202
Wales
    investiture of Charles, Prince of Wales 47, 118, 194
Walk in space 17
Wallpaper, new designs in 207
Warburg, James Paul, American financier 155
Warren, Earl, Supreme Court justice 222, picture 34
Washington, D.C. anti-war demonstration 54
Water, in a new form (polywater) 118
Water pollution 140
Waterpower see Hydroelectric power
Weather 388
Webster, Daniel, commemorative stamp 200
Weinberg, Sidney J., American financier 155
Wiesner, Dr. Jerome, American scientist 379
Welfare, Public see Social Welfare
West Berlin see Berlin
Western Samoa 272
West Europe 174–78
West Germany see Germany
West Indies, islands in Caribbean Sea 389–92
    status and heads of government 391
West Irian (western New Guinea) 89–90
White, Edward, American astronaut 17
White, Josh, American singer 155
Wildlife, preservation of 134–37, 140
Wilson, Harold, prime minister of United Kingdom
    195–96
Woodstock Rock-Music Festival, Bethel, N.Y. 180–81,
    259
Words, New 399–406
World Council of Churches 303, 307
World Series results, in baseball 330
Wright, John, Cardinal, American churchman 305
Wyoming 398

X Y Z

X-15, rocket-powered airplane 12
X rays 96

Yachting 332
Yellow Caterpillar, painting by Frankenthaler 273
Yemen 251
Yorty, Samuel, Los Angeles mayor 380
Young, John Watts, American astronaut 42, 282
Young people
    books for boys and girls 237
    crime rate, cause of 142
    fashions 180–83
    sports 342–46
    unemployment 162
    UN seeks to attract young people 364, 365
Young Sabat Maker, painting by Tanner 274
Youth see Young people
Youth organizations 393–98
Yugoslavia 52, 171–72

Zambia 71
Zinsou, Emile Derlin, Dahomey leader 62
Zionism 243

ILLUSTRATION CREDITS

The following list credits, by page, the sources of illustrations used in THE NEW BOOK OF KNOWLEDGE ANNUAL. Credits are listed illustration by illustration—left to right, top to bottom. Wherever appropriate, the name of the photographer or artist has been listed with the source, the two being separated by a dash. When two or more illustrations appear on one page, their credits are separated by semicolons.

10	NASA	72	*Farm Journal*
12	NASA	74	*Farm Journal; Farm Journal*
13	Sovfoto; NASA	76	Hubert Le Campion, *Life* magazine © Time Inc.
14	NASA		
15	Sovfoto	78	Harvard University
16	NASA	79	Harvard University
17	NASA	81	Ezra Stoller
18	NASA	82	Ezra Stoller
19	NASA	83	Norman McGrath
21	Reprinted from RCA *Electronic Age*	84	Morley Baer
22	NASA	85	Ezra Stoller
23	NASA	87	UPI
24	NASA	88	UPI
25	NASA	90	Empire News, John Finn—Black Star
26	U.S. Geological Survey	93	UPI
28	NASA	94	NASA; NASA
29	NASA	97	UPI; Leo Rosenthal—PIX
30	NASA	98	U.S. Navy
31	North American Rockwell	101	Ford Motor Company
32	George Sottung	102	Dennis Brack—Black Star
34	Pictorial Parade	103	Sovfoto—Tass; UPI
36	Rapho-Sauterean	105	Dr. Lorne MacHattie, Harvard University
37	Ian Berry—Magnum	107	Paul Conklin—PIX; Paul Conklin—PIX; Fred Ward—Black Star
38	*Life* magazine © Time Inc.		
40	J. Pavlovsky—Rapho-Guillumette	108	UPI
41	John Launois—Black Star	110	Central Press—Pictorial Parade
42	NASA—Black Star	111	Annan Photo Features
43	Pictorial Parade	112	Pictorial Parade
44	Fred Ward—Black Star	114	National Film Board of Canada
45	UPI	117	National Film Board of Canada
46	NASA	119	Eastfoto
47	Norman Parkinson—Camera Press—PIX	120	Eastfoto
48	Harry Benson—Black Star; Walter Rutter—Black Star	121	Eastfoto
		122	UPI
49	Bunte—Black Star	123	UPI
50	UPI; Baldev—PIX	127	Dennis Brack—Black Star; Dennis Brack—Black Star
51	John Olson, *Life* magazine © Time Inc.		
52	Ben Ross—Multi-Media Photography	128	Fred Ward—Black Star; Pictorial Parade
53	William A. Grahm—Camera 5; Dan McCoy—Black Star	129	Fred Ward—Black Star
		134	Bill Eppridge, *Life* magazine © Time Inc.
54	Wally McNamee, *Newsweek*	136	John Dominis, *Life* magazine © Time Inc.
55	NASA	138	© Martin Schneider
56	Philip Jones Griffiths—Magnum	143	Black Star
57	Philip Jones Griffiths—Magnum; UPI; UPI; UPI	145	Bill Eppridge, *Life* magazine © Time Inc.
		146	Marbeth
58	John Jones	147	MIRA, courtesy Hurok Concerts, Inc.
60	Pictorial Parade	148	Dennis Brack—Black Star
64	Murali—PIX; UPI	151	Pictorial Parade; UPI; *London Daily Express*—Pictorial Parade
65	Mohamed Amin—Keystone; PIX—Africapix		
67	Pip—Mondial Press	152	Photo Trends; UPI
68	Marc and Evelyn Bernheim—Rapho-Guillumette	153	Pictorial Parade
		154	Pictorial Parade; UPI

155 Kennedy Galleries
156 Camera Press—PIX
157 Hugh Rogers—Monkmeyer
158 *The New York Times; The Long Island Press*
161 UPI
163 B. Curtis—Black Star
165 UPI
166 Doug Anderson © 1969 *Saturday Review*
168 Sovfoto
171 Sovfoto
172 Sovfoto
174 Cartier Bresson—Magnum
176 Mike Kerr—Black Star
178 Photoreporters; *Paris Match*—Pictorial Parade
179 UPI
180 Ralph Lewin; Mr. Pants Inc.
182 Central Press Photos—Pictorial Parade
183 Rosenau Brothers; Central Press—Pictorial Parade
184 Pepsi Cola Company
186 J. P. Bonnotte—Gamma-PIX
188 Ideal Toy Corporation
189 Remco Industries Inc.; Multi-Media Photography; Skil Craft Corporation
194 Fox Photos—Pictorial Parade
195 Central Press—Pictorial Parade
197 Estes Industries
198 Estes Industries; Estes Industries
199 Multi-Media Photography; Multi-Media Photography
201 The Smithsonian Institution
204 *London Daily Express*—Pictorial Parade
206 Gimbels, New York
207 Gene Laurents
208 Bloomingdale's, New York
209 *The New York Times* Studio
210 Photoreporters
211 Gene Forte—Pictorial Parade
213 UPI
215 UPI; UPI
216 UPI
217 UPI
219 UPI
222 Pictorial Parade; Fred Ward—Black Star
223 Fred Ward—Black Star; Michael Sullivan—Black Star
225 UPI; UPI
227 UPI
228 Harper & Row; Harper & Row
231 © Karsh, Ottawa—Rapho-Guillumette
233 From *Apricot ABC* by Miska Miles, illustrated by Peter Parnall. Published by Little-Brown
234 From *The Fool of the World and The Flying Ship* by Arthur Ransome, illustrated by Uri Shulevitz. Published by Farrar, Straus & Giroux
236 From *Goggles* by Ezra Jack Keats. Published by Macmillan
238 Merck, Sharp and Dohme
239 Wide World
240 Wide World
243 Diana Davies
244 George Buctel
246 Geneviève Chauvel—Gamma-PIX
247 Simonpietri—Gamma-PIX
249 UPI
253 Columbia Pictures
254 Paramount Pictures
255 Cinerama Releasing Corporation
256 Santa Fe Opera
259 Sol Goldberg, Cornell University
261 Peter Mitchell/Colin Davey—Camera Press-PIX
263 George Buctel; Holmes/Lebel—PIX
265 UPI; UPI; UPI
266 Lamont—Doherty Geological Observatory of Columbia University
267 Lamont—Doherty Geological Observatory of Columbia University
268 UPI
269 Grumman Aerospace Corporation; Grumman Aerospace Corporation
271 New Zealand Information Service
273 The Metropolitan Museum of Art; Don Christensen
274 Mrs. Sadie T. M. Alexander, Philadelphia
275 The Hyde Collection, Glens Falls, New York
276 John Hill, Museum of Primitive Art
278 Peace Corps; Peace Corps; Peace Corps
279 UPI
280 New York Philharmonic
281 UPI; UPI
282 UPI
283 UPI; UPI
285 Dennis Stock, *Travel & Camera;* Dennis Stock, *Travel & Camera*
286 Richard Selby, *U.S. Camera World Annual 1970*
287 Len Steckler, *U.S. Camera World Annual 1970;* Jerome Ducrot, *Photography Annual 1970;* Carl Purcell, *Photography Annual 1970;* Pat Caulfield, *Photography Annual 1970.*
288 The Metropolitan Museum of Art; The Museum of Modern Art
290 Sovfoto
293 Marc and Evelyn Bernheim—Rapho-Guillumette
294 From *The Year 2000* by Herman Kahn and Anthony J. Wiener. Published by Macmillan; Population Reference Bureau; From *World Population Problems* by Philip M. Hauser
295 From *The Year 2000* by Herman Kahn and Anthony J. Wiener. Published by Macmillan
296 *The New York Times*
298 The Saturday Evening Post Company; The Saturday Evening Post Company
299 *Chicago Tribune*
300 Houghton-Mifflin Company
301 The New American Library; Henrik V. Boudakian
302 Pictorial Parade
304 Religious News Service
305 Religious News Service

306	Israel Information Service	347	NBC
307	*Paris Match*	349	DePatie-Freleng; DePatie-Freleng
308	Lebeck—Black Star	350	Friedman-Abeles
310	George Buctel	351	Martha Swope
312	NASA	352	Friedman-Abeles; Friedman-Abeles
314	NASA	354	George Buctel
315	Photo, NASA	355	Humble Oil
316	NASA	356	U.S. Department of Transportation
317	NASA	360	Novosti—Sovfoto
319	Hughes Aircraft Company	361	George Buctel
320	North American Rockwell	362	Tass—Sovfoto
321	UPI	364	United Nations
324	UPI	367	United Nations
325	UPI	369	*The New York Times*
326	UPI	370	Washington Reporters—PIX
327	UPI	371	UPI; UPI; NASA; Warren Uzzle—Black Star
328	UPI	373	Deborah K. Kaplan—Multi-Media Photography
329	UPI		
331	UPI	375	Paul Conklin—PIX
333	UPI; Evelyn Shafer	376	UPI; Jack Hubbard—Black Star
334	UPI	380	Arnold Sacks—Pictorial Parade
336	UPI	381	*The New York Times*
337	UPI	382	Bill Strode—Black Star
338	UPI	383	UPI
339	Wide World	384	UPI; Tass—Sovfoto
340	UPI	385	George Buctel; Gamma-PIX
341	UPI	388	ESSA 9
342	Lynn Pelham—Rapho-Guillumette	389	Keystone
343	Pictorial Parade	393	Boy Scouts of America
344	Burk Uzzle—Black Star	394	Boys' Clubs of America
345	Fred Ward—Black Star	396	Future Farmers of America
346	Peter Miller—Rapho-Guillumette	397	Girl Scouts of the U.S.A.

ARTISTS: Verne Bowman, George Buctel, Alan Colby, John Jones, George Sottung, Joe Stonehill, Blaise Zito